Dispatches from a Time Between Worlds

PERSPECTIVA

Introducing Perspectiva Press
Soul food for expert generalists

Perspectiva seeks to understand the relationship between systems, souls and society in a time of crisis, and to develop methods, grounded in an applied philosophy of education, to help us meet the challenges of our time.

As part of this broader endeavour, Perspectiva Press will specialise in short books with occasional longer works. These books will be well-presented and distinctive. Their purpose is to shape and share thinking that helps to:

- create a community of expert generalists with skills of synthesis and epistemic agility
- envisage a world beyond consumerism, and pathways for how we might get there
- support sociological imagination in a dynamic ecological and technological context
- cultivate spiritual sensibility; clarifying how it manifests and why it matters
- encourage a more complex and systemic understanding of the world
- commit to going beyond critique, by developing vision and method
- indicate how we can do pluralism better; epistemic, cultural, political, spiritual
- clarify what it means to become the change we want to see in the world
- develop the authority of people doing important work aligned with Perspectiva

It is unusual for a charity like Perspectiva to become a publisher, even a small one, but we value books as dignified cultural artefacts with their own kind of analogue power, and we believe ideas travel further and connect more deeply when they are rooted in the mandate of a publication designed to last for years, not merely moments. We also see a gap in the market for books that specialise in the kinds of integrative and imaginative sensibilities that speak to the challenges of our time.

Already published

The World We Create: From god to market   *Tomas Björkman*
An entrepreneur offers an historical perspective on achieving a more meaningful and sustainable world

To be published in 2021

Unlearn: A compass for radical transformation   *Hanno Burmester*
A compass for societal transformation, arising from the personal testimony of coming out in the shadow of Nazi Germany

Collective Wisdom in the West: Beyond the shadows of the Enlightenment   *Liam Kavanagh*
A cognitive scientist and contemplative on the nature of 'collective wisdom' and what we need to do to get there

The Politics of Waking Up: Power and possibility in the fractal age   *Indra Adnan*
A psychosocial therapist on refashioning politics by meeting people where they are

The Entangled Activist: Learning to recognise the master's tools   *Anthea Lawson*
A seasoned campaigner on how your sense of agency changes when you realise 'getting the bastards' is not working

Dispatches from a Time Between Worlds

Crisis and emergence in metamodernity

edited by

Jonathan Rowson

Layman Pascal

Perspectiva Press, London, UK

systems-souls-society.com

First published in 2021

ISBN (pbk) 978-1-9998368-0-1

ISBN (ebk) 978-1-9998368-9-4

© 2021 Jonathan Rowson, Layman Pascal, Zak Stein, Bonnitta Roy, Daniel Görtz, Lene Rachel Andersen, Sarah Stein Lubrano, Minna Salami, John Vervaeke and Christopher Mastropietro, Tom Murray, Mark Vernon and Jonathan Jong, Siva Thambisetty, Brent Cooper and Jeremy Johnson assert their moral right to be identified as the author of their work within this book.

All rights reserved. No part of this publication may be reproduced, stored in a retrieval system or transmitted in any form without the prior written consent of the copyright owners, other than as permitted by UK copyright legislation or under the terms and conditions of a recognised copyright licensing scheme.

Cover design Studio Sutherland

Typesetting www.ShakspeareEditorial.org

Printed by TJ Books, Cornwall

Dispatches from a Time Between Worlds
A new anthology series

THIS ANTHOLOGY is the first volume in a series of *Dispatches from a Time Between Worlds* that Perspectiva Press plans to publish annually. Dispatches are timely and often time-sensitive messages, while the idea that we are living *between* worlds is partly a provocative heuristic, partly a playful mystical trope and partly a fully fledged historiographical status claim.

In his acclaimed book, *Education in a Time Between Worlds*, Zachary Stein introduces the 'time between worlds' notion and offers a wide-ranging theoretical and empirical grounding for the claim that is somewhat beyond our scope here. However, since Perspectiva is committing to the idea that we are in a time between worlds as a premise of sustained enquiry for a series of anthologies, a short overview to clarify the idea's intellectual dignity seems appropriate.[1]

The premise of this series is that the myriad forces that shape global history are now burgeoning to such an extent that our conventional patterns of collective understanding, sentiment and expectation are failing to make sense of how we should act. Sometimes it feels like even the best we can do won't be good enough to save ourselves from ourselves. For instance, human rights and international law often look insipid in the context of transnational financial power, the political spectrum seems otiose when policy proposals are subsumed by culture wars, and metrics like IQ and GDP seem increasingly quaint because they are ostensibly solid empirical ground, but when we inspect them for their fidelity to the world as we find it, they lack a sound meta-theoretical basis, appear to lie on conceptual quicksand, and fail to guide discerning action.

While we are struggling to make sense of the world we have known, an experience of ambient potentiality is arising within and between people too. This *metamodern* feeling is not only shaped by our global digital context and ecological reckoning but also by cosmological re-enchantment, in which our shared insight into the precarity of planetary life and its elusive meaning heightens our sense of intimacy and elicits new impulses of wonder and tenderness. These sentiments are also manifesting in intellectual and creative output, and in design and policy processes that seemed far-fetched until recently, but are clearly emerging: for instance, bioregionalism, universal basic income, land reform, post-growth economics, wiser cryptocurrencies, and the transformative civic education known as *Bildung*.

These new patterns of living have not yet matured or coalesced, and may not, because they lack political capital and nor have they been properly tested by time, so the better world that might arise is merely intuited, glimpsed and not quite tangible. Yet we cannot but hope that something is arising that will speak to our pervasive sense of intellectual disorientation and aesthetic longing. That sense of discomforting betweenness is sufficiently strong that the attempt to wholeheartedly consider the nature of 'truth' and 'we' and 'time' that define our experience is not of mere philosophical interest but part of saving civilisation from itself. These philosophical considerations may appear niche, but they are about our place in the evolution of consciousness and history's great cosmic unfolding, detailed by visionaries like Teilhard de Chardin and Sri Aurobindo and reappraised in recent scholarship on Owen Barfield and Jean Gebser.[2]

The notion of 'worlds' is about the evolution of (inter)subjective and (inter)objective aspects of our shared reality, while the idea of being *between* worlds is meta-historical and historiographical, concerned with how the meaning and pattern of events and processes of history might best be organised through the designation of epochs, periods and phases of transition. The subjective (psychology) and intersubjective (culture) aspect of being in 'worlds' stems from social theories about patterns of common understanding, meaning and expectation sometimes called our social imaginary, which Charles Taylor describes as 'a wider grasp of our whole predicament ... not a set of ideas; rather it is what enables through making sense of, the practices of society.'[3]

And yet our imaginary arises through the objective (material) and inter-objective (institutional) features of reality. These features of 'worlds' are disclosed not by human experience as such, but by data, though it is only through theoretical concepts derived from our imaginary that we can turn data into information, and thereby decipher trends about underlying dynamics in demographics, economics and politics. Immanuel Wallerstein's research on world system dynamics and Peter Turchin's on 'secular cycles' lend empirical weight to the idea that we are between worlds, as do the growing fields of Big History and cliodynamics (history as science) more generally.[4] For example, periods of relative stability in prices, labour practices and inter-elite competition predictably lead to eventual increasing economic inequality, price instability and increases in war. There follows another stable period, until the situation begins to unravel again, only at increasingly greater scales. In forthcoming work on the visionary educator John Amos Comenius for Perspectiva, Zachary Stein goes deeper into the idea of a time between worlds, and argues that there are two phases over the last 500 years or so where data-rich meta-historical trends appear to coincide to reflect moments that can meaningfully be said to be 'between worlds'; namely the years surrounding the turnings of both the 17th century and now the early 21st century:

> In these epochs we find the ramification of new technologies, wholesale new beginnings of economic hegemons, and sweeping changes in the nature of culture and consciousness .... It is reasonable to think that during each of these transformational epochs there is an inordinate amount of thinking and innovation in the realms of basic organisational design and culture, patterns and symbols. In particular, conceptions of knowledge and education, religion and government, would all be in the process of being rethought .... A time between worlds is turbulent to say the least. It involves not just *more of the same kind of society*, which is what happened during the four centuries between 1600 and 2000, but instead, *the emergence of a new kind of society*.[5]

While meta-historians reveal remarkably similar trends in the data, I feel the extent to which history has a pattern and the extent to which we give it one for more or less strategic reasons remains a useful open question.[6] For all our woes, we are a uniquely well-informed civilisation. In theory at least, we should be able to use our understanding of meta-historical patterns to change how patterns unfold in future. That is partly what this series is about.

The purpose behind anthologising the idea of betweenness and how it manifests thematically is to show how the present is saturated with debate on particular issues but rarely do we encounter discussion about the relationships between such issues or the perception of the context that defines them. There is no shortcut to that fuller perspective and, to move in that direction, it helps if a wide range of perspectives can be seen alongside each other. Each of those perspectives needs to be capacious and reflective enough to show an awareness of an enquiry's edges and pores, allowing each perspective to be situated within modes and fields of enquiry that are to some extent isomorphic. The point is actually *not* to be 'interdisciplinary' because what is at stake is life in its fullness, not disciplines, and in most cases our responsibility is not to scholarly fidelity but the world as a whole. Our hope is that the reader can see different substantive plots arising from a shared historical setting, and understand more deeply why the meaning of the setting is contested, and what that entails for establishing the plot lines of their own lives.

Breadth and depth need each other more than ever. We hope to publish writing which reveals that – and how – any given issue can be seen from multiple vantage points simultaneously. In the case of this book, that means we have chapters covering (within and between them) terrain that is philosophical, historical, sociological, educational, technological, psychological, spiritual, theological, economic, political and legal. Giving voice to the relationship between these multiple ways of viewing our liminal predicament is difficult intellectual work. We hope this book will help all who read it to better understand the calling of this time. It's for the reader to judge whether we have succeeded in our first attempt.

This 2021 publication features an exploration of the context, coherence and scope of what has come to be known as the *metamodern* sensibility: a structure of feeling, cultural ethos, epistemic orientation and normative outlook that has arisen in response to the impact of the internet on our lifeworld and the spiritual and ecological exhaustion of modernity and postmodernity. In 2022 our *Dispatches* will examine the many senses in which 'the feminine' might be part of the response to the challenges of our times, and in 2023 and thereafter, we will respond thematically to unfolding cultural contexts.

'Crisis and emergence in metamodernity' is our opening theme because while this 'time between worlds' does not have a widely accepted name, it *can* be described as metamodern, the term that helps to capture the quality of betweenness as being a feature rather than a bug of our time. This first edition of *Dispatches from a Time Between Worlds* therefore seeks to be a major contribution to metamodernism, which is explored further in the Preface.

Notes

1 Stein, Zachary, *Education in a Time Between Worlds*, Bright Alliance, 2019.
2 Johnson, Jeremy, *Seeing Through the World*, Revelore Press, 2019 and Vernon, Mark, *A Secret History of Christianity*, Christian Alternative Books, 2019.
3 Taylor, C. (2002) Modern Social Imaginaries. *Public Culture* 14(1): 91–124.
4 See, for instance, Wallerstein, Immanuel, *World Systems Analysis: An Introduction*, Duke University Press, 2004, and Turchin, Peter, *Ultrasociety: How 10,000 Years of War Made Humans the Greatest Cooperators on Earth*, Beresta Books, 2016.
5 Stein, Zachary, *When and How Education Makes History: John Amos Comenius, the Pansophic College of Light, and Education for World-System Transformation*, forthcoming for Perspectiva Press.
6 For instance, there are significant divergences of interpretation on the meaning and timing of the Axial Age, presumed to apply to the first millennium BCE and associated with the spread of five major ethical religions, now described as Confucianism, Buddhism, Judaism, Zoroastrianism and Greek philosophy. And yet a new database that informs world history called *Seshat* partly seems to undermine the much loved grand narrative about an orchestrated shift in human consciousness, which now appears to be somewhat at odds with anthropological and archaeological research. See: Whitehouse, Harvey, Religion and Human Flourishing in the Evolution of Social Complexity. In *Religion and Human Flourishing*, edited by Adam B. Cohen and published by Baylor University Press, 2020. Or to go direct to the database: http://seshatdatabank.info.

Contents

Contributors   xv

Preface: Metamodernism and the perception of context:
the cultural between, the political after and the mystic beyond   xxi

Introduction: The end of the beginning of metamodernism   1

Part 1 Synoptic Context

1 Tasting the Pickle: Ten flavours of meta-crisis and the appetite for a new civilisation   15
Jonathan Rowson

2 Time, Change and Causality: Notes towards a metamorphosis of mind   53
Bonnitta Roy

3 Becoming the Planetary   71
Jeremy D. Johnson

Part 2 Metamodern Conundrums

4 Disarm the Pedagogical Weaponry: Make education not culture war   85
Zachary Stein

5 Metamodernism, Simplicity and Complexity: Healing developmental models through involutionary descent   105
Tom Murray

6 Metamodern Sociology: An ironically sincere invitation to future scholars   135
Daniel P. Görtz

7 Liza's Bucket: Intellectual property and the metamodern impulse 157
  Siva Thambisetty

8 But Do You Have A Vegetable Garden?: Cultural codes and the preconditions for a successful metamodern economy 175
  Lene Rachel Andersen

9 The Conundrum of Cognitive Dissonance: On the uneasy relationship between agency and understanding, and why it matters 201
  Sarah Stein Lubrano

Part 3 New Frontiers

10 Manifesting Mass Metanoia: Doing change in trying times 219
  Brent Cooper

11 Gnosis in the Second Person: Responding to the meaning of crisis in the Socratic quest of authentic dialogue 241
  John Vervaeke and Christopher Mastropietro

12 Identity Erotics: A metamodern alternative to 'Identity Politics' 271
  Minna Salami

13 On Committed Uncertainty: A dialogue concerning mystery, metaphysics and metamodernism 281
  Jonathan Jong and Mark Vernon

14 The Metamodern Spirit: Approaching transformative integration in psyches and societies 293
  Layman Pascal

Index 317

Figures

Preface
Figure P.1 The metamodern perception of context distilled to a basic four-quadrant map   xl

Introduction
Hexagram 64 'Before'   1
Hexagram 3 'The Initial Difficulty'   2
Hexagram 25 'Innocence'   3
Hexagram 4 'The Envelope of Growth'   4
Hexagram 53 'The Need for Development'   4
Hexagram 60 'The Limits of Things'   5
Hexagram 19 'The Approaches'   5
Hexagram 55 'Shifting Towards Abundance'   6
Hexagram 35 'The Conditions of Progress'   7
Hexagram 38 'Forces in Opposition'   7
Hexagram 39 'Dealing With Obstruction'   8
Hexagram 13 'The Exchanges of Fellowship'   8
Hexagram 54 'The Sign of Coupling'   9
Hexagram 2 'A New Receptivity'   10
Hexagram 63 'Afterwards'   10

1 Tasting the pickle
Table 1.1 – The pickle we're in   20

8 But do you have a vegetable garden?
Figure 8.1 Cultural codes   176
Figure 8.2 That for which we have mainstream economic theory   180
Figure 8.3 Evolution: loops of life   181
Figure 8.4 A complex system of loops within loops   182

11 Gnosis in the second person
Table 11.1 Ways of knowing   247
Figure 11.1 Ways of knowing   248

14 The metamodern spirit
Figure 14.1 Game denial, game acceptance, game change   297
Figure 14.2 Modes, genres, subsystems   298

Contributors

Lene Rachel Andersen is an economist who studied theology and wrote comedy for Danish television until she decided to become a full-time philosopher, author and futurist. She is the primary founder of the think tank Nordic Bildung in Copenhagen, an activist in the European Bildung Network, and a full member of the Club of Rome. Andersen has written 18 books, several of them about the challenges technological development poses to freedom and democracy.

Brent Cooper is a geopolitical sociologist, avant-guardian of metamodern thought and savage constructive-critic of his peers and opponents alike. His transdisciplinary approach draws focus to paradoxical knowledge–power dynamics and dysfunctional elite–mass relations, with particular attention to systemic conspiracy, globalisation and culture wars. He founded TATO (The Abs-Tract Organization) to promote abstract thinking, abstractivism and understanding of abstraction as a social-material process. As a filmmaker, he created *The Abs•Tract: Core Philosophy*, a sweeping allegory and social experiment about metaphysical fitness. Beyond making critical thinking cool again, the meta-mission of TATO is to create political climate change by practising public sociology, catalysing paradigm shift and building the peace-industrial complex. His contribution to this volume is a call to readers and co-authors to radically change and convert towards revolutionary intellectual synthesis and spiritual solidarity, or die trying. Anything less is insufficient to solve the meta-crisis. He holds a BA in International Relations from the University of British Columbia and an MSc in Political Sociology from the London School of Economics.

Daniel P. Görtz (Hanzi Freinacht) is a political philosopher, historian and sociologist, author of *The Listening Society*, *Nordic Ideology*, and upcoming books *The 6 Hidden Patterns of History* and *Outcompeting Capitalism*. Much of his time is spent alone in the Swiss Alps, where he lives a strange life at the crossroads of fact and fiction, available in cyberspace but not for live encounters.

Jeremy D. Johnson is a philosopher, editor and Senior Research Associate at Perspectiva. His academic research, writing and publishing advocates new forays into integrative thinking and praxis – aligning the scholastic, poetic and spiritual – as existentially crucial work for pathfinding in a time of planetary crisis. He is the author of *Seeing Through the World: Jean Gebser and Integral Consciousness*, editor of *Mutations: Art, Consciousness and the Anthropocene* (2020) and host of the Mutations podcast. Jeremy currently serves as president for the International Jean Gebser Society and is working on his second book, *Fragments of an Integral Future* (2021).

Jonathan Jong is a social psychologist and a priest in the Church of England. His research is mainly in the psychology of religion, and especially about the motivations behind religious belief and disbelief. He is currently working on a collection of essays about how experimental psychologists study religion. He is an Assistant Professor at the Centre for Trust, Peace and Social Relations at Coventry University and Research Associate at St Benet's Hall, the School of Anthology and Museum Ethnography, and the Ian Ramsey Centre for Science and Religion, all at the University of Oxford.

Christopher Mastropietro is a philosophical writer with interests in dialogue, symbols and the concept of self. He is a co-author of *Zombies in Western Culture: A Twenty-First Century Crisis* (Open Book Publishers, 2017) and 'Diagnosing the Current Age: A Symptomology of the Meaning Crisis' (The Sideview, 2020), among other forthcoming publications.

Tom Murray is a research scholar, publishing in the fields of adult developmental theory, meta-theory (including integral and metamodern theory), and advanced learning technologies. He is a Senior Research Fellow at the University of Massachusetts School of Computer Science, is an associate editor at *Integral Review* journal, and is Chief Visionary and Instigator at Open Way Solutions LLC (which merges technology with integral developmental theory). He has published articles on developmental theory and meta-theory as they relate to wisdom skills, education, deliberative skills, contemplative dialogue, leadership, ethics, knowledge-building communities, epistemology and post-metaphysics. He loves improvisational dance and authentic collective inquiry. See www.tommurray.us.

Layman Pascal is from Sointula, British Columbia. Imagine that was my whole biography? Just that obscure hint of the misty green isles of Canada's Pacific coast where I was born. Beautiful simplicity. Shall I say more? I seriously doubt the details will be an improvement. Nonetheless, I am co-editor of this volume as well as an author, business owner, public speaker, meditation teacher and co-chair of the Foundation for Integral Religion and Spirituality. Still more? I am a former admin for the Integral Life forum, contributor to *ReVision*, *Integral Review*, Voices with Vervaeke, etc. (and that's a big 'etc'!). Perhaps I am primarily a philosopher dealing with nonduality, integral theism, postmetaphysical spirituality, meta-progressive politics, planetary shamanism, meta-theory, coaxial developmental models, the cultivation of subconscious intelligence, the metaphysics of adjacency (MOA) and the so-called 'integration-surplus model of spirit'. Recently I have been acting as Chief Podcaster for The Integral Stage, wherein I have hosted diverse interview series about meta-theory, depth sexuality, meta-level authors, integrative podcasters, spiritual transmission and political transformation. You are also welcome to follow me at laymanpascal.substack.com, where I compose articles upon private request.

Jonathan Rowson is co-founder and Director of Perspectiva. He is also a research fellow at the Centre for the Understanding of Sustainable Prosperity at the University of Surrey and a former Open Society Fellow. His work has been published in *The New York Times*, *The Guardian* and profiled in *The New Statesman* magazine. He was previously Director of the Social Brain Centre at the RSA, where he authored a range of influential research reports on behaviour change, climate change and spirituality, and curated and chaired a range of related events. Jonathan is an applied philosopher with degrees from Oxford, Harvard and Bristol universities. He is also a chess Grandmaster and was British Champion in three consecutive years (2004–6). He views the game as a continuing source of insight and inspiration, and his book, *The Moves that Matter – A Grandmaster on the Game of Life*, was published by Bloomsbury in 2019. He lives in Putney, London, with his wife Siva and their two sons, Kailash and Vishnu.

Bonnitta Roy is the founder of Alderlore Insight Center, an education and retreat centre that offers collective insight retreats for people interested in breaking away from limiting patterns of thought. She teaches a master's course in consciousness studies and transpersonal psychology at the Graduate Institute. Her teaching highlights the embodied, affective and perceptual aspects of the core self, and the non-egoic potentials from which subtle sensing, intuition and insight emerge. Bonnitta is an author and fellow at Perspectiva, where she writes about emergent themes in education and spirituality. She is a contributor to and associate editor of *Integral Review*.

Minna Salami is a Nigerian, Finnish and Swedish writer, feminist theorist and the author of the internationally acclaimed book *Sensuous Knowledge: A Black Feminist Approach for Everyone*, published in March 2020. Translated into five languages, *Sensuous Knowledge* has been called 'intellectual soul food' (Bernardine Evaristo), 'vital' (Chris Abani) and a 'metaphysical journey into the genius the West hasn't given language to' (Johny Pitts). Minna has written for *The Guardian*, Al Jazeera and *World Literature Today* and is a columnist for *Esperanto Magazine*. She has presented talks at prominent institutions such as the UN, EU, Oxford Union, Cambridge Union, Yale University and Singularity University at NASA. She is co-director of the feminist movement Activate, and a Senior Research Associate at Perspectiva. She sits on the advisory board of the African Feminist Initiative at Pennsylvania State University and the editorial board of the *Interdisciplinary Journal for the Study of the Sahel*. She lives in London.

Zachary Stein is a philosopher of education working at the interface of psychology, metaphysics and politics. He has published two books, including *Education in a Time Between Worlds*, along with dozens of articles. He has co-founded a not-for-profit and think tank, taught graduate students at Harvard and consulted with technology start-ups. Zak is a long-time meditator, musician and caregiver. He lives with his wife in Vermont.

Sarah Stein Lubrano is a learning designer, content strategist and researcher. For many years she was the Head of Content at The School of Life in London. She is currently reading for a DPhil in Political Theory at Oxford University, studying the relationship between cognitive dissonance and politics in democracies. In previous lives, she worked as a prison tutor, student welfare officer and obituary writer. See more of her work at www.sarahsteinlubrano.com.

Siva Thambisetty is Associate Professor of Law at the London School of Economics. Her research interests lie in comparative patent law, the impact of transnational rules on developing countries, and the value of interdisciplinarity in the legal protection of inventions. She studied at the National Law School of India and earned her DPhil on a Felix Scholarship at the University of Oxford. She has published on emerging technologies, the equitable use of genetic resources, pharmaceutical innovation and biotechnology, and has worked on consultancies with the Nuffield Council on Bioethics, the UK Commission for Intellectual Property Rights, the UK Intellectual Property Office, and Lord Justice Jackson's Review of Civil Litigation Costs. She often works with scientists, policymakers and practitioners to develop sector- and technology-specific critiques of intellectual property systems. Dr Thambisetty enjoys teaching and citizenship work in higher education.

Mark Vernon is a writer, psychotherapist and associate of Perspectiva. He contributes to and presents programmes on the radio and writes for the national and religious press and for online publications. He also podcasts, in particular The Sheldrake–Vernon Dialogues with Rupert Sheldrake, gives talks and leads workshops. He has a PhD in ancient Greek philosophy, and other degrees in physics and in theology, having studied at Durham, Oxford and Warwick universities. He is the author of several books, including his latest, out in 2020: *A Secret History of Christianity: Jesus, the Last Inkling and the Evolution of Consciousness*. He used to be an Anglican priest and lives in London, UK. Mark is working on the notion of spiritual intelligence with Perspectiva, which is not about problem-solving but about the roots of awareness, as well as events. For more information, see www.markvernon.com.

John Vervaeke is an Associate Professor in the teaching stream. He has been teaching at the University of Toronto since 1994. He currently teaches courses in the psychology department on thinking and reasoning with an emphasis on insight problem-solving, on cognitive development with an emphasis on the dynamical nature of development, and on higher cognitive processes with an emphasis on intelligence, rationality, mindfulness and the psychology of wisdom. He is the director of the Cognitive Science programme, where he also teaches courses on the introduction to cognitive science, and the cognitive science of consciousness, wherein he emphasises 4E (embodied, embedded, enacted and extended) models of cognition and consciousness. In addition, he teaches a course in the Buddhism, Psychology and Mental Health programme, on Buddhism and Cognitive Science. He is the director of the Consciousness and the Wisdom Studies Laboratory. He has won and been nominated for several teaching awards, including the 2001 Students' Administrative Council and Association of Part-time Undergraduate Students Teaching Award for the Humanities, and the 2012 Ranjini Ghosh Excellence in Teaching Award. He has published articles on relevance realisation, general intelligence, mindfulness, flow, metaphor and wisdom. He is first author of the book *Zombies in Western Culture: A Twenty-First Century Crisis*, which integrates psychology and cognitive science to address the meaning crisis in Western society. He is the author and presenter of the YouTube series, 'Awakening from the Meaning Crisis'.

Preface – Metamodernism and the perception of context
The cultural between, the political after and the mystic beyond

Jonathan Rowson

If, dear reader, you do not feel called to understand what metamodernism means, I cannot blame you, and even envy you a little. Life is short, there is work to do, and we cannot dance with every ism that gives us the eye. You are welcome to give this preface a miss and enjoy the chapters. The theoretical struggle that follows – and it really has been a struggle – is mostly for the benefit of those who are invested in the meaning of metamodernism or are curious to become so. The chapters all have purposes of their own, but the nascent, capacious and ambiguous meaning of metamodernism informs the intellectual setting that all our authors are contending with, and therefore speaks to the purpose of the book as a whole.[1]

THIS BOOK was originally going to be called *A Metamodern Reader*. In 2018 my co-founder of Perspectiva, Tomas Björkman, was keen to compile a range of visions of society and methods to get there to help move intellectual life beyond postmodern critique; it seemed like a timely idea to me too. In all friendly candour, there was a collateral strategic aim in revealing the richness and diversity of metamodern thought, namely to widen the appeal of metamodern thinking and sensibility and thereby dilute the strength of the association between metamodernism and Hanzi Freinacht's iconoclastic books.[2] There are many other metamodernisms, as we'll see, but such is the strength of that association that a critical mass of prospective writers and editors became uneasy with providing tacit support for a fledgling movement they did not identify with. Moreover, the idea of a metamodern reader began to feel oxymoronic; as if a canonical text could hope to tame a concept in the semiotic wilds and digital storms of the early 21st century. There also seemed to be a case for ostensive illustrations of the style and substance of the post-postmodern impulse, rather than circling around an ambiguous term. For those reasons, the chapters in this compilation are mostly about grappling with the cultural and historical setting that has been called metamodernity, with an emphasis on the nature of the crises and meta-crises faced at a planetary level, and intimations of responses that are emerging to contend with them.

To paraphrase from Shakespeare's *Twelfth Night* then, some are born into metamodernity, some become metamodern and some have metamodernism thrust upon them. I am mostly in the latter camp. I didn't seek out this word, concept, ideology, pattern, movement, structure of feeling, state, stage, sensibility, episteme, movement, idea, notion … yet somehow metamodernism found me. Since it found me, I've used the term in my writing periodically, I have even been called a metamodernist, and now I find myself with editorial responsibility for publishing a compilation with metamodernity in the subtitle. As an adoptive parent of sorts, I feel compelled to take some responsibility for metamodernism, and perhaps even help it mature in some way.

Metamodernism is a feeling, and all that constitutes the feeling and flows from it. Our perception of context stems from a felt sense of what is happening, which is the cutting edge of our relationship to reality. When we consider the mystery of consciousness and the human drama playing out on this charming anomaly of a planet, feelings are far from trivial – they have cosmological significance. The metamodern feeling co-arises with the perception of context writ large; it is aesthetic in nature, epistemic in function, and historical in character, and it serves to call into question the purpose of the world as we find it, and the meaning of life as we know it.[3]

It might appear that metamodern*ism* emerges from within the early 21st century internet-infused cultural epoch of metamodern*ity*, but the relationship between the two is more interesting than that.[4] While the meaning of the term modern is notoriously contested, few doubt the validity of the idea of modernity as a grand epoch as such (more below), nor that we are now in the latter stages of it, but what we should *call* this phase of late modernity is contested, and is mostly a matter of choice of perceptual framing. The other contenders, like hypermodernity, supermodernity and even ecomodernity, all focus directly on the implications of technological developments. The meta prefix is distinctive, however, because it is generatively reflexive and tacitly humanistic. One way to grasp the value of the idea of *metamodernity* is to say it's about focusing our attention on our subjective and inter-subjective relationship to these times we live in, when we stand, in some quaveringly uncertain sense, after, within, between or beyond modernity.[5]

I believe the point of invoking metamodernity is not to insist on this name for a chronological phase of time but to resolve to characterise a cultural epoch with a Kairological quality of time.

What this approach discloses is not just that it's simply the early 21st century but that it's in some meaningful sense *the time*, more precisely perhaps our time, to look within, between and beyond. It is time to reappraise our inner lives and relationships by grappling with the apparent spiritual and material exhaustion of what has passed as normal and normative for a little too long: the presumed progress of science, reason, bureaucracy and industrial capitalism, the limitations of perspective and the failure of critique. We are now obliged to create meaning and fashion agency within the context of a *meta-crises* of perception and understanding relating to ecological, social and institutional breakdown, where one world seems to be dying, and another is trying to be born (as indicated in my chapter on the meta-crisis). The point of metamodernism is therefore to help us better perceive our historical context by developing theories and practices that allow us to *feel into* what it means to be in a time between worlds, where meta-crises relating to meaning and perception abound and we struggle to perceive clearly who we are and what we might do; where meta-theories seem friendly because mere theory feels absurdly specific; where nostalgic longing feels like it is as much about the future as the past, and where we sometimes feel like being ridiculously romantic and romantically ridiculous. To be metamodern is to be caught up in the co-arising of hope and despair, credulity and incredulity, progress and peril, agency and apathy, life and death. I had mixed feelings about metamodernism until I realised it is *about* mixed feelings.

The perception of context

What is at stake here is how the perception of context shapes the world. Over the last quarter of a century we have been scrambling to find language forms to help us catch up with what our shifting sense of context means for who we are, and how we should live. For many millions of people, cultural and technological developments have outpaced our conceptual grasp of them. Whether it is the sight of huge swathes of Australia on fire, the miasma of misinformation on so-called phones that have commandeered human eyes and hands, or the world apparently brought to its knees by a wayward bat in Wuhan; we are struggling to *grok* what is happening. In light of that ambient confusion, we seem to face what Graham Leicester and Maureen O'Hara call 'a conceptual emergency'.[6] We struggle to perceive our contexts clearly enough to be confident in our theories and our actions, and since the perception of context is a dynamic variable within and between people and a generative capacity in any normative vision for the world, a prima facie case arises for concepts that help us to perceive context better.[7]

The challenge is that in a digitalised, ecologically compromised and politically charged world, where hyper-objects abound, context writ large is impossible to perceive precisely or even accurately.[8] At the planetary scale, contexts are myriad, layered, contested, incommensurate and cross-pollinating, and our perceptual apparatus is often overwhelmed, if not deliberately distorted by mediating influences. In such a world there can be no conceptual panaceas, so we have to make do with our best available approximations. Meaning-making animals that we are, we hide our confusion under capacious conceptual canopies such as *modernism*, *postmodernism* and *metamodernism*, and by taking shelter there we allay our sense of feeling completely lost. While the use of such clunky terms is not always edifying, it is forgivable, and for some purposes, necessary. Just as we like to know the name of a person after talking to them for a while, but still don't pretend to really know them, it is natural to seek to name the cultural and historical context we are living through, and to try to discern a telos for ourselves and others within it. This inclination is especially true when we sense that our place, our telos, our entelechy, may not be in this world as such, but somehow *meta*: after, within, between or beyond it.

The point of grappling with metamodernism, then, is not about passive conceptual nourishment but is rather a way of taking intellectual and moral responsibility for the critical active ingredient in play – the perception of context in our lives and our times. The implicit question of this book is not really what does metamodernism mean – which presupposes that people can care, do care or should care. More profoundly, we are asking, what distinct perceptions of context does the notion of metamodernity elicit, disclose and support, such that it might be worthy of our attention and support?

I hope to show the following: first, while metamodernism has divergent interpretations, it functions as an orienting theory to describe (and, for some, prescribe) our relationship (which is in some sense meta) to the cultural and historical context of late (post)modernity. In this role, metamodernism is coherent, rich, illuminating and challenging enough to help us orient ourselves towards context writ large – a context that has shifted abruptly in this century through technological developments and ecological collapse, and now poses an existential test in terms of human understanding and cooperation. Second, modernism and postmodernism have their own capacious dignity, and both live on with us. The distinctiveness of metamodernism is often hard to discern, but that distinctive meaning can be teased out in a way that is generative, and the personal work involved in the teasing-out is part of its value. Third, metamodernism has more than one genesis story and is in every sense diverse in its origins; it is as much about protecting human dignity and interiority from the techno-capitalist dystopias of hypermodernism as it is about the particularly funky relationship between modernism and postmodernism. Fourth, metamodernism is grounded in the importance of aesthetic understanding as a form of epistemic orientation. The structure of feeling at the heart of it – whether described as neo-romantic, post-tragic or otherwise, is not background music but the active ingredient itself. Fifth, Hanzi Freinacht's contribution to metamodernism is substantial but controversial, and it is primarily about the shift in register from theory to meta-theory, thereby effectively historicising Integral Theory and politicising the metamodern sensibility. Sixth, while Hanzi helpfully distinguishes six different ways in which metamodernism is used (in recent talks and in his chapter here), the question of what exactly metamodernism *is* remains somewhat moot. For instance, it is an open question to what extent the impetus that drives developmental metamodernism is orthogonal or even antithetical to the aesthetic understanding of cultural metamodernism. Seventh, the cross-currents of metamodernism can perhaps best be distilled into three main patterns: the cultural between, the political after and the mystic beyond. Eighth, most attention has been focused on the former two, but an engagement with metamodern metaphysics is the new frontier. Ninth, while metamodernism remains variegated, I suggest the perception of context it offers can be distilled into four main themes corresponding to each of the four integral quadrants: interiority, intimacy, ecology and historicity, all of which are in some sense *developing*. Tenth, and – mercifully – finally, the broad, elusive and contested nature of metamodernism will remain; this is not a sign of weakness, but precisely what we would expect for a conceptual holding pattern of context writ large in a time between worlds. All other things considered, I contend that when viewed as a whole, metamodernism has its own coherence, dignity, relevance and timely generativity, and I hope the chapters that follow help to develop that.

Modernism and postmodernism as dysfunctional but loveable parents

We cannot hope to make friends with metamodernism if we are going to caricature or patronise her parents. We need to understand the relationship between Mr Modernism and Mrs Postmodernism well enough to enjoy gossiping about it (there is a significant age gap for a start …). Part of the challenge is that there are so many modernisms and postmodernisms that it is not surprising metamodernism is a wayward child, taking some time to find itself. And we see the same tensions between cultural, literary and political expressions of modernism and postmodernism in metamodernism today, which suggests this is a feature and not a bug of any catch-all term for the perception of context writ large. Making exhaustive sense of these conceptual thickets calls for an elaborate scholarly performance to disclose the multiple meanings of modern/ity/ism and postmodern/ity/ism and reflections on their interpretations and relationships, while also giving a respectful nod to wayward cousins like hypermodernity, altermodernity and so forth. Mercifully, many others have tried to do that work for us already. What follows is based on a conscientious reading of the relevant literature, but my aim is less an academic exegesis than an attempt to share my process of forming a relationship with metamodernism, to help the reader forge their own.[9]

The term 'modern' is derived from the Latin *modo* and simply means 'of today', distinguishing whatever is contemporary from earlier times. Modernity refers to our contemporary civilisation built over the last 400 years or so through scientific, industrial and technological revolutions, but what makes modernity is not just method or machines. We are not, as sociologist Peter Berger puts it, ancient Egyptians in airplanes, not least because so many of us are future-oriented, at least in our younger years. Indeed, Habermas's description of modernity is precisely about that. In *The Philosophical Discourse of Modernity*, he writes: 'the concept of modernity expresses the conviction that the future has already begun: it is the epoch that lives for the future, that opens itself up to the novelty of the future.' As we open up to the future, and as the world changes, we change too. And so modern*ism*, although voluminous and outrageously ambiguous, refers to the worldviews that arose from human culture stewing in the juices of modernity for decades. Modernism expressed itself in art, architecture and literature and evolved into political institutions and ideologies. Science is quintessentially modern but capitalism and communism are also modernist endeavours, and so is the organised aspect of religion and human rights law. Perhaps most relevant for current purposes is that modernism entails an irresolute process of secularisation and also the growth of civic and commercial institutions powered by bureaucratic and instrumental rationality and an exploitative relationship to nature. Modernism is therefore about presumed material and scientific progress, but it is often accused of wearing blinkers about its collateral damage. For instance, colonialism, slavery and fossil fuels drove much of modernism's so-called progress. In a related sense, in Habermas's later work, *Modernity: An Unfinished Project*, he argues that modernity is characterised by the separation of truth, beauty and goodness; of science, art and morality. That separation of our value spheres was a source of fragmentation and alienation that lived on in postmodernism, and part of the purpose of metamodern metaphysics mentioned below is to somehow bring them back together.[10]

Like modernism, postmodernism is polyform and enigmatic. Some see the very idea of summarising as antithetical to the reflex pluralism, perspective-taking and reactivity of postmodernism, such that any definition of postmodernism can be seen as performative contradiction. However, one defining quality of postmodernism is that it is modernism turned in on itself: the tools of reason questioning their own reasonableness; the idea of progress noticing, as a kind of progress, that it is indeed an idea. This spirit of recursive awareness is present in the emphasis on the relationship between knowledge and power and social (de)construction of reality rather than its simple presentation; presumptions of depth and origin and authenticity are questioned, and there is even some revelling in superficiality as its own kind of profundity. With postmodernism there is an emphasis on plurality rather than unity, and a preference for the experienced immanence of life over its putative transcendence. However, these are matters of disposition and emphasis, course corrections for modernism that, yes, sometimes entail over-corrections, but they are not typically doctrinal in nature, yet are often misunderstood as such. This refrain makes more sense when we grasp that postmodernism arises within a relatively short time frame. Some see Nietzsche as a kind of postmodern prophet writing before the 20th century; for instance, in *Twilight of the Idols* he noted that the 'will to a system lacks integrity', which anticipates perhaps the signature postmodern line of Jean-François Lyotard in *The Postmodern Condition: A Report on Knowledge* in 1979, that the postmodern condition is characterised by 'incredulity towards metanarratives'.[11] Yet, as always, Nietzsche is sui generis; it wasn't until the sixties counter-culture that postmodern vibes started to tingle from the sprouting San Franciscan flowers, the spirit of norm-breaking, self-discovery through oppositional identities (e.g. anti-Vietnam war) and the challenge to hierarchical and conventional power structures. That spirit lives on in today's 'identity politics'. However, my impression is that what Jeremy Gilbert calls 'the long nineties' may be the best temporal locus for the postmodern sensibility, especially if we allow it to be so long that it sneakily includes some of the seventies, eighties and noughties too. That quarter of a century or so before and around 2000 is when disquisitions about key postmodern thinkers (who were saying very different things and often didn't identify as postmodern) like Michel Foucault, Jacques Derrida, Richard Rorty, Donna Haraway, Frederic Jameson and Jean Baudrillard were at their height. This was also a time of the Cold War coming to a gradual end, when one side appeared to win the ideological battle, and for a time global politics felt *relatively* stable. In the pre-internet calm, and before climate collapse seemed credible, millions were at peace with their modernist gizmos – microwaves, washing machines, televisions – and yet some restless ironic detachment was setting in. The American rock band Talking Heads, formed in 1975, were quintessentially postmodern; they sang about their beautiful house not being *their* beautiful house after all, their lyrics observing moments of realisation that our lives are often a dream created for us rather than by us. Meanwhile, Hue and Cry sang about not needing 'your ministrations, your bad determinations' and having had enough of the 'pseudo-satisfaction' on offer.[12] And yet still, and even for some years later, we could go to the movies to distract ourselves with *Pulp Fiction* (1994) and *Fight Club* (1999), films that did not pretend to be deep but spoke to us by highlighting our misplaced sense of narrative coherence. When all that was too much, we could chill at home and watch simulated realities in *Friends* or *Seinfeld* or *The Simpsons*; and we could laugh along because while we were still grappling with the human condition, and there were still problems outside, everything felt more or less under control.

That is not today's world of course, and postmodernism, though still relevant and pervasive, does not feel adequate to our species-specific task of survival or renewal at scale in the context of ecological peril in particular and the context that gives rise to it: the *meta* challenge of saving civilisation from itself.

Origin stories and forgotten prophets

Metamodernism began ripening in the early 21st century, but it has a meaningful pre-history that should not be overlooked. The term was first mentioned by American literary scholar Zavarzadeh Mas'ud in 1975,[13] to describe patterns of aesthetics and attitudes that he had been observing since the 1950s, including the co-presence of fact and fiction, art and reality, manifest most tangibly in the hybrid genre of 'the nonfiction novel'. Those who know his work inform me that since he was writing before the term postmodern was in wide circulation, Zavarzadeh may have been using meta in the most straightforward sense of 'after', synonymous with 'post'. This would help explain why metamodernism took a while to get into its stride, and beyond the occasional reference in literary journals, there were perhaps only two important but somewhat neglected sources in the nineties inspired by liberation theology – Albert Borgmann and Justo L. Gonzalez – recently uncovered by Brent Cooper. These sources point to a broader (and perhaps deeper) origin story about the provenance of metamodernism that challenges the academically orthodox view that it is primarily a literary or artistic affair.[14]

In the field of technology studies, Albert Borgmann (1992) juxtaposed hypermodernity with metamodernity in a way that clarifies the two incipient worlds that we live with today. One is a dystopian future we often feel we are drifting towards, while the other is the future we are called on to fight for. For Borgmann, postmodernity bifurcates into a runaway hyperreality where we become increasingly lost and exploited through technological servitude. He refers to 'the fatal liabilities of the hypermodern condition, of a life that is enfeebled by hyperreality, fevered by hyperactivity, and disfranchised by hyperintelligence.' And yet, if we can muster the courage, guile and coordination, we can instead create a world of metamodernity where humans reclaim control of the capacities required to shape our lives, through what

Borgmann calls 'focal attention': 'Focal things cannot be secured or procured, they can only be discovered, revered, and sustained in a focal practice. Such focal things and practices are well and alive in our artistic, athletic, and religious celebrations.' Borgmann's framing of the metamodern impulse is echoed in the challenges of addiction and attentional capture highlighted by the recent documentary *The Social Dilemma*, and also in Matthew Crawford's applied philosophical work on the need for 'focal activity' and an 'attentional commons'.[15]

Another figure largely ignored by the field of metamodern studies is Cuban-American liberation theologian Justo L. Gonzalez, who connected metamodernism to the postcolonial struggle in *Metamodern Aliens in Postmodern Jerusalem* (1996). Gonzalez sees a legitimate use for meta, in the sense of going beyond the modern, such that the enduring postcolonial struggle of many millions around the world is not subsumed within postmodern critique but is grounded in a generative vision of reality in turn grounded in liberation from enduring colonialism in all its forms. Cooper suggests that Alexandra Ocasio-Cortez embodies Gonzalean metamodernism: 'A young female minority leader of a new progressive coalition … Pragmatic idealism is back with a playful vengeance.'[16]

Borgmann and Gonzales did not build their intellectual identities around metamodernism; they used the term almost incidentally in fairly obscure sources, and did not initiate discourse around metamodernism. Nonetheless, in their own ways Borgmann and Gonzalez exemplify an impulse that could be distinctly and meaningfully metamodern, namely the desire to disclose perceptions of context (meta as within and between) that are saturated with history, meaning and perspective (because modernism and postmodernism have done their work) but nonetheless remain ours to shape; and that perception of context is therefore potentially liberating (metamodern). While these sources uncovered by Cooper are not an explicit part of the conceptual scaffolding on which contemporary 'metamodernism' has been built, I am impressed by the fact that they both exemplify a perception of context that traverses political and spiritual features of human experience and proactively seek to combine them for normative ends. These sources speak to me because in my own way I have been trying to do similar work for the last decade, starting with the realisation, while working at The Royal Society of Arts in London, that my policy research work on climate change and my public enquiry into spirituality were grounded in the same perception of context.[17]

In what might playfully be called the mid-history of metamodernism, there is also an intriguing and underexplored relationship between metamodernism and Yoruba culture that is intimated by Moyo Okediji in the late nineties, the spirit of which can be discerned today in Bayo Akomolafe's poetic and prophetic thought, and which Minna Salami is currently researching for Perspectiva. Some have described reggae music as inherently metamodern in its awareness of an interiority characterised by the co-presence of suffering and joy, which we can sense for instance in Bob Marley's line about some people feeling the rain while others just get wet. More broadly, a case has been made for Black metamodernism.[18] Historic figures including Martin Luther King and contemporary figures like Cornel West are thought to exude the metamodern sensibility. For instance, when asked what to do about racism in news interviews, West often quotes Samuel Beckett: 'Try again, fail again, fail better.'[19] I am not sure where one might begin to place the metamodern in South or East Asian culture, but *Meta Modern Era* by Shri Nirmala Devi gave a quasi-Vedantic spiritual conception of the idea in 1997,[20] and much of the paradoxical and playful nature of Taoism sometimes feels metamodern in spirit, even if the Chinese Communist Party does not.[21]

Discussions of the genealogy of metamodernism also draw attention to a range of sociopolitical developments that shifted the world beyond the postmodern into something qualitatively new and ideationally up for grabs. Seth Abramson has written widely on metamodernism and emphasises the advent of the internet as seismic and pivotal, changing our capacity for self-expression and collective sense-making as a key driver of metamodern sensibility.[22] Zachary Stein emphasises our reckoning with a shift in geological time through the dawning of the Anthropocene (and Jason Moore's Capitalocene) in which humans discover they are unwitting agents of accelerating geological time.[23] The events of 9/11 and its aftermath have also been highlighted as the moment it became obvious that Fukuyama's 'end of history' had ended, where history was recommencing with a vengeance with no obvious telos in sight.

A structure of feeling

This brisk genealogy of some major aspects of metamodernism is important because it shows that the term can be seen as variegated, expansive and cross-cultural in scope. However, it is also true that metamodernism only really started to get noticed and respected by a critical mass of discerning people when two young Dutch cultural theorists, Timotheus Vermeulen and Robin van den Akker, published *Notes on Metamodernism* in 2010 – responding mostly to cultural developments in the first decade of the 21st century. The VandvdA (a useful shorthand which I hope they'll permit me) paper is commendably rich and detailed and well illustrated with examples that disclose the 'structure of feeling' that characterises our metamodern predicament, including this signature line:

> Ontologically, metamodernism oscillates between the modern and the postmodern. It oscillates between a modern enthusiasm and a postmodern irony, between hope and melancholy, between naïveté and knowingness, empathy and apathy, unity and plurality, totality and fragmentation, purity and ambiguity.[24]

Since the authors of these words are invoking ontology rather than just speaking figuratively, it is worth asking whether 'oscillation' is precisely the right term. 'Juxtaposition' (Seth Abramson) or 'superimposition' (Daniel Görtz) or 'interconnections' (Alexandra Dumitrescu) or 'braiding' (Greg Dember) might work just as well or better. That is the kind of nuanced enquiry the field of cultural metamodernism explores, usually with examples from contemporary culture, and I wish this community of scholars well.[25] Those working in the field advise me that there are metamodern elements in many of the popular culture shows I have recently enjoyed – *Stranger Things* and *Cobra Kai* on Netflix, for instance, share the postmodern feature of ironic self-reference and yet clearly transcend that with a sincere depth of enquiry into the interior states and learning journeys of the protagonists; the irony is sincere and the magic is real. Moreover, it is worth considering that *Time Magazine* listed Phoebe Waller-Bridge as one of the 100 most influential people in the world in 2020 for her work on the hit television series *Killing Eve* and *Fleabag*, both of which I loved. The nature of that influence was cultural, and metamodern, in spirit.[26]

I confess that I only read VandvdA's seminal *Notes on Metamodernism* paper properly quite recently. I say 'confess' because it made me feel sheepish about having used the term metamodern as if I knew what I was talking about, while not having digested this deep and prismatic consideration of it. This feeling of sheepishness is all the more real because there was a large community on an active website or 'webzine' between 2009 and 2016 that shared the enquiry that I was completely unaware of until a few months ago.[27] It feels absurd to apologise on behalf of people I am only loosely affiliated with, to a research community I have barely met, but in a sense I am sorry. There is a significant body of diligent and heartfelt scholarship on the idea of metamodernism that has mostly been ignored by those who encountered metamodernism, as I did, via Hanzi Freinacht, and while we can make some sense of how that came about (and I do below) it still feels somehow *impolite*.

Since *Notes on Metamodernism* was published in 2010, Google Scholar mentions of 'metamodernism' moved from single digits in that year steadily into the hundreds, and the number is now over 400, with over 2,000 in total, overwhelming in reference to Vermeulen and van den Akker and other scholars considering metamodernism in similar ways. VandvdA also published an updated reflection on responses to their paper in 2015, which is recommended reading.[28] The VandvdA perspective on metamodernism generated a whole community of enquiry, and the Arts and Humanities Research Network in the UK has supported related work on metamodernism since 2018.[29] Moreover, much of the scholarly leadership comes from women. In her PhD (2014) and subsequent publications Alexandra Balm (née Dumitrescu) offers a spiritual emphasis within a broader societal vision, including a close examination of Arundhati Roy's Booker Prize-winning novel, *The God of Small Things*. It is important to note in passing that Balm (then Dumitrescu) appears to have theorised metamodernism as a category in literature *before* Vermeulen and van den Akker, and she offers a related but distinctive emphasis, locating the metamodern patterns of integration between masculine and feminine, rational and emotional and in 'recuperating traditions'.[30] In a similar, but again distinct, vein of enquiry, Linda Ceriello links the metamodern sensibility to forms of mysticism grounded in secular spirituality, illustrated, for instance, in Russell Brand's rhapsodic flirtations with transcendence.[31] Alison Gibbons emphasises 'the resurgence of historicity' in the context of reckoning with the Anthropocene after the perpetual present of postmodernism.[32] My overall impression is that metamodernism is no passing fad. The term is here to stay.

A successful kidnap?

There is an open question now about the legitimacy of the term's scope and remit outside of academia, especially because many people who invoke metamodernism to make sense of their work are para-academic or post-academic, often writing as intellectual journalists or policy researchers and often having advanced degrees, but mostly having little inclination to confine themselves to scholarly captivity or write for academic journals. It just somehow doesn't feel metamodern to play the academic game. In so far as this observation is accurate, it may say something about the epistemic and scholarly style of metamodernism, which acts as a tacit and sometimes explicit critique on conventional academic knowledge production.

For instance, I came across metamodernism through Hanzi Freinacht's first book *The Listening Society*, in which the primary author is an academically trained sociologist who happened to undertake what sounds like a life-changing apprenticeship in Michael Common's theory of cognitive development called The Model of Hierarchical Complexity (MHC), and his political vision is informed by cross-disciplinary understanding. Hanzi's first book is insightful and referenced, but it is written in an essayistic style and it is mostly a vision of a deliberately developmental society rather than anything self-evidently metamodern in the prior meanings of the term, in culture theory at least. In the appendices of that book, which is the literary equivalent of behind the bike shed in the playground, Hanzi even describes their adoption of the term metamodern as an act of 'idealistic piracy' and claims they are 'shanghaiing' (kidnapping) it for the greater good.

With all due respect to the victims, it was a successful kidnap. Indeed, Hanzi's books are now synonymous with metamodernism for many. On reflection, however, *The Listening Society*'s main contribution to metamodern thinking is less about original intellectual substance or even innovative rhetorical style (though it has both) and more about the fact that it enriched existing metamodern theorising with integral *meta-theory* and thereby deepened its significance and broadened its applicability.

James Hillman's *Puer/Senex* distinction is useful here. *Puer* embodies a kind of creatively destructive and self-confident energy with a wide-ranging spirit of eager fantasy, while *Senex* is the established and orderly understanding or wisdom; and there is naturally tension and competition between them. Hanzi is very much writing in the spirit of *Puer* rather than *Senex*, but it seems implicit, and has to some extent been conceded explicitly, that the spirit of the *Senex* role in the book is not so much academically established metamodernism, but the progenitor of Integral Theory, Ken Wilber. To put it straightforwardly, the subtext of Hanzi's books is that he is saying: Integral Theory has failed, and metamodernism is now called for. In that quest, Hanzi attempts to use the sensibility of cultural metamodernism that he has kidnapped to usurp Integral Theory and to subsume it within political metamodernism.[33]

For those familiar with Wilber's work, even his most basic conceptual map of the four quadrants of reality, a meta-theory stripped to its barest essentials helps us to understand the evolution of metamodernism.[34] Those familiar with integral thinking use this meta-theoretical tool to locate the provenance and application of phenomena, and to make sense of existing theorising. From that perspective alone, VandvdA metamodernism looks 'true but partial' (an integral term of art) for two main reasons: it's primarily a left quadrant's endeavour (I and We, psychology and culture) and it is implicitly but not explicitly developmental in outlook. By implicitly developmental I mean that the metamodern sensibility does not entail the normative vision of a deliberately developmental society at all, but it does co-arise in response to a new cultural curriculum, as developmental theory would expect. For instance, in Robert Kegan's constructive developmental terms, the neo-romantic, post-tragic and planetary aspects of the cultural sensibility of metamodernism is 'the hidden curriculum' of metamodernity and corresponds to what he calls 'constructive postmodernism', something we learn to grow into through the coalescence of cultural evolution and personal maturity.[35]

To a relatively young and integrally informed mind, unfamiliar at that stage with Borgmann or Gonzalez or others, *Notes on Metamodernism* (and its subsequent elaborations) is therefore crying out for expression in the other quadrants, for a developmental appraisal of how the metamodern sensibility comes into being, and for a blueprint of what might follow normatively for individuals and cultures. And here is perhaps the key point. That impulse to combine cultural metamodernism and Integral Theory is not just intellectual but is also intensely and self-consciously political.

Integral Theory is not particularly political and in some ways can even be seen as anti-political; it is famed for its balance and perspective on competing points of view. The politically metamodern impulse, on the other hand, arises because today we are living with a world that feels like it's unravelling through climate change, culture war, bio-precarity, political corruption and myriad economic failures. In that context Integral Theory *has to* evolve to *something* post-integral, if only because it feels like the bottom right quadrant (the systems and structures of society) is on fire; the conflagration is already figuratively spreading to the other quadrants on the map, and literally in the sense of houses, cities and even countries burning to the ground. Any model or outlook that ignores the need for a new politics, including cultural metamodernism, therefore risks looking obtuse. Enter Hanzi Freinacht, who speaks *with* an integral understanding and with an apparently intuitive metamodern sensibility but *to* that prevailing common-sense understanding that 'something must be done'.

There are some chicken-and-egg dynamics here. On the one hand, metamodernism comes after Integral Theory and tries to supersede it, but it is only because of the historical conditions of metamodernity – culture saturated with decades of intellectual and cultural (post)modernism – that meta-theory as such becomes *possible*, as well as necessary. In this sense, metamodernity gave birth to Integral Theory, not the other way round. The conditions of metamodernity and its historical antecedents provide the raw materials and impetus for Integral Theory, alongside other meta-theoretical frameworks that contend with the relationship between the spiritual and material features of life including, for instance, Iain McGilchrist's neurocultural analysis and Roy Bhaskar's critical realism.[36]

In that fuller meta-theoretical and historical context, Hanzi deserves to be widely read and admired, regardless of inevitable critiques of his work; for instance Sarah Stein Lubrano amusingly quipped that political metamodernism is just 'Hegel for hippies' and Minna Salami notes in her chapter in this book that Hanzi's ideas often look suspiciously like feminism in disguise. However, we can all admire *any* attempt to use the intellect in good faith to try to forge a pathway to a viable and desirable future. My pragmatic inclination is therefore to hope that there is scope for a fertile dialogue between different kinds of metamodernism and that, as Daniel Görtz elegantly put it on the Metamoderna mailing list: 'There is plenty of champagne to go round.'[37]

Conundrums of metamodern normativity

Perhaps there is a figurative champagne reception to be had, but would the people present be celebrating the same thing? There are significant divergences between these two major streams of metamodern endeavour. For instance, Hanzi speaks of 'dividuals' rather than individuals, to reflect the extent of our historical and biological inheritance and networked interdependence and our reciprocal malleability, while cultural metamodernism would be more inclined to protect our uniquely *individual* interior experiences from that kind of systemising abstraction. Moreover, cultural metamodernism tends to locate the active ingredient of metamodernism in the relationship between the cultural artefacts and the interiority of people, rather than in the people as such; for some, metamodernism is a phenomenon, not a field, and certainly not a programmatic agenda that seeks to bring about a different world.

I have mixed feelings here. I am inclined to say that political and cultural metamodernisms are both completely distinct endeavours *and* part of the same pattern of meaning. As an 'intuition pump' way of resolving this tension, I wonder – since Jean-François Lyotard summarised the postmodern attitude as 'incredulity towards metanarratives' – what the metamodern attitude might be incredulous towards. There are many possible answers here, including incredulity towards technological solutionism, which is better characterised as hypermodern. I notice, however, that my personal answer appears to involve tacitly 'picking a side' in metamodernism's internecine cold war. In so far as I am metamodern or understand metamodernism, my incredulity is towards neutrality, by which I mean disavowal of our role in the direction of everything that is underway. By implication, I mean incredulity towards those aspects of cultural metamodernism that insist they are not normative in nature.

I think Hanzi should have been more generous and transparent about his kidnapping-is-the-new-adopting use of the term metamodern, but when he says he did it for the greater good, I feel he is in good faith. There is a curious streak of something like purist humility in van den Akker and Vermeulen's cultural metamodernism that resembles the contested logic of the old-fashioned is/ought distinction in ethics, which, roughly, contends that you cannot derive normative implications from statements of how things are. In their 2015 'Corrections and Clarifications' piece especially, VandvdA are keen to delineate their descriptive take on metamodernism from anything more prescriptive. That is their prerogative, but I am just not sure that descriptive/prescriptive distinction holds, especially when what is being *described* often stems from a background sense that the world as we have known it is collapsing, which means that something is tacitly prescribed in the process too, not necessarily in Hanzian terms, but in the feeling that *something must be done*.

And yet I suppose there is some hubris there too, because humans are never as in control as we think we are. Covid has taught us that, and much else besides. Moreover, normativity is vexing in all sorts of ways. For instance, as I became familiar with postmodernism I began to feel some generosity of spirit towards it, which obliged me to work harder to identify what exactly metamodernism *could* add at a normative level — the first of many conundrums of metamodern normativity. A lazy summation of postmodernism is that it is about style rather the substance, that it lacks depth and soul, easily collapses into mad relativism and gets lost in critique, self-reference and endless perspective-taking; on this view of it, postmodernism lacks generativity and cannot help us to save ourselves from ourselves. None of that is strictly false, but it is straw-man-like, and there are other ways to see it. For instance, Derrida appears to contend that there is nothing outside the text or no context that is outside-text (il n'y a pas de hors texte),[38] but what he really means is that there is nothing outside of hermeneutic context, and it follows that it's incumbent on us to understand the context in which meaning arises; that sounds like an invitation to back up all the way to our collective imaginary — a key metamodern focus for some that is perhaps quintessentially postmodern. And Lyotard does not say there can be no metanarratives of big stories, just that we are right to be sceptical about them (and surely that's sound advice?). Moreover, he suggests knowledge has a narrative character and that our responsibility is to own up to the implicit ethics and metaphysics in the stories we live by (the problem with modernism is that it disavowed those commitments), which sounds a lot like the metamodern lingo of 'co-creating a more conscious society'. And the putatively metamodern emphasis on serious irony would not be new to the apparently arch postmodernist Richard Rorty, and nor is solidarity with all beings and all perspectives; consider the title of his classic text: *Irony, Contingency and Solidarity*. Moreover, it's not true of postmodernists that 'they have no positive ideas'; for starters, philosophical pragmatism can be seen as postmodern and the putatively metamodern reappraisal of Bildung looks quite a lot like Rorty's pragmatic case for sentimental education.[39] And in today's context of data extraction, behavioural manipulation and smartphone addiction, who better than Michel Foucault to remind us of the link between knowledge and power, the surveillance (panopticon-like) apparatus of the disciplinary society and our scope for emancipation? My impression is that in the battle for the perception of context and the creation of tools to remake the world, postmodernism is better armed and more versatile than we tend to think.

I share this short appraisal of postmodernism to contextualise a second conundrum of metamodern normativity about Hanzi in particular. However well developed the vision of a deliberately developmental society may otherwise be, it is unclear whether Hanzi really shifts the dial of our experience and perception beyond (post)modernism. Hanzi's iconoclastic writing style is designed to bamboozle and thereby circumvent postmodern cultural reactivity. I believe he does achieve forms of metamodern oscillation in his readers between, for instance, hope and despair, and sincerity and irony, and he does help move us beyond postmodern 'whataboutery' to something that feels closer to the whole truth of our experience and scope for normative directionality within it. Yet the idea of a listening society (and the ecosystem of political institutions and practices designed to facilitate it outlined in *Nordic Ideology*) can be seen as more like a hybrid than a synthesis: two distinct things characterised as being one thing that is two things, or a third thing that emerges from the *relationship* between the two.

In a morphological sense, the Hanzi vision is inherently multi-perspectival in nature ('Solidarity with all beings means solidarity with all perspectives'[40]) which can be seen as primarily *postmodern* in spirit. And the underlying vision of a self-consciously therapeutic and deliberately developmental society is arguably *modernist* in its system-building, universalising and emancipatory spirit. In the comment thread to an online essay mostly targeting Hanzi that was later republished by Perspectiva, Samuel Ludford puts the challenge like this: 'Postmodern discursive norms and modernist politics does not amount to a developmental synthesis at either level. What it amounts to is the cultural logic of late capitalism writing itself an alibi.'[41] On reflection, this line might not be as clever as it sounds, but it brought to mind the idea of surveillance capitalism, which is defined with analytical precision by Shoshana Zuboff, but can perhaps be seen more loosely as a totalising modernist infrastructure that monetises postmodern cultural tropes of hyperreality and identitarian polarisation.[42] Surveillance capitalism is clearly part of the context of metamodernity, and it influences our structure of feeling, but there is no oscillation to speak of, nor any enchanting emergent properties up for grabs. I think this means that metamodernism has to reckon more clearly with its defining structural and cultural limitations in metamodernity. Since that context is both modern and postmodern, but without necessarily having any higher-order synthesis or funky oscillation beyond our own projection, metamodernism struggles to create a distinctive normative vision without losing its conceptual fidelity to metamodern context and sensibility. To be fair, and in response to my incredulity towards them, this subtle point may already have been intuited by Vermeulen and van den Akker.[43]

The third and directly related conundrum of metamodern normativity is that it is not straightforward for metamodernism to be political as such. Although there is a subculture of 'The New Left' that links metamodernism to progressive policy programmes, and Hanzi's think tank, Metamoderna, flirted with calling itself The Alt-Left to offer an alternative to the Alt-Right, there have been many right-wing appropriations of the term metamodernism. For instance, Greg Dember writes of the Alt-Right as follows:

> While their behaviour is frequently vile and degrading towards others, from their own vantage, they are engaging in ironic play disrupting a hegemonic culture that leaves no room for their inner world. 'Metamodern' helps describe the cultural-behavioral reaction observed here. A descriptive, epistemic theorization of metamodernism allows for exemplars not favoured by the theorist. Put plainly, if 'metamodernism' is used to refer only to content you agree with and like, it's probably not metamodernism.[44]

Whatever one's relationship to metamodernism, saying that it is fundamentally left-wing or right-wing or centrist is not going to work, or help. In a world shaped by the private co-option of the public realm, myriad addictions, ecological collapse, governance failure, reassertions of identity and pleas for survival, the old-fashioned binaries of individual/collective, freedom/equality, state/market and tradition/change are otiose. There is scope for conceptual renewal here grounded in a new aesthetic, and *that* feels like a metamodern enterprise to be encouraged.

I am not saying that metamodernism should be post-political in the sense of equating politics with technocracy. On the contrary, I feel metamodernism *has to be* more astutely and deeply political in its offering (both to meet the needs of the time and to be true to itself). Metamodernism can influence events by being in some way *quasi-political*, for instance influencing politics through cultural or educational innovation, or *pre-political*, through the cultivation of relational and civic virtues. Most fundamentally, metamodernism can be *meta-political* in the sense that the structure of feeling that defines our time may contain clues to what politics as a whole should be about; that is arguably what The Alternative political platforms in, for instance, Denmark and the UK are about. However, any successful meta-political venture, for instance Bildung at scale as the organising principle of society, needs a strategy for outcompeting other meta-political movements, for example, QAnon or Neoliberalism, and such a strategy may have to be concerned directly with how to attract and wield power, and therefore be more conventionally political in nature. None of this is easy.[45]

The third refrain on metamodern normativity is actually a celebration, because the view of metamodernism as a path-forging and future-creating endeavour is by no means exclusive to Hanzi, and there are already quasi-political, pre-political and meta-political ventures under way. For instance, in addition to those mentioned above, Tomas Björkman invokes metamodernism as the cultural inheritance that behoves us to consciously fashion a more viable and desirable collective imaginary.[46] In a similar spirit, Lene Rachel Andersen uses the term to describe the construction of a new cultural code that works for our times, transcending and including prior cultural codes, including the indigenous, the premodern, the modern and the postmodern. Both Björkman and Andersen lay out normative pathways, often relating to the praxis of transformative civic education called Bildung.[47]

Metamodernism is also used as an umbrella term to describe the overarching pattern of enquiry and endeavour that connects the work of The Alternative political parties in Denmark and the UK, who seek 'a new politics', Daniel Schmachtenberger's Epistemic NGO The Consilience Project, the spirit of ontological design in the Game B community, and a range of theorists and practitioners working on regeneration, such as Joe Brewer on bioregionalism, perception-generating methodologies like Nora Bateson's warm data labs, Jason Snyder walking the talk of 'cosmo-localism' and Michel Bauwens' advocacy of peer-to-peer practices. Also sharing this inclination to connect inner and outer change, we could mention Giles Hutchins and Laura Storm on Regenerative Leadership, Gregg Henriques' Theory of Knowledge community and Daniel Christian Wahl on Designing Regenerative Cultures. We might also include Otto Scharmer and Katrin Kaufer in their work on Leading from the Emerging Future, Elizabeth Debold and Thomas Steininger's work on Emergent Dialogue, and Frederic Laloux's *Reinventing Organizations*.[48]

These theorists and practitioners do not necessarily call themselves metamodern, but they are operating in 'a time between worlds' and are responding to the metamodern structure of feeling. And yet there's a twist, because as this discussion moves towards a close, I notice an elision and conflation (not oscillation!) between two kinds of betweenness in metamodernism discourse – the time *between* worlds and the relationship *between* modernism and postmodernism. Clearly, these are ontologically and historiographically distinct phenomena, and that begs the question of just how much work the meta in metamodernism is doing.

Meta as a triple agent

It has taken me five years to make friends with metamodernism. For too long I had been looking at the meta in the 'metamodern' without really seeing her, without grasping that she, *Meta*, is a kind of triple agent, hiding inside the concept as a protean spy, and using the modern as an elaborate cover story. The meaning of metamodernism is notoriously elusive, but it becomes enchanting when we notice that it varies depending on which features of herself the beguiling host discloses at any given moment; the cultural *between*, the political *after* or the mystic *beyond*.[49]

As indicated, we learn from literary scholars and cultural theorists that metamodernism is discerned in cultural artefacts with qualities of signification that are in some sense oscillating *in between (metaxy)* the apparent progress and optimism of modernism and the critical and subaltern perspective of postmodernism. Yet the initiatives and practices that are derived from that sensibility can only arise *after* postmodernism. If that paradox of *the after* being a kind of *in between what went before* isn't confusing enough, many who identify with metamodernism at its most broadly conceived seek, somehow, to move *beyond* all forms of the modern, *including* the metamodern. It's exhausting being a triple agent. Meta wants to break free.[50]

If you'll permit the indulgent metaphor, one way to see this improbable analytical love story is that the main protagonists' 'after' and 'betweenness' enjoy conceptual coitus and create a higher-order betweenness that is not merely in between the modern and postmodern but is open to the possibility of a different kind of *after* that is truly new, *the out-between* that is implicit in 'a time between worlds' where we metamoderns seek to move *beyond* the old relationship in between 'Mo' and 'Pomo'. We move out of *that* betweenness to being between the metamodern moment and whatever is beyond the modern, which has been envisaged by many great sages and prophets like The Mother and Sri Aurobindo, or Jean Gebser, but it remains, for now, inherently mysterious.[51]

The fact that the meta inside metamodern *itself* points towards at least three ontologically distinct phenomena (between, after and beyond) gives metamodernism valuable heuristic vitality and agility. Indeed, in Hanzi Freinacht's chapter in this book he references Sean Esbjörn-Hargen's (2010) idea of a metamodernism as a 'multiple ontological object'. Hanzi goes on to distinguish between six *uses* of metamodernism, but these are arguably different functionalities, not different ontologies, and the question of what metamodernism qua metamodernism is remains moot and it helps to show the different work 'meta' is doing in each case.

When metamodernism is a cultural phase with a corresponding 'sensibility' (e.g. Vermeulen and van den Akker), meta is *after* and *between*.

When metamodernism is a developmental stage of society and its institutions (e.g. Lene Rachel Andersen), meta is mostly *after*.

When it's a meta-meme (e.g. in the study of history), meta is *after* and *between*.

When it's a relatively late and rare stage of personal development (e.g. Hanzi Freinacht), meta is *after*.

But when metamodernism is used to speak for a new paradigm with its own philosophy with accompanying theologies, and when it's used to mean a movement or project, meta is used partly as after, but also as *beyond*, as is the case, I hope, with many of the chapters in this book.

To look at this another way, what comes *after* modernism and postmodernism is that (pace Kegan) we are *not subject to them* in the way we used to be. Like some kind of Escher drawing, we are after them only when we *see* they are still with us. The point is that we can relate to them better as objects of enquiry *as well as* sometimes being subject to their patterns of continuing influence in our experience. And yet surely that kind of betweenness, that after, is not the end of the road? Hanzi says there is no cultural code beyond the metamodern. More generally, metamodernism is sometimes presented as a kind of Hotel California, where you can check out, but never leave.

That's not my metamodernism. I risk caricaturing the views of others here, but I do so to get to the underlying tension between 'the after' and 'the beyond' that I think is a critical feature of the next wave of metamodernism. If the limitation of cultural metamodernism is its political ambivalence, the limitation of political metamodernism is its ambivalence towards metaphysics.

Metamodern metaphysics

Zachary Stein targets this issue directly in his extraordinary Integral Review paper, 'The Metamodern Return to a Metaphysics of Eros' (2018) where he draws on Charles Sanders

Peirce to make the case for the need for metaphysics in general.[52] Stein argues that the way we answer 'What is the human?' is now critical, given that the emerging power of new technologies now renders the human malleable in unpresented ways. The paper develops Marc Gafni and Kristina Kincaid's work to advance a particular metaphysical view called 'cosmo-erotic humanism', which is grounded in a deep appreciation for the evolutionary process of love and contains a central place for 'the structure of feeling' as a unit of analysis, suggesting it is a generative feature of collective human life. In his conclusion Stein signals the scale of the ambition:

> There is no longer any prospect for premodern forms of metaphysics after Kant, Darwin and planetary-scale computation. Yet the modern and postmodern absence of metaphysics has created its own problems by leaving a vacuum where answers to the most important questions used to be found. The metamodern return to metaphysics seeks to fill this vacuum of meaning by providing a new context for human self-understanding – a new Universe Story that includes a new story of self and community.

The case for the return to metaphysics is also indicated by Bonnitta Roy, who has argued that metaphysics matters because we need 'a new mind' and metaphysics is required to help us foster new architectures of thought, an idea further developed in her chapter here:

> The new architecture would cut out the epistemic complexity and more perfectly cohere with the rich elegant complexity of the real. By adopting a process understanding of reality, metaphysics could become a suitable guide for a Metamodern praxis, one which integrated perception and participation with the free play of imagination and memory.[53]

A feature of the new metaphysics is that it will have to integrate the immanent and the transcendent. Many of the more promising initiatives for societal renewal have distinctly premodern or indigenous features relating to returning to the land, the soil, the seasons. And although not explicitly metaphysical as such, recent scholarship by Jeremy Johnson on Jean Gebser's aperspectival consciousness and by Mark Vernon on Owen Barfield's 'participatory knowing' is consonant with 'the evolutionary process of love'.

The point of metamodernism for me is that it takes root in the best kind of soil, the new mixed in with the old, and that it has the potential to give rise to new life. The emergent properties that are evoked by the concept for me are not merely about the maturation of the relationship between modernism and postmodernism. What is exciting for me is *our relationship to that relationship*, because *that* relationship is potentially fecund, world-creating and metaphysical in character. The meta in metamodern that is most worth caring about is not passive and descriptive but is generative of the kinds of creative energy we need for what my co-editor Layman Pascal calls a new renaissance. That renaissance will grow in metamodern soil, so the final turn in the argument is to clarify the nature of its main nutrients.

Metamodern touchstones: interiority, intimacy, ecology, historicity

You've been very patient, dear reader, but please allow me to share just one more simple conceptual frame before I put my case to rest. To again borrow the simplest version of the simplest meta-tool at hand, we can map the sources of the emerging metamodern perception of context on to a four-quadrant map, derived from the most basic expression of Integral Theory, which in this context also acts as a helpful creative constraint. There are philosophical risks in any distillation, but I do this in the pragmatic spirit of 'thus far and no further' which I think is a valid use of this integral heuristic.[54] In doing so, I had the following criteria in mind: they can be seen as meaningfully post-postmodern, they have descriptive validity in our cultural context and under-developed normative potential, they are clearly cross-pollinating but ontologically distinct from each other, there is validity in their quadrant placement, and they all contain aspects of meta that offer scope to speak to the cultural between, the political after and the mystic beyond. That's my self-imposed test to probe the scope for metamodern touchstones, and here is my answer, which by this stage in the essay, I can only sketch.

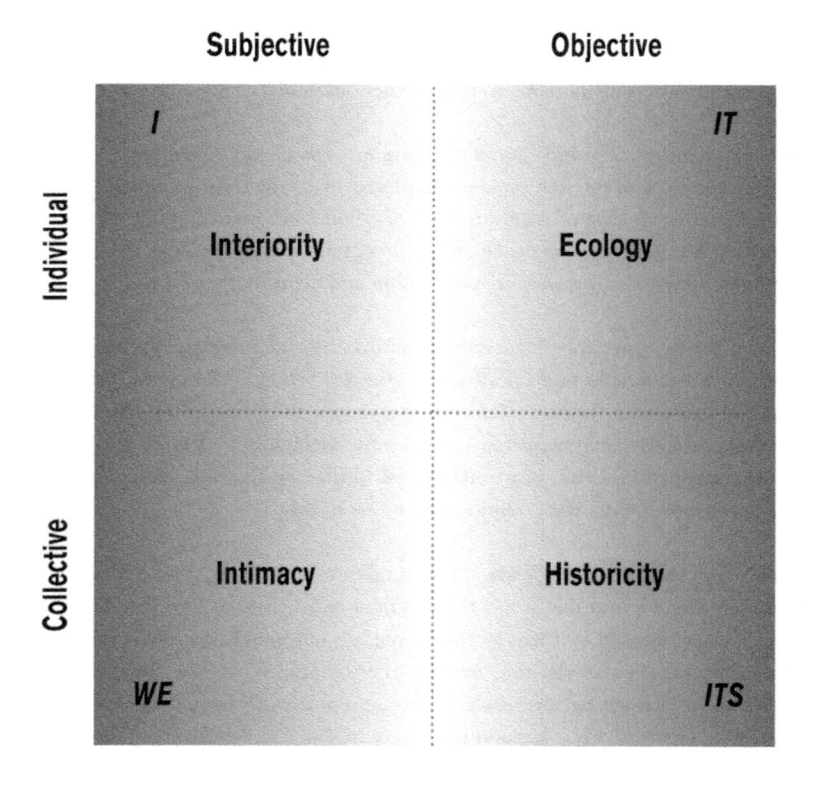

	Subjective	**Objective**
Individual	*I* — Interiority	*IT* — Ecology
Collective	*WE* — Intimacy	*ITS* — Historicity

Figure P.1 The metamodern perception of context distilled to a basic four-quadrant map

In the top left, metamodernism affirms our *interiority* as being non-reducible, despite being as plural as it is singular and as relationally embedded as it is existentially unique. As Greg Dember puts it, informed by Raoul Eshelman:

> The movements of metamodernism, classically characterised by
> oscillation, are driven by 'a need to safeguard the individual's interior
> experience against postmodern ironic relativism, modernist reductionism,
> and also from the ontological inertia of premodern tradition'.[55]

In the bottom left, typically conceived of as 'culture', there is a new form of intimacy arising from our sense of coexistence, what Sam Mickey calls 'the unbearable intimacy of ecological catastrophe' and in particular our inability to exit from the kinds of relationships that are defined by our metamodern plight, including the relationship to, for instance, mass extinction. This intimacy in the face of planetary peril is contrasted with the representation, construction and distancing irony of postmodernism, and indeed with the postmodern abuse of 'the meta move' as a way of subverting intimacy in general.[56]

The metamodern sensibility also seeks a deeper appreciation of how past, present and future fold together along many entangled pathways, so in the bottom right there is a revived sense of historicity, which might also be rendered as simply 'history' or more subtly as 'temporics'. This sense of historicity manifests both in the public appetite for 'Big History' books like Harari's *Sapiens*,[57] and 'meta-history' in Hanzi's forthcoming work, but also in what Alison Gibbons observes as a new temporal logic driven by the need to 'reopen the possibilities of the future' in the context of global warming and other mass-scale crises.

> The historical thinking required to understand climate change, in turn,
> necessitates narrative thinking; and precisely because anthropocentric
> narratives call for collective imagination, they are mythic structures or,
> in other words, grand narratives. Grand narratives of the Anthropocene
> fundamentally require future thinking and, resultantly, they have the potential
> to engender change, or at least some form of environmental intervention.[58]

In the upper right, there is a reorientation towards Gaia, not so much in terms of Lovelock's hypothesis but in terms of a new appreciation and a new philosophical seriousness towards the objective features of Planet Earth. There has been a reckoning with our bio-precarity through the pandemic, an epic encounter between human biology and planetary geology in the Anthropocene, and an increasingly popular object-oriented ontology that entails an acceptance of processes of reality that are indifferent to human desire. We could call this 'living systems' or even 'Gaia' but I prefer ecology. I realise this term slightly subverts the spirt of the upper right as Wilber conceived of it (extant material bodies from microcosm to macrocosm), but it serves to remind us that the objective exterior material features of reality are processes and relationships. Another way to see this is in terms of World One of Karl Popper's Three Worlds Hypothesis, whereby the world of physical objects and events have their own pre-epistemic ontology; they can be *understood* ecologically, and, from a metamodern perspective perhaps even *should* be.[59] I agree with William Ophuls that 'ecology' has to become our master discipline, not merely a field of practice but an ontological presupposition:

> Ecology contains an intrinsic wisdom and an implied ethic that,
> by transforming man from an enemy into a partner of nature, will
> make it possible to preserve the best of civilization's achievements
> for many generations to come and also to attain a higher quality
> of civilized life. Both the wisdom and the ethic follow from the
> ecological facts of life: natural limits, balance, and interrelationship
> necessarily entail human humility, moderation, and connection.[60]

I accept that the validity of the simple quadrant map is creaking under the ambiguity of those four metamodern touchstones, but it is my initial attempt to distil the perception of context that metamodernists, broadly conceived, share. These are just four words, but together they contain a distinctive perception of context, and they are juxtaposed with the modern and postmodern perceptions of context that we are outgrowing. Interiority is about reasserting the depth of consciousness against modernism's reductionism and postmodernism's flirtation with superficiality. Intimacy highlights forms of relational beauty and is contrasted with modernist universalism and postmodern distancing. The reopening of time through historicity is contrasted not only with modernist grand narratives but also with postmodernism's perpetual present. And ecology affirms the need to reorient ourselves to the relational and process nature of material reality, while being contrasted with the environmental blindness of modernism and the miasma of hyperreality in postmodernism.

At home in a world that might not be falling apart

When seen in this light, whereby meta is a sincerely ironic 'trinity' of between, after and beyond, and metamodernism has four orienting touchstones of interiority, intimacy, historicity and ecology, what is on offer is a lodestar that helps to orient our perception of context. The metamodern orientation towards meaning in that context is more soulful than propositional because it involves juxtaposing and reanimating concepts that have their own ambiguities, and it therefore relies on the dignity of paradox in which several things that are not mutually consistent appear to be true at once. Indeed, physicist Niels Bohr anticipated the metamodern sensibility when he wrote: 'How wonderful that we have met with a paradox, now we have some hope of making progress'.[61]

Metamodernism, then, is not so much a word for a new historical epoch, but rather a new disposition towards the experience of history unfolding. It is not merely an idea but an invitation to an imaginary that seasons our taste for ideas. It is not only an epistemology that studies understanding but also an *episteme* that emphasises a certain kind of aesthetic understanding. And it is not a metanarrative as such, but an outlook that restores the dignity of the metanarrative impulse without being subject to it. And it's not merely one feeling, but a whole structure of feeling; and that structure of feeling *matters* because it is prior to the structures of thought and society and the domains of the political and epistemological. As indicated, the metamodern notion contains a cultural between, a political after and a mystic beyond. In light of this sweeping scope and elastic structure, the test of the value of metamodernism is no less than this: whether it helps us feel at home in a world that might not be falling apart.

And does it? That's the test for the chapters that follow.

Jonathan Rowson
Putney, London, UK
April 2021

Notes

1. I am grateful to the following people for feedback on drafts of this preface: Zachary Stein, Anna Katharina Shaffner, Bonnitta Roy, Layman Pascal, Tomas Björkman, Ian Christie, Daniel Görtz, Jeremy Gilbert, Minna Salami and Ivo Mensch. A special thank you to Greg Dember for a range of perspectives I would otherwise not have known, and for helping me to silently 'think out loud' on Twitter Direct Message exchanges as I attempted to find connections between different forms of metamodernism.
2. In *The Listening Society* (2017) and *Nordic Ideology* (2019), both published by Metamoderna.org, the author Hanzi Freinacht is an invented character representing the combined efforts of Daniel Görtz and Emil Friis.
3. Damasio, Antonio, *The Feeling of What Happens*, Vintage, 2000, is a classic text in this domain. In recent years, popular books that highlight the centrality of feeling to human consciousness, culture and politics include Haidt, Jonathan, *The Righteous Mind* (Penguin, 2013), Mishra, Pankaj, *The Age of Anger* (Allen Lane, 2017), Nussbaum, Martha, *Political Emotions* (Harvard University Press, 2013) and Davies, William, *Nervous States* (Jonathan Cape, 2018).
4. Some benign confusion and gentle weariness over terminology in this terrain is a feature, not a bug. In fact, it's a sign that we are paying attention. I am reminded of Bonnitta Roy's paraphrasing of Dogen, the 13th-century Japanese philosopher poet: 'If you make the difference, you suffer the sameness. If you make the sameness, you suffer the difference'.
5. At first blush, that may not look new, because postmodernity is already characterised as a time that is reflexive about modernity, albeit usually from a critical distance, and with ironic detachment, rather than from a spirit of existential tenderness, openness or vulnerability. To help clarify the difference, consider Umberto Eco's reflection in the postscript of his novel *The Name of the Rose*: 'I think of the postmodern attitude as that of a man who loves a very cultivated woman and knows that he cannot say to her "I love you madly", because he knows that she knows he knows) that these words have already been written by Barbara Cartland. Still there is a solution. He can say "As Barbara Cartland would put it, I love you madly".' Eco goes on to say that since the man has avoided false innocence, he will nevertheless say what he wanted to say to the woman: 'That he loves her in an age of lost innocence.' This perspective is reflexive about modernity and postmodernity and in that sense post-postmodern and perhaps proto-metamodern, but I think a metamodern approach would be simply to say 'I love you' with all the rest taken as a shared given as part of the intimacy being conveyed, or perhaps to do something more profoundly neo-romantic like reading aloud from a Barbara Cartland book for amusement value before expressing similar thoughts in one's own words.
6. *Ten Things to Do in a Conceptual Emergency*, Triarchy Press, 2009.
7. The nature of the relationship between perception and conception is well-worn terrain in analytic philosophy that could easily swallow me whole, but it helps to keep it in the frame when we find ourselves wondering 'why should I bother with a word like metamodern?' For species-specific reasons relating to our survival, for social and emotional needs, and as a basis for action, we seek to perceive the world and our place in it more clearly, and we use concepts of various kinds to do so. When those concepts cease to help us perceive what's going on, we reach for new ones. These new concepts often become available to us through some kind of historical upwelling or cultural osmosis, and they appear as new affordances that guide action in the context of a conceptual emergency.
8. Morton, Timothy, *Being Ecological*, Pelican, 2018.
9. In addition to various primary textual sources, on the nature of modernism and postmodernism, I can recommend: Watson, Peterson, *A Terrible Beauty: The People and Ideas that Shaped the Modern Mind*, Phoenix Press, 2000; Cahoone, Lawrence (ed), *From Modernism to Postmodernism*, Blackwell, 1996; Truett Andersen, Walter (ed), *The Truth about the Truth*,

A New Consciousness Reader, 1995; Malpas, Simon, *The Postmodern*, Routledge, 2005; Smith, James K.A, *Who's Afraid of the Postmodern?*, Baker, 2006; Gergen, Kenneth, *The Saturated Self*, Basic Books, 1992; Lifton, Robert J., *The Protean Self*, Basic Books, 1993. There is a good chapter, 'The Modern and Post Modern Worlds', in Iain McGilchrist's *The Master and his Emissary* (Yale University Press, 2009). Ken Wilber covers this terrain in several places, but the clearest expression is probably in his book about science and religion, *The Marriage of Sense and Soul* (Broadway Books, 2000). I also benefited from listening to a three-hour podcast on the meaning of postmodernism by Jeremy Gilbert: Culture, Power and Politics, 'What is (or was) Postmodernism? – 3 hour version!', (December 2020): https://culturepowerpolitics.org/2020/12/20/what-is-or-was-postmodernism-3-hour-version/. On metamodernism in particular, I am grateful to Brent Cooper for his heroic and compendious efforts to keep track of writing and research relating to metamodernism, which has been invaluable. You can find a range of his articles on his Medium pages at https://medium.com/@brentcooper. I would also draw attention to his attempt to integrate aspects of metamodernism in 'Mapping Metamodernism for Collective Intelligence', The Side View, May 2020. Available at: https://thesideview.co/journal/mapping-metamodernism-for-collective-intelligence/. I am also grateful to Greg Dember for drawing my attention to a range of sources relating to cultural metamodernism, and some of their backstories that I would not otherwise have known about.

10 Much as I would love to have had the time to read all of Jurgen Habermas's books, I confess that I could only read extracts and summaries relating to *Discourses on Modernity* (1987) and *Modernity: An Unfinished Project* (1996).

11 Nietzsche, Friedrich, *Twilight of the Idols*, OUP (Reissue, 2008); Lyotard, Jean- François, *The Postmodern Condition: A Report on Knowledge*, Manchester University Press, 1984.

12 The lyricist Pat Kane, who also sang this song, said of these lines in a personal communication on Twitter that they were 'Straight out of Stuart Hall … don't forget the left postmodernism that was all about taking "the cultural turn" seriously … the whole song is about what it takes to resist interpellation (Althusser)/subjectivication (Foucault)'.

13 Zavarzadeh, Mas'ud, 'The Apocalyptic Fact and the Eclipse of Fiction in Recent American Prose Narratives', *Journal of American Studies*, 9(1) (1975) 69–83. ISSN 0021-8758. JSTOR 27553153.

14 Brent Cooper has provided significant service to the idea of metamodernism, and much of what follows is gleaned from his series on alternative histories of metamodernism and his bibliographic tracking of the use of the term. See for instance: Cooper, Brent, 'Metamodernism: A Literature List: Tracking the Scattered Use of the Term', Medium (July 2019): https://medium.com/the-abs-tract-organization/metamodernism-a-literature-list-91272fa32b9d and 'Missing Metamodernism: A Revisionist Account of the New Paradigm', Medium (June 2019): https://medium.com/the-abs-tract-organization/missing-metamodernism-5da6b0b35dde

15 For a full discussion of Borgmann and related sources, see: Cooper, Brent, 'Borgmannian Metamodernism: Philosophy of Technology and the Bifurcation of Postmodernity', Medium (June 2019): https://medium.com/the-abs-tract-organization/borgmannian-metamodernism-8ed5e275f3ae. For Matthew Crawford on the Attentional Commons, see: Crawford, Matthew, 'Matthew Crawford: In Defense of the Attentional Commons', *Texas Architecture* (October 2016): https://soa.utexas.edu/events/matthew-crawford-defense-attentional-commons

16 Cooper, Brent, 'Gonzálezean Metamodernism: Post-colonialism, Alter-globalization, and Liberation Theology', Medium (June 2019): https://medium.com/the-abs-tract-organization/gonz%C3%A1lezean-metamodernism-c9343d2f4e0.

17 See for instance, Rowson, Jonathan, 'A New Agenda on Climate Change', *The RSA* (December 2013): www.thersa.org/reports/a-new-agenda-on-climate-change ; Rowson, Jonathan, 'Spiritualise: cultivating spiritual sensibility to address 21st century challenges', *The RSA* (October 2021): www.thersa.org/reports/spiritualise-cultivating-spiritual-sensibility-to-address-21st-century-challenges

18 Cooper, Brent, 'Black Metamodernism: The Metapolitics of Economic Justice and Racial Equality', Medium (June 2019): https://medium.com/the-abs-tract-organization/black-metamodernism-a72d24da6f0f

19 See: www.youtube.com/watch?v=JNfqr-rzj5I (06.50 mins in).

20 Shri Nirmala Devi, *Meta Modern Era*, Divine Cool Breeze Books (5th edn, 2012).

21 For a wonderful overview of spiritual life in modern China, I can heartily recommend Johnson, Ian, *The Souls of China*, Allen Lane, 2017.

22 Seth Abramson has written a range of articles about metamodernism for Huffington Post, on Medium, and on the website, Metamoderna.org. I have read most of this material and my impression is that he is eager to disclose the breadth and generativity of the domain of inquiry, to highlight some of its main patterns, and to improve dialogue within it. However, I have been unable to discern whether Abramson has a distinctive take or angle on metamodernism that others do not.

23 See Moore, Jason, *Capitalism in the Web of Life*, Verso Books, 2015. There are various shorter versions of this argument online, for instance: Moore, Jason W., 'World accumulation and Planetary life, or, why capitalism will not survive until the "last tree is cut"', *Political Economy Research Centre* (December 2017): www.perc.org.uk/project_posts/world-accumulation-planetary-life-capitalism-will-not-survive-last-tree-cut/

24 Vermeulen, T. and van den Akker, R. 'Notes on metamodernism', *Journal of Aesthetics and Culture*, 2(1), (2010) DOI: 10.3402/jac.v2i0.5677.

25 One of the better disquisitions is Greg Dember's 2018 Medium article (arguably a metamodern medium!) 'After Postmodernism: Eleven Metamodern Methods in the Arts'. These are, illustrated with examples: 1. Hyper-Self-Reflexivity ('Life as Movie'); 2. The Narrative Double Frame (Eshelman's *Performatism*); 3. Oscillation Between Opposites; 4. Quirky; 5. The Tiny (metamodern minimalism; 6. The Epic (metamodern maximalism); 7. Constructive Pastiche; 8. Ironesty; 9. Normcore; 10. Overprojection (Anthropomorphising); and 11. Meta-Cute. Dember, Greg, 'After Postmodernism: Eleven Metamodern Methods in the Arts', Medium (April 2018): https://medium.com/what-is-metamodern/after-postmodernism-eleven-metamodern-methods-in-the-arts-767f7b646cae. It is also worth considering the brief 'Metamodern Manifesto' by Luke Turner (2011), which begins with the line: 'We recognise oscillation to be the natural order of the world' and ends with 'We must go forth and oscillate!' Available at: www.metamodernism.org/

26 Fleabag, for instance, is a character who has undergone tragedy that she struggles to discuss with anyone in the show. While there is some ironic detachment, we projectively identify with the character and we are clearly invested in her inner life; that is the emotional context in which she 'breaks the fourth wall' to confide in the audience. That much could be postmodern, and familiar from, for instance, *House of Cards*. As Fleabag gets increasingly romantically embroiled with a priest in the second series, however, he spots her doing something while we witness her breaking the fourth wall. In this way, the dramatic performance is reified and rendered real – a kind of true fake. Another perspective is that the priest observes her spacing out, such that we come to see the exchanges with the audience as internal experiences. A deeper and more speculative take is that the fourth wall is a kind of coping mechanism when she is otherwise unable to process her trauma, and the priest is the first person with whom she is actually able to share it. In all cases, something meaningful and beyond the postmodern seems to be happening. Perspectiva, 'The secret to *Fleabag*'s success: it's metamodern', YouTube (September, 2020): www.youtube.com/watch?v=sAxUan3xvA8

27 The website is www.metamodernism.com and the archives contain the sub-categories of architecture, art, fashion, film and tv, literature, music, network culture, politics, theatre and theory. In light of the challenges in establishing a clear relationship between cultural metamodernism and other forms, it seems particularly worthwhile to read the politics section, which is quite extensive: www.metamodernism.com/category/politics-2/. I have not yet managed to do that, but can recommend Timotheus Vermeulen's (2013) essay 'Thirteen Theses on (the end of) Liberal Democracy': www.metamodernism.com/2013/02/25/thirteen-theses-on-the-end-of-liberal-democracy/

28 van den Akker, Robin, and Vermeulen, Timotheus, 'Misunderstandings and Clarifications', *Notes on Metamodernism* (June 2015): www.metamodernism.com/2015/06/03/misunderstandings-and-clarifications/

29 *Metamodernism: Historicity, Affect, and Depth after Postmodernism*, van den Akker, Alison Gibbons and Timothy Vermeulen (eds), Rowman and Littlefield International, 2017.

30 Although I am not well versed in her scholarship or poetry, my impression is that Alexandra Balm's work deserves more attention than it has received. She appears to have noted metamodernism as a distinct phenomenon quite a few years before *Notes on Metamodernism* was published, and her work appears to connect the spiritual to the pre-political in a way that is resonant with the 'beyond' feature of meta that I highlight towards the end of this essay. For instance, see the 2004 paper: Dumitrescu, Alexandra, 'Foretelling Metamodernity: Reformation of the Self in Jerusalem', Babes-Bolyai University (2004): https://metamodernism.files.wordpress.com/2013/11/metamodernism-towards-a-new-paradigm-identity-conference-cluj-2004.pdf

31 Ceriello, Linda C., 'Metamodern Mysticisms: Narrative Encounters with Contemporary Western Secular Spiritualities', *Rice Digital Scholarship Archive* (April, 2018):https://scholarship.rice.edu/handle/1911/103873. See also: Ceriello, Linda C., 'Metamodernism, Russell Brand and Spiritual-But-not-Religious Soteriology', Medium (October, 2020): https://medium.com/what-is-metamodern/metamodernism-russell-brand-and-spiritual-but-not-religious-soteriology-c66ac8515a62

32 Gibbons, Alison, 'Metamodernism, the Anthropocene, and the Resurgence of Historicity: Ben Lerner's 10:04 and 'the utopian glimmer of fiction', Sheffield Hallam University Research Archive (2020): http://shura.shu.ac.uk/26465/

33 I am grateful to Zachary Stein for highlighting the relevance of this distinction to Hanzi's energy in the metamodernism mailing list. The original source is: *Senex and Puer: 03*, James Hillman Uniform Edition, Spring Publications, 2005.

Preface – Metamodernism and the perception of context

34 The four quadrants have significant heuristic value and some limitations, which Wilber was and is aware of. The metatheoretical basis for them is described most accessibly in his *A Theory of Everything* (Gill Books, 2001). The four quadrants are sometimes described as I, We, It, Its; or interior individual, interior collective, exterior individual and exterior collective; or subjective, intersubjective, objective and inter-objective; or Psychology, Culture, Science and Society.

35 Kegan, Robert, *In Over Our Heads: The Mental Demands of Modern Life*, Harvard University Press, 1995.

36 I discerned this point by listening to Zachary Stein's first appearance on The Emerge podcast: Emerge: Making Sense of What's Next, 'Zak Stein – A Metaphysics of Love for a Time Between Worlds' (October, 2018): https://radiopublic.com/emerge-making-sense-of-whats-next-Gby9N8/s1!74237

37 I agree with much of Elke Fine's considered critique of *The Listening Society* in *Integral Review*, where in essence she argues that in his cavalier dismissal of other theorists, Hanzi does not walk the talk of a listening society: https://integral-review.org/the-listening-society-a-metamodern-guide-to-politics-book-one/. I also found the political vision of *Nordic Ideology* over-prescriptive, spiritually somewhat oblique, and ultimately unpersuasive. Most fundamentally, the core theoretical premise of *The Listening Society*, the effective value meme, may not be philosophically coherent and sufficiently empirically grounded. It is hard to see how the four main elements of stage (cognition) state (phenomenology) code (cultural psychology) and depth (autoethnography) could ever be ontologically commensurate enough to provide an empirically valid composite measure for the purposes of social policy, which begs the question of how it could ever gain political traction. However, it does appear to work at an heuristic and sense-making level, which is its own kind of validity.

38 Derrida, Jacques, *Of Grammatology*, Baltimore and London: Johns Hopkins University Press, 1997.

39 In his 1993 Oxford Amnesty Lecture, Richard Rorty presented 'Human Rights, Rationality, and Sentimentality', where he argues that we cannot *justify* human rights, that reason cannot really help to promote or protect them, and that we should concentrate our energies instead on *sentimental education*. The paper is one of Rorty's most famous, gives a powerful statement of applied philosophical pragmatism and is available in the book, *On Human Rights: The Oxford Amnesty Lectures*, edited by Stephen Schute, Basic Books, 1994.

40 Freinacht, *The Listening Society*.

41 Dember, Greg, Ludford, Samuel, and Rowson, Jonathan, 'Is oscillation the beating heart of Metamodernism? If not, does it even have a heart?', *Perspectiva* (March, 2021): https://systems-souls-society.com/is-oscillation-the-heart-of-metamodernism-if-not-does-it-have-a-heart/

42 Zuboff offers eight short definitions at the start of the text, and a more elaborate analytical and empirical case throughout her lengthy book. The first definition on offer is simply: 'A new economic order that claims human experience as free raw material for hidden commercial practices of extraction, prediction, and sales'. Zuboff, Shoshana, *The Age of Surveillance Capitalism*, Profile Books, 2019.

43 One way to resolve these kinds of question about what is or is not metamodern theoretically is to establish a position on the ontology of the relationship between modernism and postmodernism. While it looks indulgently niche at first, it really does appear to matter whether the relationship between the sentiments and proclivities of modernism and postmodernism is characterised as a form of oscillation, juxtaposition, superimposition or braiding. And yet insisting on the importance of that discussion feels somehow silly, a kind of meta-metamodernism, and that makes me wonder if I have lost my way, not just in this analysis, but in life more generally. For more details, and indulgence, see Dember et al, 'Is oscillation the beating heart of Metamodernism? (note 40)

44 Dember, Greg, 'What Is Metamodernism and Why Does It Matter? Metamodernism and the structure of feeling', The Side View (May, 2020): https://thesideview.co/journal/what-is-metamodernism-and-why-does-it-matter/

45 In my open letter to the human rights community, for instance, I indicated that the Universal Declaration of Human Rights in 1948 was a kind of metapolitical move, and that the Human Rights Movement needs to make a similar metapolitical move by becoming a human capability movement: Rowson, Jonathan, 'Human Rights: What are the questions that really matter?', Open Global Rights (October, 2020): www.openglobalrights.org/human-rights-what-are-the-questions-that-really-matter/ I am grateful to Zachary Stein for introducing me to the idea of Metapolitical Practice, for instance here: Stein, Zak, 'Metapolitical Practice', zakstein.org (October, 2018): www.zakstein.org/metapolitical-practice

46 Björkman, Tomas, *The World We Create*, Perspectiva Press, 2019.

47 See Andersen, L.R. and Björkman, T., *The Nordic Secret* (2018) and my own essay on Bildung: Rowson, Jonathan, 'Bildung in the 21st Century – Why sustainable prosperity depends upon reimagining education', CUSP (June, 2019): www.cusp.ac.uk/themes/m/essay-m1-9/; see also Andersen, L.R., *Metamodernity: Meaning and Hope in a Complex World*, Nordic Bildung 2019.

48 It feels excessively diligent to cite references for the work of all those people, but please contact me if online searches are not yielding good results.

49 This preface was written several months after my chapter 'Tasting the Pickle' was complete, where a slightly different, but compatible view of metamodernism is described. I had already picked up a certain amount of theorising about metamodernism through online reading and from network osmosis, but I only gave the subject dedicated attention when considering in what ways this book might help to develop the field.

50 'Beyond' is a relatively rare but still legitimate meaning of meta. I devised this three-part way of considering metamodernism before reading 'Periodising The 2000s, or, The Emergence of Metamodernism' by Robin van den Akker and Timotheus Vermeulen in the 2017 book *Metamodernism: Historicity, Affect and Depth after Postmodernism*, where they have a three-way reading of 'with or among', 'between' and 'after', which is still confined to an analysis of a structure of feeling. Their reading seems a tighter analysis of the cultural sensibility in question, but I feel my trio maps better onto the broader meanings of metamodernism.

51 See Aurobindo, Sr,i *The Life Divine*, Lotus Press, 2nd edition, 1990. I can recommend Jeremy Johnson's excellent summary of Jean Gebser's work in *Seeing Through the World*, Revelore Press (2019) as well as his essay 'Meta, Modern' in The Side View (2020): https://thesideview.co/journal/meta-modern/. Blake's distinction between Beulah and Eternity as features of imagination might help us distinguish between the metamodern 'after' and the metamodern 'beyond', but that lies beyond our scope here. For context see: Vernon, Mark, 'The four fold imagination', Aeon (September, 2020): https://aeon.co/essays/what-we-can-learn-from-william-blakes-visionary-imagination

52 Stein, Zachary, 'Love in a Time Between Worlds: On the Metamodern "Return" to a Metaphysics of Eros', *Integral Review* (August 2018): https://integral-review.org/love-in-a-time-between-worlds-on-the-metamodern-return-to-a-metaphysics-of-eros/

53 Roy, Bonnitta, 'Why Metaphysics Matters', *Integral Review* (August, 2020): https://integral-review.org/why-metaphysics-matters/

54 I have tried to be conscientious in my use of Ken Wilber's material and commentaries on it, but I am not a scholar of Integral Theory, and I am using the model in a heterodox way here, so let me acknowledge the following qualms. First, if the fabric of reality is comprised of 'holons' (wholes containing interior, exterior, individual and social aspects that are parts of other wholes), 'heaps' (mere stuff without sentience or consciousness) and 'artefacts' (patterns or functions derived from the agency of holons that do not themselves have interiority), and if the various ways in which holons evolve and develop and thereby transcend and include each other varies, then a single term used to encapsulate the metamodern perception of context should be capacious and versatile enough to honour both the antecedent process that gives rise to our context *and* our divergent perceptions of context as we currently find it. That may well not be possible, or wise, to even attempt, but I have done so anyway! I feel it's important to be able to quickly point out what the metamodern perception of context entails in a way that is *sound enough* to make sense for those who are new to it, to quickly show its breadth of application, and yet also acknowledge its loose affiliation to Integral Theory. Whether such a distillation's heuristic value is worthy of the analytical concessions made to acquire it is a judgement call. A second qualm is that 'interiority' sounds like a mere description of what 'subjective and individual' means, and therefore doesn't add anything substantive. That seems valid, and 'depth of consciousness' would be an alternative descriptor for the upper left. Yet if one way to understand the metamodern perception of context is that the bottom right (exterior objective) quadrant is 'on fire', another is that the upper left (interior subjective) has become all the more precious and valuable because it is partly what we are trying to protect, and it has in recent history been explained away as a reducible epiphenomenon; so to call it 'interiority' is simply to resolutely reaffirm for our present times: Yes! I exist! This experience I am having matters! A further qualm is that 'ecology' is a highly peculiar term to use for the upper right, which is more often described as the realm of behaviour (empirically observed action) or science (not the institution or culture, but the subject matter studied) and it is often understood as the full range of material bodies in the known universe from, for instance, atoms to planets. Moreover, ecology implies, to some extent at least, 'ecosystem', but 'system' would typically be used to describe the bottom right features of holons. Even if you accept that reality is best understood as being comprised most fundamentally of holons, artefacts and heaps rather than processes or things or events, part of the perception of context, including the metamodern return to metaphysics, might well be to view the objective and exterior features of life in process-relational terms. For those eager to go further down this rabbit hole, I can recommend Wilber, Ken, *Sex, Ecology and Spirituality*, Shambhala (2nd edition, 2000), particularly Book One in general and chapter three in particular. See also 'Holons, Heaps and Artifacts (And their corresponding hierarchies)' by Fred Kofman in January 2001, published at www.integralworld.net/kofman.html, and for an excellent short overview of what a process-relational philosophy entails, I recommend Mesle, C. Robert, *Process-Relational Philosophy: An Introduction to Alfred North Whitehead*, Templeton Press, 2008.

55 Dember, Greg, 'What Is Metamodernism and Why Does It Matter? Metamodernism and the structure of feeling', The Side View (May, 2020): https://thesideview.co/journal/what-is-metamodernism-and-why-does-it-matter/
56 Mickey, Sam, *Coexistentialism and the Unbearable Intimacy of Ecological Catastrophe*, Lexington Books, 2018.
57 Harari, Y.N., *Sapiens*, Harvill Secker, 2014.
58 Gibbons, Alison, 'Metamodernism, the Anthropocene, and the Resurgence of Historicity: Ben Lerner's *10:04* and "the Utopian Glimmer of Fiction"', Sheffield Hallam University Research Archive (2020): http://shura.shu.ac.uk/26465/. Gibbons, Alison, 'Metamodernism, the Anthropocene, and the Resurgence of Historicity: Ben Lerner's *10:04* and The Utopian Glimmer of Fiction', *Critique: Studies in Contemporary Fiction*, Taylor and Francis Online (Website), (June 2020): https://doi.org/10.1080/00111619.2020.1784828
59 See: https://tannerlectures.utah.edu/_documents/a-to-z/p/popper80.pdf
60 Ophuls, William, *Plato's Revenge*, MIT Press, 2013, p. 29.
61 Moore, Ruth E., *Niels Bohr, The Man, His Science and the World They Changed*, MIT Press, 1985, p. 196.

Introduction
The end of the beginning of metamodernism

Hexagram 64
'Before'

Metamodernism has a richer and deeper history than is expressed in any particular version of itself. As indicated in the preface, these variants are haunted by a discernible yet elusive thematic consistency, a cognitive style and a persistent tension between reflecting upon the conjunction of the premodern, modern and postmodern, and a desire to go beyond that reflection.

Perhaps we are finally in a position to integrate the initiatory phase of metamodernist thinking, and in doing so we realise ourselves to be on the precipice of another possible wave. We may have arrived at *the end of the beginning*, which is the correct moment to open a new set of pathways that could carry the *before*, through the *between*, into the *after* and perhaps even *beyond*! By taking seriously each argument for the nature of metamodernity and broadening our scope to place old and new domains of metamodern enquiry alongside each other in a putatively shared pattern or even field, we are drawn to the question – *what comes next?*

The organisation of chapters follows a general pattern, flowing from the introduction of the meta-crisis in a fairly comprehensive sense, through various perspectives on how we got here, where 'here' actually is and what kinds of pathways of thought, behaviour and social organisation might lead beyond the current sense of precarious stagnation towards the type of civilisational renaissance that has a fighting chance to make our current technological, economic, intellectual and emotional world into a deeper, more meaningful, more sustainable and more beautiful civilisation.

Each of the chapters that follow contains aspects of critique, vision and method, and most are at least somewhat cross-disciplinary and often transdisciplinary in spirit. There are many possible taxonomies, and we have chosen to group them in three sections. Part One, Synoptic Context, offers a philosophical overview of our societal predicament in this time between worlds. Part Two, Metamodern Conundrums, explores a range of challenges in education, sociology, psychology, economics, law and politics. While all chapters are forward-looking in their own way, in Part Three, New Frontiers, the chapters directly advocate their own ways forward.

Part One: Synoptic context

**Hexagram 3
'The Initial Difficulty'**

Perspectiva Press's Editor-in-Chief Jonathan Rowson's chapter, 'Tasting the Pickle: Ten flavours of meta-crisis and the appetite for a new civilisation', is an exercise in what he refers to as 'discriminating bliss', conceptual distinctions that disclose the nature of our predicament as a whole and thereby help clarify the scope of our individual and collective agency. He distinguishes between the pandemic as a *reckoning*, climate change as an *emergency* and our political economy as a *crisis*, and then he looks more deeply at a range of related but distinct socio-emotional, educational, epistemic and spiritual *meta-crises*, of which he lists ten. Together, these different features of our predicament form 'the pickle' that we are in, which he encourages the reader to *taste* in the sense of experiencing them viscerally and aesthetically as far as possible. The question 'Have you tasted the pickle?' is therefore a way of asking, 'Have you given sufficient attention to our context writ large, and your place within it?'

There is more than one way to conceive of the pickle we are in, and many ways to taste it, but however the current predicament is framed or experienced, all chapters in this book to some extent seek to answer the questions: how did we get here, and where might we go from here?

**Hexagram 25
'Innocence'**

In 'Time, Change and Causality: Notes towards a metamorphosis of mind', Integral Process philosopher Bonnitta Roy explores the metaphysical assumptions of modernity that may still underlie and perpetuate our strategies for change. These background assumptions appear to be untenable in complex systems of all kinds and no longer resonate with subjective human experience in a universe wherein causes and effects are often opaque, uncertain and plural. Roy makes a fascinating distinction between the chrysalis and the cocoon, suggesting that the former, the time in between, is never invited and hardly ever welcomed. 'A cocoon is an external enclosure spun out of silk that covers the pupa stage of a moth. The chrysalis of the butterfly, however, grows from within the caterpillar's insides, eventually erupting through the skin. The caterpillar then is the appropriate metaphor for the times we live in, where our identities at every scale – individual, social and planetary – are dissolving by forces erupting from within.' Roy goes on to suggest that we who navigate this time between worlds think of ourselves as 'the extemporarians': 'the people to create enduring acts of inspiration and imagination for others to find when this world finally comes to an end.'

Hexagram 4
'The Envelope of Growth'

In 'Becoming the Planetary', Jeremy Johnson highlights a growing awareness of the planet as our cosmological context, an object of enquiry that is both vast relative to our own agency and tiny relative to its interstellar setting, but it's now where we glimpse our own contingency and fragility, and in which we navigate the interagency of the human and the non-human. As he puts it: 'The planetary assists us in our own process of decoupling from our fixation with the modern, post-, meta- or otherwise. If we are to go meta, then we should bring the concept of the planetary with us.'

Part Two: Metamodern conundrums

Hexagram 53
'The Need for Development'

In 'Disarm the Pedagogical Weaponry: Make education not culture war', philosopher of education Zak Stein examines the contemporary predicament of education in the shadow of the culture war. What is novel today, argues Stein, is that a generation growing up in relative physical safety is nevertheless endangered in the crossfire of a *culture war*. The chapter looks deeply at the idea of culture war and its broader ramifications for societal continuity and renewal in the context of education broadly conceived, in a time when the boundaries between education, culture and technology are increasingly hard to draw. 'What does it really mean to have a war without physical violence, to have a *culture war*? It means simply that the drivers (motivations, generators, incentives) of cultural production and innovation are made akin to those of warfare, where dynamics of force and power override action oriented towards mutual understanding and cooperation … the deep structure of "war" is something like *a competitive social situation of pure strategic interaction in which the motive for optimising personal advantage is primary because the costs of failure are catastrophic.'*

Hexagram 60
'The Limits of Things'

In 'Metamodernism, Simplicity, and Complexity: Healing developmental models through involutionary descent', Integral philosopher and educationalist Tom Murray explores the risk that we are constrained by our models of growth, development and change. Our tendency to fetishise either simplicity or complexity as a linear aspiration can sabotage the general applicability of the ideas with which we approach problem-solving and human maturation. As Murray puts it: 'learning and growth do not progress through a pure "simplicity" that "transcends and includes" the best of prior forms, but rather they inevitably introduce elements of shadow, demi-reality, contradiction and/or trauma into psychological and social systems … any theory of human development must explicitly include processes for release, unlearning, healing, and/or "shadow work" in addition to modelling complexity.'

Hexagram 19
'The Approaches'

Hanzi Freinacht lives 'at the crossroads of fact and fiction' and his chapter, 'Metamodern Sociology: An ironically sincere invitation to future scholars', is introduced by Daniel Görtz, who finds him there. Daniel wonders on Hanzi's behalf: 'If sociology is the social science that views society *as society*, is then there not an intrinsic link between, on the one hand, sociological understanding and research and, on the other hand, a philosophy that seeks to eject itself from the conceptual, cultural, political and spiritual confines of modern society – metamodernism?

Hanzi argues that, yes, this is the case.' One of the major contributions of this chapter is the sixfold classification of metamodernism already mentioned: 'Metamodernism is thus a cultural phase, *and* a developmental stage of society, *and* an abstracted meta-meme, *and* a stage of personal development (with different, complexly intertwined subcategories thereof), *and* a philosophical paradigm, *and* a movement with a certain project for culture and society.' Hanzi argues that it is imperative to specify which of these is being invoked at any given moment, and that seems right, although due to their overlapping and cross-pollinating nature, that is easier in slow-motion analysis than in most communicative contexts.

Hexagram 55
'Shifting Towards Abundance'

In 'Liza's Bucket: Intellectual property and the metamodern impulse', legal scholar Siva Thambisetty calls upon an old folk song to explore some root causes of the apparent sclerosis of our current economic system and sketches out the contours of a metamodern analysis of intellectual property law, particularly patents. The rationales that lead to our legal organisation of the ownership of ideas are almost entirely hidden from public view, and yet they manifest as pervasive institutional logics that reinforce forms of thinking, valuing and justifying that militate against many of the proposed transformative approaches outlined in the other chapters here. In her own language, we need to better understand 'the psychoactive content' of intellectual property (IP) rights that shape our inner lives and therefore our experience of culture and politics.

Hexagram 35
'The Conditions of Progress'

In 'But Do You Have a Vegetable Garden? Cultural codes and the preconditions for a successful metamodern economy', philosopher Lene Rachel Andersen, co-author of *The Nordic Secret* and author of *Metamodernity*, offers the contours of a new economic model inspired and informed by metamodernity that takes the best from the 'four main cultural codes' of human history, prehistoric indigenous, premodern, modern and postmodern, each with its unique kind of economy. The underlying principle is to model the economy on life, manifest as patterns of evolving self-organising complex systems, with what Andersen describes as 'loops': 'multitudes of parallel loops within loops allow systems that are open and dynamic to be stable and self-coherent over time.' The challenge at scale is to somehow gradually incorporate the right kinds of loops from the best and most complementary features of each of the cultural codes, such that the economy undergoes a beneficial phase transition; in that case capitalism becomes one mechanism among many in a much richer economic paradigm or fabric: a truly mixed economy.

Hexagram 38
'Forces in Opposition'

In 'The Conundrum of Cognitive Dissonance: On the uneasy relationship between agency and understanding, and why it matters', political theorist Sarah Stein Lubrano reflects on the nature of political agency, whether it might be thought of as a necessary illusion, and the kinds of discomfort that follow from the experience of having it, particularly in relation to cognitive dissonance. Is it possible that the intense discomfort of such dissonance may lie at the root of political apathy? Stein Lubrano writes: 'Passionate certainty and disengagement may *appear* to be opposing tendencies, but in many cases these are fuelled by the same underlying motivation: the desire (sometimes unconscious) to avoid facing and feeling responsibility for one's ambivalence, uncertainty and contradictory beliefs.' The challenge is to collectively rework our relationship with decision-making so that we are less pressured into strong opinions or disengagement, such that we become more free than we currently are, if only in our capacity to change our minds.

Part Three: New frontiers

Hexagram 39
'Dealing With Obstruction'

In 'Manifesting Mass Metanoia: Doing change in trying times', political sociologist and metamodern activist Brent Cooper writes about 'mass metanoia – a social transformation, paradigm shift, systems change, etc.' which is described as 'a *necessary possibility*'. While some limit metamodernism to a broadly descriptive endeavour, Cooper makes an impassioned case for why metamodernism can and should be politically normative. He describes seven major interrelated 'turns' of metanoia for the metamodern spirit: to know the history of metanoia; to see the cognitive roots of metanoia and its social implications; to use metanoia as leverage to intervene and overturn capitalism's pathologies; an explicit metamodern turn in sociology and society; the role of religion in the post-secular age; feminist praxis; and, finally, the fundamental choice between metanoia over paranoia in the context of our historic bifurcation in which postmodernism morphs into metamodern or hypermodern trends.

Hexagram 13
'The Exchanges of Fellowship'

In 'Gnosis in the Second Person: Responding to the meaning crisis in the Socratic quest of authentic dialogue', John Vervaeke and Christopher Mastropietro explore the art of intersubjectivity as a means of self-transformation, cultural production and shared sensemaking necessary for the stabilisation and furtherance of a metamodern civilisation. If we are trapped with the limitations of first- and third-person ways of knowing, we need to restore and reimagine the intellectual dignity of the art of conversation, which is viewed here as 'second person'. Vervaeke and Mastropietro introduce the idea of *dialogos*, which they describe as 'a practice of *onto-intimation* that discursively disciplines our existential attitudes by arranging our loves to seek self-transformation'. This line, like many in the chapter, is extraordinarily rich and challenges the reader to pause and reflect. Stated somewhat more directly, in the authentic discourse of dialogos, 'you cannot know without also being known, cannot be known without also being changed, and cannot be changed without changing your capacity to know.' Grounded in a meta-theory of (embodied, embedded, enactive and extended) cognition, the authors explore dialogos in the context of four main ways of knowing: propositional, procedural, perspectival and participatory. With these tools, and many others, the authors provide a philosophically profound exploration of the need to resurrect the art of dialogue as a crucial transrational skill set for sensemaking and meaning-making, and perhaps even the encounter with Spirit.

**Hexagram 54
'The Sign of Coupling'**

In 'Identity Erotics: A metamodern alternative to "Identity Politics"', feminist theorist Minna Salami proposes the radical idea, distantly inspired by Elinor Ostrom, that identity itself should be viewed as a kind of commons. She indicates that when we pay closer attention to identity formation, the human tendency is 'to anchor a sense of self in parameters of meaning, rather than towards a particular group'. In that sense, the idea of identity erotics, characterised not merely as sexual desire but as intimate togetherness in all its forms, is a relatively untapped parameter of meaning available within our shared social reality. The challenge is to situate ourselves and each other in patterns of togetherness characterised by the reciprocated awareness of unique, manifold and evolving interiorities. Salami suggests that this 'embodied, embedded and relational dynamic' may be necessary to move beyond identity politics. Ultimately, identity erotics can help to foster a relational sensibility of connection and care for strangers simply based on the shared, intimate complexity of being human.

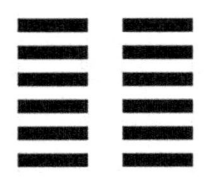

Hexagram 2
'A New Receptivity'

In 'On Committed Uncertainty: A dialogue concerning mystery, metaphysics and metamodernism', psychotherapist, philosopher and ex-Anglican priest Mark Vernon speaks with theologian and cognitive scientist Jonathan Jong 'On Committed Uncertainty'. Today's religion often expresses a limited dogmatic view and focuses on the individual's personal beliefs about reality rather than open-minded, interpersonal relational exchange. Theology and faith are limited in ways we must escape, and have given rise to the current stand-off between spirit and science. This discussion also serves as a somewhat sceptical and cautionary note on metamodern zeal, or relies too much on that term and what it represents. With this context in mind, Jonathan Jong suggests 'we don't have to *make* – inevitably by force – this world into some other world of our fantasies. It already is heaven.' Mark Vernon expresses a similar underlying counterpoint like this: 'Postmodernity or metamodernity or hypermodernity has an epicycle feel, like a series of footnotes to modernity. The way out is to make the inward turn, to foster the capacity to perceive further dimensions to the world, upon which the world rests.' Jonathan Jong later responds: 'You ask about the 'problem of *meta*modernism, but if this incarnation of the eternal recurrence of prefixes entails a retrieval of *meta*physics – in a second naivete, as Paul Ricoeur might say – then this time, we might have a way out of our rut after all. Much depends on whether our cynicism will triumph over our courage to believe in things unseen, or at least to essay towards such mysteries.'

Hexagram 63
'Afterwards'

Finally, in 'The Metamodern Spirit: Approaching transformative integration in psyches and societies', co-editor of this volume, postmetaphysical spiritual philosopher, co-founder of The Integral Stage podcast, Layman Pascal contemplates the production of spirit in a metamodern epoch. How do we access edifying motivations, existential comfort, creative energy and transcendental satisfactions in a time between worlds and an intellectual landscape beyond postmodernism? Generalising his integration-surplus model of spirituality and religion, and revisiting several major themes and thinkers explored earlier in the volume, Layman treats metamodern betweenness as the context of all integration – sketching a speculative vision of the deep resonances between the cognitive style of metamodernism, the architecture of numinous experience and the moral urgency to enable a new individual and social flourishing. *Only a renaissance can solve a metacrisis.*

We are delighted to bring this volume into the world, thank all the authors for their considerable efforts, and look forward to preparing the second volume of *Dispatches* in the near future.

Our 'signature' as authors/editors of the introduction
Jonathan Rowson
and
Layman Pascal

Part 1 Synoptic Context

1 Tasting the Pickle
Ten flavours of meta-crisis and the appetite for a new civilisation

Jonathan Rowson

I AM NOT sure I am worthy of a spiritual name because for the last decade I have lived a bourgeois family life in London and enjoyed my share of boozy dinner parties. Yet there is a corner of the world where I am officially *Vivekananda*, a name conferred on me somewhat hastily in 2016 at a nondescript temple that doubled as a religious office in Kerala, South India. I came up with the name *Vivekananda* myself, which is not how it's supposed to happen. I liked that it means discriminating (vivek) bliss (ananda) because it chimed with my experience of getting high on conceptual distinctions; my wife Siva and my Indian in-laws agreed it was fitting and I was sent to photocopy my UK passport in a nearby booth on the dust roads. I returned with a piece of paper that detailed what I was ostensibly about to surrender, and it happened a few minutes later on a cement floor with chalk drawings, where I sat cross-legged under a ramshackle plastic sheet protecting us from the heat of the sun. I don't remember the priest's features and he didn't speak English, but I knew the fire he created would be our witness, and when he invoked me to chant, those ancient Sanskrit sounds would resonate beyond that day. I was undertaking apostasy. This act of spiritual sedition felt political because it so often goes the other way in India, and I still feel the solemnity of that moment in my body. I did not seek to flirt with the sacrilegious and nor did I wish to renounce a faith I never really had, but I was sure that faith as such would always be my own, as would my Christian name.[1]

I am still Jonathan, but technically renouncing my presumed Christianity to become Vivekananda was the only means by which I could be initiated into *Arya Samaj* (noble mission), which is a reformist branch of applied Vedantic philosophy within the religious orbit known as Hinduism. This conversion was neither doctrinal nor devotional, but it was undertaken quite literally to get closer to God, whom I hoped might exist, understand and perhaps even laugh with. After several years of sitting it out in a nearby air-conditioned hotel, the certificate I received after the ceremony was the only way I could, for the first time, join my family and enter the nearby pilgrimage site at Guruvayur, which is strictly for Hindus only, and purportedly Krishna's home on earth. Whatever the fate of my soul, family pragmatics meant that my upper body was needed to carry our second son, Vishnu, and his abundant baby paraphernalia. I was never asked for my certificate, and were my skin brown I would not have needed it. Yet it was only because Jonathan doubled as Vivekananda that the rest of his family could pay obeisance alongside thousands of other pilgrims. I watched them queue for hours to see idols bathed in milk, offer their weight in bananas to God, feed the temple elephants and pray. At one moment, tired but grateful, I looked down at baby Vishnu in my sling, not yet a year old, and it felt like the temple's host was smiling back. I was there under false pretences, but those false pretences were true.

Swami Vivekananda was a celebrated spiritual figure and a disciple of the mystic Ramakrishna, which, curiously, is my father-in-law's name, which he also chose for himself. Vivekananda was known, among other things, for receiving rapturous applause for the acuity of his opening line at the Parliament of World Religions in Chicago in 1893: 'Sisters and Brothers of America,' he said. That line seems quaint now, but it was catalytic at the time for a Hindu to speak in such resolute solidarity with an international audience, an encapsulation of the emergence of a global consciousness that now reverberates everywhere, though not within everyone. To become worthy of the name Vivekananda would mean learning to speak with similar precision and to delight in the power of the intellect in service of higher ends, a manifestation of *Jnana Yoga*. Spiritual names are often aspirational like that, reflecting latent qualities that might yet be realised. I am not worthy to use the name Vivekananda in that way, but I mention it here to atone for the pragmatism that acquired it, and to inform the spirit of what follows.

There is a process of *reckoning* going on around the world, heightened by the conditions of the pandemic and the palpability of our fragility, inequality and interdependence. There is a climate *emergency* that requires urgent action, but the precise nature, cost, location and responsibility of that action is moot. There is a broader *crisis* of civilisational purpose that appears to necessitate political and economic transformation, and there are deeper socio-emotional, educational, epistemic and spiritual features of our predicament that manifest as many flavours of *meta-crisis*: the lack of a meaningful global 'We', widespread learning needs, self-subverting political logics and disenchanted worldviews. These different features of our world are obscured by their entanglement with each other. It is difficult to orient ourselves towards meaningful action that is commensurate with our understanding because we are generally unclear about the relationship between different kinds of challenge and what they mean for us. That's what this chapter is about. The world is in a pickle and, daunting though it is, we need to learn how to taste it. Tasting the pickle relatively well requires, in the spirit of Vivekananda, finding joy and releasing energy through the right kinds of discrimination.

The English word 'pickle' comes from the Dutch word 'pekel' but there are related terms in most languages. For several centuries vegetables of various kinds have been preserved in a brine-like substance like vinegar or lemon. Depending on where you are on the planet, 'pickle' is likely to evoke images of stand-alone gherkins, jars of pickled vegetables or perhaps composite substances with fermentation or spice. Due to the south Indian influence in my family, I know pickle mostly as lemon, garlic, mango or tomato pickle, condiments *reduced* to intensify flavour, usually in small amounts at the side of the plate that enhance the whole meal (not all reductionism is bad!).

Whichever image or feeling is evoked by the idea of 'the pickle', one major point of the metaphor, in a time of difficult decisions, is to help avoid various kinds of sweet-tasting spiritual bypassing, by reminding us of the importance of good and necessary but challenging tastes in a satisfying meal – salty, sour and spicy.[2] Pickles are also about the latter stages of a process that begins with ripening and it therefore highlights the will to preserve – to hold back entropy and decay. To buy time. The expression 'in a pickle' also alludes to difficulty in the sense of being as *trapped*, *mixed up* and *disoriented* as the pickled vegetables in a jar. The etymological fidelity of such claims matters less than whether the phrase helps us sense how we are all mixed up with myriad things, somehow stuck, entangled and unable to change in ways we otherwise might. There are early uses of the term by Shakespeare that relate to being drunk, and sometimes being drunk *while not knowing we're drunk*; and that's also appropriate for our current predicament. Most people still appear to be running on autopilot with an outdated kind of fuel, drunk on ideas of progress, our own significance and the notion things will somehow be ok. As my colleague Ivo Mensch put it to me, we're collectively living a life that no longer exists.

For many years I took pleasure in the study of conceptual frameworks, diagrams and maps, and I was excited by developmental stage theories in particular.[3] These days I sense that the wellspring of life is not cartographical in nature, but more like a quality of experience that we should not be too quick to define. I am still vulnerable to outbreaks of cartological hedonism, but I am now in remission, looking for new ways to think and write that allow me to apply my intellect in the service of qualities of life that are not merely intellectual. The idea of tasting the pickle flows from that incipient change of direction. Rather than produce a framework, the idea is to imbibe a distilled version of our historical moment, that is, verbally warming up a set of situational ingredients to intensify their taste, and then, in ways that have to be unique to each of us, *taking it in*. The point of the practice is to make sufficient distinctions among the figuratively bitter, astringent, salty and sweet flavours of 'the pickle' we are all in to properly digest what is happening for us personally, and thereby improve our chances of living as if we know what we are doing, and why.

The pickle also alludes to unity in diversity – several tastes that are also one taste. A visual analogy to tasting the pickle is The Waterboys and seeing the whole of the moon, but *the tasting* of the pickle is key. I believe we expect too much from 'vision', as if sight alone could ever save us. The tasting in question is about introjecting world system dynamics rather than spiritual realisation, but there are some parallels to the 'one taste' (which is every taste) developed in Ken Wilber's basic map of evolution from matter to mind to soul to spirit, and involution from spirit to soul to mind to matter. Much of the theorising in the meta-community is tacitly about evolution in the former sense, about the purported need to become 'more complex' to deal with the complexity of the world. Tasting the pickle is mostly about the simultaneous necessity of countervailing movement, so that we can return home from our exalted abstractions, even if we may need to head out again (some of the dynamics of this kind of process are developed in Tom Murray's Chapter 5). Wilber makes the point that the process of involution happens at the Big Bang, when we are born, and most profoundly at every waking moment if we know how to grasp it. But 'one taste' is not a specific state, more like wetness is to all forms of water. The pickle is more exoteric than esoteric, but it shares this fractal and permeating quality.[4]

Finally, it matters that *taste* has an aesthetic orientation. At a time when most attempts to diagnose the world's challenges appear to have an economic, epistemic or ethical emphasis, emphasising the need for qualities of taste that are not primarily cognitive seems worthwhile. The pickle is figurative, not mythical, but there is a useful parallel in James Hillman lamenting the loss of mythic understanding as a concomitant loss in the epistemic status of our capacity to relate to the world aesthetically, that is, to be beguiled, horrified, delighted, enchanted.[5] Learning to 'taste the pickle' is a training in the cultivation of *epistemic taste* that can be seen as an aesthetic and embodied sensibility in which ideas are tested not merely for analytical coherence or explanatory power but also for the beauty of their acuity and discernment in otherwise vexed problem spaces.

I am thinking here as a chess Grandmaster who knows that the quality of beauty in *a single move* typically arises from the cascade of ideas that can only arise from a particularly refined grasp of the truth of the position *as a whole*. In a different context, I remember being asked to read Schiller's *On the Aesthetic Education of Man* as an undergraduate (in the late nineties) and I didn't grasp it at all;[6] the idea that cultivating the sentiments through aesthetic education might have tempered some of the fury of 'The Reign of Terror' that took hold after the French Revolution seemed obtuse to me. Now I see that it is about the importance of individuals having sovereignty over their attention, emotion and experience so that they are less likely to be engulfed by ambient hysteria, but it's deeper than that too. Aesthetic education is also about acquiring a taste for beauty as a gateway to the fuller truths of life that temper the fervour of ideology because they seem more fundamental. In this sense the aesthetic dimension of tasting the pickle can be seen as a training in love in Iris Murdoch's celebrated definition: 'the extremely difficult realisation that something other than oneself is real.'

The underlying contention is that it is when we come to know and feel things in their sameness *and* their particularity that they really come alive for us. Even with very complex and variegated issues such as climate collapse, democratic deconsolidation, widespread economic precarity, intergenerational injustice, race relations, cultural polarisation, loneliness or depression, part of the metamodern sensibility is the inclination to feel incredulity towards seeing such problems as distinctive domains of inquiry, because they are always as polyform, co-arising and cross-pollinating. There is ultimately one predicament, but that predicament can and should be viewed in many ways from multiple perspectives. Tasting the pickle entails using *the right kinds of discrimination* to clarify relationships and what they imply for our individual and collective agency.

To put it plainly in today's context:

The Covid-19 *reckoning* says: Reflect and contend with what really matters.

The climate *emergency* says: Do something! Act now!

The political and economic *crisis* says: Change the system! Transformation! Regenerate!

But our portfolio of *meta-crises* all ask: Who? How? With what sensibility and imagination?

One of the worst forms of pretence is the truism that everything is connected, because it frees us of the responsibility to disclose the provenance and meaning of those connections. Mythic soothsaying is rarely as helpful as compassionate discernment. Most of the things worth fighting for are grounded in the active ingredient of at least one good distinction. For instance, as Donna Haraway puts it, although everything is connected to something, nothing is connected to everything.[7] To really taste the pickle then, you need to taste its ingredients, to distinguish between different features of the predicament as a guide to wise perception and constructive action, all the while knowing those features also exist *as one thing*. It is hard to overstate the importance of this point. In a noteworthy remark in *History, Guilt and Habit*, Owen Barfield writes of the 'obsessive confusion between distinguishing and dividing'.[8] For instance, we can distinguish, he says, between thinking and perceiving, but that doesn't mean we can divide them. Table 1.1 is, forgive me, 'my last cigarette' as a cartological hedonist – someone who takes pleasure in maps. I am aware that it looks somewhat ridiculous, but some people like to see the ingredients on the side of a jar before they open it and taste what's inside.[9]

Table 1.1 can be seen as the map of the *pickle* but not the pickle itself. The value of *tasting* the pickle is that while it helps to recognise the plurality and vexation of our predicament as a whole as far as possible, it is important not to get lost in it, and important to keep it connected to the beating heart of the emergency, the realpolitik of the crisis and the circumstances of our own lives. The point of 'tasting the pickle' then, is to put everything together with wholehearted discernment and then ask:

Have you tasted it yet? Can you feel what it means for you?

The pickle is personal: metaphor, distinctions, sensibility

In what follows I seek to establish what makes the experience of tasting the pickle personal to each of us, and then I consider how I have come to see it politically, philosophically and professionally; this overview of the pickle is a key strategic premise for Perspectiva's work, which is why I have highlighted some of our emerging responses.

Dispatches from a Time Between Worlds

Table 1.1 The pickle we're in

What's happening?	Reckoning (Covid)	Emergency (climate)	Crisis (societal)	Meta/Crisis (socio-emotional)	Metacrisis (educational)	Meta-crisis (epistemic)	Meta crisis (spiritual)	After Pickle
Description	Situation	Process	Predicament	Relationships	Confusion	Self-subversion	Meaninglessness	Diaphaneity
Experience	Dissonance	Urgency	Despair	Tribalism	Exhaustion	Frenetic inertia	Delusion	Post-tragic
Image	Portal	Fire	Fork	Battlefield	Tangle	Gas/brake	Hall of mirrors	Tesseract
Domain	Health	Climate	Political economy	Culture	Education	Ideology	Arts and humanities	Pan-contextual
Injunction	Survive, reflect and contend	Act	Do almost everything differently	Love your neighbour as yourself	Transcend and include perspective	Awaken	Imagine	Taste
Pathway	Vision and method	Socio-technical transition	New economic praxis/ governance	Expanding circles of belonging	Global paideia, Bildung	Reflexive transcendental design	Cultivate spiritual sensibility	Realisation
Obstacles	Fetishising normality	Competing commitments	Vested interests and hidden assumptions	Culture-shaping technologies	Human capital theory of education	Allergies and infatuations; hegemonic co-option	Consumerism	Imaginary
Virtues	Painful truths	Courage and speed	Resolve and collaboration	Whole-heartedness and friendship	Curiosity and teacherly authority	Discernment	Beauty	Wisdom
Illustrative issues	Can there be a new normal?	How can we live without relying on fossil fuels?	How to create a regenerative economy?	How to achieve polycentric governance and 'glocal' harmony?	How should we contend with smartphone addiction?	How can we create a healthy information ecology?	Could we create a spiritual commons?	Metanoia

It matters that the pickle is tasted personally, that each of us struggles and succeeds in fathoming how we are implicated in what is happening at scale, even if that struggle inevitably takes place with, through and for other people; indeed, to be perennially 'alone with others' is a major ingredient of the pickle and sometimes its main flavour.[10] But what I have in mind is more profoundly personal. While many are familiar with the maxim that 'the personal is political', tasting the pickle is more about grasping the subtle contention of the psychotherapist Carl Rogers: 'What is most personal is most universal.'[11]

When we are invited to see the world through a conceptual map, we might feel some intellectual orientation but we don't always see ourselves on it. When we are invited into the uniqueness of another's experience and vantage point, however, our own sense of personal possibility comes alive. The more deeply and uniquely a personal experience is conveyed, the more keenly the latent possibilities of our own uniqueness are felt. Why does that matter today? In the first two decades of the 21st century we typically spoke about global collective action problems with words like 'regeneration', 'transformation' or 'systems change'. While that kind of amorphously ambitious language does help to elevate discussions beyond narrow or naive concerns, the aspirational feels amoral, and it is *insufficiently personal* to have universal validity and resonance. As part of helping the reader taste the pickle, then, it feels incumbent on me to start with some personal disclosure, to help you find your own place in what follows.

I was born in 1977 and grew up in Aberdeen, Scotland, in the context of the Cold War and Thatcherism. My main formative influences include becoming a type-one diabetic at the age of six and my father and brother developing schizophrenia while I was a boy; I know how it feels to be a visitor in a psychiatric hospital, certainly one of the outer circles of hell. I pretended not to notice or care too much about my parents divorcing and I sublimated all adolescent growing pains through an intense dedication to chess and later became a Grandmaster; that process entailed lots of travel, but much of the sightseeing was on chess boards and computer screens within hotel rooms. There were eight years in three parts of looking for an academic home in philosophy and social sciences but not really finding it, including a PhD on the concept of wisdom. There were seven years in public policy research, latterly in a polite renegade capacity where I was rethinking prevailing approaches to climate change and leading an exploration into the place of spirituality in public life. And I've spent the last five years as an ideas entrepreneur, building the organisation, Perspectiva, that is publishing this book.[12]

There has been a lot to learn and unlearn along the way, but by far the biggest intellectual influence on my life has been the experience of parenting. Apart from a few short sanity breaks masquerading as work trips, I've been with one or both of my sons, Kailash and Vishnu, for about 4,000 days now. I say *intellectual* influence not to beguile the reader with the folksy half-truth that my children are my teachers, because they are also my tormentors. Their influence on me has been intellectual in a more grounding and exoteric sense, training me to attend to quotidian matters like finding missing socks or sought-after ingredients as if they matter – although I mostly fail – and helping me to contextualise the intellect in the kinds of daily life enjoyed and endured by millions. Marriage has been another major influence, not least because on those 4,000 days of parenting I've coordinated activity with my wife Siva, who is a legal scholar and also has other things to think about. We both struggle to think and write while updating each other on whatever needs to be cleaned, bought, cooked, fixed, found or otherwise organised. Being busy is often lame excuse doubling as a status claim, but I am busy, so much so that I'm not always fully awake to myself as one week becomes another and I get steadily older. In his epic poem *Savitri*, Sri Aurobindo speaks of 'a somnambulist whirl', and that's what I notice I am caught up in, especially when I have moments alone.

While waiting for the water to boil in my kitchen, I sometimes imagine myself as one of millions of passengers standing in line for coffee, travelling on a wet spaceship that twirls in a galactic trance to the tune of the sun. The cosmological setting for the plot of our lives is a geological niche too remote from human experience to be known like a particular tree or river can be known, but it is nonetheless *very particular*. Our planet is not merely a place that happens to be our home, but a process that gives, sustains and destroys abundant life, uncannily blessed by mathematical and mystical details that allow evolution towards language, consciousness, culture and the creation and perception of history. There may be kindred processes out there, but there is a distinct possibility we are alone; all eight billion of us. Our situation is laughable, and heartbreakingly beautiful.[13]

God knows what we're doing here, but there's a real chance we might screw it all up. In fact it's looking quite likely. The agents of political hegemony that are invested in the reproduction of the patterns of activity that cause our destructive behaviour might just be conceited and blinkered enough to destroy our only viable habitat beyond repair (*The Bastards!*). Alas, those who see it coming and watch it unfold might be too irresolute, disorganised and wayward to stop them (*The Idiots!*). The regression to societal collapse within the first half of this century is not inevitable, but it's not an outlier either, and it may be the default scenario. Are we really condemned to be the idiots who blame the bastards for the world falling apart?

At times, it can feel like we really are that wayward and deluded, but there are many scholars, mystics and visionaries who see the chaos of our current world as an unfolding evolutionary process that has reached its limits of unfolding. What they see in the world today is the necessary and perhaps even providential dissolution of our existing structures of consciousness and their manifestations, including our conceptual maps, so that another way of seeing, being and living can arise.

Something or perhaps *somehow* is emerging. It might be an impending disaster that looms. But our growing awareness that the first truly global civilisation is in peril is also an active ingredient in whatever is going on. Therefore, the most important *action* we can take – and it is a kind of action – is cultivating the requisite qualities of perception and awareness. In order for new ways of seeing ourselves and the world to arise, we need not so much to resist our current predicament, which often serves to reinforce it, but to reimagine it.

As developed further below, imagination is indispensable to help us to transgress our limitations, and while we like to think there are no limits to imagination, it is shaped and to a large extent constrained by the world as we find it. Our task, then, is to *allow* the intellectual premises of the process of destruction that is underway to be *dismantled*, which requires acute discernment about what exactly is going wrong and where precisely the scope lies for what Layman Pascal, in Chapter 14, calls *renaissance*. When the intellect serves the imagination without seeking to fragment it, distinctions begin to feel like our friends.

To say societal collapse is inevitable is not shocking: it's a truism. Societies and civilisations are mortal, and we even have reason to believe that, regardless of human activity, our planet and solar system are time-limited. As Bonnitta Roy highlights in Chapter 2, the issue at stake is a matter of timing and our relationship to time, and what follows for our responsibility to attend, feel and act with a discerning sense of priority. The American writer and leadership theorist Meg Wheatley is one of few with the resolve to contend that we simply cannot effect systems change at scale in the way we keep saying we have to; there is simply too much cultural inertia and economic and political interest inside our figurative ship to turn it around in time. In the context of that hysteresis (though she doesn't use that word), we should not expect too much from the elixir of emergence. Emergence is highly probabilistic in nature, and at present, in aggregate, most outcomes appear likely to be bad.[14]

Objectively, I see that, but I don't yet feel it. I am not sure if that's a kind of denial, or immaturity, but I feel the world is just so darn surprising that things will not unfold as we expect them to, and that there are latent immunities and antibodies that are treated like wildly optimistic unknown unknowns, but are in a sense more like viable known unknowns – nebulous intangibles that we nonetheless have sound reasons to believe in.

To make the most of whatever chance we have to protect what is most precious about life, we need to grow out of wishful thinking. We need, for instance, to get over the idea that widespread integral consciousness will forge within everyone's hearts and minds any time soon. And yet forms of sensibility *are* arising that are captivated by beauty, imagination and calling, and less bound to identity and materiality, although still dependent on them too, as intimated in Minna Salami's Chapter 12 on 'Identity Erotics'. It seems wise not to attach to specific outcomes, but I am thinking, for instance, of abundant renewable energy, wise polycentric governance, universal basic income linked to land reform, a peaceful global paideia and just enough optimal conflict in the world to keep us keen. At a species level, there are still viable and desirable ways of living to fight for, but it is not clear how we might find the heart for the scope and scale of the renaissance required to get us there.

In a geological sense, planet earth is becoming less hospitable to human life, and in an historiographical sense something epochal seems to be ending. Our intellectual function cannot fully grok what is happening, and it is far from clear what, if anything, is beginning.

We can't just make do and mend, we cannot redesign it all from scratch while we're still here, and I don't anticipate a mass 'shift in consciousness' any time soon. Still, it is clear that some beneficent forms of life are emerging, and whether they will scale in time to put out the fire or arise from the ashes is unclear. As poet W.H. Auden put it: 'We are lived by powers we pretend to understand.'

The pickle as political economy: reckoning, emergency and crisis

The reckoning

Like a new child in the playground who has not yet found their place, the Covid-19 pandemic has been called by many names. In the *Financial Times*, Arundhati Roy called it a *portal* between one world and the next and 'a chance to rethink the doomsday machine we have built for ourselves'. Writing in *The Guardian*, Rebecca Solnit said that in times of immense change, '[w]e see what's strong, what's weak, what's corrupt, what matters and what doesn't.' Writing for Emerge, Bonnitta Roy suggested we should see the pandemic as, in the terms of her title, *A Tale of Two Systems*: the relatively new system of global financial capitalism looking brittle, in the process of collapsing, while another system, ancient and resilient based on mutual aid and collective intelligence, was coming back into its own. Zak Stein captured this sense of burgeoning awareness evocatively in the title of another Emerge essay: *A War Broke out in Heaven*. There he writes: 'Alone together, with imaginations tortured by uncertainty, we must remake ourselves as spiritual, scientific and ethical beings.'[15]

With these influences in mind, contending with the disequilibrium caused by Covid-19 is fundamentally a *reckoning* to see more clearly all the entanglements we are caught up in. Poetry makes this point better than prose. Fichte said that to be free is nothing, but to *become* free is heavenly. That line makes sense of another by John Keats: 'nothing ever becomes real until it is experienced.' Many events, processes and things in the world that *are* objectively real can only *become* real within us or between us when we are directly implicated in that process of becoming. On this reading, the Covid-19 pandemic means that the systemic fragility of a planetary civilisation that was already real just *became real* for millions of people. Our shared mortality, biological inheritance and ecological interdependence became real. The vulnerability of our food, water and energy supplies became real. The deluded nature of plutocratic, extractive, surveillance capitalism became real. The value of care-based relationships and professions, and the solidarity of strangers became real. The need for good governance of scientific knowledge and technological innovation became real. The plausibility of a universal basic income became real. And since much of the attempt to avoid the spread of the virus is about avoiding untimely deaths, it begs the question – why are we alive at all? – thus the purpose of life as such for all of us became real. In Chapter 7, on intellectual property law, Siva Thambisetty highlights how these kinds of questions arise through any critical reflection on this legal basis for capitalism, and yet they are rarely articulated as such.

The taste of the reckoning is mostly a kind of dissonance. For those whose health is not directly compromised, the pandemic is difficult precisely because day-to-day things are *not that bad*. It's not a time for heroism in war or resistance under occupation. Instead, there's a strange co-presence of normal and abnormal life. The protracted dissonance is tiring, or in some contexts even *painful*, as Sarah Stein Lubrano puts it in Chapter (, but I think it is possible to see dissonance as a kind of collective growing pain too, and the longer it endures, the less the desire to go back to normal will feel normal. And rightly so, because if we were in our right minds, normal would be a state of emergency.

The emergency

Prior to Covid-19, the declaration of climate *emergency* by Extinction Rebellion and many political leaders was (and is) legitimate because it is grounded in an objective characterisation of our time-sensitive ecological plight.[16] As David Wallace Wells said at the RSA in London, 'Everything we do in this century will be conducted in the theatre of climate change.'[17] Urgent action *of some kind* is called for, but the declaration of emergency seems eerily obtuse, because it suggests we can disentangle climate collapse from the broader plight of a multifaceted and mortal civilisation, as if climate change were a deviant variable to be brought back into the fold with those purportedly benign constants called macroeconomics and politics. Alas, even during a pandemic, emissions are not falling even close to the extent that we need them to, and the idea of emergency is powerless to change that, because our problems are altogether deeper, broader and more entangled.

I like the fact that climate pronouncements have qualifications, textures and layers: the most authoritative consensus, on our best available evidence, indicates that humanity, *as a whole*, only has a small and diminishing amount of time, to have a fighting chance of maintaining a viable habitat in many places in the world, and eventually all of the world. A recent paper in *Nature* is one of numerous respected sources to make that kind of case, particularly in relation to the probability of tipping points that could hasten a cascading collapse of ecosystems that give us the kinds of temperature, air, food and water we need for a decent quality of life, if not merely survival.[18]

The statistical focal point that made the greatest emotional impact on me is the one that suggests our chances of even *failing well* are vanishingly small. The Intergovernmental Panel on Climate Change states that for a two-thirds chance of limiting warming to the relatively modest constraint target of a two degrees Celsius rise in mean surface temperature since pre-industrial levels, emissions have to decline by 25 per cent by 2030 and reach net zero by 2070. But it is 2020 at the time of writing and emissions continue to rise, even in a pandemic, and show no sign of abating. Climate campaigners advise everyone to speak of the ambitious 1.5 degree target constraint, because several low-lying countries depend on that to remain above water, and it is good to establish a new norm, but it seems all but impossible given that this entails lowering our 2010 emissions levels by 45 per cent before 2030, to achieve net zero emissions around 2050.[19]

The idea of an emergency is useful as a call to action in the fierce urgency of NOW, because, as Rebecca Solnit notes in a *Guardian* essay, it signifies 'being ejected from the familiar and urgently needing to reorient'. However, the idea of emergency is conceptually mute on what discerning action would look like, and why it's not forthcoming. Ecologically we have knowledge, which we keep at bay through unconscious grief and terror, that we are inexorably destroying our only home. In its complexity, magnitude and consequences, climate change is an emergency unlike any we have confronted before, but it's a collective action problem that is also laced with dissonance. Calls for action feel hollow because nobody seems quite sure *how* to do what we *have* to do. The collective challenge is therefore to attend wholeheartedly to the deeper variables in which the climate issue is entangled and, unless we do that, we have little chance of even limiting temperature rises to 3 degrees Celsius or more.[20]

The crisis

In almost every part of the world, our scope for action on the emergency is constrained not by the lack of calls for an emergency, but by a *crisis – a very different phenomenon*. Crisis is derived from the Greek *krisis* and is about the necessity for judgement in a state of suspension between worlds, characterised as a juncture or crossroads that may soon reach a turning point. To be in a *critical* condition, medically or otherwise, means that even if the dice might be loaded, things could yet go either way. Or more positively, as Will Davies puts it, 'To experience a crisis is to inhabit a world that is temporarily up for grabs.'[21]

For several decades now, there have been reductions in absolute poverty, improvements in literacy and life expectancy, and significant technological and medical progress. And yet there is also cascading ecological collapse, socially corrosive inequality and widespread governance failures, many of which relate to apparent technological successes. The simultaneous presence of progress on some metrics and collapse on others is a feature of the crisis, not a bug, because it drives concurrent narratives that obscure our sense of what's happening and confounds consensus on how radically we should seek to change our ways. The crisis is not that everything is going wrong, but more like some things are going very well, some are going very badly. We cannot collectively decipher what this means, we need to change several things at the same time, but cannot articulate the relationships to build a compelling political case to even try.[22]

Our evaluative metrics work on a piecemeal basis, saying X is doing well but Y is doing badly, but they struggle to evaluate the whole. While our intuition may be that this co-arising of positive and negative features of our planetary civilisation suggests the truth lies somewhere in between, complex systems dynamics means it is more likely that because everything is inextricably linked, that we live at a particularly unstable moment. As we look to the future, the chance of dynamic equilibrium in perpetuity is very small indeed. Civilisations are mortal, the end sometimes comes quickly, and this one may well be near the end. Even for those with an instinctive both/and mentality, it looks a lot like the world system will either evolve to a higher state of resilience, complexity and elegance, or collapse under the strain of its own contradictions.

Daniel Schmachtenberger is one of many to call this predicament 'the hard fork hypothesis' – the contention is that we may have to go one way or the other. I agree with the underlying sentiment about instability, but there are other possibilities, including a system that becomes more resilient and less complex, and I am not sure whether to consider the hard fork hypothesis idea axiomatic, a plausible and useful heuristic, or an article of faith. The theoretical basis for these ideas arise beyond my own competence, from bifurcation theory in mathematical modelling, Prigogine's theory of transitions in complexity in chemistry and Wallerstein's work on world system dynamics. What I can surmise, I think, is that in the context of socio-economic systems, we do not have the kind of data that would indicate whether we are approaching a bifurcation event (as they are known) but it's important to understand that we *could* be.[23]

The design process for the kind of thinking that is discerning enough to offer an alternative to collapse is what Forrest Landry calls Transcendental Design, and that has to be a design process that is inherently reflexive because the humans undertaking it are simultaneously affected by it, because they are both constants and variables. Nobody yet knows what a viable destination will look like institutionally, nor how it will vary across the world. Some speak of this kind of approach as 'Game B', in which a world of non-rivalrous games is built from within 'Game A' – the world as we find it. Others, including Vinay Gupta, point to basic ecological and ethical constraints relating to stringent reductions in the per capita use of carbon and the ending of de facto slavery. Whatever the precise model or terminology, it seems clear that the desirable destination is less like a new place and more like a renewing and regenerative process that will include:

- A relatively balanced picture of self in society, free from the alienation of excessive individualism and the coercion of collectivism, with autonomy grounded in commons resources and ecological interdependence.

- A more refined perception of the nature of the world, in which discrete things are seen for what they have always been – evolving processes.

- A dynamic appreciation of our minds, which are not blank slates that magically become 'rational' but constantly evolving living systems that are embodied, encultured, extended and deep.

- An experience of 'society' that is not merely given, but willingly received or co-constructed through the interplay of evolving imaginative capacity.

- A perspective on the purpose of life that is less about status through material success and more about the intrinsic rewards of learning, beauty and meaning.

- An understanding of our relationship with nature that is less about extraction of resources for short-term profit and more about wise ecological stewardship (some would add, for the benefit of all beings).

- Patterns of governance that are less about power being centralised, corrupt and unaccountable and more 'glocal', polycentric, transparent and responsive.

- A relationship to technology in which we are not beholden to addictive gadgets and platforms but are truly sovereign over our behaviour, and properly compensated for the use of our data. (And where, in Frankfurt's terms, we 'want what we want to want'.)

- An economy designed not to create aggregate profit for the richest, but the requisite health and education required for everyone to live meaningful lives, free of coercion, on an ecologically sound planet.

- A world with a rebalancing of power and resources from developed to developing worlds, and men to women, and present to future generations.

These are not necessarily the transitions that will work best, nor the only transitions that could help, but they describe the *pattern of transitions* we need based on our current historical sensibilities, transitions that are of sufficient scope and concern for the interconnected nature of our predicament. In Chapter 8, on the metamodern economy, Lene Rachel Andersen gives some pointers to what this kind of transition might entail in practical and policy terms, but many questions remain, for instance on the technological nature of the money supply or the provision, storage and transportation of energy; it is likely to mean a very different kind of world, and getting there is unlikely to be costless for everyone. Even if we seek an 'omniconsiderate' world of win-win scenarios and believe such a place is possible, there will certainly be winners and losers on the way there. And because there are winners and losers in parts of the necessary process of transition, and not all of them can be expected to defer to the presumed wisdom of the improvement for the whole, there will be conflict, and possibly war. The world as a whole is not loyal to game theoretic assumptions about Pareto optimal outcomes, and we should not expect it to be, nor imagine that we can ever bend it with our wills to be so.

In the context of crisis and the hard fork hypothesis, political hope no longer seems to be about electing the right political parties and campaigning for a policy tweak here and there. Our ecological situation is so dire and our prospective technological changes so profound that it seems implausible we will somehow 'muddle through'. The critical idea to grasp this point is *hysteresis* – the dependence of the state of any system on its history. We are already underway, and we have been since the Industrial Revolution, if not before. Things already in motion cannot be easily changed, but they *can* be better understood, and that understanding influences their direction. The notion that we are responding to a crisis is not therefore about a litany of problems or a general call to arms but is the recognition of the need for intentional action in the context of seismic changes that will either happen to us unwittingly and unwillingly, or through us creatively and imaginatively.

The crisis, then, is about misaligned interests, confusion over the co-arising of success and failure and the path-dependent nature of entropy and hysteresis that oblige us to change course. The emergency *is* the crisis in this sense: it's not just that we have to *act* fast, but that we have to *get it right* fast, where 'it' is something like the underlying logic, the source code or the generator function for civilisation as a whole. That source code is not just in the world outside, but within us, between us and beyond us too. How we understand and react to our crisis is an *endogenous* part of our crisis and our emergency, and at a species-as-a-whole level, at a political level, at a business level, we don't understand it very well at all.

All of our rallying cries for action and for transformation arise in cultures and psyches riddled with confusion and immunities to change. We have to better understand *who* and *what* we are, individually and collectively, in order to be able to fundamentally change *how* we act. *That* conundrum is what is now widely called the meta-crisis lying within, between and beyond the emergency and the crisis. That aspect of our predicament is socio-emotional, educational, epistemic and spiritual in nature; it is the most subtle in its effects but is the roots of our problems, and the place we are most likely to find enduring political hope.

Pausing the pickle: we need to 'go meta' while realising we are already there

I have three main things to say about the wisdom of going meta. First, there are several meanings of meta. Second, there is epistemic skill involved in knowing when and how to go meta, and when not to. Third, we are already meta.

At its simplest, meta means *after*, which is why Aristotle got to metaphysics after writing about physics. It can also mean 'with' or 'beyond' but these terms can mean many things. *With* can mean alongside, concomitant or within. *Beyond* can mean transcending and including, superseding or some point in the distance. In most cases 'meta' serves to make some kind of implicit relationship more explicit. The 'meta' in 'metamodernism' can simply mean 'after modernism', but a more precise way to capture what that means is with another kind of 'meta': *metaxy*. Metaxy is about between-ness in general, and the oscillation between poles of experience in particular. Being and becoming is a metaxy, night and day is a metaxy, and modernism and postmodernism is *the* metaxy that characterises metamodernism. Hanzi Freinacht further clarifies the many uses of the term metamodernism in Chapter 6, but Jeremy Johnson put the point about metaxy particularly well in his feedback on this chapter:

> This is why I think it's helpful to keep returning to the etymological roots, re: metaxy. Charging the word with its quicksilver, liminal nature, it approximates both the magical structure of consciousness (one point is all points), it provides a mythical image (Hermes, anyone?), it elucidates a healthy mental concept (oscillation, dialectics, paradoxical thinking), and in a back-forward archaic-integral leap, it challenges us with the processual and transparent systasis ('from all sides'). Tasting the pickle.

One additional point on the meaning of meta is that it is invariably used as a prefix and it appears to have a chameleon nature depending on what it forms part of. As indicated in Brent Cooper's chapter, the meta in metanoia is mostly *beyond*, as in the spiritual transformation of going beyond the current structure of the mind (nous). The meta in metamorphosis and metabolism is a kind of 'change', and the meta in metaphor has the composite meaning of the term because metaphor literally means 'the bearer of meta'. The point of showing the multiple meanings of meta is not to get high on abstraction – though there is that – but to illustrate that meta need not be, and perhaps should not be, thought of principally in semantic terms as a word with its own meaning. Adding the prefix 'meta' introduces a shift in gear or register that can take us to several different kinds of place. It's a manoeuvre in our language games that changes the mood and tenor of a discussion or inquiry.

As Zak Stein argues, however, there are also limits to the wisdom of going meta, which can easily become a pseudo-intelligent love of infinite regress disconnected from the pragmatic purposes of thought. Worse still, the constant availability of the meta-move creates the kind of 'whataboutery' that makes it difficult to create a shared world. For instance, when someone says: 'this conversation is going nowhere', they are going meta in a way that unilaterally ends whatever collaborative spirit of inquiry may have characterised it up to that point. To paraphrase Aristotle on anger, anyone can go meta – that is easy; what is difficult is to go meta in the right way, at the right time, for the right reasons. Going meta in the wrong way can feel strenuously abstract or even absurd, but when done well, going meta should feel more like a return to sanity or a step towards freedom.

The good news is that it should not be particularly difficult to go meta in the right way because we do it all the time. Meta-phenomena are more diverse and pervasive than we typically imagine – the meta world arises from our relationship with the world as sensemaking and meaning-making creatures. Meta is *already here* with us, within us, between us, beyond us, waiting to be disclosed and appreciated. We are already meta. Learning how to learn is meta – and schools increasingly recognise the need for that. A speech about how to give a speech is meta – and people pay to hear them. Parents of young children experience meta whenever they feel tired of being tired. For a different take, if you 'go meta' on oranges and apples you get fruit (or seeds, or trees). If you go meta on fruit you may get to food, and if you go meta on food you may get to agriculture, and then perhaps land and climate, and then either soil and mean surface temperature, or perhaps planet and cosmos. Meta is also what happens in meditation (meta-tation!) when the mind observes itself in some way: there I go again, we think, without pausing to feel astonishment at being both observer and observed. Meta themes abound in popular culture, for instance in *Seinfeld*, where comedians successfully pitch for a television show in which nothing of significance ever really happened; that idea was the explicit expression of the implicit idea that made the whole series funny.[24]

The meta-move is often noteworthy because it tends to happen when normal moves exhaust themselves. For this reason, 'going meta' is a key feature of metamodernity, characterised by our encounter with the material and spiritual exhaustion of modernity and the limitations of postmodernity. Going meta is therefore important and necessary, and it's already a part of popular culture, so we should not fear talking about it as if it was unacceptable jargon. But we do need to be a bit clearer about why and when we use it, not least when acting in response to 'the meta crisis'. Since I have argued that crisis has a particular meaning relating to bifurcation and time sensitivity, and we often use the terms meta and crisis to describe our predicament as a whole, the relationship between meta and crisis deserves closer attention.

Here is how I see it. The idea of the meta-crisis is pertinent and essential, and the term offers the kind of creative tension and epistemic stretch that we are called upon to experience. However, in our social change efforts we need to remember that language is psychoactive, and it matters which terms we use to attract, persuade and galvanise people. I don't think the aim should be to stop talking about meta as if it was a secret code we had to translate to make it more palatable. Instead, I think the aim should be to disclose that what is meta is so normal and even mundane that we don't need to draw special attention to it.

While most developmental progress is about the subject-object move, in the case of meta-phenomena, I wonder if this is an exception that proves the rule. What we appear to need is for whatever is meta in our experience and discourse to become subject again, such that it becomes a kind of second nature that we simply 'do' rather than reflect on or talk about. The aim is to close the observational gap by integrating what you previously exorcised by making it object, moving from unconscious, to conscious and then not back to unconscious as such, but to dispositional and tacit. In this sense, the aim is to know the meta-crisis well enough that it ceases to be 'meta', and ceases to be a 'crisis', and frees us of the need to speak in those terms. The aim is to get back to living meaningfully and purposively with reality as we find it.

Some of the most profound and promising theorising in this space comes from those who suggest we might precipitate the new forms of perception we need by understanding the provenance of our current sense of limitation more acutely. Jeremy Johnson puts it like this:

> If we wish to render transparent the true extent of the meta-crisis, to get a clear sense of how to navigate through it, then we need to thoroughly identify the foundations of the world coming undone. In order to navigate this space 'between worlds', we need a phenomenology of consciousness that can help us to trace, as it were, the underlying ontological 'structures' of the old world, the constellations of sensemaking we have relied on up until now. We should do this so that we can better recognise what the new world might be like – to re-constellate ourselves around that emergent foundation.[25]

I have endeavoured to try to do that in what follows. Once you take the idea of meta-crises seriously and start looking at them closely, it seems we are caught up in something oceanic in its depth and range, and *plural*. The idea of trying to define *the* meta-crisis as if it could be encapsulated as a single notion and conceptually conquered is a kind of trap. I have come to think it helps to *distinguish* between different features of an experience that ultimately amount to the same underlying process. In fact, that's how I see the meta-crises writ large: they are the underlying processes causing us to gradually lose our bearings in the world.

There are many ways to parse the different qualities of meta-crisis, which are of course interrelated, but I have alighted on four main patterns, unpacked as ten illustrations.

- The socio-emotional *meta/crisis* (meta as with/within; the crisis of 'we') concerns the subjective and intersubjective features of collective action problems relating to management of various kinds of commons, not least digital and ecological. In essence it's the problem relating to the limits of compassion and projective identification, and of the world not having a discerning sense of what 'we' means in practical, problem-solving or world-creating terms.

- The epistemic *meta-crisis* (meta as with/self-reference; the crisis of understanding) concerns ways of knowing that are ultimately self-defeating, underlying mechanisms that subvert their own logics. In essence it's the problem of ideological and epistemic blind spots.

- The educational *metacrisis* (meta as after/within and between; the crisis of education) concerns the emergent properties arising from all our major crises taken together, which entail learning needs at scale, particularly how to make sense of the first planetary civilisation; how to confer legitimacy transnationally; how to do what needs to be done ecologically; and how to clarify collectively what we're living for without coercion.

- The spiritual *meta crisis* (meta as beyond; the crisis of imagination) concerns the cultural inability or unwillingness to 'go meta' in the right way, for instance to think about the political spectrum rather than merely thinking with it, or for economic commentators to question the very idea of the economy or the nature of money. More profoundly, it is about being cut off from questions about the nature, meaning and purpose of life as a whole as legitimate terrain in our attempts to imagine a new kind of world.

The philosophical pickle: tasting ten flavours of the meta-crisis[26]

Do we even know what we want? If pushed for an answer I would say I seek a world of ecological sanity that delights in its own abundance, societies with dynamic equilibriums where everyone can develop skill and taste and relationships, and forge meaningful purpose, and education that leads us to seek truth, feel moved by beauty and experience joy, but these intimations and sketches I am never quite sure what to hope for. I also feel that that desirable world is already with us to a large extent, and it would be foolish to wish it all away. There are certainly socio-economic and ecological problems to be solved, but I don't have a working vision of utopia as a lodestar, and doubt those who do. I notice that life is defined by processes of change that feel endemic and pervasive, that struggle is part of that process, but often a friend in disguise, and although I have no direct experience of war, widespread calls for peace on earth don't ring altogether true; I wonder if our darkness is a feature rather than a bug, and perhaps we can only ever repress the patterns of ambitious coercion that are baked into human desire. Whatever its woes, and there are many, the world we are called upon to love is always the one we are already living in.

What should we work towards, then, and how? It is precisely when we take this question seriously – the question of what to do about the emergency and the crisis – that the full range of meta-crises reveal themselves. What follows, then, is a performance of my own tasting of the pickle, of what it feels like to dive into the jar as it were, and play with all the elements that seem to be swirling around in the meta-crisis discourse. It is hoped that by conveying my experience of the pickle, others may think and act with an enriched set of reference points.

1. The meta/crisis of cosmopolitics: we don't have a viable We

The slash in meta/crisis signifies that the meta/crisis is *almost* indistinguishable from the crisis as such. The term also helps sharpen the distinction between emergency and crisis by highlighting perhaps the most fundamental feature lying *within* our crisis. The main limitation with the idea that we face an emergency is that there is no 'we' as such to address it. The We that wants to say there is an emergency is not the same We as the We that needs to hear it, and the We that needs to hear it has several different ideas about the nature of the We that should do something about it. As I argued in the second edition of *Spiritualise*, 'we' is usually an injunction in disguise.[27]

Perhaps spiritually we are One, or could be, but politically we are many, indeed for many how we decide to demarcate our 'we' is the fault line of politics.[28] Many believe political polarisation is the defining challenge of our time; it is certainly one of them. Fascism has been described as 'the politics of them and us', and while it is not a term to be used lightly, many countries are at least somewhat closer to the spirit of fascism than they have been for years. One way of looking at The 2019 Citizenship Amendment Act in India for instance is that it effectively makes Hindus 'more Indian' than Muslims. The Indian 'We' may still be secular and legally plural, but politically that ideal is increasingly contested under the ethno-nationalist claims from incumbent powers that proclaim India to be a Hindu nation.

More generally, there are competing tribes, perspectives, interests and factions in the world, and perhaps there always will be. You don't need to travel far to realise that, but I found it helps to do so. For me, spending some time in Sarajevo as part of my Open Society Fellowship was particularly useful, because it revealed how easily and tragically war can arise when a collective sense of We-ness shatters into lethal shards of them and us. At almost every level of analysis, from sclerotic global governance to quarrelling spouses, we appear to lack sanctified mechanisms to resolve what kind of *We* we want ourselves to be. Ecological sanity depends upon the recognition of some kind of unity in diversity, and that should not be impossible to obtain. For instance, Elinor Ostrom's work reveals that collective action solutions are every bit as real as collective action problems.[29]

However, in the absence of a wholehearted commitment to something like the human rights framework or the sustainable development goals at an international macro level, or the rapid deployment of polycentric governance to coordinate meso levels, or the spread of methodologies of interpersonal micro-solidarity (e.g. micro finance) at a micro level, or a combination of all of the above, the widespread misalignment of our identities and priorities will remain problematic. Competing and incommensurate political aims undermine the *stability* of the kinds of cooperation and sacrifice that may be necessary for the greater good at a planetary scale in a time of emergency. That *realpolitik* is part of the crisis.

As Bonnitta Roy reminded me in a personal communication, while people make a lot of conceptual statements around 'us' as unity, the problem is that it doesn't turn into units of action – the appropriate scale for 'we' as a unit of action is the critical question, and an urgent one at a time of global collective action problems where the presumptive global we is *not* a unit of action. I felt the acuity of this point even more profoundly in a personal exchange with Dougald Hine, who noted that whenever people travel and converge for conferences of various kinds, the question invariably arises: 'What should we do?' And yet there is usually no 'we' in the room that is capable of coordinated action because they are all away from their contexts and networks where each of them may more readily establish units of action, and that recurring confusion wastes precious time.

To take an example at a larger scale, we need to keep most oil and gas reserves in the ground and virtually all coal in the ground to give us a fighting chance of staying within the relatively ambitious 1.5 degrees Celsius above pre-industrial temperatures. There's a compelling case for pursuing that global objective if you are one of the thousands of inhabitants of Tuvalu or any other low-lying small island state with non-amphibious humans who simply wish to live above water. However, if your political remit is to do something about energy poverty affecting millions of families in a coal-rich part of rural India or China, you may see things differently. Likewise, if you are one of many rapidly developing African countries seeking to catch up with Western living standards and you notice that a lack of an international airport places you at an economic disadvantage, it won't look obvious that 'we' shouldn't build any more airports.

The identity crisis about our 'we' is compounded by the confusion about our *success as a we* – a species. Many people feel an understandable desire to continue being 'successful' without really knowing what that means. One recent expression of this aspect of meta/crisis is an impressively reasoned paper in the journal *Science* about the lack of acuity and coherence in the idea that Green Growth or The Green New Deal, which is the policy that advocates 'winning' on all fronts – economically and ecologically – is the preeminent response to our plight. It would make sense if it worked, and it might even be a necessary step forward, but after reading the meticulous takedown of the assumptions behind the idea, it is hard to see how it could ever be credible as a global strategy. Let's imagine then that a significant majority of powerful people read that paper, agreed with all of it, and decided resolutely that growth in developed countries is the wrong goal, and then acted on that post-growth understanding in a fundamental shift in policy goals and political messaging. How likely is that? Not at all likely, and that's the crisis too – some apparent truths are deeply unacceptable politically, in the literal sense that we, writ large, are not *able* to accept them and sometimes also not *willing* to accept them, in the sense of not knowing *how* to do it.[30]

No wonder people will continue to ask: What should I do? What *can* I do? If we don't really know who they are (and often they don't really know either) all we can offer are lowest-common-denominator things we don't wholeheartedly believe in anymore. Recycling is good, but feels lame when your country is on fire, and writing to your elected representative feels quaint when *their* leaders brazenly lie. And climate activists rightly remind us that we are running out of time, so there is no time to waste.

Perhaps we save time by reminding ourselves that the question, what should I do, is always asked by particular, knowable, historic, geographic, embodied, learning individuals. The answer can and should therefore be unique to their pattern of character formation, their professional skill, social influence and growth potential; and it usually comes down to this: do what you are best at to address whatever is most generatively helpful, and collaborate with other individuating people. A deeper exploration of individuation, as a mostly Jungian concept traversing psyche and character and journey, is beyond our scope, but in terms of its implication for *action* it is closely related to the achievement of autonomy, and the best short definition of autonomy is an open system that is capable of closing itself. That, in essence, may be what we need at scale – open systems capable of closing themselves. The 'We' required to collaborate for the greater global good depends on individual capacities and sensibilities that are not just insufficiently abundant, but insufficiently autonomous because they are also, qua Carl Rogers mentioned earlier, insufficiently personal. So when one of the eight billion asks us then: What should I do? At least part of the answer has to be: You tell me.

At a time when requisite action – on consumerism, on smartphone addiction, on political polarisation – is often a kind of restraint, one of the psychological variables we need to understand is *the provenance of agency*, because that determines the extent to which an action is volitional or habitual, chosen or coerced. One of the reasons the collective action problems of our time seem overwhelming therefore is that we sense that they are actually problems of *collective individuation* in disguise. There is a necessary realisation waiting for all of us that yes, we are utterly contingent and interdependent, but we are also uniquely relevant and ethically singular. While the kind of We that might actually be fit for purpose cannot be wished into existence, then it can perhaps be forged. That forging process, an educational process, is a collective effort to allow all the *I*s that we are to begin to know, find and create themselves through a collaborative institutional and cultural effort that speaks to that endeavour. Technology alone will not save us from the sensibilities that lead to the misuse of technology. What we need to mitigate ecological collapse, cultural fragmentation and political and economic breakdown is the widespread internalisation of a global commons, such that people *feel* their individual actions are a palpable part of a global web of life. Getting to that kind of collective sensibility will not happen if your raw ingredients are eight billion or so pieces of generic collaborative fodder. There is no such 'We' to be mobilised, and we know it. Cooperation at scale may nonetheless be possible, but we should consider what follows if it depends on the resolute, discerning and skilled collaboration of *individuals* worthy of the name.

This challenge of collective individuation applies across contexts, and in the context of his relationship to Buddhism, Stephen Batchelor puts the underlying aim as follows:

> The Dharma needs to be individuated in the Jungian sense, meaning differentiating yourself from the collective, from archetypes, from the norms or traditions, and so forth, in such a way that you become increasingly your own person. That doesn't mean you become an egoist, but it means that you've teased out your potential in such a way that you can optimally flourish to be the person that you aspire to be, that may have elements of Buddhism or Christianity or socialism or whatever fed into it. The mix is uniquely your own. It's your own voice that you find. That, to me, would be a vision of where we're going.[31]

The majority of the world's population may remain highly suggestible, and susceptible to manipulation by plutocratic alchemists who stoke base impulses and appetites and turn them into figurative gold for private gain. A critical mass, however, can become relatively discerning and act according to their own judgement, ideally with some care for the greater good and capacity to help others find their own unique contribution. I reflect further on the idea of collective individuation in forthcoming publications. For now, it is sufficient to understand that the individual and the collective are profoundly co-constituted, and our predicament calls for a planetary-scale response that is both profoundly collective and deeply personal. This 'We' challenge of collective individuation is at the heart of the new strategy for Perspectiva's Emerge project.

2. Metacrisis in world system dynamics: we're not good at joining the dots

The composite word '*metacrisis*' is inspired by our German friends, and is useful for resolving to speak to the cross-pollinating crises of our time as one whole thing. Here, the aim is to better 'join the dots' between apparently disparate phenomena while recognising, as Gödel helped us discern, that no single grand vision or narrative, however textured and inclusive, can fully make sense of itself. The simplest view of the metacrisis then, is that it's about whatever underlying crisis is driving a multitude of crises, not just ecological collapse (which is certainly bad enough) but also a range of governance and security issues, alongside global economic instability and inequality within countries, a steep rise in mental health problems and a decline in social trust. It's as if we have a civilisation-level wicked problem.

This idea of an underlying problem behind, within and between all problems goes back at least to the 1970 Club of Rome report that describes 49 'continuous critical problems' which they also call 'meta-problems'.[32] More recently, in a talk at Google, the philosopher and entrepreneur Terry Patten reflected on the need to speak to meta-crisis as 'the sum of our ecological, economic, social, cultural, and political emergencies'.[33] When the first Covid-19 lockdown began, Elizabeth Debold argued in our first Emerge online gathering that one collateral benefit of *the reckoning* was that many thousands of those who were just beginning to think systemically (a non-trivial cognitive achievement) would have accelerated their development. As the nature of the world's interdependence and the reality of the relationship between apparently different 'things' became palpable, so did a growing awareness of the metacrisis. This way of seeing the metacrisis – as a descriptor for the pattern that connects various crises – is perhaps the most conventional use of the term, and it is the premise for Perspectiva's encapsulation of the scope of our inquiry as 'systems, souls and society'.

3. Metacrisis in historiography: modernity and postmodernity struggle to procreate

The composite metacrisis can also be seen as the failure of culture to evolve quickly enough to save itself from itself. Cultures vary enormously of course, and different kinds of changes are called for in different parts of the world, but the active ingredient in question here is shared across cultures, and called by various names: cultural code, hidden curriculum, consensus reality, paradigm, collective imaginary, value memes, shared story, sacred canopy, social surround. All of these terms mean something a little different, and sometimes they apply to particular places and at other times to the world as a whole, but they all refer to the prevailing pattern of norms and forms of life and the assumptions they entail; at its most abstract and generic we can think of it as a semiotic fabric that acts as an ideational ozone layer for humanity. When the late anthropologist Clifford Geertz said that we are creatures suspended in webs of meaning that we ourselves have spun, he was referring to something like this.

This metacrisis is mostly a metacrisis of modernism – the world of the presumed universality and beneficence of science and reason and progress – and the battle that we have not yet fought and won to transcend and include that presumption. Many, including Jürgen Habermas, appear to view postmodernity as a phase within the modern historiographical epoch in which the critical tools of modernity were turned back on itself. While the postmodern critical inflexion has value and is necessary, in terms of cultural renewal and adaptation, it also appears to be a kind of dead end.

Post and meta can both mean 'after', but while the after in postmodernism is more like modernity's after party – a continuation of the same party, or 'afternoon' – a later stage of the same day, 'meta' has a notion of after that is more than mere temporal extension. Meta here signals that a qualitatively different kind of relationship has arisen. When meta is placed in this context, and understood in this way, the cultural meta-crisis is about our apparent failure to cultivate metamodern sensibilities with sufficient permeation at scale to adapt to our historiographical epoch of metamodernity. This qualitatively new epoch has been with us to some extent since the birth of digitisation, and its impact on the lifeworld has arisen alongside the apparent spiritual and material exhaustion of modernity. We all know from abundant misquotations of Einstein that cultural and moral progress needs to keep pace with technological and economic developments, but that's not happening.

Viewing the metacrisis in this way helps illuminate why metamodernism as a normative endeavour matters, as argued in greater depth in Hanzi Freinacht's chapter. I feel Greg Dember puts the case for why metamodernism matters mostly acutely when he argues that we need it to protect our interiority from capture on either side of the oscillation of the dominant cultural codes. Each of us risks losing the meaning of our lives to either the scientific reductionism and instrumentality of modernism or the identity politics and irony of postmodernism. The primary function of metamodernism may therefore be to safeguard interiority. Curiously, and perhaps excitingly, the resources for that task are as likely to be found in indigenous and premodern cultures as in untethered futurism, and that may simply be because we need to rediscover our place in nature, and patterns of activity and meaning that fall out of that.[34]

The metamodern sensibility is described in the works of cultural studies scholar Timotheus Vermeulen, professor of philosophy Robin van den Akker and literary theorist and political activist Seth Abramson, and more recently there have been strains of political metamodernism in the work of Hanzi Freinacht, Brent Cooper and Tomas Björkman. The modernist in me senses the progress in the exposition of the idea, while the postmodernist notes the predominance of Anglo-Saxon White males. For metamodernism to flourish it will have to deepen and widen its sense of itself, which is one of the underlying purposes of this compilation, and perhaps Perspectiva Press more broadly.

4. Metacrisis in philosophy of education: we are failing to learn how to learn

In his 2014 essay, *Spirituality and Intellectual Honesty*, German philosopher Thomas Metzinger offers the following dark prognosis:

> Conceived of as an intellectual challenge for humankind, the increasing threat arising from self-induced global warming clearly seems to exceed the present cognitive and emotional abilities of our species. This is the first truly global crisis, experienced by all human beings at the same time and in a single media space, and as we watch it unfold, it will also gradually change our image of ourselves, the conception humankind has of itself as a whole. I predict that during the next decades, we will increasingly experience ourselves as failing beings.[35]

The educational question hidden within this statement is: what are our present cognitive and emotional abilities, and how much capacity do we have to improve them at sufficient scale and speed?

As argued by Zak Stein in Chapter 4, on the impact of culture war on education, this feature of the metacrisis arises in a time when the distinction between technology, culture and schooling is barely perceptible, but ecological collapse is cascading, children's mental health is deteriorating and governance failures abound. When learning is as much tacit and informal as formal and the gap between digital and analogue sensibilities widens, the proper place of intergenerational transmission is difficult to discern. We appear to be unable to adapt to the challenges of our time because our goals (e.g. getting a job; increasing national GDP), our methods (e.g. teaching to test) and our metrics (e.g. school admission results) are perpetuating ways of being and living that are destructive in aggregate. In response, Perspectiva plans to develop a Transformative Educational Alliance (TEA) based on five questions for the future, which are educational in the sense that they beg the question of what and how we need to learn to address them, and what that means for designing institutional forms and cultural practices that may take us beyond conventional schooling and assessment.[36]

Intelligibility – what's going on, and how do we know?

Capability – do *we* have what it takes to do what we need to do?

Legitimacy – who gets to say what *we* should be doing and why?

Meaning – what ultimately matters and how do we live accordingly?

Imagination – what does a viable future look and feel like?

These questions permeate Perspectiva's *Realisation* strand of work, which includes an annual festival and the building of our own transformative education curriculum within an already established growing network around the idea of *Bildung*, which may be loosely translated as transformative civic education.[37]

5. Meta-crisis in ideology: our underlying mechanisms subvert their own logics

The hyphen in '*meta-crisis*' speaks of a crisis of self-reference and sometimes a paradoxical failure of achievement; too much liberty may kill liberalism, too much democracy can weaken democracies, and we don't always understand how we understand, we tend to deny our denial, and we are struggling to imagine a new imaginary.

In *The Politics of Virtue*, Milbank and Pabst describe a wide range of meta-crises, mostly characterised by a kind of self-referential excess.[38] So the meta-crisis of democracy is about *too much* democracy leading to the weakening of non-democratic elements that keep democratic systems stable; and the meta-crisis of capitalism arises from capital being too free, leading to its abstraction and reification, as money becomes increasingly untethered to the actual material world. In his review of their book, Rowan Williams frames this view of the meta-crisis as follows:

> There are crises and there are meta-crises: a system may stagger from one crisis to another but never recognise the underlying mechanisms that subvert its own logic … If we are now panicking about the triumph of a politics of resentment, fear and unchallengeable untruthfulness, we had better investigate what models of human identity we have been working with. Our prevailing notions of what counts as knowledge, our glib reduction of democracy to market terms, our inability to tackle the question of the limits of growth – all these and more have brought us to the polarised, tribal politics of today and the thinning out of skill, tradition and the sense of rootedness. Treating these issues with intellectual honesty is not a sign of political regression but the exact opposite.[39]

On this logic, the meta-crisis of liberalism is that it is too liberal, encapsulated in Patrick Deneen's saying that liberalism has failed because it has succeeded. For instance, through its emphasis on the protection of the individual by the state, liberalism weakened the power of intermediate institutions and became simultaneously more individualist and statist; and by supporting the apparently free market, it has facilitated the coercive power of commerce in ways that make us less free: 'Liberalism created the conditions, and the tools for the ascent of its own worst nightmare, yet it lacks the self-knowledge to understand its own culpability.'[40]

Backing up, the meta-crisis refers to our inability to see how we see, our apparent incapacity to understand how we understand; our failure to perceive how we perceive or to know how we know. In this sense, the hyphenated term meta-crisis is valuable because that conjunction of words encapsulates our problem: we are struggling to understand our predicament well enough to conceive of intentional action that appears to be meaningful in the context of the challenges we face, and mostly we amble on towards probable catastrophe.

This feature of the meta-crisis might even have something resembling a neurophysiological basis, although it certainly cannot be reduced to the brain. The psychiatrist and philosopher Iain McGilchrist speaks of our current problems in terms of our need to escape 'a hall of mirrors', patterns of attention arising from conceptual constructs of our own making and their institutional expressions, that arise from an overly dominant left hemisphere. In so far as that is correct, and I worked with Iain to clarify the nature of the claim as far as possible, the way out of such self-reference lies in reclaiming sovereignty over our attention, feeling into details, retaining embodied presence, appreciating context and enjoying nuance; there are also contemplative practices that allow us to develop these capacities.[41]

Perspectiva's *Praxis* strand of work seeks to address these kinds of self-referential challenges, including our work on metaphor design, constellations inquiry and improvisation. In each case there is an embodied and relational attempt to see ideological and conceptual confinement more clearly, and move beyond it where possible.

6. Meta-crisis in epistemology: the territory is full of maps

The *Vox* journalist David Roberts has written influentially about epistemic bubbles, reality tunnels and the need to grasp that different tribes increasingly live in different kinds of epistemic reality, where there appears to be no neutral terrain to decide what is true. In his most recent memoir, ex-US President Barack Obama brought 'epistemological crisis' into mainstream language. These are important developments, because the increasingly public language of 'the epistemic' is a healthy form of cultural incorporation of the meta, because when we are arguing about what is understood, and known and true, it helps a lot to have a broader holding pattern to make better sense of understanding, knowing and partial and whole truths.

This development appears to arise from an even deeper issue. As my friend David Rooks puts it, in the context of failing to feel that the world is intelligible through conceptual maps, there is a curiously recursive problem: 'The reason "the map is not the territory" is because the territory is full of maps'. It is not as though there is a shared world and competing sensemaking perspectives to make sense of it. It's more like the shared world is defined by that competition, and the challenge is to make sense of *that world*. This idea is actually one of the premises of what makes a wicked problem wicked, namely, that there is disagreement about the nature of any given problem at hand, and those disagreements are an enduring feature of the problem, not something to be resolved and eclipsed. Climate change is a good case in point – there is genuine disagreement on the maps of the territory, such that nobody seems sure if the situation is challenging, grim or apocalyptic – and the point is that the range of maps that make the cases for those claims are part of the reality that confounds our capacity to address it.

The way out of this feature of the meta-crisis will probably not be a map, or even maps, but it will come down to a collaboration of organisms who cannot help but be constituted by their own mapping processes. This is the terrain of neo-Piagetian developmental theory and the literary exploration of Jorge Luis Borges and others. I see this idea as an important part of the meta-crisis because we are mapmakers who struggle to experience and gain perspective on the reality of our own mapping process.

Grasping this complex map-territory relationship is an important aspect of what is sometimes called the sensemaking or intelligibility crisis. In Chapter 11, on 'Gnosis in the second person', Vervaeke and Mastropietro suggest part of the challenge of meaning and intelligibility more broadly at this time may be to recover the praxis of knowing through dialogue – *dialogos* – which has been somehow squeezed out by the over-emphasis on first- and third-person forms of knowing. Perspectiva's main approach to this problem is the development of the antidebate praxis, which is about combining methods of debate and dialogue to enhance and promote epistemic literacy and the intellectual humility that goes with it.

7. Meta-crisis in design: we have a suicidal generator function

In the language of meta-design used by gamers (principles that influence coding decisions), the meta-crisis is about a code reaching its own computational limits, like cultural software running out of ecological hardware. The problem lies in our 'underlying generator function' (Daniel Schmachtenberger) or 'source code' (Jordan Hall) being 'self-terminating'.[42]

The most straightforward expression of this idea is that in a world of 'rivalrous dynamics' (win-lose zero-sum games) that characterise our capitalist world system, where there are strong incentives to damage shared long-term (commons) resources for short-term gain, combined with the multiplying force of 'exponential tech' (forms of technology that lead to further technology and further incentivise or at least make possible this kind of behaviour), civilisation 'self-terminates'. This formulation can be seen as a more abstract and analytically precise formulation of the limits to the growth theory of the seventies, but with a technological emphasis.[43]

This way of viewing the meta-crisis is palpable in that it points to our apparent inability to prevent our own suicide. Perhaps the most evocative expression of this idea is

Schmachtenberger's idea that in a world where technology gives us the destructive power of gods, we need to develop the wisdom of Boddhisattvas. In his interview with Eric Weinstein, Schmachtenberger even spoke of 'Bodhisattva engineering', which is an amusing and somewhat oxymoronic term, but perhaps a good way to characterise the purpose of the new global paideia outlined in Zak Stein's advocacy, but in a language more likely to receive the investment it requires.[44,45]

Perspectiva does not currently work at the level of transcendental or ontological design, but our work on praxis is distantly inspired by the idea of 'Boddhisattva engineering'. We observe the community loosely defined as 'Game B' with interest in a collaborative spirit, but we are more inclined to cultivate receptivity to forms of life and ways of living that are also emergent but perhaps more open to transrational phenomena. A commitment to praxis is a necessary part of creating this receptivity. In an essay by Perspectiva's Senior Associate Mark Vernon, on Blake's imagination, he puts the point somewhat more strongly than I would, but the underlying emphasis is shared:

> [Blake's] vision for ecology is, therefore, not one of managed exploitation (Ulro), managed consumption (Generation), or even managed cooperation (Beulah), but instead one aimed at radically extending awareness of the ecologies of which we're a part. It means embracing not just the environments and organisms studied by the natural sciences but the divine intelligences appreciated by the visionaries, plus a panoply of gods, spirits and daemons that our ancestors took as read.[46]

8. Meta crisis in consciousness: we are increasingly disabled by dissonance

The adjectival form of 'meta crisis' says that's the kind of crisis it is – a crisis defined by a debilitating lack of perspective and abstraction – if an economic crisis is a crisis in the economy, the meta crisis is a crisis in the meta. To clarify, with reference to the discussion on meta above, our widespread inability or wilful refusal to a 'go meta' in the right ways is giving rise to a pervasive sense of dissonance. The experience of dissonance arises when we try to align our thoughts, values and actions, but fail, and notice we have failed, but don't quite understand why.

We live in an age of dissonance. The complexity and pace of events has long since eclipsed the complexity of human consciousness, yet social, political and professional conventions oblige us to talk and act as if we know what we are doing.[47] What dissonance highlights that concepts like alienation, false consciousness and dislocation do not is the idea that our experience is defined by a lack or loss of *agreement*, the sense that things that should fit together do not. Opposites of dissonance include agreeable and harmonious. Dissonance is a relational idea at its heart, but the relationship in question is the most fundamental relationships of all, between the subject of experience and the object of inquiry, between an organism and its environment, between ourselves and the world.

The experience of dissonance is prismatic of that relationship between subject and object being in a state of disequilibrium. This relationship can be seen as 'the form' that shapes our perception and understanding, and for millions around the world this form is in the more or less slow process of 'trans-forming'. Such development involves creating an observational gap between subject and object, such that we can observe and relate to whatever we were previously embedded in and defined by. That happened when we first saw Earth from space. That happens when we stop saying 'left wing' and 'right wing' and start asking: is this political spectrum really helping us and should we perhaps create a new one? That happens when we move from commenting on the economy to questioning the very idea(s) of the economy and, for instance, the idea of 'money' within it. That happens when we suggest, as Joe Brewer does, that the default unit of coordinated action may not be city or state, but something more like a bioregion. But this *kind* of 'healthy meta' thinking remains painfully niche.

On this framing, the meta crisis arises from large swathes of the population being unable or unwilling to make such meta moves or consider them worthwhile. A recent example would be the debate over Brexit in the UK when, at various stages of the process, numerous ideas or proposals were described as being democratic or anti-democratic, but almost never did the broader question of what democracy might mean seem like a permissible inquiry – it was right at the heart of the public argument for months and yet still apparently too abstract to consider as a question of shared public interest. A similar point applies to the apparent inability of the media to view climate collapse through anything other than an environmental frame.

Dissonance may now be a feature of life, and we need to learn to dance with it; through cognitive development and emotional maturity, dissonance can perhaps become less painful and more playful and paradoxical. One of the most hopeful developments in this space is a new institutional form – the Epistemic NGO – called The Consilience Project, founded by Daniel Schmachtenberger and developed by Zak Stein and others, which Perspectiva hopes to learn from and contribute towards in due course. The aim is to show that news (what's happening), meta news (*why* some sites/people are presenting the case in particular ways and others seeing it differently) and education (what the underlying issues/backstories are that are needed to understand what's going on in the news and meta news) belong on the same platform. By making the information ecology more transparent to itself, we may all be better placed to see the *basis* of the disagreement between ourselves and others, and any disagreements within ourselves, and perhaps also learn and grow through the epistemic fuel of any dissonance that remains.

9. Meta crisis in arts and humanities: the imagination is limited by the imaginary
Where are the prophets and the rishis? Does anyone have a notion of what a viable world could look and feel like in the 21st century, one that is not naive, or coercive, but which might actually arise from the world as we find it, and the people that shape it? The meta crisis in imagination may be the most important ingredient in the pickle, and again it's a crisis of what is in some sense meta, in this case an inability to adequately relate to what we are constructed by in a way that would allow us to conceive or create something new.

To come back to where we started this reflection, in the spirit of *Vivekananda*, one way to grasp the relative difficulty of imagining the end of capitalism is by distinguishing between the imagination, the imaginary and the imaginal, but the distinctions that follow seek to be heuristic rather than canonical. It helps to think of the imagination as a distinctly human *capacity* that is *in some sense real*, cultivated most directly in the domain of the arts and humanities, as detailed for instance in Northrop Frye's classic CBC lecture series in the sixties: *The Education of the Imagination*. The imaginary is more helpfully thought of as a minimally malleable *constraint*. This concept from social and cultural theory is about the limits of what we can imagine and the idea is developed explicitly by, for instance, Cornelius Castoriadis, Charles Taylor and former Perspectiva researcher Sam Earle; it is also tacit in the idea of *The Sociological Imagination*, which is also the title of Wright C. Mill's 1959 classic text.[48] And the *imaginal* is neither a capacity nor a constraint, but more like a *cornucopia* to be discovered in the terrain of depth psychology, mythology and comparative religion. Almost anything by James Hillman is of value here, but the classic text might be Jung's autobiography, *Memories, Dreams, Reflections*.[49]

With these distinctions in mind, while the end of the world is a mere act of *imagination* – an event characterised by stock imagery and widely portrayed in cinema, capitalism has become a defining feature of our collective *imaginary* – a shared social construction that circumscribes our relationship to imagery and our imagination. Moreover, the impact of social media (there are approximately two billion Facebook users and 1.5 million regularly using YouTube) might be that because we pass each other so much of the same imagery, our imaginations are becoming less individuated and more collectivised, such that the renewing power of the individual imagination is at ever greater risk of being subsumed by the collective imaginary. And perhaps the reason we appear to be struggling to see and think beyond our imaginary is partly because we don't take the *imaginal* realm – our psychic, mythic and archetypal resources – seriously. Indeed we may need our theories of change to be premised on something like what Cynthia Bourgeault calls 'imaginal causality', which taps into a source that is deeper than ideas and values and habits, and powerful enough to change them fundamentally.[50]

I am out of my depth here, and I say that because my experience of dreams and therapy and synchronicities lead me to feel that the imaginal realm is in some meaningful and non-reductive sense real; and yet it is still mostly terra incognita, for me at least. I don't know what follows, but I see the imagination as a frontier and our last best hope to loosen the grip of the collective imaginary may well be forms of praxis that explore the imaginal. Those forms of praxis may arise from socially acceptable forms of artistic endeavour. However, they may also be relatively transgressive forms of shamanic inquiry, psychedelics and everything between and beyond. We will need courage and discernment as we go.

10. Meta crisis in cosmovision: a weakness for one of two kinds of spiritual bypassing

Following the sequence of the pickle tasting from the Covid *reckoning*, to the climate *emergency*, to the political and economic *crisis*, to the mostly social and emotional *meta/crisis*, the mostly educational *metacrisis*, the mostly epistemic *meta-crisis* and the mostly spiritual meta crisis, it is time to take stock of the most fundamental holding pattern for those underlying features of our predicament, namely our cosmological framework, religious outlook or worldview – this is the terrain considered in Chapter 13's discussion between Jonathan Jong and Mark Vernon.

At the Museum of Anthropology in Mexico City I learned a great term to meet our conceptual needs here: 'cosmovision'. This charming Mesoamerican word is indigenous and centred around premodern practices of world-making, world-centring and world-renewing, but morphologically those same practices are needed today, and cosmovision deserves a modern reappraisal as a way to describe our perception of our place in the universe as it informs our everyday lives. The meta crisis here, which the term 'cosmovision' perhaps helps us see, is that many people currently fall into one of two main forms of spiritual bypassing that undermine generative forms of spiritual life.

In my 2017 book *Spiritualise*, I query the value of definitions, but go on to define spiritual sensibility as a disposition characterised by concern for the fullness of life and experienced through simultaneous intimations of aliveness, goodness, understanding and meaning. Those glimpses of wholeness and integration have a texture that is at once emotional, ethical, epistemic and existential – respectively, the feeling of being alive, the conviction that something matters, the intuition that the world makes sense, and the experience that life is meaningful.

Spiritual bypassing is classically conceived of as the tendency to look for spiritual answers to psychological problems at a personal level and, less often perhaps, political problems at a societal level. Many of those who sense the need to bring 'the inner world' to bear on the crisis and emergency fail to connect the case for spiritual sensibility to inner life as a whole, including its darker emotional and psychological aspects and, further, to its historically situated nature in all our systemic and structural complexity. I think this kind of spiritual bypassing is a neglected part of the meta crisis precisely because it's often pseudo-meta in nature; it does not entail a cosmovision at all but more like an adherence to consensus reality with some aspirational identity markers. As Robert Augustus Masters puts it in his classic text on Spiritual Bypassing:

> Authentic spirituality is not some little flicker or buzz of knowingness,
> not a psychedelic blast-through or a mellow hanging-out on some
> exalted plane of consciousness, not a bubble of immunity, but a vast
> fibre of liberation, an exquisitely fitting crucible and sanctuary, providing
> both heat and light for the healing and awakening we need.[51]

That resolute statement helps to disclose another way to think of spiritual bypassing, not as a misapplication of the spiritual, but the complete ambivalence towards or disregard for it. This kind of spiritual bypassing is about more than an intellectual wariness towards the ambiguous term 'spiritual', as I learned from the project I led at the RSA in London, which was more or less premised on the question: 'Why don't we speak more of spiritual matters in the public domain?' In this context, however, I am concerned mostly with metaphysical openness, whereby mind is not assumed to be merely irreducible to matter but also potentially in relationship with transpersonal forms of life that are simply not perceptible in a materialist ontology or naturalist epistemology. And for the avoidance of doubt, yes, that means I am just not sure about, inter-alia, the existence of ghosts, life after death, telepathy, divination, the reality of God and so forth. While it is important to retain one's critical faculties, and social and academic conventions make many of these subjects taboo, when we don't really understand time, consciousness or life as such, I think we need to remain curious about our metaphysical assumptions.[52]

The book that has made a big impression on me on this matter is Jeffrey Kripal's *The Flip*. The most notable claim is that an acceptance of consciousness as an irreducible feature of reality, and a concomitant acceptance of a range of apparently 'paranormal' phenomena, is not primarily a spiritual achievement, but more like a cultural correction at the level of intellectual leadership; that it is something I feel can happen in a number of years rather than decades or centuries. This point matters profoundly because many discussions of our planetary predicament are characterised by a misplaced presumption of secular liberal atheistic materialism, despite the fact that over 80 per cent of the world's population identify as being in some sense religious.[53] There is a kind of cosmovision among our ruling elites, but it's mostly a limited one, and it precludes the kinds of vision, sentiment and realisation that is in some fundamental sense spiritual. It does not follow that we invite in old time religion by the back door. As Kripal makes clear, the case for the irreducibility and/or primacy of mind often points towards an uncanny and even disturbing view of reality that is at odds with much of religion. He also argues that we need 'a new metaphysical imagination that does not confuse what we can observe in the third person with all there is'.[54]

I feel a certain hopefulness towards the flip, related to the limitations of what Jean Gebser calls the mental mode of consciousness; we flip partly because it's a source of epistemic and spiritual renewal; otherwise, things make less and less sense and we grow increasingly exhausted. The flip is not a transformation of consciousness as such, but perhaps a precursor to it. From a more spiritually ambitious integral and evolutionary perspective, this new metaphysical imagination may give rise to a growing awareness of *Spirit* as such. *In Ever Present Origin*, Jean Gebser describes what is needed as follows:

> A mere interpretation of our times is inadequate … This new spiritual reality is without question our only security that the threat of material destruction can be averted. Its realization alone seems able to guarantee man's continuing existence in the face of the powers of technology, rationality, and chaotic emotion. If our consciousness … cannot master the new reality and make possible its realization, then the prophets of doom will have been correct. Other alternatives are an illusion; consequently, great demands are placed on us, and each one of us has been given a grave responsibility, not merely to survey but to actually traverse the path opening before us.[55]

It is far from clear what follows, but the point is that we just don't know what is really going on. In Perspectiva's *Insight* work, including our essays, books and podcast, we are therefore keen to apply our powers of reason and discernment to metaphysical and cosmological perspectives that may help to make better sense of how we should recalibrate or reimagine life for the greater good in this time between worlds. To put it in secular business terms, when we are tasting the pickle, we may have pragmatic reasons to focus on the emergency and the crisis, but cosmovision has to be 'on the table'.

Tasting the pickle in practice: Perspectiva's purpose

Many of the thoughts above were gleaned but not fully articulated when I collaborated with Tomas Björkman to found Perspectiva as a charity in 2016. We are now on a secure financial and operational footing, and describe ourselves as a community of expert generalists working on an urgent one-hundred-year project to improve the relationships between systems, souls and society in theory and practice. We have evolved into a community of scholars, artists, activists, futurists and seekers who believe credible hope for the first truly planetary civilisation lies in forms of economic restraint and political cooperation that are beyond prevailing epistemic capacities and spiritual sensibilities. Our charitable purpose is therefore to develop an applied philosophy of education for individual and collective realisation in the service of averting societal collapse; and in the spirit of serious play and ambitious humility to cultivate the imaginative and emotional capacity required to usher in a world that is, at the very least, technologically wise and ecologically sound.

Over the next few years we will be pursuing four main thematic strands of work that help others to taste the pickle with us, to help us all work better on the crisis and the emergency.

> *Realisation* is our response the educational metacrisis. It's about building an alliance of transformative educators, and features an annual festival 'for the soul' in collaboration with St Giles House in Dorset, and intellectual inquiry on the frontlines of activism and 'the digital ego'.
>
> *Insight* is our response to our epistemic meta-crisis, our intellectual vision work in our essay series, journal, podcast and book publishing arm, Perspectiva Press, which offers 'soul food for expert generalists'.
>
> *Praxis* is our response to the spiritual meta crisis in which we attempt to turn theory into practice, currently through improvisation, metaphor design and the antidebate methodology, but potentially through innovative approaches to the imaginal, temporics and Logos.
>
> *Emergence* is our response to the 'we' problematic of the meta/crisis, and is about building a pre-figurative social movement through whatisemerging.com for wise global transitions.

There is a long road ahead, so if you have reached this far, thank you for tasting the pickle, and good luck!

Notes

1 With thanks to Bonnitta Roy, Mark Vernon, Layman Pascal, Ivo Mensch, Hannah Close, Ian Christie, Minna Salami, Jeremy Johnson and Zachary Stein for their feedback on various drafts of this chapter.
2 Masters, Robert A., *Spiritual Bypassing: When Spirituality Disconnects Us from What Really Matters*, North Atlantic Books (2010).
3 Rowson, Jonathan, 'The Unrecognised Genius of Jean Piaget', Medium (2016) https://jonathanrowson.medium.com/the-unrecognised-genius-of-jean-piaget-78c2914e306
4 Wilber, Ken, *One Taste*, Shambhala Press (2000), p. 315.
5 Intellectual Deep Web, 'James Hillman – Why Study Greek Mythology', YouTube (2017) www.youtube.com/watch?v=blF0NdSm1lQ
6 Schiller, Friedrich, *On the Aesthetic Education of Man*, Penguin Classics (2016).
7 Haraway, Donna, *Staying with the Trouble*, Duke University Press (2016).
8 Barfield, Owen, *History, Guilt and Habit*, Barfield Press (2006).
9 Table 1.1, especially the last column, includes several terms that are not introduced in the text, but act as placeholders for related terms and issues that are. Diaphaneity, for instance, is a Gebserian term that refers to 'seeing through the world'. A tesseract is a shape thought to best illustrate Robert Kegan's fifth-order of consciousness. Pancontextual just means across all contexts, a variant of Nora Bateson's terms 'transcontextual'. Metanoia is examined in more depth by Brent Cooper in Chapter 10.
10 Batchelor, Stephen, *Alone with Others*, Grove Press (1983).
11 Rogers, Carl, *On Becoming a Person: A Therapist's View of Psychotherapy*, Mariner Books (1995), p. 83.
12 I write about all these details in considerably more depth in my book, *The Moves that Matter: A Chess Grandmaster on the Game of Life*, Bloomsbury (2019).
13 I enjoyed the discussion between Forrest Landry and Jim Rutt on the possibility that earth might be unique in producing life like ours: The Jim Rutt Show, 'EP31 Forrest Landry on Building our Future', (2019) https://jimruttshow.blubrry.net/forrest-landry/
14 State of Emergence, 'EP028 Meg Wheatley – Warriors Wanted: It's Time to Defend the Human Spirit', (2020) https://dispatchesfromterrypatten.libsyn.com/028-meg-wheatley-warriors-wanted-its-time-to-defend-the-human-spirit
15 Solnit, Rebecca, 'The Impossible Has Already Happened', *The Guardian* (7 April 2020) www.theguardian.com/world/2020/apr/07/what-coronavirus-can-teach-us-about-hope-rebecca-solnit; Roy, Bonnitta, 'Corona, A Tale of Two Systems', Emerge (15 April 2020): www.whatisemerging.com/opinions/corona-a-tale-of-two-systems-part-one; Stein, Zachary, 'Covid-19: A War Broke Out in Heaven', Emerge (26 March 2020): www.whatisemerging.com/opinions/covid-19-a-war-broke-out-in-heaven; Roy, Arundhati, 'The Pandemic is a Portal', *Financial Times* (3 April 2020): www.ft.com/content/10d8f5e8-74eb-11ea-95fe-fcd274e920ca
16 Gautier, Chappelle, Rodary, Daniel, Servigne, Pablo, and Stevens, Raphael, 'Deep Adaptation opens up a necessary conversation about the breakdown of civilisation', *Open Democracy* (2020). www.opendemocracy.net/en/oureconomy/deep-adaptation-opens-necessary-conversation-about-breakdown-civilisation/
17 RSA Minimate: Climate Change and the Future of Humanity (2020): www.youtube.com/watch?v=eUh-TXKIdiE
18 Lenton, Timothy M., 'Climate tipping points – too risky to bet against', *Nature* (November, 2019), Vol 575, pp. 592–595: www.nature.com/articles/d41586-019-03595-0

19 McIntosh, Alastair, *Riders on the Storm: The Climate Crisis and the Survival of Being*, Birlinn Ltd (2020).

20 Less public, but uncannily similar to the climate emergency in its prospective tipping point when you begin to grasp it, is an emergency in the world of machine learning. We are in the process of creating theory-less knowledge and accruing 'intellectual debt' – namely the number of systems functioning in our lives that appear 'to work', but often in ways even the AI designers/engineers don't understand, gradually moving into a world where decisions will be taken on an algorithmic basis that is opaque to everyone. This time-sensitive lock-in risk is a quieter and less palpable emergency than climate change, but may be 'an emergency' nonetheless.

21 Davies, William, 'The Last Global Crisis Didn't Change the World, But This One Might' (2019): www.theguardian.com/commentisfree/2020/mar/24/coronavirus-crisis-change-world-financial-global-capitalism

22 For further details and sources see: Rowson, Jonathan, *We've Never Had it so Good, but Everything has to Change*. The Centre for the Understanding of Sustainable Progress (2017): www.cusp.ac.uk/themes/m/never-so-good/

23 Related issues are discussed at length in an excellent interview between Daniel Schmachtenberger and Jim Rutt: The Jim Rutt Show, 'Transcript of Episode 7 – Daniel Schmachtenberger', (December, 2019): www.jimruttshow.com/the-jim-rutt-show-transcripts/transcript-of-episode-7-daniel-schmachtenberger/

24 'Seinfeld – The Nothing Pitch', YouTube (2010): www.youtube.com/watch?v=EQnaRtNMGMI

25 Johnson, Jeremy, 'Meta, Modern', The Side View (2020): https://thesideview.co/journal/meta-modern/

26 Meta-crisis has a particular meaning below, but I also use it here, and above, as the default way of writing the term that captures all the different kinds of meta/crisis, metacrisis, meta-crisis, and meta crisis.

27 Rowson, Jonathan, *Spiritualise: Cultivating spirituality sensibility to address 21st century challenges* (2nd edition) Perspectiva/The Royal Society of Arts (2017): www.thersa.org/globalassets/pdfs/reports/spiritualise-2nd-edition-report.pdf

28 Schmitt, Carl, *The Concept of the Political*, Rutgers University Press (1932).

29 Ostrom, Elinor, *Governing the Commons: The Evolution of Institutions for Collective Action (Political Economy of Institutions and Decisions)*, Cambridge University Press (1991).

30 Jackson, Tim, and Victor, Peter A., 'Unraveling the claims for (and against) green growth', *Science*, Vol. 366, Issue 6468, pp. 950–951 (November 2019): https://science.sciencemag.org/content/366/6468/950

31 'Solitude Will Change Your Life: How to Be Alone With Others. Author and ex-monk Stephen Batchelor on the ageless practice of self-reflection', *Psychology Today*, September 21, 2020: www.psychologytoday.com/us/blog/the-seekers-forum/202009/solitude-will-change-your-life-how-be-alone-others

32 The Club of Rome, 'The Predicament of Mankind: Quest for Structured Responses to Growing World-wide Complexities and Uncertainties – A Proposal', *Demosophia.com* (originally published 1970): https://demosophia.com/wp-content/uploads/Predicament-Club-of-Rome-1970-1.pdf

33 Talks at Google, 'Confronting The Meta-Crisis: Criteria for Turning The Titanic – Terry Patten', YouTube (2019): www.youtube.com/watch?v=jHxTvvPZUuI

34 Perspectiva, 'What is Metamodernism?', YouTube (2020): www.youtube.com/watch?v=d9_TbQvgapM

35 Metzinger, T. 'Spiritual and Intellectual Honesty' (2013): www.blogs.uni-mainz.de/fb05philosophie/files/2014/04/TheorPhil_Metzinger_SIR_2013_English.pdf, p. 2.

36 These five questions arose collaboratively at Perspectiva. I am grateful to Zak Stein for his earlier version of four questions and latterly to Mark Vernon for suggesting imagination should be added. For an exposition of their importance and relationship, see my talk at the Das Progressive Zentrum conference on bringing the future back to Democracy in October 2020: Das Progressive Zentrum, 'Bringing the future back to democracy with Helena Marschall, Jonathan Rowson and Jens Südekum', YouTube (October, 2020): www.youtube.com/watch?v=iKETkVzmXYI

37 Rowson, Jonathan, 'Bildung in the 21st Century – Why sustainable prosperity depends upon reimagining education', CUSP essay series on the Morality of Sustainable Prosperity, No9, CUSP (June, 2019): www.cusp.ac.uk/themes/m/essay-m1-9/

38 Milbank, John and Pabst, Adrian, *The Politics of Virtue*, Rowman and Littlefield (2016).

39 Williams, Rowan, 'Liberalism and capitalism have hollowed out society – so where do we turn now?' *New Statesman* (October 2016): www.newstatesman.com/culture/books/2016/10/liberalism-and-capitalism-have-hollowed-out-society-so-where-do-we-turn-now

40 Deneen, Patrick, *Why Liberalism Failed*, Yale University Press (2018).

41 McGilchrist, Iain, and Rowson, Jonathan, 'Divided Brain, Divided World: Why The Best Part Of Us Struggles To Be Heard', *The Royal Society of Arts*, London (2013): www.thersa.org/reports/divided-brain-divided-world

42 Schmachtenberger, Daniel (2019), 'Self-terminating Civilization': www.consciousevolution.co.uk/otherinterviews/daniel-schmachtenberger-self-terminating-civilization

43 The Jim Rutt Show, 'Transcript of Episode 7 – Daniel Schmachtenberger', (December 2019): www.jimruttshow.com/the-jim-rutt-show-transcripts/transcript-of-episode-7-daniel-schmachtenberger/
44 Stein, Zak, *Education in a Time Between Worlds*, Bright Alliance (2019).
45 Daniel Schmachtenberger on The Portal (with host Eric Weinstein): On Avoiding Apocalypses: www.youtube.com/watch?v=_b4qKv1Ctv8)
46 Vernon, Mark, 'The Fourfold Imagination', Aeon (2020): https://aeon.co/essays/what-we-can-learn-from-william-blakes-visionary-imagination
47 As Jeremy Johnson puts it in his essay Meta, Modern: 'This uncanny world of hyperobjects we have entered defies categorical and compulsory mapping. There really are "No Maps for these Territories".' Johnson, Jeremy, 'Meta, Modern', The Side View (2020): https://thesideview.co/journal/meta-modern/ and Gibson, William, *No Maps for These Territories* (2000).
48 Wright Mills, C., *The Sociological Imagination*, Oxford University Press (1959).
49 Jung, C, *Memories, Dreams, Reflections*, HarperCollins (2019).
50 Bourgeault, Cynthia, *Eye of the Heart: A Spiritual Journey Into the Imaginal Realm*, Shambhala (2020).
51 Masters, Robert A., *Spiritual Bypassing: When Spirituality Disconnects Us from What Really Matters*, North Atlantic Books (2010), p. 3.
52 Emerge Podcast, 'Soryu Forall – Manufactured Awakenings', (March 2020) About 52 minutes in: https://podcasts.apple.com/us/podcast/soryu-forall-manufactured-awakenings/id1057220344?i=1000468307893
53 Rowson, Jonathan, *Spiritualise: Cultivating spirituality sensibility to address 21st century challenges*, RSA/Perspectiva (2017): www.thersa.org/globalassets/pdfs/reports/spiritualise-report.pdf
54 Kripal, Jeffrey, *The Flip: Epiphanies of Mind and the Future of Knowledge*, Bellevue Literary Press (2019), p. 107.
55 Gebser, Jean, *The Ever-present Origin: The Foundations and Manifestations of the Aperspectival World, Part One*, Ohio University Press (April 1986): www.jean-gebser-gesellschaft.ch/Dokumente/Considerations.pdf

Dispatches from a Time Between Worlds

2 Time, Change and Causality
Notes towards a metamorphosis of mind
Bonnitta Roy

Dispatches

THE WORD 'dispatch' means to send someone or something off to a destination. It has often been associated with sending a letter or report from a frontier or war zone back home so others might bear witness to the incredible or atrocious experiences of the writer. This is the meaning captured here in this anthology, except that we are not dispatching from place to place, but from one time zone to another. These writings are dispatches from a time between worlds, to a time when a new world takes its place. They come from writers who consciously acknowledge we are in a time zone that has the characteristic of being both a frontier and a war zone. We are explorers and survivors, and we are writing *to you*, the people of the future. Perhaps you will be able to make sense of the things that elude us here. Perhaps these dispatches will help you make sense of where you are, knowing how perilous and wayward a journey we have undertaken to get there.

The philosopher Jean Gebser (1985) looked back in time and saw that cultural artefacts – art, oral history, philosophy, religion and science – could be read as dispatches from their times. In taking this approach, he saw there were times of deep epochal change when one form of human consciousness was replaced by another. He characterised these epochal shifts as 'leaps' because each new structure was so radically different, they seemed to be discrete, discontinuous events. Gebser describes a 'latent' period of 'in between' when the old structures are no longer working, but the new structure has yet to fully emerge. Gebser identifies key artefacts where the old consciousness can be seen to be losing hold, and yet the new consciousness is not fully formed. Similarly, writing this article, from this place of in between, I have a strong feeling that my ideas are half-born and thus what are dispatched are fragments of a mind that is itself undergoing profound metamorphosis. A mind whose mental structures and conceptual frameworks have been dismantled to make way for the new structures, new frameworks, new categories of understanding, to emerge. This experience of reckoning with crisis and emergence and endings and beginnings is being dispatched from this time between worlds.

Metaphor

The prefix 'meta' in metamodernism points to the ability to take a perspective on modernity, to examine it as if 'from without'. This was the goal of the postmodern turn towards deconstruction and critique. I would argue, however, that because they share the same fundamental metaphysical categories of time, change and causality, the critique is not 'from without' but stuck on the inside. Hence both the modern paradigm and its critique tend to escalate risk and exacerbate crisis. In Gebser's terms, modernity is the efficient mode of the mental structure of consciousness, while postmodernity is the deficient mode. Our working hypothesis is that metamodernism is the latent mode of an emerging structure of consciousness. To exercise a metamodern view, then, simply means to see that modernity and postmodernity are self-enclosures tightening in on themselves inside a metaphysical loop.

This chapter shows how the metaphysics that underpins both modernity and postmodernity have not only primed the current meta-crisis, but also how they continue to exert 'upward pressure' towards civilisation's collapse. Here I use the term 'upward pressure' because postmodernity's response to crises has been in the direction of ever higher complexity and on an ever greater scale. Graham Harman used the term 'reducing upward' to characterise this tendency of the postmodern critique and its exorbitant systemisation of everything to produce conceptual paralysis (Harman, 2011; Roy, 2019). If we could reckon with the underlying paradigm instead, I believe that we would greatly release the complexity of the challenges we face. In other words, we are not so much working for greater systemic reach or to identify all the links in an enormous causal chain; rather we need to closely examine the metaphysical operating system of our minds, and participate in the creative emergence of a new structure of consciousness. This participation would of necessity include both thinking *and acting* and, as I argue in the section Causality, in an era of conceptual and planetary *closure* we must become the *first mover*. As Chandler (2018) puts it, we would need to become experimenting, compositional and playful persons 'fully aware of [our] lack of causal knowledge and confident and at home with contingency and the unexpected' to 'creatively engage with emergence itself, thus turning problems or threats into new opportunities', and to see that the problems themselves point to openings where new opportunities lie.

In this chapter, I do not intend to drive thinking 'up' towards increasing levels of complexification. Rather, I am attempting to drive thinking 'down' to the metaphysical roots of the modern/postmodern mind (Gebser's mental structure of consciousness). I refer to these roots as 'metaphysical primes' to connote that, like mathematical primes, they cannot be divided or reduced piecemeal but must instead be replaced entirely, and also that like 'priming a pump', they set the conditions for thought to happen. I address three metaphysical primes – Time, Change and Causality. I will show how these are deeply implicated in the meta-crisis, and how they are keys to the metamorphosis of our minds, which I argue is already underway, albeit in latent forms. This metamorphosis is driven by pressures that run counter to the modern mind's upward path. It operates through what David Chandler (2020) calls 'counter-systemic' approaches which destabilise the modern imaginaries of 'progress', 'civilisation' and 'development' while challenging our 'fixed and empty framework of time and space with ourselves at the centre'. As we face environmental destruction at a planetary scale and existential risk at a global scale, we should examine our stories that stick firmly to the modern imaginaries, since they emphasise our separation from nature, and de-story our shared genealogy with the life force of the earth. These stories, of separation and alienation, are consequences of reasoning from a particular set of metaphysical primes associated with the mental structure of consciousness, from which the modern world and its sequel, the postmodern, are scripted. Perhaps the term 'modern' in 'metamodern' reflects the continuance of the same old metaphysical architecture, in new conceptual bottles. But for me, it signals a response, of looking at modernity from somewhere else. And this 'somewhere else' is our period of latency, a time between worlds.

Our conceptions of Time, Change and Causality are based on a certain class of metaphors named 'interaction metaphors' by Max Black (1979). Interaction metaphors do not merely convey a definite conjunction between like pairs or systems. Rather, they have the property of *catachresis* – the ability to remedy gaps in vocabulary in order to lead to a synesthetic understanding. Black thought interaction metaphors were useful in science when the explanation was otherwise lacking precision. That employing interaction metaphors could lead towards greater precision. Richard Boyd (1979), however, pushed the usage of metaphor deeper into the heart of the scientific enterprise. He argued that certain classes of interaction metaphors – which he called theory-constitutive metaphors – helped scientists 'accomplish the sorely needed task of accommodating language to the causal structure of the world'.

> In the first place, the role of theory-constitutive metaphors in science reflects in a perhaps surprising way the epistemological necessity for the accommodation of conceptual structures to the causal structure of the world. Scientific kinds and categories must be defined in ways which reflect a deference to the world even at the cost of conceptual complexity. The fact that scientific investigation sometimes requires reference to kinds whose definitions are necessarily causally rather than conceptually unified indicates the depth of that necessity. (p. 485)

In this moment in history, in our time between worlds, we can no longer afford our usual sense of time, change and causality to remedy the gaps in our understanding. On the one hand, we feel time is accelerated and 'going somewhere' and that we need to 'get ahead of it', and so we speed ourselves up and in speeding ourselves up, accelerate time. On the other hand, there is still a great deal of inertia in the systems and institutions that are failing us. Even the resurgence that is screaming for reform and revolt has turned into a brutal and ongoing spectacle for the media complexes. In this chapter I am arguing that in order to constitute a new world, one that replaces the old, powerful new metaphors must shift our ways of relating and choosing against our own wellbeing and against the natural processes of the earth, towards generative behaviours and actions that nourish us and enable all life to flourish.

Time

Time is an invention, or it is nothing at all. Henri Bergson

Jean Gebser (1985) described how each structure of consciousness featured a unique relationship to Time which he called its particular 'temporics'. The temporics of the magical structure of consciousness was undifferentiated. The temporics of the mythic structure was dominated by past-consciousness, its reproduction, repetition and recurrence. With the mental structure of consciousness, our temporics becomes predominantly future-oriented. This manifests in our compulsion towards progress, purpose and pursuit of goals. Contrast for example, the modern notion of progress with the Aboriginal notion of 'increase' (Yunkaporta, 2019). Unlike growth and progress, which are matters of scale and quantity, increase is a precious quality that allows something to penetrate further or to ripen. To increase wellbeing, vitality and aliveness is to make them richer, just as frost concentrates the sugar in the fruit, or the way in which conflict concentrates our conversations.

Our preoccupation with progress, however, rejects such 'ancient wisdom' because we conflate the past with 'primitive' and the future with 'complex' and thereby equate anything that is more complex or more progressive with 'more good'. Yet Gebser (1985) admonished that progress is not a positive concept. He equated the modern era of 'progress' with the era of machine technology and the two world wars. Today, progress is associated with exponential tech, escalating complexity and accelerating existential risk. Gebser wrote, 'Progress is also a progression away, a distancing and withdrawal from something, namely origin' (p. 41). We therefore think of cosmogenesis as something that is done and over with, and 'our evolution away from the animals' as something that has happened in the past. Contrast this with Tyson Yunkaporta's (2019) view:

> Creation is not an event in the distant past, but something that is continually unfolding and needs custodians to keep co-creating it by linking the two worlds together via metaphors in cultural practice. (p. 110)

Note the notion of metaphor in Yunkaporta's view as 'interaction', which extends to images that serve as pattern languages, along with dance, song, culture, objects, ritual gestures and more (p. 110). In Yunkaporta's view, metaphors are the language of spirit which closes the gap between the abstract space and the real world – something that echoes Boyd's notion of theory-constitutive metaphor from an indigenous perspective. Metaphor, Yunkaporta says, is a relationship between theory and practice. We have to be careful with the metaphors we use, Yunkaporta says,

> because metaphors are the language of spirit and that's how we operate in our fields of existence either to increase or decrease connectedness within creation. We are the custodians who are uniquely gifted to do this work, so we need to do it consciously and with mastery, within cultural frameworks aligned with the patterns of creation. (p. 119)

As moderns, we 'spatialise time'. We employ mental models of time as a dimensional coordinate, predominantly linear like a time *line*, but often radial as in an event *horizon* or the time–space cone that traces the universe from the Big Bang out. Along these coordinates we arrange types of existence from less to more complex. This is a substance view of reality, which Whitehead and other process thinkers reject. In the substance view, only actual things are counted, whereas the potential state of the ground processes are ignored. Whitehead's process-relational philosophy entails a new time-consciousness. Consider the possibility of space as an infinite array of dimensionless dots of infinitesimally small but non-zero capacity to connect with another dot. The array is infinite, so the potential is also infinite. What actually exists is a small fragment of what potentially exists, with all that is latent potential composing a background that remains implicit in what actually exists. In a sense, new relationships are always 'threatening to appear'. Whitehead used the term 'subsist' to capture their continual participation as open potentials, as background capacitors.

Gebser said that the integral structure of consciousness would have the character of *time-freedom*. Humanity would no longer be concerned with securing its future position, which has the aroma of conquest over natural processes. We must drop the question of escaping the dangers of what lies up ahead, and concern ourselves instead with the question of 'what is future in us?' Gebser called forth this latency – that which is concealed, the demonstrable presence of the future, the ever-present potential that has been passed over because they are construed to have occurred in an irretrievable, dead past.

The Greeks had two words for time: *chronos*, and *kairos*. *Chronos* refers to chronological time, the spatialised sequence spread out across a line. It has the aspect of quantity and measurement like ticks along that line. *Kairos* has a qualitative aspect to it, which refers to a proper or opportune moment. *Kairos* has the quality of being saturated with resonance and meaning. Donna Haraway (2016) uses a third Greek word *kainos*, which she translates as 'now, a time of beginnings, a time for ongoing, for freshness'. 'Nothing in *kainos* must mean conventional pasts, presents or futures,' she writes,

> There is nothing in times of beginnings that insists on wiping out what has come before, or indeed, wiping out what comes after. *Kainos* can be full of inheritances, of remembering, and full of comings, of nurturing what might still be. I hear *kainos* in the sense of thick, ongoing presence, with hyphae infusing all sorts of temporalities and materialities. (p. 2)

Kainos resonates with Yunkaporta's (2019) time, where there are spheres of existence all coming into being simultaneously and where time and space form a unity of relationships. Perhaps these ideas intersect in what is already (past) latent (future) in us today (present): the potential to be in resonance with this moment in between worlds, to savour its precious flavours, instead of rushing to overcome it using artifices of one that is falling away, returning as it were to the background, to the world of dis-appearance. To be sure, the kind of change we need today is of such radical proportion, that if we were to gaze on the humans of tomorrow, they would barely be recognisable. To our modern eyes, they would seem to be travellers from another planet. We would peer into the future and see our future selves as somehow *other than us*, in the same way we peer at the animals and see them as other. By spatialising time in this way, we are destined to be forever 'in between', never having completely left, never having fully arrived. It has become our modern outlook – the proposition of our era, to be 'in a time between worlds', unable to reside among them, in resonance with their perpetual fluxes and flows.

We need a new temporics that is resonant with a deeper ontological reality of the human condition. Time is a powerful interaction metaphor that is constitutive of our theories of change. From these we derive all our contemporary models around individual development, evolutionary biology, ecological adaptation, resilience thinking and the new sciences of complexity and emergence. If our conceit of *time* is up for grabs, then so are all of these models. We are weavers of time. We do this freely. But we have been weaving unconsciously and so we trap ourselves in our own nets of knowing. Time-freedom, for Gebser, meant becoming aware of our weaving skills, rendering time itself transparent to us as *an activity of consciousness*. This process, which Gebser called a-waring, was for him essentially a spiritual encounter. Like Yunkaporta, whose people consider metaphors as the language of spirit that save us from abstraction by reconnecting us with the real world, Gebser called for a new kind of statement 'to make the strength of spirit perceptible' to express the energies of the psyche, the self, the soul and the culture. He declared that philosophy based on abstract representations was coming to an end and that the new form would render spirit transparent to us, would allow it to enter our awareness directly.

Gebser experienced his own time as in between worlds. He understood the need to address the inherent fatalism at the heart of our relationship with time. *Kainos* means each moment is replete, precious and precarious. But our modern fatalism presents itself as a continuous process of escaping death and rushing to get ahead, if we are ever to get there at all. It presents itself as our addiction to exponential technology, which makes us willing to destroy the village, the forest, the wetland, the tundra, in order to modernise them. It presents itself as a feeling that we are listing towards collapse without ever having noticed that things had been going terribly wrong all around us all along. For Haraway (2016), to be able to notice such things means 'staying with the trouble', which is a kind of in-dwelling that 'does not require such a relationship to times called the future'.

> In fact, staying with the trouble requires learning to be truly present,
> not as a vanishing point between awful or edenic pasts and apocalyptic
> or salvific futures, but as mortal creatures entwined in myriad
> unfinished configurations of places, times, matters, meanings. (p. 1)

And this kind of presence has everything to do with how we relate to change.

Change

'Panta rhei' – all things are in flux.   Heraclitus

There is a meaning to being 'in between' that relates to how we conceive of change as being between two forces. One force, which is fuelled by our addiction to progress, pulls us towards the future. The other force is our Darwinian attitude, which drives us from behind. One is the carrot forever ahead of us; the other is the stick always threatening to strike from behind. The Darwinian attitude shows up in thinking of human evolution in terms of escape velocity, as a force so great it has enabled us to exit the orbit of natural history. It makes us view evolution as a prologue to human emergence and to assume that everything of significance thereafter happens on *our branch* of the tree. It justifies techno-popular notions that humans are merely prologue to the Borg, and planetary evolution is merely an 'on ramp' to the stars.

The modern mindset struggles with change. We establish laws and ideas to be eternal and solid despite the ongoing change in society. In the same manner, we build 'permanent' structures on landscapes that meander and erode. Sedentary habits and modern needs for stability compel us to confine naturally moving forces, like culture as well as rivers, to narrow, predictable passageways. Viki McCabe (2014) chronicles the efforts the US has made over the years to contain the Mississippi to controlled boundaries. For 200 years the Corps of Engineers claimed that they could make the Mississippi River go anywhere the Corps directed it to go. The engineers focused on the physical properties of water, mass and gravity, while ignoring the geological, hydrological, meteorological and oceanological forces of the planet. And yet these are the very forces that *are the Mississippi* and can never be quelled. So of course, confinement only made the forces stronger. Hundred-year events began occurring at ten-year intervals, and unprecedented disasters loomed. On 29 August 2005, when Katrina hit, the devastation was incalculable. The timing was unpredictable, but like the Covid pandemic, it shouldn't have come as a surprise. Meteorologists long predicted such events *as an outcome of the intervention of the engineers*, while geologists and environmental scientists studying the delta topography specifically blamed the Corps for causing 'catastrophic structural failure' of the flood-waters system that protected New Orleans (McCabe, 2014).

Rivers and deltas, like human economies and cultures, are complex dynamic systems that cannot be understood through simple laws and predictable constants. C.S. Holling (Gunderson and Holling, 2001) crafted a model of change called the panarchy cycle as a way to re-conceive change in complex ecological systems. The panarchy model comprises four phases that cycle through different types of change. One phase, termed the Kappa or K-phase, correlates to development – the long slope of progress where energy is increasingly captured by dominant forms such as a dominant species, climax forests and relatively few stable ecological niches. We can think of the dominant forms of energy capture on the planet today in terms of humans, livestock animals and pets, corn and soy, and urban landscape features. Similarly, we can conceive of the current economy and contemporary culture as being in the K-phase, where more and more wealth is captured by fewer and fewer people, and global secular culture comes to dominate all other social niches. The K-phase is characterised by more tightly connected couplings and centralised relationships that increase systemic fragility. If the system seeks to stabilise by tightening couplings and increasing centralised response – in other words, by ramping up the same strategies – a threshold can be breached where catastrophic collapse is inevitable. The panarchy model suggests that resilient systems must move into a phase of 'creative destruction' before the threshold is breached. This is a phase of release where the stored energy is redistributed in a system that undergoes revitalisation through the making of new relationships and the creation of new identities and niches. New ways of living and world-building emerge.

This 'release' phase of the panarchy cycle has been called the 'back loop' (Wakefield, 2020; Chandler, 2020), and Holling himself has identified the Anthropocene as 'a very big back loop'. According to Holling, the back loop is fundamentally a situation of unknowns and unknown unknowns (Wakefield, 2020). Here *all explanations break down*. Here *we should expect explanations to break down*. We may be surprised to be here, but we should not be surprised that we cannot make sense of things here, where previously centralised narratives give way to a Pandora's box of alternative narratives. The point here is that back-loop dynamics are supposed to surprise and confound us. Yet we seem not to be able to resist trying to control them. Wakefield notes that while in city after city, people faced with the inevitability of crisis and change have switched from thinking in terms of sustainability to resilience, their responses have been patently front-loop action logics that emphasise security and centralised governance.

It is not only that our attitude conjugates the very crises we are purporting to avoid, but it also reflects itself in the means we apply in our 'experiments' – those very same layers of concrete, pipelines, mines, power plants, transportation and finance systems, governance policies and surveillance – that represent the ongoing commitment to front-loop action logics. Wakefield summarises it this way: 'Resilience designs thus work in *conjunction* with front-loop infrastructures, which continue to produce the disasters resilience intervenes upon' (p. 50). Back-loop dynamics defy front-loop logics of planning, entanglement, strong couplings and instrumental acts upon which global resilience responses rely. The logics of the back loop include surprise, autonomy, loose couplings and random acts. From the vantage point of the front, these are seen as illogical, irrational or written off as 'primitive'; the net result is to ward off other ways of living that are possible, many of which already function in the shadows of modernity, in urban slums, rural wastelands, indigenous communities and enclaves of experimental neighbourhoods and outposts of emerging culture. People who inhabit these places are already skilled at 'experimenting in unsafe operating spaces' – a phrase taken from the subtitle of Wakefield's book.

Resilience thinking is a powerful way to make sense of our time of exceptional volatility and the threat of catastrophic collapse. It asks some of us to be patient, steadfast and to endure, while strategically adapting on large and small scales in order to stay safe and survive. For others, the call is to keep moving. In any case, the application of the panarchy model to this time between worlds gives us a sense that because things are becoming simultaneously more exceptional and steadily worse, we must be somehow getting very close to a threshold. This is the persistent dramaturgy that accompanies our sense of change. It reflects the narrative arc of movies, where the future of the protagonist is available only after surviving a series of 'final' blows. Contemporary dystopic series such as *Falling Skies* intentionally disrupt this narrative arc, which is characteristic of modernity. Agreements between creator and viewer that once were sacrosanct, such as which favourite characters must never be killed off, are being violated in these series, in ways that reflect a growing zeitgeist. We have acted, as moderns, as if we have entered into a contract with the earth, and the contract says that humans are to be spared. The contract is signed with our signature intelligence and technological prowess, and our belief that the arc of history 'bends towards progress'. Each blow, the atrocities we have inflicted on each other, as well as the 'natural' disasters inflicted on us, are interpreted as signs that we must be getting close to the end of a tunnel, where the light will appear, or the end of a story where everything is made whole. Perhaps it is time to imagine a kind of change that has no instrumentality at all, has no eschatology or apocalypse, and signifies nothing beyond the meaning we give to it with the metaphors and models we use to reckon with it.

We give different meanings to the notion of resilience based on how and where we assign the conceptions of continuity and change. Consider a lowland forest that becomes flooded by beaver dams and turns into a wetland ecology. The trees die off and eventually the wetland, sustained by beaver construction, becomes a pond. Where are we willing to claim continuity and where are we compelled to claim a change? Is the lowland forest resilient because it can change into a wetland pond? Or is it fragile because it succumbs to the flooding? Think further ahead, when the pond is abandoned, and fertile sediments turn it into a fragrant meadow. Do we see continuity or change? Eventually the meadow is reclaimed by the signature species of the forest. Now we might say, the forest is indeed resilient, because it has come back!

Reconsidered in this way, resilience comes to be associated with the notions of appearance and disappearance. For something to be resilient means to maintain the potential to appear, even after it disappears. The 'system' that turns a forest into a pond, into a meadow, into a forest, is inclusive of all the relationships that can generate those varieties. Somehow, the potentials to do so subsist, even when they are not realised as actual appearances. Change, as it happens for us, is the dropping in and out of observable reality, those sets of relationships that have been afforded their time and space of appearance. This is as true for language and cultures, regimes and civilisations as it is for forests and ponds. Political change, for instance, requires that people who share visions of potential worlds, such as a democratic and egalitarian society, come together in public spaces to make their appearance through speech acts, and to form relationships that can actualise them. Hannah Arendt (1958) saw this confluence of speech and action and the space of appearance in the Greek word *polis*, which for her expressed the conviction that action and speech create a space of appearance that can find a location almost any time and anywhere:

> The space of appearance comes into being wherever men are together in a manner of speech and action, and therefore precedes all formal constitution of the public realm and the various forms of government. Its peculiarity is that, unlike the spaces which are the work of our hands, it does not survive the actuality of the movement which brought it into being. (p. 199)

Arendt saw that civilisations were held in the balance between the potential for speech and action to appear and disappear, and the choices of people to actualise the *polis*:

> Wherever people gather, it is potentially there, but only potentially, not necessarily and not forever. That civilisations can rise and fall, that mighty empires and great cultures can decline and pass away without external catastrophes – and more often than not such external 'causes' are preceded by a less visible internal decay that invites disaster – is due to this peculiarity of the public realm, which, because it ultimately resides on action and speech, never altogether loses its potential character. (p. 200)

Causality

The crisis of our times and our world is in a process ... of complete transformation, and appears headed toward an event which, in our view, can only be described as a 'global catastrophe'. This event, understood in any but anthropocentric terms, will necessarily come about as a new constellation of planetary extent. Jean Gebser

Causal reasoning is so fundamental to our way of life that few people realise that our ability to make if-then propositions emerged only 3,000 years ago in the Axial Age (Bellah, 2012; Gebser, 1985). Without if-then propositions, scientific reasoning is simply not possible. Without them, there could be no hypotheticals, and hence no experiments to test them. This led to a Western form of enlightened reasoning. In the East, if-then thinking led to a spiritual form of enlightened reasoning that traces back to Gautama Siddhartha, who applied if-then reasoning to construct a model of the causal links of suffering. His model, the 'Wheel of Samsara', identifies the 12 causal links in an action-reaction cycle that includes cosmological, phenomenological and psychological factors. The scholastics associated with Nagarjuna (~150–250 CE) investigated the causal implications between human minds and external reality. They demonstrated how mental events and phenomena are causally implicated in physical events. Consider an extreme case of a person with paranoid delusions. The delusions themselves are subjective phenomena. Yet the subjective state of the person leads to actual behaviours in the objective world, such as the person killing someone, and those actual events have their own objective and subjective repercussions. Yet, to say that the subjective state 'leads to' certain behaviours is not the same as saying it 'causes' that behaviour in a direct, predictable fashion. Rather, in the Eastern understanding, causal entanglement between mind and world was construed as something numinous – everywhere and nowhere at the same time. Here, inside this numinous reality, simple if-then propositions break down. This is the hallmark of our time.

Part of why I am pointing to this is because it shows that our mental models of causality are themselves causally implicated in the objective world. Our belief in what *causes* climate crisis, for example, or what *causes* the breakdown of global supply chains during a pandemic, will insert itself into that very same causal loop, whether they are 'true' explanations or not. It is increasingly the case that the causal assumptions embedded in our systems thinking around complex problems, make us prepare for a collective response on a grand scale. Once these preparations are in place, they actually increase the likelihood that we will experience the very effects we hoped to avoid. If I prepare for a battle I believe is coming, I increase the likelihood that you will ramp up your army, increasing the likelihood that that battle will happen. This is only one of the strange causal loops we will see in what follows.

The Western enlightenment in general and Newtonian physics in particular ushered in the modern dualistic approach to causality. Newton's laws of motion codified forces that acted upon (cause) and objects that were acted upon (effects) and the billiard-ball collision model of causality came to predominate. It is this tendency to animate some parts of a causal system and to de-animate other parts that sticks stubbornly to our modern minds when we reason in terms of (animated) cause leading to (de-animated) effects. This is as true for the billiard player and his balls as for climate science and contemporary excursions into complex systems thinking. This dualistic mentality was applied in the West to investigate the relationship between subjective mental phenomena and objective real-world events.

How can the mind insert itself into the chain of physical forces? How does this unique sort of efficient cause operate? What kind of force could that be? (Juarrero, 2002) Some modern materialists reconciled dualism by trying to identify all the points of collision in the casual chain: the factors in the external world that trigger the neural correlates that activate the body. According to Juarrero, 'One part triggers another, which pushes a third, and so on until something shoves the skeletomuscular system into action' (p. 23). This is the modern view of 'cause as only collision' that emerges from the Newtonian assumptions of resting objects that require an external force to push them along the chain of events. In such cases of reductive causation, the whole is construed to consist of atomised parts governed by immutable laws. The individual parts are seen as points of leverage for directing the system. Once we understand the physical properties of the parts, we can leverage the system. This is our approach when addressing climate change. Carbon is seen as a critical point of access to the entire planetary crisis, just as vaccines are seen as the critical point of access to our immune system. But is this kind of reductive causation adequate to address complex dynamic systems, where mental and physical phenomena are entangled across all scales, from self to body to local environment, to ecological range, to world, society and planet? And if, at the bottom of our systems approach, there is a reductive kind of causality, where some of the parts are animated and some are de-animated (waiting to be pushed along), then perhaps our interventions are actually creating the very conditions for the problems we are hoping to mitigate, and our responses in turn are closing in on themselves, increasing the complexity of the situation and escalating risk. Might this be the very possibility that is hidden in plain sight, here at the edge of the known world?

The question posed here is not only what is ethical action in such a world, but also how can we choose our actions at all, when intention and outcome have become causally indeterminate? In her book *Dynamics in Action* Alicja Juarrero (2002) attempts to overhaul the modern assumptions around causality and the paradox of human action by describing intentional behaviour through the lens of complex systems. The trick when combining issues of causality within complexity science is to get out of the tendency to extend vitality and free agency (intention) to some aspects of the system and not to others. In other words, to make sure that the system does not foreground the actor subjects as causal agents, while inadvertently hiding the acted-upon objects as determined effects. For embodied action this gets even trickier. In some instances, some of the parts act as free agents, while other parts are merely receptors, as for example, the mind that moves the body or the intention that raises the arm. In other instances, this tendency can be masked by systemic complexity, for example, in the case of dual causation where the member parts act to create the system, which then acts upon the members themselves. This leads to the notion of 'formative causation' when the system is construed to constrain the member's behaviours through its own system's properties, as expressed in the popular phrase, 'we create our systems and thereafter our systems create us.' Still, in more complex systems, the system itself is conceived as a higher-order causal agent that 'supervenes' on the parts such that the system determines the actions of the parts, but the parts are incapable of acting on the system. For example, how we might describe the way that the person 'supervenes' on her cells when she walks across the room in the sense that her cells have no say in the matter?[1] In addressing causality in a deeply entangled reality, we must avoid de-animating some of the parts while assigning causal efficacy to others. This is the core error in ecological management thinking, where humans are construed to be actors who can manage (act upon) ecological systems. The same kind of thinking is involved with climate science, which assumes that humans can access a privileged position in which to act on the climate without the climate acting on us in response. Chasing just one half of the equation exacerbates the negative effects coming from the other half. Yet nor can we contend that we are subject to 'systemic forces' of such power that we cannot turn the tide around and change the system. These are the key concerns in addressing crises in our world today.

The Darwinian attitude slips into this discussion through the language of complex adaptive dynamics where agents (populations of individuals) are the foreground and the environment is backdrop. The backdrop operates without intention even as it exerts pressure on agents to respond. Random differences in individuals' ability to adapt give some individuals greater odds for survival and better breeding prospects. Note that, in some contexts, humans are the agents adapting to pressures exerted by natural processes. In other cases, humans, animals and plants are being pressured to adapt to human processes. The orangutan suffering the pressures of palm oil harvesting is conceived as adapting to a changing backdrop, not as suffering the intentions of any individual human. This way of conceiving adaptive pressure as unintentional processes rids the system of critical ethical and moral implications. Today this simplistic construction of an ethical gap between agents as foreground and environment as backdrop is breaking down. Where for example, is the backdrop for how the climate is adapting to human activity? The point of leverage is not somehow in outer space. Rather it is here, in our own intentional space and actions (Arendt, 1958).

> Without actually standing where Archimedes wished to stand (*dos moi pou stō*) still bound to the earth through the human condition, we have found a way to act on the earth and within terrestrial nature as though we dispose of it from the outside, from the Archimedean point. (p. 262)

Neither can we afford the simplistic construction of the earth as backdrop, and we as merely sufferers of its forces. Here the Darwinian attitude and the language of complex adaptive systems slips into our imagination as 'survival drives'. This means we are beginning to think of ourselves, individually and collectively, as 'people under siege'. Yes, life is precarious. We need not pretend we are discovering this for the first time. But precarity is not the same as predation. And while it might be useful to adopt the Darwinian attitude in circumstances between actual predators and prey, if we address our existential condition of precarity in the same manner, we might come to think of the very forces and systems that life depends upon as the forces and systems that must be stopped or destroyed: 'Modernist assumptions of securing the human against the world are held to be precisely the problem that needs to be overcome' (Chandler, 2018, p. 10). Hence, the world is not an environment that requires an *adaptive* response from us. What is required from us is a *transformation* in perception of the world, from 'threat to be solved' to a field of mutuality and possibility.

Complex adaptive systems (CAS) is a powerful theory-constitutive metaphor for how we currently conceive of causality in complex systems. The danger is that once we extend the metaphor to include the backdrop, we become hopelessly embroiled in a loop that we ourselves have closed. Here all agents across all contexts are merely *reactive*, and the system functions as a perpetual motion machine escalating towards catastrophic bifurcation. This is an implicit warning in Juarrero's (2002) model of intentional behaviour as complex systems where the 'wave as a whole imposes (top-down) … constraints on the behaviour of the individuals' and there are 'suddenly ways in which they cannot behave at all'.

> [Once closure] takes place, second-order, context-dependent constraints (from whole to part) suddenly appear on top of the first-order contextual constraints …. The newly created 'structured structuring structure' in which the components … are now situated as a whole changes the prior probability of their behavioral options and, as such, alters their degrees of freedom. (p. 141)

This then eventually turns out to be another (albeit very sophisticated) kind of de-animation. Whether we conceive of this happening because of objective systemic properties, as in autopoietic closure in dynamical systems (Juarrero, 2002), or due to subjective states primed by theory-constitutive metaphors such as complex adaptive systems, is probably a matter of emphasis. Yet what we choose to emphasise makes a difference in terms of our behaviour. In the first case, where the emphasis is on the objective properties, we might behave as if we were suffering neglect from a benign system. In the second case, where the emphasis is placed on the subjective qualities of our intentional state, we might believe that we can create new imaginaries that do not rely on the same metaphors of time, change and causality that have tightened the causal loop. This is not a trivial epistemic shift. It has ontological repercussions because, for human beings, our intentional states and mental models are causally implicated in our actions. In fact, the notion of complex adaptive systems is itself epistemically suspect since it *necessarily implies closure*, because everything is adapting to everything else, and every adaptation to pressure simultaneously injects more adaptive pressure into the system. It is a continuously escalating, perpetual motion machine of antibiotics and bacteria, insects and pesticides, markets and trade, nuclear arms and weapons defence, viruses and vaccines. Inside complex adaptive systems thinking, closure may be predicated on the very properties of the model itself.

Perhaps, then, the primary imperative of our time in between worlds is to *become the first mover*. In the face of adversity, precarity and uncertainty, we must create actions *de novo* out of pure imaginative will. We must act with regard to a kind of numinous causality, which could not be pegged to a single event, speech or deed, but would be something percolating in the hearts and minds of people. 'We are never merely a doer,' wrote Hannah Arendt (1958), 'but always also a sufferer of our actions.' In this 'medium' which is the human condition of plurality, every process set in motion is not a cause of an 'equal and opposite' or even 'adaptive' reaction, but the cause of other *new* processes. As such, the consequences of every new act, although it may be singular and may emerge *de novo*, are boundless.

> This boundlessness is characteristic not of political action alone, in the narrower sense of the word, as though the boundlessness of human interrelatedness were only the result of the boundless multitude of people involved, which could be escaped by resigning oneself to action within a limited graspable framework ... because one deed and sometimes one word, suffices to change every constellation. (p. 190)

The Darwinian attitude and the language of complex adaptive systems are based on causal metaphors of response and reaction. What if instead we adopt metaphors such as Openings, Offerings and Welcomings to formulate new approaches to complex systems thinking? If we combine these kinds of metaphors with a process metaphysics of time, change and causality, we end up constituting a theory based on something that could be called 'complex potential states' thinking. Unlike the logic of complex adaptive systems, which ask, 'what do we do now?', the logics of complex potential states leads to the question 'what can we do from here?' Here, systems are construed to be complexes of potential states, which include both threshold (actual objective occasions, conditions and events) and subthreshold (potential occasions, conditions and events) processes that are causally entangled. The subjective state of the person would represent the subthreshold potentials of the actual events that flow forth from them. Yet every subthreshold potential is encapsulated in a subthreshold micro-action in the same way that every threshold event unfolds from a subjective force from within. In his book *Facing the Planetary* William Connolly (2017) describes Whitehead's notions around potential states as 'a stream brimming with pluripotentiality flowing toward action'. The coherent state that emerges as action taken enfolds only some of the potentials. Those not selected are in a sense 'left behind', but they are not eliminated. Connolly writes: 'The open plurality that preceded the selection now simmers in the background of being, available to enter into future vibrations when a new situation arises.' In fact, the coherent state that emerges due to the remarkable processes of relationship 'adds to' the collection of potentials that subsist in the adjacent possible.

> So loose instinctual residues from a past that never was periodically exert pressure on life. The scar left behind, however, bristles with uncertain potential. It may be activated under new circumstances, forging an

> uncanny relation with the new situation from which a new bout of creative energy arises. ... A new idea, feeling, tactic, perception, desire, plan of inspiration may bubble into being as if from nowhere. (p. 77)

This gives Connolly reason to hope that the 'uncanny processes of creativity' are causal forces of change.

> Creativity thus forms an uncanny element of human relations. Creativity is a critical *element* because freedom would be flat or dead if it did not radiate with the potential to become something new; the process is *uncanny* because creativity is neither the simple result of a preformed intention nor the realisation of a preordained principle waiting to be elaborated. (p. 77)

This gives us another meaning of being in a time in between. Perhaps we are inhabiting a world of subsisting potentials, a world of 'partially formed tendencies that are not consolidated because another fork had in fact been forged and taken'. Perhaps this world in between is the 'fork not taken' that now 'subsists as a partially crystalised instinct of collective, arrested, thought-imbued energies'.

Crisis and metamorphosis

> *... if we do not overcome the crisis it will overcome us; and only someone who has overcome himself is truly able to overcome.*   Jean Gebser

Whether framed in terms of development, adaptation, resilience or a dynamic balancing act, there is a sense of wanting to calibrate the human experience to a greater perfection in the metamodern mind, which I believe is its predominantly modern mentality. As moderns, we only value change in the direction of 'progress' because these are models of change that preserve the identity of the thing, the individual, the process, without having to undergo the kind of metamorphic transformation which replaces the old identity with a new one. In this world, as 'modern' caterpillars, we only want to get bigger, stronger, grow more legs and devour everything. In the next world, as 'modern' butterflies we will only want to get bigger, stronger, fly faster, farther, longer and lay more eggs. The chrysalis, the time in between, is never invited and hardly ever welcomed. The metaphor of the chrysalis as opposed to that of the cocoon is particularly relevant here. A cocoon is an external enclosure spun out of silk that covers the pupa stage of a moth. The chrysalis of the butterfly, however, grows from within the caterpillar's insides, eventually erupting through the skin. The caterpillar then is the appropriate metaphor for the times we live in, where our identities at every scale – individual, social and planetary – are dissolving by forces erupting from within.

For over 3,000 years we have been transcribing our metaphysics of Time, Change and Causality into more sophisticated modern theories. Words such as resilience, adaptation and complexity and the models that they derive from – panarchy, complex adaptive systems, complexity science

– compose powerful ways to make sense of our world, help organise our collective thoughts and align our goals. Our modern system has proven to be particularly robust and has served some of us particularly well. It is quite possible that those who have been underserved, or even those who have suffered profoundly as a result, far outnumber those who have benefited, especially if we consider the other animals and the other living beings in the flora and fauna of our shared biosphere. The perception that our modern mindset is particularly robust and has served us well may very well be tautological, given its foundations on notions that equate progress with complexification, and advance with predictability and control.

I have tried to present an alternative point of view, one in which time is not linear, change is not advance, and where causal forces are not systems that de-animate their parts. It is a view where maturity and ripeness, senescence and decay as well as disappearances and vanishings create crucial openings for the game of life to go on. Neither progress, nor complexity, nor compounding evolutionary pressures can account for metamorphosis. Metamorphosis requires openings, and openings the old form to be *taken out of existence*.

When we lock ourselves inside a narrative of crisis, we isolate ourselves from the very possibilities that can help us transform. But the energies of crisis, held appreciatively, transmute to the energies of metamorphosis. Appreciation is not the same as remembering, such difference being, for example, that between remembering the dead and appreciating them. One is hopelessly frozen and we feel the chill. The other continuously revitalises us on our own journey. Appreciate Plato, Kant, the Founding Fathers, the Western canon and the ways of modernity. Appreciate them for both having brought you here *and* for leaving themselves behind. This is the spirit of emergence. Therefore, appreciate these times of crises, these times of transitions, not only because they are here, they are shaping us and they will leave their stamp, but also because of their impermanence. What these times have to offer *uniquely as theirs, as ours*, will one day be irrevocably lost to the annals of retrospective sensemaking. Juarrero (2002) notes that in the midst of phase changes, there is not enough explanatory detail for us to reconstruct the causal relations in play. We must instead defer to narrative reconstruction that relies on hermeneutical practices of meaning-making:

> Phase changes cannot be explained in terms of the dynamics from which they issued. The reason … is that phase changes mark a qualitative, catastrophic transformation in the dynamics themselves. Across phase changes, therefore, what requires explanation is how the meaning that governed one stable state is transformed into qualitatively different dynamics … . As a result, a narrative reconstruction of the genealogical, evolutionary process must explain the 'neogenesis' enabled by this strange form of causality operating far from equilibrium. (p. 124)

Bifurcation events are singularities that cannot be captured by deductive-nomological explanatory processes. They must be encapsulated in stories that evolve through other genealogical processes because the explanandum itself undergoes a leap at the bifurcation point. 'Once we recognise the astronomical multidimensionality of human experience,' writes Juarrero, 'we can use vivid detail and fresh analogies to explain action' (p. 239). In so doing, we highlight the rich complexity of our human condition, instead of abstracting it away to a false simplicity.

Thus the story of our time between worlds is hidden from us, even with the words we dispatch to readers of the future. The very richness of the in-between world makes it imperceptible to us. 'The light that illuminates processes of action,' Arendt (1958) wrote, 'appears only at the end, frequently when all the participants are dead.'

Once on the 'other side', we may forget again what it was like to be in the uncanny position of acting without knowing and moving while still wondering where to go. Here, however, we have the chance to appreciate the incredible, impossible journey of being transported from one world to another, without needing to know how exactly it is happening. Along the way, we should not hope to be remembered for our actions, because we really don't know what we are doing. Rather, our hope is to be appreciated. Nor should we expect to be understood by future generations. More likely, the mystery we are to ourselves will be permanent, just as the 'sages of old' – those forces of epochal change and emergence that the ancients reified as men – are still a mystery to us today.

Coda

> *The miracle that saves the world, the realm of human affairs, from its normal, 'natural' ruin is ultimately the fact of natality, in which the faculty of action is ontologically rooted. It is in other words, the birth of new men and the new beginning, the action they are capable of by virtue of being born.* Hannah Arendt

What, then, must we do? We are the people to create enduring acts of inspiration and imagination for others to find when this world finally comes to an end. These will be seeds that can grow in the next world, but not in ours. We will never see them bloom. It would be like planting a tamarack in the Pleistocene for someone today. We are the people to do this religiously, but not with messianic fervour, rather with loving care, trusting that our purpose is not of this world and for us, but of the next world and for them.

Who are we, then, these people assembled at the end of the world?

We are the extemporarians.

Selected bibliography

Arendt, Hannah (1958). *The Human Condition*. Chicago: University of Chicago Press.
Bellah, Robert (2012). *The Axial Age and its Consequences*. Cambridge, MA: Belknap Press.
Black M. (1979). More about Metaphor, In A. Ortony (Ed.) *Metaphor and Thought*. Cambridge: Cambridge University Press.
Boyd, R. (1979). Metaphor and Theory Change: What is 'metaphor' a metaphor for? In A. Ortony. (Ed.) *Metaphor and Thought*. Cambridge: Cambridge University Press.
Chandler, David (2018). *Ontopolitics in the Anthropocene*. New York: Routledge.
Chandler, David, Grove and Wakefield (2020). *Resilience in the Anthropocene*. New York: Routledge.
Connolly, William (2017). *Facing the Planetary*. London: Duke University Press.
Gebser, Jean (1985). *The Ever-Present Origin*. Athens: Ohio University Press.
Gunderson, Lance and C.S. Holling (2001). *Panarchy*. Washington, DC: Island Press.
Haraway, Donna (2016). *Staying with the Trouble*. Durham, NC: Duke University Press.
Harman, G. (2011). The World is Enough: On overmining and undermining. Retrieved from https://larvalsubjects.wordpress.com/2011/10/11/the-world-is-enough-on-overmining-andundermining/
Juarrero, Alicia (2002). *Dynamics in Action*. Cambridge: MIT Press.
Juarrero, Alicia and Carl Rubino (2010). *Emergence, Complexity and Self-Organization*. Litchfield, PA: Emergent Publications.
Latour, Bruno (2017). *Facing Gaia*, Cambridge. UK: Polity Press.
McCabe, Viki (2014). *Coming To Our Senses*. New York: Oxford University Press.
Palmer, Clare (1998). *Environmental Ethics and Process Thinking*. Oxford: Clarendon Press.
Roy, Bonnitta (2019). Why Metaphysics Matters, *Integral Review* Vol 15 No. 1. Retrieved from https://integral-review.org/issues/vol_15_no_1_roy_why_metaphysics_matters.pdf
Stein, Zachary (2019). *Education in a Time Between Worlds*. Occidental, CA: Bright Alliance Publishing.
Stengers, Isabelle (2011). *Thinking with Whitehead*. Cambridge: Harvard University Press.
Wakefield, Stephanie (2020). *Anthropocene Back Loop*. London: Open Humanities Press.
Whitehead, A.N. (1979). *Process and Reality*. Cambridge, UK: Free Press.
Yunkaporta, Tyson (2019). *Sand Talk*. Melbourne: Text Publishing.

Notes

1   Although this might seem intuitively correct to most people, it is actually a poorly conceived construction of what a body is. Consider, for example, saying that the earth 'supervenes' on people as it travels through space. We, of course, have no say in the matter. Yet the earth is the environment through which we move. So, does the earth constrain or afford movement? Likewise, the body is the environment through which the cells move and participate in their own societies, as in turn the cell is the environment in which subcellular agents interact.

3 Becoming the Planetary

Jeremy D. Johnson

IF WE want to cohere the emergent qualities of a 'metamodern' social imaginary, another concept becomes readily useful, even necessary: the concept of the planetary both extends the applications of the metamodern thinker into the ecological and the posthuman, and allows us to recognise new possible social imaginaries, planetary imaginaries, that are already at hand. The planetary assists us in our own process of decoupling from our fixation with the modern, post-, meta- or otherwise. If we are to go meta, then we should bring the concept of the planetary with us.

Entering orbit

'Planetary', in its sphericity, its curvature and terrain, breathing and rhythm, is a word we ought to pay special attention to. So many of our challenges today are locatable in relation to how we enact our sense of world, self and time. How we define the word 'planetary' itself reveals many things: to the Greeks, *planasthai* ('to wander', as in *planētai*, 'wandering stars'), to moderns, a world orbiting a star (Edgar Morin's 'Planetary Era').[1] And to us? Are we quite modern, any more? The word now carries a terrestrial meaning, so much so that novelist Frank Herbert's character Liet Kynes, a 'planetary ecologist' in his science fiction classic *Dune*, immediately makes a kind of intuitive sense to the reader (a sense that I'll return to in the next section).[2]

Here is a first approach: by *planetary* I mean some kind of complex interrelationship between the human and non-human world. The planetary is simultaneously climatological and biospheric, geological and astronomical; it requires us to consider a sense of evolutionary *deep time* and the interrelated processes that constitute the being and becoming, the *breathing* of the biosphere in its relation to the 'whole Earth', that is, the way in which life actively shapes global homeostasis.

The planetary denotes a certain reality *beyond* the mere conceptual. It describes an incipient *realism* we have become critically cognisant of in recent years, especially since the popularisation of the Gaia Hypothesis developed by Lynn Margulis and James Lovelock.[3]

Thinking at the planetary-scale challenges our conceptualisation of space: it is very big and very small. It requires *both* the microscope of Margulis to consider the planetary effects of the infinitesimal-yet-mighty microbiome *and* the telescope of Lovelock who, while observing the waning atmosphere of Mars, recognised Earth's remarkable ability to maintain homeostasis.

The planetary seems, at the very least, to have to do with the way in which human cultures – in particular our global, interconnected civilisation – are finding ways to internalise these realities.

But that's not quite it.

Approaching the planetary requires that we circumnavigate it – dashing in and out of the gravity well of heavenly bodies – while perhaps becoming wandering stars ourselves. So here is our second attempt to provide a working definition: *the planetary as a (still incipient) consciousness of the whole in which we participate as living organisms.*

How *do* we imagine our relationship with the climatological, or with the evolutionary processes of deep time, if we imagine these things at all? Who are *we*, homo sapiens, in relation to this manifold interagency of beings that participate in the making of the biosphere, the geosphere, 'noosphere'?[4] How do we conceptualise and visualise this extended, inexhaustible whole of who we are? And how does the whole involve itself in the singularity of a human being?

In a word, how does the planetary get under our skin?

Another concept becomes readily useful to bring these threads of inquiry into one stitch. Charles Taylor's 'social imaginary' has recently become a helpful way of talking about a kind of *collective social unconscious* that shapes the way we imagine the borders and boundaries, relationships and structures of self and society.[5] We can refine our focus in the context of what *kind* of social imaginary is actually emerging in the metamodern era, a context we can no longer avoid: the 'planetary imaginary'.

Bruce Clarke, in his recent *Gaian Systems: Lynn Margulis, Neocybernetics, and the End of the Anthropocene*, writes that, '[the planetary imaginary] is constituted whenever found or made images of worlds living or otherwise are bodied forth in some workable medium'. These images are either 'popular or artistic', but regardless, they work to nurture the 'intuitions of the actual Earth's complex interactions'.[6] This would include the aforementioned novel *Dune*, for instance, or the first 1967 photographs of the Earth from space.[7]

The most urgent and pressing expression of the planetary imaginary is that imminent global reckoning, ever on our future's horizon: anthropogenic climate change. Modernity's social imaginary is breaking down, unable to respond satisfactorily to a 'meta-crisis' that seems to challenge *every* facet of our industrial civilisation.

Repositioning 'meta' in the planetary context

Our modernist social imaginary is breaking down, and a planetary imaginary, though still incipient at best, is nevertheless cohering. We can begin to say a few words about what this restructuring is like: in the Anthropocene, human beings have begun to enfold the *non-human* world *into* their social imaginary, because that world can no longer be kept at a perceived and abstracted distance.

In this time of 'going meta', the social imaginary *is becoming* the planetary imaginary – and how can we get any more meta than that? This kind of meta is not necessarily *modern*, if by modern we mean a kind of abstraction from the non-human world. Rather, going meta is *intimate* with the whole as it is multi-layered and participatory, enfolding itself in embodiment (and if levels of abstraction *do* find their place in this definition, they are *secondary*, not primary, qualities of meta).

If those mighty microbes are responsible for Gaian homeostasis, then surely human societies must find themselves always-already embedded in the 'thick' planetary present.[8] *Going meta has something to do with becoming planetary* and, as I've suggested elsewhere, this emergent sense of the whole is precisely that: a sense. When we talk about metamodernism, we ought to remember that it begins, as Vermeulen and van den Akker have pointed out, with a structure of feeling. Nora Bateson writes: 'there is something holding all of this together ... there is an alive order that we are within and that is within us',[9] and Joshua Rothman reflected in the *New Yorker*, '[there is a] hidden sense of continuity .... Concrete details stand in contrast to the presence of an abstract whole – a whole that shapes life, but isn't wholly visible from within it.'[10] This hidden sense of continuity, this alive order, is where our planetary sensemaking ought to land.

Any discussion about going meta, in order for it *not* to become a bootstrapped reification of modernism, post- or otherwise, ought to begin and end with this felt sense, a method of integral philosophy which Jean Gebser called *kulturphilosophie*.[11] It is here where the concept of the planetary begins to help us, and arguably becomes necessary if we wish to articulate what is emerging in consciousness and culture in the present.

When we go meta, we aren't just going meta about *anything*. The metamodern era describes a de-structuring and a re-structuring of feeling that *involves each and every one of us in the planetary, churning out new images for the social imaginary*. Meta is that uncanny transparency that occurs when the tentacular world comes spilling in through the back door, or the kitchen window.[12] So, when we talk about the metamodern sensibility – a sensibility about 'the whole' – we can bring the planetary to the forefront of our discussion.

Succinctly, then, the planetary is *how we intuit, embody, conceive of and ultimately concretise the interagency of the human with the non-human world.* The planetary helps us consider how, in the age of the Anthropocene, the human being is involved in a process of mutual becoming: *we are becoming the more-than-human as the more-than-human world is becoming us.* This process of intensifying transparency between the human 'social imaginary' and the commingling agencies of the non-human world is the new, uncanny reality of the planetary. We are being invited – some might say *initiated* – to not only recognise but also creatively *realise* this way of knowing and being in our time.

On the one hand, defined initially the way that it is here, we could understand that human cultures *always* had planetary imaginaries; we have always participated in the making of the world and our worlds have always existed in relation to the non-human. Fair enough. So how do we distinguish the import of what is happening presently? How does the concept of the planetary and the development of a new planetary imaginary help us to navigate through the so-called meta-crisis?

Finally: what could it mean for us to *become planetary*, let alone *go* planetary?

Becoming planetary, or developing a planetary imaginary in our time, encourages geological allusions, terrains. It implicates us in what philosopher Timothy Morton describes as 'a fundamental shaking of being, a *being-quake*', of hyperobjects, his own conceptualisation of our age. Entangled webs of interrelated processes too big or too small to see, like climate change, hyperobjects are another way of thinking about the planetary: 'The Titanic of modernity hits the iceberg of hyperobjects.'[13]

This shift in our being *is* tectonic, restructuring our ontology, rearranging the strata upon which our present cultural sensemaking stands – and falls. It is in this sense that the transformation is *radical*, as in getting at the *roots* of us. This is good. It means that the kind of restructuring happening today *involves* us, sensemakers or not, intellectuals or not.

Questions we can then ask might be:

> To what extent am I already participating in this worlding?
>
> To what extent is my participation not only by way of thinking (i.e. representing, conceiving, abstracting), but also by taking other forms of involvement?
>
> What other kinds of knowing are possible?
>
> What images arise for me that are born of this planetary imaginary?

What modes of sensemaking are emerging in this new ontology? Or, how does my sense of self, time and space shift as I contemplate and imagine my involvement in this planetary being (being-planetary)?

What modes of sensemaking no longer serve us in their exclusivity?

And how might we repurpose these cultural modes, help them to find their proper place in the (emergent) rearrangement of the whole?

If we could work to clarify the qualities of the new, how the new is *already* shaping us, we might lessen the painful and catastrophic collision between the reality of the planetary and the runaway machinery of capitalist modernity. At a minimum, we could find ways to prepare ourselves for new ways of living and dying well in the Anthropocene.

The ruptures and quakes we experience, the vertigo of *not-knowing*, is exactly where we ought to be probing.

Orbiting the dark planetary

'We live in a culture we do not see,' the late historian William Irwin Thompson wrote, 'we don't live in industrial civilization; we live in planetization.' Marshall McLuhan often said that *we see the present through the rear-view mirror.* 'What we see as the present is really the past,' Thompson adds. He wrote the article for *The New Story* back in the winter of 1985, but like a good Philip K. Dick novel, its prescience seems to only improve with age.[14]

Think of the nostalgia-pop nineties muzak, vaporwave, proliferating *just* as the era of smartphones and Amazon were ramping up and shopping malls were shuttering their doors for good, the surge of popular 'dead mall' YouTube videos, or the idolisation of bygone eighties analogue technology (Netflix's *Stranger Things*) glimpsed through the Gorilla glass of our tablets. 'All the heavy armor we associate with the Middle Ages isn't from the Middle Ages,' Thompson says; 'it's from the 15th century.'

Nostalgia-vision is perhaps a natural response to living in a time that seems to be stuck in forward gear, where there is, as a character in William Gibson's novel *Pattern Recognition* says, 'insufficient now to stand on'.[15] But there *are* ways we can lean into the unthinkable present: if the planetary is already shaping our social imaginary, we ought to look to the dark places, where things *aren't quite* working as they should. Where things break down. Here is where we'll find the future's still-hazy shape. 'From the breach, the wound,' Jean Gebser wrote, 'a new possibility of the world emerges.'[16] *How* things fall apart can teach us a lot about what is emerging.

Thompson suggests that we have a 'civilizational unconscious' (perhaps similar to Taylor's social imaginary), and that it is where we ought to look if we want to learn more about becoming a planetary culture. 'It's expressed in negative activity ... shadowed activity ... in evil activity.'[17]

We can look at supply chain food scares during the wave of Covid-19 lockdowns in 2020, or the fragility of an economic system that threatens to collapse when it's forced to slow down its runaway growth model. And we know, as a *structure of feeling* of our times even when we can't quite articulate it, that this virus is one of *many* proliferations of a new planetary realism.

The negative image (the *whole* system is falling apart) mirrors an implicit, if latent, new planetary imaginary (there exists this whole, this planetary reality, in which we *participate*).[18]

'As this crisis shows,' Kim Stanley Robinson recently wrote for the *New Yorker*, 'we are interconnected as a biosphere and a civilization … this mixture of dread and apprehension and normality …. It could be part of our new structure of feeling, too.'[19] The kind of planetary imaginary that's possible, first as anxiety and collapse, and only later (perhaps) as constructive expression of planetary culture, would be one that has hopefully internalised what Donna Haraway calls 'sympoiesis', or a cultural cosmology of 'making-with' the kin of the biosphere, recognising the 'complex, dynamic, response, situated, historical systems … a word for worlding-with, in company'.[20] In the posthuman turn, ironically, we turn again to the creative agency of the human being – now in conscious participation *with* the rest of the marvellous biosphere.

The planetary ontology of being-*with* – with tangling, interrelated, inter-agentic, *tentacular* beings – echoes in Robinson's writing. He decries Margaret Thatcher's 'there is no such thing as a society' as the 'tottering' neoliberal zenith of the *old* structure of feeling, and affirms the transparent, multispecies interagency of the human and the non-human when he writes that 'we're beginning to understand that this "we" includes many other creatures and societies in our biosphere and even in ourselves … your skin holds inside it all kinds of unlikely cooperations … we are societies made of societies … this is shocking news – it demands a whole new world view.'[21] Societies made of societies! The individual is revivified, somehow, in spite of or better yet *because* of all that mingling. When James Joyce wrote, 'here comes everybody', is this what he had in mind?

It's here that a practice of *not-knowing* begins to yield the nascent shape of our (present) future. This past year – 2020 – has been nothing short of a 'pedagogical catastrophe', as P2P theorist Michel Bauwens calls it: *a teaching crisis*.[22] But this crisis also affords us an opportunity to learn the important lessons, to engage in a process of 'mutual learning' between human beings and the rest of the world we are already worlding-with. We appear to be breaking open the world, but in doing so, we can hope that we are also breaking open ourselves, and there is no going *back* to pre-industrialisation, nor is there any more business rushing *forward* with the civilisation we have built up until now. Rilke's 'you must change your life' takes on an evolutionary scope for human culture and consciousness.

When we approach the darkness of the planetary, we are really approaching the limits of our culture. 'Gaia, in all her symbiogenetic glory, is inherently expansive, subtle, aesthetic, ancient, and exquisitely resilient,' Lynn Margulis wrote in *Symbiotic Planet*: 'we cannot put an end to nature; we can only pose a threat to ourselves … I hear our nonhuman brethren snickering: "Got along without you before I met you, gonna get along without you now."'[23]

When we really take this to heart, we begin to appreciate why the planetary means taking on a posthuman character. The anthropocentric forms of cultural evolution that have served industrial civilisation well have no more *reality* underneath them (if they ever did!). This rocks us to our ontological core; it's *more* than trading one relatively contemporary form of cultural sensemaking for another in modernity's progressive mastery of the forces of nature and time. That march has *ended*, and even if we haven't articulated at a conscious level of our social imaginary, there is still something in us that *knows*.

'Climate change is not a problem organizations can draw lines around, encompass, or own,' Bayo Akomolafe writes, 'it is ontologically untraceable, unthinkable, and incalculable.'[24] It is this uncontainable reality that nevertheless presses upon our imaginary to somehow realise. This is where transparency concretises for the planetary: where the imagined, thinkable human world becomes uncomfortably intimate with the unimaginable, the unthinkable non-human world of hyperobjects and multitudinous agencies, even *within* the human body. 'We are no longer bounded "I"s whose task it is to study natural "laws"; we are inside the frenzied equation.'[25] The entangled threads of past, present and future bloom in the intensity of *now*.

Here, the 'dark intelligible abyss' of the planetary is approached.

Eugene Thacker's popular 2011 book, *In the Dust of this Planet*, reflects this understanding. 'The world is increasingly unthinkable,' Thacker wrote, considering the complexity of the meta-crisis and the inability for us to 'adequately understand the world at all'. For Thacker, the concept of the planetary is a way of talking about how 'anything that reveals itself does not reveal itself in total', and in that sense, the planetary goes *beyond* what we might describe as the Earth (the objective, systems approach) or the World (the phenomenological, subjective approach). There is that uncanny transparency again – where does the inside begin and the outside end? This is an 'unresolvable dilemma', Thacker continues: 'what is important in the concept of the Planet is that it remains a negative concept.'[26] Similarly, Clarke writes that 'whereas you can spin a globe so as to have no dark side … you cannot really spin an actual planet such as Earth. Its intricacies will finally surpass our technological as well as our epistemological grasp … The planetary view is always partial, and so decenters the human in relation to its worldly situation.'[27]

We remain somewhere in the middle, the liminal, and meanwhile the previously objective ground continues to splinter apart into groundless fragments and conspiracies, caricatured iterations of Cartesian thought. The epistemic import of the planetary involves the acknowledgement that 'capital-S science' is part of this exhausted and now concluding mentality, that appealing to mere objective facts 'doesn't give them [scientists] back their old authority'.[28] But in this generative tension between the failure of one cultural mentality and the existential pressure for another to take its place, mutational leaps can find their openings.

Posthuman mutations

When Gebser wrote about 'arationality' as a character of an incipient integral consciousness, he was presciently describing this mutative leap to another kind of planetary knowing, the kind that Akomolafe describes: 'invisibilized knowledges lying in the shadows of colonial sciences ... the Yoruba people of West Africa ... have always understood that everything is a crossroads ... resisting absolute determinacy.' Inhabiting this liminality of the crossroads – the rhizome – is one of the implicit themes in the field of metamodernism, that is, *metaxy*, or 'the state of being in-between'.[29] The majority of us today *do* have a felt sense about this. But the transformation taking place – folding the planetary *and* the human in the mutual becoming of the planetary imaginary – is a theme we ought to continuously revisit in order to cohere (and never expect to get to the bottom of). It requires us to forego the compulsive desire to hitch our star to systemic thinking, to instrumental rationality, measurement, even to *meta*-systemic thinking – we still wish to smuggle modernity's onwards-and-upwards impulse into these unthinkable geographies, but like capital-S science, going 'meta' (rational) is an insufficient response to the planetary. We must, as Latour suggests, come *down to Earth*, the terrestrial – to matter, to the entangled interspecies justice of a haunted terrain.

These quakes in being disrupt our colonial, *directive* sense of time and progress (from 'zombie' neoliberalism to zombie modernity!). If anything, 2020's abrupt halting of our capitalist economy and the multiple disruptions of the pace of modern life are forcing us to reckon with the reality of the planetary, *already* reshaping us, restructuring us, inducing an *orthogonal sense of time*. The future arrives not 'ahead' of us but amidst us, in the immanence of the dark imaginary, the flashing forth of the whole in its 'integral complexity'.[30]

If we can, we should try to *become comfortable with our discomfort* in this liminality, this *via negativa* path of the dark planetary imaginary. But that doesn't mean more can't be cohered about the new and ever-present modes of knowing available to us as we learn to become more attentive to the unthinkable present. If we can 'stay with the trouble', like Haraway suggests, we might be able to achieve an important leap in our sensemaking. We might enfold modernity's social imaginary, with its 'sense-directed thinking', into the increasingly transparent and unthinkable present, and awaken in this cloud of unknowing to a 'senseful awaring',[31] where our anxiety of the planetary instead becomes a creative fulfilment and spiritual participation of *the human being as planetary being*, in 'primordial trust', co-initiating Earth's posthuman future.

Postscript on planetary mythologies: poetry from the future

The planetary is not merely a 'new story' in the singular but an over-determined integral ontology and intensity that our consciousness and culture are already responding to (and in the many unfortunate ways we saw in 2020, fleeing *from*). So, we can finally return to that initial question: *how are we going planetary?* What incipient dreaming of the planetary imaginary is already present, and what does this dreaming tell us about the planetary realism we already inhabit?

Tim Morton wrote that 'art is thought from the future', and both Gebser and McLuhan knew that what is emerging in cultural evolution shows up through the intuitive sensibilities of the artist who plays with space and time and works out the latent possibilities in the social imaginary. Even those of us who aren't artists, but metamodernists and integralists of some sort, have an imperative to cultivate an artist's sensibility and become attentive to the present. We ought to look at what human creativity – always and already a place of *metaxy*, liminality – is imagining for us in our civilisational unconscious.

The planetary imaginary is already restructuring our sense of identity, our sense of space, and acutely our sense of time. If progressive, linear time has ended, what other forms of time are present? 'Time is long,' Hölderlin wrote, 'but the True comes to pass.'[32] How do we approach this 'integral complex' of time through, for instance, the aesthetic sensibilities of digital culture, which *so readily plays with time as an art form*? And lastly, to be explored in the other essays in this volume: when it comes to our new stories, what are they telling us? In these stories, implicit mythologemes or 'mythemes' get under our skin and proliferate new subjectivities, new senses of time, space and self. These are our *planetary mythologies*, and there are many lessons we can learn from them. 'Thought must veer toward art,' Morton wrote, so any approach on becoming planetary must find a way to attune to the 'poetry from the future'.[33]

Notes

1. See Morin, Edgar (1998) *Homeland Earth*. Hampton Press. p. 6.
2. Herbert, Frank (2010). *Dune*. London: Gateway, Kindle edition.
3. I'm avoiding the term 'climate realism' here due to its unfortunate, counterintuitive adoption in public discourse to mean a rejection of climate science. See 'Climate Realism is the New Climate Denial': https://newrepublic.com/article/158797/climate-change-alarmism-greta-thunberg-naomi-seibt accessed 27 January 2021.
4. Teilhard de Chardin, in *The Human Phenomenon*, helped to popularise this concept to distinguish the human species, producing a 'thinking' layer of the Earth, after the biosphere and geosphere.
5. See Emerge. 'What is the social imaginary?' 1 October 2020: https://youtu.be/iGCPcaIFHDA accessed 27 January 2021.
6. Clarke, Bruce (2020). *Gaian Systems: Lynn Margulis, Neocybernetics, and the End of the Anthropocene*. Minneapolis: University of Minnesota Press.
7. Ibid. p. 211.
8. See Haraway, Donna (2016). *Staying with the Trouble: Making Kin in the Chthulucene*. Durham, NC: Duke University Press.
9. Bateson, Nora (2016) *Small Arcs of Larger Circles*. Digital edition, p. 15.
10. Johnson, Jeremy (2020). Meta, Modern: Navigating with Crisis with Jean Gebser's Integral Philosophy. *The Side View*, 2(1), 156.
11. Ibid.
12. Haraway, Donna. *Staying with the Trouble*.
13. Morton, Timothy (2013). *Hyperobjects*. Minneapolis: University of Minnesota Press, p. 19.
14. Thompson, William Irwin. 'It's Already Begun': www.context.org/iclib/ic12/thompson/ accessed 27 January 2021.
15. Gibson, William (2004) *Pattern Recognition*. London: Penguin, p. 57.
16. Gebser, Jean (1985). *The Ever-Present Origin*. Athens: Ohio University Press, p. 75.
17. Thompson. 'It's Already Begun'.
18. This might be another way of illustrating how going 'meta' is about 'tasting the pickle'. See Jonathan Rowson, Chapter 1 in this volume.
19. Robinson, Kim Stanley. 'The Coronavirus is Rewriting Our Imaginations': www.newyorker.com/culture/annals-of-inquiry/the-coronavirus-and-our-future accessed 22 February 2021.
20. Haraway. *Staying with the Trouble*, p. 58.
21. Robinson, Kim Stanley. 'The Coronavirus is Rewriting Our Imaginations'.
22. Bauwens, Michel. 'Coronavirus and the Commons': http://liminal.news/2020/04/125/ accessed 27 January 2021.
23. Margulis, Lynn (1990) *Symbiotic Planet: A New Look at Evolution*. Amherst: Basic Books, p. 128.
24. Akomolafe, Bayo. 'What climate collapse asks of us', https://bayoakomolafe.net/project/what-climate-collapse-asks-of-us/ accessed 22 February 2021.
25. Akomolafe, Bayo. and Ladha, Alnoor (2017). Perverse Particles, Entangled Monsters and Psychedelic Pilgrimages: Emergence as an onto-epistemology of not-knowing, *Ephemera: Theory and Politics in Organization*, 17(4): 819–839: www.ephemerajournal.org/contribution/perverse-particles-entangled-monsters-and-psychedelic-pilgrimages-emergence accessed 22 February 2021.

26 Thacker, Eugene. (2011) *In the Dust of This Planet*. Alresford: Zero Books. pp. 1–8.
27 Clarke, Bruce. *Gaian Systems*, p. 212.
28 Kofman, Ava. 'Bruno Latour, the Post-Truth Philosopher, Mounts a Defense of Science', 25 October 2018, *New York Times Magazine*: www.nytimes.com/2018/10/25/magazine/bruno-latour-post-truth-philosopher-science.html accessed 27 January 2021.
29 Akomolafe, Bayo. 'What climate collapse asks of us', https://bayoakomolafe.net/project/what-climate-collapse-asks-of-us/ accessed 22 February 2021.
30 Gebser, Jean. *Ever-Present Origin*.
31 Ibid.
32 Gebser, Jean. *Ever-Present Origin*.
33 Morton, Timothy. *Dark Ecology: For a Logic of Future Coexistence*. New York: Columbia University Press, 2016, p.1; Horvat, Srećko. (2020) *Poetry From the Future*. London: Penguin, Kindle edition. A phrase borrowed from Marx: 'The social revolution […] cannot take its poetry from the past but only from the future', p. 130.

Part 2 Metamodern Conundrums

4 Disarm the Pedagogical Weaponry
Make education not culture war
Zachary Stein

Introduction

THE SO-CALLED 'culture war' is resulting in a radical and disturbing transformation of socialisation patterns. Ideas, values and memes created for the purposes of profit, strategic disinformation and political agitation/manipulation are taken up by young minds and integrated into identity structures. Because children have no choice but to engage culture as education, there should be an immediate ceasefire among those who view culture as war. Today, the adults conduct a 'culture war' while their children are caught in the crossfire, unable to escape the dangerous ecosystems of meaning in which they are socialised. The result is a growing rift in the fabric of intergenerational transmission – a generational gap – as the culture at large increasingly relinquishes its educative function, having been reduced to commodities and weaponry. Two trends in particular are noted in this chapter: 1) algorithmically directed human development in which the user (i.e. child) is on the receiving end of scientifically engineered 'cultural weaponry', including AI-enabled surveillance and psychometrics that are used to optimise and customise meme delivery (this happens on YouTube, Facebook and other platforms); 2) the strategic destruction of truth as a cultural signifier, creating a crisis of socialisation in the absence of legitimate teacherly authority (this happens in schools, colleges and public culture). There is no possible future for humans in which culture becomes reduced to an arena of strategic and exploitative agency – reduced to war. Our children have nowhere else to become educated but within the cultures we create. I recommend approaches in which culture can be freed to assume its educative function.

Cultural warfare: eclipse of education

While it is true that throughout history children have grown up in physically dangerous war zones, they have done so in the context of relatively coherent cultures. What is novel today is a generation growing up in relative physical safety who are nevertheless endangered in the crossfire of a *culture war*. The obvious difference between what has historically been called 'war' and what is now called 'culture war' concerns the presence or absence of physical violence. Culture wars are fought with ideas and memes; actual wars are fought with guns and bombs. Whereas war involves physical violence, culture war involves *educational violence*. To the degree that we engage culture as warfare, we must strategically manipulate the function of culture as education. This creates a situation in which there are incentives to systematically distort the educational dynamics of culture itself for strategic advantage. The results are all around us today: politicalisation of everything, total advertisement-saturation and the disappearance from culture of communication aimed at reaching mutual understanding.

In this chapter I discuss some of the *educational contradictions* that occur when culture is repurposed as a theatre of war. The situation today is one where the most powerful educational technologies in history (networked computers) are contradicting their own educational potentials because they have been co-opted as weaponry in a culture war. The way out is to fundamentally reimagine the institutions of education, beyond schooling. The aim should be to reimagine them enough that the dynamics of digital technology can be changed from extractive surveillance in the interest of capital to educative scaffolds in the interest of human development. If this redesign of culture as education is not accomplished, and the condition of totalised culture war continues, then humanity faces what may be the most profound educational crisis in its history.

But what does it really mean to have a war without physical violence, to have a *culture war*? It means simply that the drivers (motivations, generators, incentives) of cultural production and innovation are made akin to those of warfare, where dynamics of force and power override action oriented towards mutual understanding and cooperation. It is interesting to note that when I remove physical violence from the equation, it appears that the remaining deep structure of 'war' is something like *a competitive social situation of pure strategic interaction in which the motive for optimising personal advantage is primary because the costs of failure are catastrophic*. War without violence boils down to the reduction of social interaction to a kind of austere *zero-sum game theory*. Me (or Us [but mostly *me*]) in competition with You (or Them), with winner-takes-all stakes. This is why the structures and practices of many capitalist enterprises amount to essentially war without the violence: conquest, extraction and profit (Harvey, 2016). Therefore, by my definition, we are embroiled in culture war today because, in effect, 'everywhere is war!' (Marley, 1976). The social world of late-capitalism, sometimes called 'postmodern' (Jameson, 1992), is a world in which the logics of war and capital have been conflated, generalised and normalised. Culture has always involved a certain amount of competition and strategy, but it has seldom (if ever) collapsed entirely into the logic of war. That is, *until now*. The very structure of cultural production involves 'harvesting attention' and 'converting views to dollars' – all proxies for conquest, extraction and profit. At its core the culture war has to do with the ongoing capture of the means of cultural production, and the use of education as a means to extraction and profit (Zuboff, 2019).

Note that my definition of 'culture war' contains more than the notion as it was first coined in the 1990s by neoliberal conservatives (Hunter, 1991). The term was coined to draw attention to the increasing polarisation of public discourse in the United States (and other industrialised nations), which began to erode the once stable foundations of civil public life. According to this view, we fight with words instead of guns. Content producers stand for ideals and seek to win over the hearts and minds of the nation. You fight a culture war as a preamble to an election or as part of mobilisation for an actual war. Using this frame, I am at war whether I like it or not simply because I am an author. There is an assumed sense of knowing the good guys from the bad guys and the agreed-upon stakes and manoeuvres. It is not about truth and quality; it is about the question, 'What side are you on?'. If I mention arguments in favour of green energy and social justice, then I am on 'that side'. If I offer facts on the differences between men and women, or about the benefits of two-parent households, then I am on 'that side'. The validity of what I write is less consequential than where readers place me in their map of the many battlefields embroiled in the culture war. Is my writing useful ammunition for their cause, or dangerous incoming fire from an enemy? Because of this ongoing war of words, authors change the way they write. Everyone making and contributing to the culture begins to change their words and gestures. This is a war at the level of cultural production, a war of words, a war of ideas (Rodgers, 2011).

I am suggesting the situation has escalated. A total reframing of culture as war is now possible, I believe, because during the decline of modernity, as global capitalism strains under its own externalities, the planet has been interconnected for the first time through digital technologies (Bard and Söderqvist, 2018; Bratton, 2015). This is a simple story in which we become one world for better and for worse. The inevitability of planetisation has been demonstrated; humanity will close in upon itself as it encircles the globe, eventually reaching an epochal crescendo of incredible intimacy in the throes of planetary catastrophe and emergence (Aurobindo, 1944; West, 2018). This is one way of understanding the narratives and theories classed as 'metamodern' (Freinacht, 2017). They all come as a response to this new situation, after postmodernity, in a digitally refigured lifeworld of planetary scope. Metamodern cultural creators are working in profound anticipation and concern, actively caught up in the dynamics of the ongoing 'digital tsunami' that is the culture war. The metamodern epoch is the late-capitalist endgame, involving the emergence of a planetary networked society. In this context there is a *transformation and expansion of war* from being about land and energy to being also about data and human consciousness. This transformation is the root cause of the seemingly interminable culture war that is upon us.

My argument here hinges on the insight that underneath this obvious war over the content of culture, there is another less obvious war, a more sinister one, which is fought over who controls and defines *the means of cultural production*. Technological innovators are also driven by the frame that culture is war, but they don't create content; they create what allows you to create and consume content. The technology that structures your news feed exerts more influence on you than the content of the news feed (McLuhan and McLuhan, 1988). The technology by which you view and make culture is in fact the main theatre of conquest, extraction and profit. These technologies conquer and capture your attention, extract personal information and data about you, and then use this to make profits (Zuboff, 2019). The culture war is not only about what people are doing on social media applications; it is also (and I think primarily) about what these applications are doing to people.

An explicit public argument between polarised political viewpoints on social media appears to be where the battles are fought. The question appears to be, 'Who will win the war of words (memes)?' However, this is only a minor theatre in the broader culture war, where deep in the digital meshwork your every keystroke and gesture are tracked, your attention is systematically harvested, and your habits of mind and body are formed (ibid). On the surface, the culture war has us arguing about ideology on social media – as if we might educate each other somehow through the all caps shouting – but, remember: at its core the culture war has to do with the ongoing colonisation of the means of cultural production for the purposes of extraction and profit. The better question, therefore, is, 'Who will win the war of behavioural algorithms (that structures the war of words [memes])?'

'Data is the new oil.' This is now a mantra. The conquest, extraction and profit centres of the capitalist world system have moved beyond the mines and factories to become occluded behind screens, sensors and algorithms (Bridle, 2018). It has been estimated that approximately one fifth (1/5) of all 'discussions' on social media during the lead-up to the 2016 US presidential election involved data-guzzling AI-bots (ibid). The entirety of the online advertising during those years was delivered based on data-intensive psychological profiles lifted from the analysis of individual website-use habits (ibid). The means for producing and consuming culture now involve ubiquitous surveillance and data extraction for the sake of strategic advantage and profit, and it is only getting more sophisticated. This is culture war on a massive scale; but it has nothing to do with shouting moral ideology across politically polarised divides. This deeper culture war is played out in the bowels of server farms where ideological divides disappear into a single sea of value – follow the (meta)data! The spoils of the culture war are not won by those on the battlefield. Indeed, the so-called ideological battles are often beside the point, literally, as the war for harvesting your attention has already been won by the customised advertisement next to what you were intending to read.

Strip-mining the side of a mountain for metal ore is obvious enough to be visible from space and, therefore, often clearly appears as problematic (i.e. erosion and emissions can also be seen from space). But the strip-mining of data from human behaviours taking place through vast social media and sensor networks is basically invisible, at least at first. Once this data is processed, it is fed back into the data extraction machine as fuel. The more it learns about you, the better it gets at learning about you, the more it knows how to get your attention and influence you to do things. Data informs the design of better data extraction techniques and related behaviour-modification regimes that make data collection easier. After a few iterations, it becomes all too clear that harvesting and using data from humans is not a neutral or benevolent activity. The result is a drastic alteration of cultural forms, such as I have discussed elsewhere (Stein, 2018); the current cultural and educational crisis – the so-called *culture war* – is predicated on the following accelerating trends in the new communications technologies ecosystems:

1. The inability to distinguish non-commercially motivated from commercially motivated information;

2. The related inability to distinguish honest information from intentional misinformation that is spread for strategic advantage;

3. Decreased message length, increased message frequency, and inability to track all message sources (i.e. information overload);

4. The absence of shared overarching meta-narrative that could potentially reconcile conflicting information and perspectives;

5. Escalating emotional intensity of information (due to factors 1–4);

6. Normalisation of weaponised language (i.e. lies, slander, censorship, politicisation, due to factor 4).

These trends reflect an informational ecosystem optimised for harvesting data and manipulating users for the purposes of advertising. That is in fact why it was built, if you look at it carefully (White, 2016). The near total capture and exploitation of the means of cultural production is a new and extremely problematic extension of extractive and conquest practices that have dominated the world system for the past 400 years of capitalism (Zuboff, 2020). Whereas stripmining destroys the natural beauty of the mountains and eventually destabilises ecosystems, data extraction practices destroy cultures and eventually destabilise individual identity structures. This is what happens when culture war has escalated beyond words.

There has been a technological arms race ongoing for at least two decades as part of the culture war. Like all arms races, it is certainly farther along than anyone in the general public really knows; there has been a proliferation of secret weapons programmes. From the perspective of educational theory, the situation is something like the Manhattan Project – a vast covert effort to develop basic technologies that will change life forever – only now the goal is to change the realms of culture, consciousness and education. The culture war has created its equivalent of 'the bomb', and it has already been dropped on millions of civilians. *The technologically enabled destruction of the very notion of truth is the 'atomic' option that is now being exercised at the level of culture.* Social media platforms, YouTube and aspects of mainstream news outlets have all become fundamentally disruptive to culture, at a basic (in the sense of foundational) epistemological level. The years after 2016 have seen a kind of 'winter' or 'fallout' circulating around the planet from the nuking of American culture during that election cycle. Just as there is no going back to a time before we split the atom and held all human life in our hands, we are now forever stewarding that vast cosmic power. Today, we cannot return to a time before we split the atom of 'truth' into its constituent social and technological particles (Woolley, 2020). The idea of 'truth' can be defined in categorical terms as 'the communicative presupposition of a shared objective reality' (Habermas, 1984), that is, the idea that 'truth' exists is part of the background consensus of the lifeworld, allowing us to communicate and recognise each other as persons. We now have the power to destroy human notions of truth entirely and will thus forever be stewards of this immense power and essential cultural resource.

Today, the task of de-weaponising and then redesigning culture – *as education*, not war – is a complex technological, political and economic problem. It is a problem implicating the capacities and consciousness of people, including especially children, their self-understandings, identities, fears, hopes and the most intimate notions about the meaning of human existence. If this seems extreme to some, then they are unaware of the extent to which screens mediate identity formation in contemporary culture (Carr, 2011). Research into the dynamics of current digital socialisation patterns cannot keep pace with changes in technology use among children and adolescents, but the preliminary results are complex, and on the whole disturbing (Sheldon et al, 2019). The implication is an historically unprecedented possibility for identity formation largely outside the bounds of normal reality testing and yet within the bounds of high technology. We face an impending rift in the intergenerational fabric of the lifeworld that would be catastrophic for the continuity of civilisation (Stein, 2019). To be irrevocably cut off from functioning cultural notions of truth is an untenable situation in the context of climate chaos, impending economic disaster, and a near exponential increase in technological capacities, including in the domains of weapons and biotechnologies. Humans need to be able to convene conversations and make decisions about what is true – in public, over time – and in the context of some minimal cultural coherence. Indeed, a culture that can come together beyond difference to learn about what is universally true for everyone is probably the definition of a coherent and healthy culture.

Children in the crossfire of the culture wars

At the airport for necessary travel, I see children on smartphones and tablets, mostly watching YouTube. I am not trying to look, but it is crowded, and I am directly behind a group of kids as I try to read. They are constantly touching the screens to load new videos, probably once every three or four minutes. Cartoon voices are audible through their headphones even in the airport, which means the volumes are loud. I find that the presence of the screen in my visual field makes it hard to read, and I keep unconsciously glancing over to catch a moment of cartoon distraction. I am basically forced by the screen to stop reading because of the working memory demands of trying so hard to not be distracted (and then being distracted and looking).

Screens are not passive things that just sit there while you look at them. Although it appears like an inert tool or piece of furniture (like a chalk board or painting), the screen is far from passive. That screen in the airport was actively capturing my attention and the attention of the kids. The device was also actively capturing all kinds of information about the children using it (*it was watching them*, in a sense). The screen uses its observations of the children to structure the options and videos it plays. It knows what they click, and thus what they like and, therefore, also what they are likely to want to see more of. It can tell how old they are and what gender, race, nationality, religion and neighbourhood (it knows where these kids live, and often their exact current GPS location) (Bridle, 2018). The kids were holding something literally designed to be endlessly fascinating and thus intensely addictive. This became obvious when the mother of one of the children suggested they had watched enough. I got up to leave to find another place to read as the mother was forced to prise the iPad from the loudly protesting child, now crying.

When I was a child (in the early 1980s), there was one screen in the house and only a few options for things to view on it. Nobody knew what I was watching but my parents and me (sometimes just me). Not a single advertising or technology company had any information about me at all. Today, children are in a very different situation, which has not gone unnoticed (Pariser, 2011; Alter, 2017). But it is not only a matter of the number of screens, the time spent watching them, and the overwhelming variety of the content. If screens today were as simple as a TV with endless channels, things would be, in essence, about the same as they were when I was a kid. Nor is the difference advertisement-generated revenue, which has always been the bedrock of children's TV. Looking back, I think the example of *Sesame Street* needs to be considered carefully as a case of research-based culture design for educating kids, initially free from the demands of profit and extraction and fully actualising certain educational potentials within TV (Davis, 2009). Disney, on the other hand, was one of the first to move in the direction of harvesting children's attention and desires for profit, thus resulting in the now rampant *contradictions* of TV as an educational medium (Giroux, 1999).

The difference today is that *the screen watches the child as much as the child watches the screen*. It's not just YouTube. Regardless of the website, application or operating system, digital technologies are uploading shocking amounts of data about those who use them, and it takes being a computer security expert to have it be otherwise (Zuboff, 2019). When you say, 'let the kid watch the iPad', what you also mean is, 'let the iPad watch the kid'. When I watched the TV in the 1980s, it did not systemically surveille me, learning about my habits, and then organise my viewing options for me accordingly. In any given viewing session on YouTube, the sequence of videos watched is not the sequence that would most benefit the child in terms of their learning, or even their happiness and health (and it *could* be designed that way). The child sees a sequence of videos that is deemed most profitable for YouTube and its operating channel partners and subsidiaries. Videos are being produced to generate financial transactions that generate substantial income when videos go above the hundreds and thousands of views. Importantly, there are now AI-based approaches to creating content that has an optimal chance of being viewed and, thus, that yield maximal profit from selling ads via harvested attention (Bridle, 2018; Alter, 2017).

This can be easy to misunderstand so I will be clear: there are channels on YouTube for children (with millions of views) that consist of computer-generated cartoons that are created by computers based on automated processes for analysing the data of user behaviours on YouTube. If videos of a certain cartoon character are becoming popular, then a knock-off video can be generated by computer and posted automatically, listing the same or similar title to the original video that started the trend. This new 'fake' video catches some percentage of people looking for the original video, who now end up watching a video created by a machine only to sell the ad that plays before it or flashes next to it. The shorter the video, the more pages load and re-load during a viewing session and, thus, the more advertisements are displayed and revenue generated; this strategy incentivises short, fragmented clips. Kids can spend hours moving between snippets of videos on channels run like this on YouTube, as described by Bridle in horrific detail. This is the worst kind of 'educational' experience: too complex, confusing and *created with some other intention than the benefit of the child*.

The difference from TV cannot be stressed enough. Culture has always been used to make money for as long as making money was seen as important, which is to say forever. In modern times, advertisements and broadcast news defined the TV era, where a relatively homogeneous culture poured out into living rooms, designed to influence purchasing habits and beliefs *en masse*. Today is different: huge numbers of people (supposedly 'everyone') are making, consuming and curating cultural content. Multitudinous peer-to-peer narrowcast cultural creation was understood as the holy grail of the internet age. It worked. Everyone and her mother now has a 'social media following' or is an 'influencer', that is, has conquered and extracted profits from winning the war for your attention. But as the pundits and talking heads multiplied, each became less impactful. And as I have said, the deeper culture war went below ground, behind the layer of content production and into the technical conditions that make our new digital culture possible in the first place. While content producers proliferated and their feuds and arguments heated up, new methods of extraction and profit were being rolled out behind their backs, built into the means of cultural production and consumption themselves.

While the original TV set itself was stupid (it just sat there), today's screens are allegedly 'smart', which makes them more dangerous, even though they appear to just sit there. The feedback loop between two systems that are observing and responding to each other is different from the feedback between two systems where only one is observing and the other is simply 'watched'. This is a pattern of differences known in evolutionary biology and actor-based modelling techniques in computer science and game theory. Co-observing, co-responding systems co-evolve; whereas in cases where only one system observes and responds there are no co-evolutionary dynamics. Today, we are in a complex and intimate co-evolutionary dance with our communications technologies, which was not possible with TV.

Moreover, in the case of the child watching (and being watched by) YouTube on a tablet computer, there is asymmetric force and ability on the part of the screen. That is to say, the screen is watching the child with algorithms that cost billions to develop and that can only be run on hardware composed of rare earth minerals requiring the involvement of transnational corporations in their creation. There is a psychometric backend that is learning about the child and will create a psychological profile about her for sale to advertisers. YouTube itself will be 'optimising' what the child sees based on data about her viewing history in order to keep the child's eyes on screen. The screen is evolving faster and smarter than she is in real time. She is just a young girl who can barely read, but she can easily spend hours a day in 'dialogue' with this hidden world of algorithmic surveillance used to customise an endless stream of attention-grabbing images.

This process of getting locked into a co-evolutionary dance in which you are out-matched by your screen's ability to capture your attention is sometimes called *algorithmic radicalisation* (Bridle, 2019). I prefer the term *algorithmically directed human development*. The prior more common term points to the tendency for these 'click funnels' to send radicals and conspiracy theorists deeper into their self-confirming reality tunnels. The more general phenomena occur whenever the machine has the upper hand in the co-evolutionary dance, which means the drive of the machine to optimise viewing for advertising revenue overrides the drive of the viewer to learn. The person is watching a great deal of content they otherwise would not have even known about had the machine not retrieved it for them. Experience is shaped by the cultural content made available by the machine, which is tasked primarily with optimising attention-harvesting for profit. Now all of a sudden, you know a great deal about something you never really intended to learn about. Your knowledge and burgeoning personality are now in some measure a side effect of an *algorithmic* selection, rather than your choice-making. This is the outcome of the trends described above, which have to do with the optimising of the current informational ecosystem for harvesting data and manipulating users for the purposes of advertising. The rabbit holes of content that children and adults can be sucked down are the result of using the means of cultural production as a locus for the extraction of attention in the interest of profit.

The question must be asked: 'Is this kind of experience with screens a form of culture and thus educational?' I think we have to say 'yes', and then begin to look around at the true state of our 'culture'. Contrast the hour the child spends careening through YouTube with an hour spent listening to her grandmother tell a story about childhood in the 1960s. The experience on YouTube appears to be mostly about the manipulation of attention for extraction of profit through ad revenue, while the experience with her grandmother is mostly about acculturation and education. As screens take up more and more attention, algorithms come to shape our cultural experiences in the interest of conquest, extraction and profit. From this perspective, ideally, the grandmother would post her story to her blog, Instagram and Facebook, so that her educational moment could be repurposed as a means to harvest the attention of people who have been algorithmically determined as susceptible to (i.e. in need of) grandmother stories. Nevertheless, #grandmamoment does not have the same educational value as an actual moment with one's grandmother. This is because #grandmamoment embodies the *educational contradictions* so rampant in the new media environments. The very things we want to trust and learn from have been run through the machinations of the culture war and turned into profit-seeking ventures. Is this #grandmamoment a legitimate authentic moment? To what extent is it something designed to fool me into thinking it is authentic, as a ploy to gain followers? What happens when there is nothing left over from what used to be culture except for #culturewar? This involves looking into what cultures must be and do to assure their own continuity and survival; now we are back to the necessity of maintaining continuity in the dynamics of intergenerational transmission.

Make education, not culture war!

Cultures orient individuals participating within them towards explicitly shared contexts of value and reality (Habermas, 1984; Mead, 1970). Cultures are incredibly complex; therefore, some groups of scientists seeking to study cultural evolution have focused on simple but exemplary cases of cultural transmission. Cultural transmission, and more precisely intergenerational transmission, does not mean only preservation and passing on of culture; it also means *evolving* culture. Take for example the cultural transmission of *knots*, such as those used extensively in the ship riggings of seafaring cultures. These kinds of examples of simple cultural transmission and evolution have been studied as a way to understand the basic minimum facets of human culture (Richardson and Boyd, 2005). Without the ability to intergenerationally transmit an incredibly complex culture of knots, the ships and nets cannot be rigged, and the culture fails. There is a clear framework for 'reality-checking' that orients the teaching, discussion and application of the vast array of knots that have evolved for centuries in certain cultural pockets. An elder teaches a novice how to tie an important knot and discusses those kinds of situations in which it should be used. It is clear to everyone involved in the culture that in certain contexts a well-tied knot is good, true and beautiful: that is, the appropriate person ties it at the allotted time (goodness); the knot works physically (truth); the knot is elegant, simple and strong (beauty). Eventually, the novice becomes an expert and begins to innovate and evolve the culture of knots further. This kind of 'ratcheting' and cumulative educational transmission is part of the essence of 'culture' as a species-specific trait of *homo sapiens* (Tomasello, 1999; 2019).

Culture is everywhere for children; it is the water they swim in. Dinner conversations (or their absence), screens, commodities that structure peer cultures, and the nightly news (or newsfeed) discussed by grown-ups – these things are taken in by children without a filter as simply how the world is. Eventually, 'grown-ups' can escape this submersion in culture and begin to deliberately make and change culture. This ability to reflect and act on culture can lead to changing the very technological substrates of cultural production itself, as I have already discussed. This ability to make new culture and change the very nature of culture is one of the gifts that older generations leave to younger generations. Indeed, this ability is part of the aforementioned species-specific trait for 'culture' that sets humans apart from even the most advanced primates (ibid). This is also an interesting definition of *education*: education is simply culture *in process*, that is, as it is transformed, reworked and transmitted to younger generations.

However, when the 'grown-ups' begin to make culture a profit centre and this spirals up into deciding that *culture is war* (i.e. a theatre of conquest, extraction and profit), then this ability to transform, rework and intergenerationally transmit culture takes a dangerous wrong turn. None of the reality-checking that enables intergenerational transmission remains when we understand ourselves as in a 'culture war' – words become weapons instead of reasons. In place of truth, goodness and beauty as orientations for culture, we find profit, strategic disinformation and political agitation/manipulation. Returning to the culture of knots studied by Boyd and Richardson, the new scenario would be an elder who is seeking to disrupt the culture of knots to secure political and economic advantage. Perhaps he has a plan to discredit old knots in order to drive business to his new patented rope and techniques. Presumably, he is not the only one disrupting the traditional culture of knots for strategic advantage, which means that the reality-checking virtues that allowed for coherent and cumulative intergenerational transmission are no longer simply assumed. The journeyman novice is now subject to individuals who are purposefully misleading him about the truth, goodness and beauty of knots. Instead of socially necessary educational relationships, there are advertisements, proprietary techniques and systematically distorted communications about value and truth.

Technically speaking, from the perspective of the philosophy of language, during a culture war pragmatics and rhetoric come to override syntax and semantics; the *effect* of what is said is more important than its meaning and logical integrity. In a culture war, what matters is the *appearance* of truth and goodness insofar as these allow statements to be powerfully weaponised. Thus, simply ruining the *appearance* of truth is as good as actually proving something is wrong. Eventually, the fog of war seeps into everything, and the culture will lose its sense of what is real and valuable. The next generation could then become so miseducated that they are literally unable to tie the knots needed to hold everything together. Ships no longer sail and nets are no longer cast. The result of all-out culture war is the end of culture.

Of course, cultures involve more than knots. But the same lessons apply to all the various aspects of culture that must necessarily be handed down from generation to generation as part of the process of cultural evolution. Cultural warfare does not result in the same processes of cultural evolution; instead, culture begins to manifest *educational contradictions* as intergenerational transmission fails. During culture war, the culture *is* changing – and in a very broad sense still evolving – but it is no longer demonstrating the kinds of cumulative learning processes that characterise civilisation. Digital technologies are largely contradicting their intended and potential educational possibilities because they are designed primarily to harvest attention for the extraction of profit. Streaming videos algorithmically optimised for profit constitutes a new kind of culture, as do mass-produced, highly politicised (illiteracy inducing), postmodern children's books. This digital culture spawned by surveillance capitalism makes no attempt to educate; it only attempts to 'win' at doing something else (i.e. it is made for some reason other than to help children make sense of the world). Truly educational relationships are antithetical to the practices of culture war, which is one of the reasons that cultural warfare induces educational crises that eventually manifest in generational gaps of catastrophic breadth and depth.

Growing up a cultural warrior

To this point I have established the notion of culture war and described some of the basic dynamics that are in play, showing what is at stake in the domain of intergenerational transmission. The capture of the means of cultural production for the interests of profit stands out as the most basic underlying process at work, which then spawns a cascade of consequences throughout the many cultural landscapes of the digital. I am arguing that this kind of new digital culture is disabling or distorting the dynamics of education and intergenerational transmission in profound ways. What happens when the primary modality of enculturation and education is characterised by strategic action and cultural war? You might think that screens are not the main effect in socialisation, and in some homes this is true, but the average seven to nine hours a day that teens spend on smartphones, tablets and laptops would suggest otherwise. This amounts to being raised in an informational war zone, where everyone you meet is a strategic actor, where danger and confusion saturate the processes of identity formation. This brings us to Soph, who was, in the spring of 2019, one of the fastest rising commodities on YouTube – a right-wing, foul-mouthed, hyper-articulate, 14-year-old girl (Bernstein, 2019). She serves as a unique object lesson about the effect of the culture war on children.

Soph, as she calls herself, has nearly one million followers. Her content has been attracting attention because it is openly inflammatory and aggressive, filled with expletives and 'hate speech', as well as threats of violence against 'social justice warriors', feminists and Muslims. Rape and graphic descriptions of violence are discussed for amusement. And it is all coming from the brace-faced grimace of a freshman in high school, who seems way too smart and YouTube-savvy for her own (or anyone else's) good. The production quality and content of her videos suggest someone who has been in the culture wars for years, and this is the case: Soph began engaging like this when she was 9 years old and had gained a following and publicity by 13. It would be easy to think these videos are produced and written by adults who are manipulating a child actor, until you see the obviously unscripted interviews where she is just as articulate. She is not a scam or a put-on, but she is also not a typical 14-year-old. In one sense, she is a prodigy in the genre of do-it-yourself alt-right YouTube videos. Soph is aware of her gifts but also believes that she is a child of the incompetence and lack of oversight in the domain: 'The fact that I was 11 and could easily follow the [video] commentary formula should have been a sign that the standards for the genre were terribly low,' she said. Indeed, part of her message appears to be that the stupidity and greed of adults has created systems that spawn people like herself, that is, 'She is a problem, she seems to be saying, of YouTube's own making' (ibid).

Soph explicitly reflects, in one of her videos, on the fact that she is part of a generation raised on the internet, without 'a centralised source of information that controls what we think' (ibid). She argues that her generation is 'inoculated to the bullshit' and cannot be brainwashed. The target in many of her videos appears to be adults, as Bernstein explains:

> The ultimate target of [Soph's videos] is, finally, adults: people who just
> don't get why social justice discourse is meaningless and co-optable,
> why school can't compare to YouTube, why mass murder can be funny
> … She's sure that adults are selfish and stupid, that the people with the
> most power over her life are making it up as they go along, just like she
> is. When you look at the adults who have gotten rich off the platform
> that created Soph, she isn't completely wrong. She's been publishing on
> YouTube for years with no consequence other than becoming famous.

I would not normally quote from a *BuzzFeed* article because this 'news' outlet is precisely the kind of click-bait, advertisement-driven media that is part of the problem. However, Bernstein's analysis is apt, and easy enough to double check by going on to YouTube. Watching some of Soph's videos was an uncanny and unnerving experience for me. Some of her videos were not available because they had been removed after being declared 'hate speech' (presumably after Bernstein's article, which linked to them). I do not recommend you engage with her videos yourself. As an educator and developmental psychologist, I find the tragedy of her socialisation is apparent. She is akin to a gifted child who is neglected and bored in school only to become a drug dealer or criminal mastermind. The delinquency is spawned from the mismatch between her intellect and her environment, only in this case *culture war broadcasting* is the medium in which this adolescent pain and searching finds expression.

It is hard to find a better example of the looming generational gap and educational crisis stemming from the culture war than Soph. She is a remarkable example of *algorithmically directed human development*, or *algorithmic radicalisation*. Although she claims to be from a generation that is not brainwashable, there is no doubt that Soph herself was repeatedly subject to informational 'rabbit-holes' of extremely charged content at certain critical periods of her socialisation. By her own admission, she grew up watching (and learning how to use) YouTube and not interacting with her parents, teachers or peers. Her views are certainly not those of the schools or mainstream media – she has destroyed them as possible sources of teacherly authority. But nor are her views the product of reflective self-directed learning, such as might be undertaken by a mature and sovereign adult. Her views are to some extent the result of YouTube's algorithms, which are intended *only to maximise 'engagement'*. YouTube and related social media platforms became the ecosystem in which she socialised and constituted (by commodifying) her identity, and this ecosystem was structured to maximise views, not to maximise positive outcomes for young people who are smart, creative, alienated and angry. Soph is a useful, if disturbing, example of the nihilistic crisis of teacherly authority:

> YouTube has taken no ownership over what is happening to kids who
> grow up inhaling its trademark stench of bigotry, conspiracy and nihilism.
> Now the kids, or the smart ones anyway, seem to know it. Indeed,
> YouTube's own incompetence and lack of quality is one of Soph's
> recurring themes; she acknowledges owing her fame to them. (ibid)

Indeed, the cynicism and caustic social critique ends up ricocheting or boomeranging back, only to end up damaging the still immature person doing the talking. Soph does not appear inflated or grandiose, nor does she even appear to be having fun. There is a certain indignity and shame in her performances that I think stems from her (often stated) awareness of the stupidity of the genre in which she herself has found mastery, in effect, she says, 'The culture is terrible; YouTube is a scam!' But in the very act of saying this, she is, in fact, acting so as to 'win' at culture by having a massive following on YouTube. This is one of the self-contradictions that is slowly eating away at the most creative minds in a now almost entirely alienated generation of youth. They both hate and resent the culture war they are forced to deal with, even as they themselves are fast becoming its most talented warriors. Instead of culture, Soph was raised on war; and now she has become a talented but soulless fighter in battles she does not really understand.

This is what the future looks like if we fail to create new forms of life that are free from the dictates of culture war. As I explain at length elsewhere (Stein, 2019), *informational environments are not educational environments*. Educational environments include, among other things, shared ideas about reality and truth; non-strategic social interaction; non-commodified forms of communication and identity formation. At this point, the best educational environments still involve immediate (non-mediated) forms of cultural production, that is, there is no 'platform' on which real education is taking place these days; 'platforms' are largely manifesting the *educational contradictions* of networked computing. YouTube might conceivably be used as *part* of some educational experiences where the video serves as something like a book (i.e. as content), which is then discussed and put to use, with others, away from the screen. Leaving a child alone with a screen is almost never an educational intervention; it is usually the opposite, because screens are the locus of conquest, extraction and profit. The screen contradicts its potential and miseducates the child; this will be the case until the culture war is contained and rolled back. Soph is what the future looks like unless we begin to fundamentally rethink the domain of education.

The future of education begins now (during a pandemic)

As I finish this essay, during July of 2020, the context of a global pandemic has revealed the *fragility* of large, centralised school systems. This has been shown alongside overwhelming evidence for the *resiliency* of digital educational platforms. The tide was already shifting towards using digital technologies as the basic foundation for new forms of education, and now the tide has turned. The near-term results of this change could be disastrous, as the very foundations of enculturation and learning shift perilously close to chaos. But there is an outside chance that we stand at the threshold of the most profound transformation of education in history.

Society has been in crisis now, explicitly, for the better part of a year. Quarantines, school closures and massive unemployment combined to trap the atomic family unit at home. Kitchens, living rooms and bedrooms became classrooms, offices and gyms. Information flooded into and out of homes at alarming and unprecedented rates. With school and work miles away, and world historical events unfolding, the main educational effect was the informational ecology provided by the smartphone and computer. Most family members 'working' in one way or another at a screen, then switching chairs to 'relax' in front of one. On these screens the cultural war raged, and the pandemic fuelled the fires.

Awash in images, between worlds in the midst of crisis, a digital bardo realm was manifest. The totalised capture of attention by digital technologies and social media was achieved. The internet became everything during quarantines and lockdowns, saving lives and allowing us to connect. The value of digital interconnection and the potentials for its use became clearer. And yet the internet as we know it now is an apparatus of conquest, extraction and profit. So, the pandemic moved us all deeper into the *enclosure* of awareness and communication within digital applications, which are themselves designed to surveille and shape behaviour. Views are like cash, which means all manner of enticements to click are put on the table. This internet designed to addict adolescents has won. Schools have lost. It took a crisis to drive home what had long been the case.

There is no future for schools as we have known them. Our world needs a new form of education. Civilisation depends upon it. While the days of schools are numbered, educational transformations and innovations are at Renaissance pitch. After schooling, education will remain, to be distributed throughout the many digital information landscapes. In the terrain of these digital landscapes is found the actual future of education. As school systems continue to falter under the strain of unbearable complexities, we must be ready to abandon that form in the interest of education itself. This is key to understanding education at the edge of history, where new forms are coming into being.

Screens have beat out schools, with the pandemic finalising this transformation. As I have explored above, the means of cultural and educational production have been transferred over to digital technologies. But these applications are not designed to be educational; they are designed to capture attention for profit. The only way forward involves a redesign of digital technologies, done in the context of a rethinking of the very form of schooling itself.

Already with the advent of the smartphone, schooling had been more or less permanently disrupted. Since then, and more so every day, technology and advertising companies have captured the attention of the youth with ruthless efficiency. Digital technologies have supplanted schools as the main dynamic of childhood socialisation and enculturation (Sheldon et al, 2019). Outside of schools are emerging digital informational landscapes in which education is taking place on a massive scale, for better and for worse. Pop-culture commodifications of youth experience have been competing with schooling since the 1950s, but with the advent of digital technologies schools could not keep up.

There has been a turning over of the means of cultural and educational production, if you will, a transfer of power in the domain of who provides the main contexts, materials and scaffolds in which education takes place. Today Google, Facebook and a rotating host of other platforms own the means of educational production. The means of educational production used to be in the hands of large international publishing houses, state-run schools and universities. Before that, it was in the hands of religious communities, tribes and families. Today's changing of the guard places education firmly in the digital, which is itself in the hands of large private corporations. The implications of this turn-over are beginning to unfold around us, mostly in the form of pollution, coercion and degradation within the informational commons, and the commodification of educational contexts, that is, the culture war.

I have written elsewhere about the fact that we stand poised between different educational futures, some good, and some bad. When I published, *Education in a Time Between Worlds* (2019), the argument needed to be made that the large school systems built by modernity would soon be transformed drastically. Today it is apparent that such a process is taking place. Schools, colleges and universities across the country shut their doors and sent students home to learn in a new way. Each school has dispersed into a distributed digital educational network, mostly unplanned and makeshift. School districts are figuring out how to make learning happen without school buildings, while colleges are finding a way to operate without a campus. According to my arguments, much of the prior system of schooling would be better left 'switched off' so the opportunity can be taken to end modern schooling and to begin a new and truly digital era of education.

We are already seeing direct-to-consumer offerings, innovations in artificial intelligence-based tutoring systems, and technology-enabled pop-up classrooms beginning to reshape the educational landscape. Given this opening and fragmentation, there are sweeping science fiction-like vistas for educational futures. There are futures in which state schools have disintegrated into thousands of for-profit 'EduShops' that sell software and remote tutoring and proctoring. There are other futures in which massive online public schools teach millions of students exactly the same ideas in exactly the same ways, as kids sit at home in front of state-distributed screens for hours on end. These are some of the futures we must fight.

Although what I am saying may seem radical (i.e. schools as we have known them are dead), I am actually fighting for a future that embraces the civilising accomplishments of the public schools built by nation states around the planet. These vast school systems of the modern world are not simply to be dismantled or shut down, nor should they be sold off to private enterprises, as is now happening worldwide in what is the largest privatisation of educational institutions in history (Stein, 2019).

Our great school systems need to be repurposed and redesigned – and now is the time. The school buildings themselves could be transformed into unprecedented institutions that are a combination of public libraries, museums, co-working centres, computer labs and cooperative childcare centres. Funded to the hilt and staffed by citizen-teacher-scientists, these public and privately supported learning hubs would be the local centres of regionally decentralised pop-up classrooms, special interest groups, apprenticeship networks and career counselling.

Giant schools built on the model of early 20th-century factories can be gutted, remodelled and reborn, metaphorically and literally, to create the meta-industrial one-room schoolhouses of the future – 21st-century temples of learning. Technologies will enable the formation of peer-to-peer networks of students and teachers of all ages, from all across the local region (or the world through video), without coercion or compromise. What enables these safe and efficient hubs of self-organising educational configurations are fundamentally new kinds of educational technologies, which put almost unlimited knowledge in the palm of every person's hand.

The new sciences of learning are largely ignored or misused in the design of most educational technologies. The digital technologies we know are not optimised as *educational* technologies, not even close. For decades, research has told us that learning is optimised when it involves sustained interpersonal relationships, emotional connection, embodiment and dynamically interactive hands-on experiences. Based on the best of what we know about the dynamics of learning, educational technologies should be bringing people together *away* from screens – *not* isolating individuals alone in front of screens. Technologies ought to help us customise learning and provide universal access to information through useful, well-organised and curated content. They should not be the primary focus of attention or the main source of interaction and instruction.

Right now, throughout the United States and the world, many schools are being forced to patch together something like the technological backend of a digital system of education. With makeshift stacks of existing educational technologies, we are experimenting on a massive scale with spoke-and-hub networks of decentralised mini-classrooms. During a stay-at-home order, every house in the country becomes a school, at least for a certain amount of time each day. That has not been the case since the era of the one-room schoolhouse (i.e. not since pre-industrial education). Under the strain of social crisis, education retreats to its first and truest bastion: the relationship between children, their parents and a network of concerned and responsible adults.

We should not think that keeping schools running now means having students sit at home in front of their screens all day. We must innovate, radically and quickly. If we do so, it may happen that communities and families will realise that the power of education has been put back in their hands. And although it may feel like a relief when the schools reopen, there is the possibility that most of the learning stays on screens, and that the experience of a decentralised, resilient and innovative digital education makes schools as we have known them appear obsolete.

But none of this is possible without reclaiming the means of cultural production and making good on the promise of the digital. The difference is between a pop-up classroom in a park and sitting in a chair watching a YouTube video. Compare a long conversation in real time to the asynchronous text-based exchanges found on platforms like Twitter. There is a stark contrast between actual embodied problem-solving in the world and massive online multiplayer video games. The choice is between reality and the screen, between the freedom of attention or its imprisonment.

Digital technologies could be designed to liberate attention, rather than capture it for profit. Bending history in the direction of a learning-centric (or human development-centric) civilisation requires that educational vision takes precedence over business as usual. It is still possible to repurpose digital technologies for different ends, to recapture the best potentials of the planetary computational stack, and to avoid a catastrophic disruption of intergenerational transmission. It is not too late to save the very possibility of education from the clutches of total capture by capital.

The way forward involves, as I have been suggesting here, the end of schooling and the end of digital technologies as we have known them. What could emerge, what we know is possible, is a future in which truly unprecedented educational configurations become the new normal. The vision of a decentralised education hub network as outlined above offers one way forward. This can locate the seat of education within the community again, outside school walls, beyond campuses, engaging young people in the problems and processes of their community.

The secondary effects of the pandemic include fundamentally new economic realities, with radical changes in the dynamics of labour markets. The college-to-job-pipeline looks complex to say the least, let alone the school-to-college transition. Should the youth be sent back to schools as if they are being prepared to enter pre-pandemic higher education and labour markets? No. They should be released from this misconceived notion about the function of schooling.

Intergenerational transmission and education can be liberated from outmoded forms of schooling through digital technologies. But this can only be done if technologies are designed with educational value as the bottom line. Digital tools can enable people to safely find each other in actual embodied community, to collaborate, learn and contribute to community problem-solving. It may be that the only way out of the multifold crises cascading around us is to tap the wellspring of human potential. School-aged children and adolescents can help actively solve many of the problems facing their communities if the right tools are put in their hands. Without this possibility, with only a vision of 'returning to school', there will be a long, drawn-out and painful period of educational decline.

We stand poised between a new dark age or a new enlightenment, with the future depending on who controls the means of cultural and educational production.

Bibliography

Alter, A. (2017). *Irresistible: The Rise of Addictive Technology and the Business of Keeping us Hooked*. New York: Penguin.
Aurobindo, Sri. (1944/2005). *The Life Divine*. Pondicherry: Lotus Press.
Bard, A. and Söderqvist, J. (2018). *Digital Libido: Sex, Power, and Violence in the Network Age*. Stockholm: Futurica Media.
Bernstein, J. (2019). YouTube's Newest Far-Right, Foul-mouthed, Red-pilling Star is a 14 Year-old girl. BuzzFeed.News, May 13: www.buzzfeednews.com/article/josephbernstein/youtubes-newest-far-right-foul-mouthed-red-pilling-star-is
Bratton, B.H. (2015). *The Stack: on software and sovereignty*. Cambridge: MIT Press.
Bridle, J. (2018). *The New Dark Age: Technology and the End of the Future*. New York: Verso.
Carr, N. (2011). The *Shallows: What the Internet Is Doing to Our Brains*. New York: W. W. Norton and Company.
Davis, M. (2009). *Street Gang: The Complete History of Sesame Street*. New York: Viking Books.
Freinacht, H. (2017). *The Listening Society: a metamodern guide to politics*, book 1. Metamoderna ApS.
Fuhs, C. (2017). The hidden story of the Marc Gafni smear campaign and the people who want him dead. Medium.com. Retrieved from: https://medium.com/@clintfuhs/the-hidden-story-of-the-marc-gafni-smear-campaign-919b9cdd044f
Giroux, H. (1999). *The Mouse that Roared: Disney and the End of Innocence*. New York: Rowman and Littlefield.
Habermas, J. (1984). *The Theory of Communicative Action, Vol. 1: Reason and the Rationalization of Society*. Boston: Beacon Press.
Harvey, D. (2016). *The Ways of the World*. New York: Oxford University Press.
Hunter, J.D. (1991). *Culture Wars: The Struggle to Define America*. New York: Basic Books.
Jameson, F. (1992). *Postmodernism, or, The Cultural Logic of Late Capitalism*. Durham, NC: Duke University Press.
Kripal, J. (2007). *Esalen: America and the Religion of No Religion*. Chicago: University of Chicago Press.
Kripal, J. (2017). *Secret Body: Erotic and Esoteric Currents in the History of Religions*. Chicago: University of Chicago Press.
Kripal, J. and Shuck, G.W. (2005). *On the Edge of The Future: Esalen and the Evolution of American Culture*. Bloomington: University of Indiana Press.
Mansbach, A. (2011). *Go the Fuck to Sleep*. New York: Akashic Books.
Marley, B. (1976) 'War.' *Rastaman Vibration*. Jamaica: Island Records.
Mead, M. (1970). *Culture and Commitment: A Study of the Generation Gap*. New York: Doubleday.
McLuhan, M. and McLuhan, E. (1988). *Laws of Media: The New Science*. Toronto: University of Toronto Press.
Mumford, L. (1970). *The Myth of the Machine, Vol. 2: Pentagon of Power*. New York: Harcourt, Brace and Co.
Nargara, I. (2013). *A is for Activist*. New York: Triangle Square.
Pariser, E. (2011). *The Filter Bubble: How the New Personalized Web Is Changing What We Read and How We Think*. New York: Penguin Books.
Richardson, P. and Boyd, R. (2005). *Not by Genes Alone: How Culture Transformed Human Evolution*. Chicago: University of Chicago Press.
Rodgers, D.T. (2011). *Age of Fracture*. Cambridge: Harvard University Press.
Sheldon, P., Rauschnabel, P.H. and Honeycutt, J. (2019). *The Dark Side of Social Media: Psychological, Managerial, and Societal Perspectives*. Cambridge: Academic Press.
Stein, Z. (2011). On Spiritual Teachers and Teachings. *Journal of Integral Theory and Practice*, 6(1), 57–77.

Stein, Z. (2014). On Spiritual Books and their Readers: a review of Radical Kabbalah by Marc Gafni, 2012. *Integral Review*, 10(1), 168–178.

Stein, Z. (2015). Beyond Nature and Humanity: Reflections on the Emergence and Purposes of Metatheories. In R. Bhaskar, S. Esbjörn-Hargens, N. Hedlund, and M. Hartwig (Eds.), *Metatheory for the Twenty-First Century: Critical Realism and Integral Theory in Dialogue*. New York: Routledge.

Stein, Z. (2018). Love in a Time Between Worlds: On the Metamodern 'Return' to a Metaphysics of Eros. *Integral Review*, 4(1).

Stein, Z. (2019). *Education in a Time Between Worlds: Essays on the Future of Schools, Technology, and Society*. San Francisco: Bright Alliance.

Thompson, W. I. (1971). *At the Edge of History: Speculations on the Transformation of Culture*. New York: Harper and Row.

Tomasello, M. (1999). *The Cultural Origins of Human Cognition*. Cambridge: Harvard University Press.

Tomasello, M. (2019). *Becoming Human: A Theory of Ontogeny*. Cambridge: Harvard University Press.

Werczberger, R. (2017). *Jews in the Age of Authenticity: Jewish Spiritual Renewal In Israel*. New York: Peter Lang.

West, G. (2018). *Scale: The Universal Laws of Life, Growth, and Death in Organisms, Cities, and Companies*. New York: Penguin.

White, M. (2016). *The End of Protest: A New Playbook for Revolution*. Toronto, ON: Knopf Canada.

Woolley, S. (2020). *The Reality Game: How the Next Wave of Technology will Break the Truth, and What We Can do About It*. New York: Hachette.

Zuboff, S. (2019). *The Age of Surveillance Capitalism*. New York: Public Affairs.

5 Metamodernism, Simplicity and Complexity
Healing developmental models through involutionary descent

Tom Murray

Introduction

It appears that humanity is at a critical juncture – a time where our choices may determine the survival of our species and of many planetary life forms. Our historical moment has been described in terms of the successes and failures of modernity, and what comes before and after modernity. Modernity in this context refers to dominant (or dominating) cognitive and cultural, social and technological processes driven by abstract logical thinking, individualism, capitalism, democracy and material 'progress'. The significant achievements of modernity, as well as its potentially catastrophic manifestations (aggregated into the so-called 'meta-crisis' – Williams, 2016; Stein, 2019), will be familiar to most readers of this volume. Our predicament is often described in terms of increasing *complexity*. It is now practically a platitude that 'we live in a complex and fast-changing world', a VUCA world (of volatility, uncertainty, complexity and ambiguity), requiring humanity to step up to the challenge by increasing the complexity of our thinking and collaborative problem-solving. In this narrative, complexity must be met with complexity.

This dominant narrative about increasing complexity, building momentum over centuries and perhaps millennia, has perennially called forth a counter-narrative, appearing in waves within cultural movements such as romanticism, traditionalism, postmodern critique and New Age culture. Although some aspects of these counter-narratives add complexity by taking a critical meta-perspective (e.g. to deconstruct underlying assumptions), for the most part they point to *less* complex forms of being. The contrasting narratives critique sophistication, complication, progress, expansion and power, and aim towards *simplicity* suggesting: slowing down and looking inward; going 'back to the land', orienting towards matters of holism, spirit and soul; emphasising simple acts of care and selflessness; and the humility of not knowing or beginner's mind. In this chapter I use a developmental lens to look closely at how complexity and simplicity are understood and misunderstood in certain narratives on the human condition.

Metamodernism is often described in terms of the cultural tensions between modernism, traditionalist appeals to return to premodern ways, postmodern critiques that analyse the problems of modernity without offering solutions, and New Age movements that are a confusing combination of naive utopian vision and back-to-nature regression that ignores pragmatic givens (Vermeulen and van den Akker, 2010; Turner, 2015; Abramson, 2015; Cooper, 2018; Freinacht, 2017). The emerging metamodern mindset or culture can be defined in terms of a synthesis that seriously considers the postmodern critique, does so without jettisoning the positive contributions of modernity, and re-integrates, rather than regresses to, aspects of the human condition that were exorcised by modernity. Although metamodernity originally was a descriptive term tracking cultural trends, our focus here is on the more prescriptive orientations towards metamodernism. Neither describing nor achieving that emergent synthesis can be adequately accomplished through simple processes of pruning, mixing, oscillating and balancing the simple versus the complex, or the modern versus the non-modern. To understand this terrain, one must look deeply into the dialectical relationship between complexity and simplicity in human development. *Developmental theory* is primarily the study of learning as increasing complexity in human thought, and by extension, culture. It offers important conceptual tools for understanding the dynamics related to metamodernism. Yet it can achieve even more explanatory and emancipatory power than it has done thus far. Here I will argue that developmental approaches must be supplemented with more rigorous treatments of *simplicity* as well as complexity, and in particular that such approaches must consider processes of *unlearning* and *releasing complexity*.

Although themes of complexity and simplicity permeate narratives about our moment in history, the relationship between complexity and simplicity is often misunderstood. Complexity is a theme central to thinking about development, evolution, learning, problem-solving and transformational change. Simplicity is a common theme in diverse areas that include spirituality, pragmatism, ethics, embodiment, romanticism and ecological living. Approaches drawing on theories of human development and evolution often invoke a quasi-teleological notion of 'simplexity' – the emergence of a 'simplicity on the other side of complexity', borrowed from the study of complexity and self-organising systems in nature. I argue that in the domains of human ideas, abstractions and plans, as opposed to 'natural' systems, learning and growth do not progress through a pure simplicity that 'transcends and includes' the best of prior forms, but rather that they inevitably introduce elements of shadow, demi-reality, contradiction and/or trauma into psychological and social systems. Thus, again, any theory of human development must explicitly include processes for release, unlearning, healing, and/or 'shadow work', in addition to modelling complexity.

To address the dilemmas and apparent paradoxes within the meta-crisis and contemporary culture wars, it is imperative that we turn around problematic trends of increasing human-systems complexity, abstraction and dissociation, and re-orient to fundamental (perhaps 'simple') values of care and integrity. But this must be done through a wisdom that does not pit simplicity *against* complexity, nor goes by a simplistic model that believes simplicity is approached easily *through* complexity, nor that sees the issue merely in terms of *balance* and harmony within a polarity. Our developmental framework is summarised by 'wisdom skill = complexity capacity + spiritual clarity', where complexity capacity is growth in hierarchical complexity, spiritual clarity is related to depth, unlearning, simplicity and releasing complexity, and wisdom skill is related to ego development and meaning-making maturity.

This chapter contains only a brief summary of a more extensive treatment found in Murray (2020, in press). Along the way I hope to remedy common confusions about the relationship between *transcendence* and *embodiment*, and between *ascending* and *descending* metaphors of psycho-spiritual growth. These distinctions are important because ascending (towards developmental/evolutionary complexity) and descending (towards involutionary release, re-membering, and simplicity), while both critical, are distinct cognitive or transformational processes, achieved after overcoming distinct motivational and social challenges, and matched to distinct types of resultant capacities.

Preliminaries

On the importance of complexity. Although this chapter focuses on elaborating negative consequences of complexity, I should ground the narrative by noting its positive significance. The dynamics of the evolution of the cosmos and of living systems can be described in terms of hierarchically emerging levels of complexity, in which, as Ken Wilber puts it, each level transcends and includes (or embraces and transcends) the prior, resulting in entities that are more than the sum of their parts (Wilber, 1995; Koestler, 1967). Emergence is not predictable or guaranteed, and in fact is a barely understood process, yet complexity science has become a powerful tool for understanding reality (Stacey, 1995; Bar-Yam, 2002; Allen et al, 2014). Here I focus on complexity in human systems and human cognition, including the capacity of cognition to make sense of a complex reality.

Critiques of complexity (and of development or hierarchy) often ignore the importance of foundational strata. It is easier to critique than to propose a practical solution – easier to dismantle than to construct – because crafting sustainable reality-based solutions requires understanding and honouring how each level builds upon prior structural levels. For example, many 'radical' critiques of modernity don't acknowledge that the intelligence needed to craft a good argument, the political freedom to critique the status quo, and the technology used to disseminate critical perspectives, rely directly on those structures that the radical critique proposes to tear down – for example, educational systems, democratic political systems and technological tools forged in the cauldrons of capitalism. Applying this theme to cognitive and ego development, we can note the importance of healthy foundational levels of cognition and culture. 'Traditional' values of honour, respect, teamwork, appreciation and gratitude speak to the importance of sturdy foundational strata. Expertise born of experience is also a form of complexity, and attitudes that devalue expertise in favour of bottom-up power or egalitarian consensus, although well intentioned, risk ultimate failure. Although radical transformation and deconstruction are indeed necessary for humans to survive the meta-crisis, most revolutionary or radical proposals to dismantle existing structures do not understand what is lost in regression into social or cognitive chaos.

Development is largely the study of how knowledge and skill *build upon* prior knowledge and skill – that is the essence of hierarchical complexity. Many believe that the territory of complexity and depth implicit in metamodern cognition necessarily includes at least an informal intuitive understanding of how developmental factors pertain to the human condition. Hanzi Freinacht's seminal book on metamodernism (*The Listening Society*, 2017) describes a developmental approach to metamodernism, basing its model on Commons' Hierarchical Complexity Theory. Our treatment here expands on Freinacht's treatment of developmental 'depth', which he says 'is a person's intimate, embodied acquaintance with subjective states' (ibid, chapter 14). Rather than base depth on states, we integrate development with a descending or involutionary movement that involves *releasing* complexity as an essential component (following Roy, 2018; Roy and Trudel, 2011). We agree with Freinacht's notion that depth is 'a kind of existential or spiritual wisdom' but believe that it is not best described in terms of state experiences, but rather by using processes of deconstruction, shadow-work and insight-generation that we call 'spiritual clarity' – but more on that later.[1]

Some problems of complexity, and the importance of simplicity. In natural processes of evolution, development and emergence, complexity simply happens, and it is not something one can or should critique per se. But in the domain of human consciousness and culture, actions and beliefs can be judged as right/wrong and true/false (as ethics and propositions are among the newly emergent properties of the human life domain over the animal life domain). Within the human realm of beliefs, ideologies, egoic choices, invented technologies, group conflict and hierarchical regimes of power, increasing complexity is a mixed bag of benefits and disasters.

Cognitive complexity, that is, learning and belief formation, can contain what Roy Bhaskar calls 'demi-reality' – explicit beliefs and implicit assumptions that do not correspond to reality. Demi-reality refers to people's disconnection from others, nature and self, in forms such as deception, denial, grandiosity, oppression, alienation and fragmentation (Bhaskar, 1975; 2017; Collier, 1994), and is related to Carl Jung's notion of individual and collective shadow. The contemporary 'meaning crisis' in human sensemaking stems from our inability to see and eliminate forms of demi-reality (Vervaeke et al, 2017). Demi-reality can also be embedded within social, economic and political systems, in how their supposed purpose is at odds with their actual effect. For theories of human development and complexity to be maximally relevant to our times, they must have something to say about demi-real complexity and knowledge, that is, about the moral implications of hierarchical complexity.

Clearly, increasing complexity in cognitive, cultural, political and technological domains is not guaranteed to produce 'good' ends. Complex thinkers and geniuses can be malevolent or oblivious to the needs of others. Complex technology can be used to harm. Complex laws, policies and bureaucracies, although sometimes seemingly necessary, are at best 'necessary evils', and at worst oppressive, inefficient and extractive. The paradox is that, to understand and address complex problems, one must reflect upon them fully and deeply, which, by definition, must be done from an even *more* complex vantage point (as in Einstein's well-known adage that 'we cannot solve our problems with the same level of thinking complexity that created them').

One might think that the resolution to this paradox is that somehow it is 'good complexity' that is used to understand and reduce 'bad complexity'. But this principle is flawed because of another paradox, captured by the adage that 'every solution creates new problems'. We cannot predict the complex outcomes of introducing new complexity.[2] The downsides of increased complexity are usually unintended and rarely anticipated (and all too often, through human greed and haste, potentially negative outcomes are conveniently ignored and denied). Even with the best of intentions it is not possible to predict or avoid the negative consequences that will accompany any positive outcomes of increased complexity.

We are born into (thrown into) families and cultures that inculcate us with forms of learning and complexity that we do not choose and cannot predict. Thus, simply avoiding the negative outcomes of complexity will not do, but we must also identify and release complexity, that is, dismantle structures and unlearn beliefs and habits, when they are revealed as problematic. Above we touched on how external forms of complexity tend to create negative externalities, and later we will show how *internal* complexity, that is, cognitive hierarchical complexity, also leads inevitably to demi-realities. For a variety of reasons, intentionally releasing complexity seems much more difficult than adding complexity. Again, our suggestion is the regular reflective practice of assessing, undoing, unlearning or releasing complexity, at many levels of human systems. Doing so involves skilful means, which implies that one must have a 'theory of change', which we attempt to contribute to here. But we should not forget that moving in this direction is also a matter of virtue and moral will, and an orientation to 'basic goodness', not merely abstract understanding.

Usually in these fields people think that 'higher is better'. But, following developmental theory and its emphasis on built-up strata of complexity, one could argue that the earlier or 'simpler' levels are, in a sense, *more* important than the later more complex levels. Just as the structural integrity of a building's foundations is more important than the structural integrity of the top floor, the health and robustness of foundational layers of the psyche (or of social systems) is of utmost importance. Calls to 'meet complexity with more complexity' miss the fact that often complexity is part of the problem, not the solution, and that the real culprit is weak or misshapen foundational structures. For example, members of a dysfunctional (maladaptive) family or organisation will adopt complex coping mechanisms, and sometimes there is an escalating 'arms race' of complexity when each member tries to out-strategise the other to get their needs met. Resolution or healing for such a system requires *releasing* complexity in individuals and their strategies. For example, psychotherapeutic modalities can strengthen safety, self-worth, trust and empathy at foundational levels, leading to less complex and more coherent and fluid interactions and less need for complex strategies or bureaucratic rules.

As noted, many narratives respond to the potential dangers of hierarchical growth and increasing complexity with calls for simplicity or recovering foundational psychic assets. Spiritual and contemplative discourses refer to concepts such as *letting go*, *purity*, *emptiness* and *stillness*. Psychotherapy points to *uncovering* and transforming early schema. The ethical gestures of forgiveness and acceptance are also types of release. Spiritual growth in the many religions includes processes of *purgation* or *purification*, and Buddhist meditation orients to *deconstructing*, *dismantling*, *cutting-through*, *dis-integrating* or *eradicating* mental 'impurities'. Psychological/spiritual growth is sometimes understood as a *healing* process of removing psychic injuries or shadow material, and is sometimes described in terms of disidentification and the tearing down, *dissolution*, de-composition or releasing of boundaries; and at other times in terms of *loss* and death of parts of the self. Psychological/spiritual maturity is said to involve 'waking up' from the 'cultural trap' or 'consensus trance', and *seeing through* conditioning and *laying bare* deeper truths. All of these terms form a conceptual cluster that has a very different (*descending*) felt sense as compared to terms used in positivist discussions of (*ascending*) hierarchical complexity, growth and advancement. Even sentiments such as 'be here now', and 'accept what is' are about releasing complexity – in this case, of beliefs and mentations that occlude experiential reality.

As another example of the importance of simplicity, consider how scholars, professing on abstract theoretical aspects of important issues, inevitably must respond to audience questions that include 'so what can one *do concretely* to implement these ideas?' In my experience, the vast majority of such answers are rather mundane, in that the principles of concrete action boil down to simple aphorisms and perennial truths and values: show love, compassion, forgiveness, gratitude, tolerance, self-control, curiosity, perseverance and so on; know thyself, love yourself, let go, think for yourself, speak the truth, accept what is, follow your dreams (or bliss, or gut ...), be open to grief and loss, act locally (clean your room) ... breathe!

The desire for simplicity comes in part from the fact that, as we will elaborate later, human development and learning is never ideal – it does not simply 'transcend and include' in a purely additive and transformative sense, but rather it inevitably *leaves things behind* as it moves forward into new territory. Everyday observation shows us that, without exception, people leave things behind as they mature from childhood into adulthood. One can lose playfulness, innocent curiosity, earnest honesty, hopefulness, openness, trust of others, self-acceptance, perceptual clarity, an affinity for the natural world, fluid imagination, dedication to the values of one's tribe, trust in logic and science and so on, at different junctures on the developmental path into maturity.

These foundational capacities are primitive psychic capacities that need to be recovered or re-membered, more than built anew. Regardless of how complex our world becomes, our survival and happiness depend in large part upon the simple forms of wisdom and truth that, because of the nested structure of development, sustain all later levels. It is self-evident that these resources are sorely depleted in modern life and one could argue that the urgent problems of organisations and societies are caused more by the atrophy or shunting of these foundational capacities than by a dire need for more complex thinking. These early modes of being are *critical psychic resources* needed to endure hardship and to balance negative emotions (from both real and concocted negative and stressful experiences) in any challenging or complex context. The essentials of trust, love, playfulness, curiosity, forgiveness and so on, don't need to be understood metaphysically as essential truths or principles that must drive and permeate all life – this risks turning them into idealisations and ideologies. Rather, we argue that we need robust access to these modes of being to balance and complement other capacities, and that not having the skilful means to access them greatly diminishes resilience, robustness, wellbeing and sanity.

Patternings such as psychological shadow, denial, and repression all fall within the rubric of what we will call *occluded/occluding* knowledge and skill. Occluded cognitive structures are those left behind, hidden, rejected, forgotten or distorted through the imprints of later (occluding) experiences and structures. Occlusions are not necessarily negative, and can serve important purposes in an individual's (or group's) survival, coping or thriving during specific conditions. Also called lacunas, they can be useful during one period and become undesirable under a new context. One sometimes needs to push prior ways aside or beneath to make room for the new, as when one becomes disgusted with one's family's 'old time religion' and its contradictions. But what was rejected can later be re-integrated, when the time is right – just as one realises there was important gold in the dross that was rejected.

Perhaps the most extensive occlusions come through modernity's adoration of abstract/ rational thinking as it pushes much of the 'magical' strata of the psyche into the inaccessible unconsciousness (Donald, 1991; Hutson, 2012; Jung, 1968). That strata of cognition is (practically) always active (see Brown, 2002), yet all too rarely listened to. It operates unreflectively through associations, at a level of processing that does not clearly separate self from other, imagination from sensory reality, or impulse from action. This magical strata of mind produces images, associations and feeling states – often vivid, pregnant or disturbing – that point to deeper truths about one's being, sometimes called the *imaginal* realm. To the extent that modernity has inhibited this layer of information and processing, we miss vital truths, perceptions and intuitions. One aspect of metamodern cognition or consciousness is the 're-enchantment of the lifeworld', that is, maintaining an open channel to information and experiences from the lower strata of the psyche. While modernity rejected this information as fanciful or emotion-laden, it can and should be understood as having a type of truth and validity on its own terms, within its own domain.

By now it should be clear that our notion of 'simplicity' is often about recovering developmentally *earlier* or structurally prior modes. They are simpl-*er* in that they are prior to structures built after and on top of them, which, by definition, are more complex. But they are not simple per se. The unconscious, including processing at the perceptual and magical strata, is quite complex of course. The child learning to walk or talk is complex beyond our understanding, and even a cell contains complexities beyond comprehension. Further, primeval aboriginal cultures practise sophisticated modes of perception and hold complex wisdoms that modern man has long forgotten and desperately needs.

Pathologies of simplicity. Having argued on the side of simplicity, we must now caution against simplistic approaches to simplicity, and re-engage the theme of complexity. Above we argued against a type of simplistic thinking that ignores the role of the foundational strata of the psyche. We have also noted that regressive appeals to return to earlier states (or stages), and anarchistic appeals to deconstruct (blow up) existing structures are inherently naive, although they may arise from valid concerns. Also to be avoided are progressive forms of simplicity, including: hippie romanticism (e.g. the literal interpretation of 'all you need is love'), New Age ideology (the unexamined metaphysics of misplaced concreteness, as in the 'law of attraction'), so-called bleeding heart liberalism or 'idiot compassion' (that can feel deeply but cannot act wisely to impact positive change) and 'spiritual bypassing' (confusing state experiences for wisdom and using spiritual ideas to avoid concrete realities). All of these approaches, if held too tightly or exclusively, contain a regressive naivete in terms of the practical complexities of life that prohibit them from serving as the basis of successful actions in a complex world.

The simplicity we are championing is not about regressing to earlier modes of being but rather about recovering lost psychic resources which are 'simple' in that they originally develop in childhood, and, in their pure or original form, are not complicated by the machinations of abstraction and reflective problematisation. These resources are to be recovered and *re-integrated* in later action logics, where mature forms of sensemaking are operational. In other words, romantic injunctions to return to states of emotional intensity, simple living and natural beauty are important when they point to the need to recover and integrate these resources, but are naive and dangerous when they suggest a return to modes of consciousness associated with the magical and mythical strata of the mind. Regression means that one accesses an earlier developmental level without keeping 'on line' the reflective and regulatory functions of later, more complex levels, so that the more primitive levels dominate decision-making. One can release higher-level functions temporarily to open to non-ordinary states or healing experiences, but usually one is supported by others who temporarily take on the higher-order 'executive functions' of the situation.[3]

The *positive* functions of the simplistic mind and heart are salient to romanticists, who often ignore the *disturbing* parts of the magical world of the infant – the impulsive, the narcissistic and even the proto-psychotic and hallucinatory. On the flip side of openness and wide-eyed awe is the terror of magical forces beyond one's control; on the other side of blissful oneness is co-dependent merging and weak personal boundaries; and on the other side of hugging the cute puppy is the unbridled rage or terror of upsetting events (see Hutson, 2012; Murray, 2019, p. 144).[4] The early action logics are *dangerously pre-ethical* – arising from that strata of mind that knows undifferentiated connection, but cannot take perspectives. During non-ordinary state experiences in which one is resting openly in the expanded magical or mythical strata of consciousness, one is open to manipulation as well as love; rage as well as rapture (as they say, 'set and setting' is key). The universe might seem blissful and oceanic until someone gets in one's way or disagrees, and then the expansiveness collapses into suffering unless one can readily access rational functions, such as objectively analysing the situation, and taking multiple perspectives to reason with others. The romantic's plan to live in simplicity rightly banishes cruel complexity, but there must still be 'an adult in the room' (or in the presidency, etc.).

To prioritise or choose among options requires a higher developmental level than understanding the choices in isolation. For any given context there are likely to be conflicting directions implied within our list of important resources at foundation levels (respect, playfulness, etc.). Thus, once one removes barriers or blind spots and gains access to foundational psychic resources, there is still the more complex task of *discerning* when and how to apply or embody what one encounters there, which might include both intended and unintended emanations.[5]

The paradox of desiring simplicity while acknowledging Einstein's principle (that one needs additional complexity to understand a situation) is resolved in understanding that untangling a knot might require a moment of additional complexity (a meta-perspective) to figure out how to *release* the problematic complexity, but once complexity serves that purpose it can be put aside, rather than built up. For example, a problem at complexity level 4 may require a level 5 analysis, but the goal of that analysis can be to reduce the whole system to a level 3 complexity, or to make levels 1, 2 and 3 more healthy and robust so that level 4 operations function better. Note that for many problems the level 5 meta-view is only required by a few leaders or influencers, who can then guide other stakeholders. For example, when members of an organisation do not trust each other, arcane and complex interaction patterns can emerge. A skilful intervention might be to remove complex-thinking narcissistic individuals and complex bureaucratic systems, and then realign organisational systems towards supporting participants in resourcing the foundational capacities of trusting self and other, orienting to perception over analysis, and eliminating complex barriers to communication (see Roy, 2016). A leader or leadership team might accomplish this intervention without needing the majority of participants to understand the system at the level of complexity that the leaders do.

All of this is does not discount the often important and marvellous outcomes of hierarchical development or the value of theories of hierarchical development. But caution is warranted, especially for those oriented exclusively to ascending paths and progress into later stages.

On developmental theory and dangerous tools

Developmental models and complexity. In the Preliminaries section we summarised the contours of a ubiquitous tension between complexity and simplicity, closely related to the tensions between modern and romantic movements that postmodernism reveals and critiques, and metamodernism aims to resolve. We spoke to the detrimental and pathological manifestations of complexity, as well as its importance. And we spoke to the importance of acknowledging foundational structures. We emphasised that the recovery of early psychic structures should not be a regression, but a release (ablation) of occlusions to regain access to lost resources, which can then be evaluated and re-integrated by more mature cognitive functions as needed.

But these distinctions and principles are too crude to address the significant problems we face. Developmental models can bring us closer to an adequate understanding of the complexities involved. They help us move away from a simple bi-polar or linear understanding of simplicity versus complexity, or rationality versus non-rationality and so on, which tends to limit us to considerations of choosing, mixing, oscillating, balancing or harmonising, and allows for a more nuanced, dialectical and dynamic non-linear understanding of these relationships, showing how simplicity and complexity entwine and co-emerge. Developmental models paint a detailed spectrum of unfolding strata of cognition and consciousness.[6] They use principles from dynamic systems theory, which were designed to characterise different forms of complexity and explain how complexity arises from simplicity.[7] Developmental theories allow us to measure strata of hierarchical complexity to a resolution of about a dozen levels, or even dozens of sub-levels, depending on the context and theory.[8] They explain factors in how skills grow horizontally and vertically/hierarchically, what drives growth and what inhibits it. Our interest here is with the general principles that operate all along the developmental spectrum, rather than with descriptions of each level.

Developmental theories explain the growth of cognitive complexity and sophistication in any area and, most importantly, they help explain the challenges to manifesting personal happiness and a just and compassionate society in a modern world profuse in diverse belief systems and lifestyles (Kegan, 1994; Cook-Greuter, 2004; Kohlberg, 1973; Habermas, 1990). Applied broadly to human meaning-making, these theories describe the journey from black-and-white, narcissistic and impulsive, us versus them, short-sighted, shallow and simplistic action logics (worldviews or modes of meaning-making) into more complex, nuanced, expansive, layered, flexible, adaptive, reflective, empathic, multi-perspectival and/or pro-social action logics. Developmental complexity has also been used (though somewhat less empirically or rigorously) to describe the evolution of cultures – including their systems of values and ethics, their modes of communication and commerce, and their technological achievements (Beck and Cowan, 1996; Hall, 1990; Zak and Knack, 2001; Freinacht, 2020). In this short text we assume that the reader has at least a slight familiarity with some adult developmental models (e.g. by Kegan, Torbert, Cook-Greuter, O'Fallon, Fischer or Commons; with many such models summarised in Wilber, 2000), as our goal is to renovate how they are interpreted and used.

Development as building upon prerequisites. The central contribution of developmental theory is in the meticulous mapping of *prerequisite skills*. That skills build upon each other seems an obvious fact, but the full implications are surprisingly absent from most analyses of social, political or cultural phenomena. Developmental principles help us avoid asking, expecting or wishing that people would do or understand something when, in fact, they lack the developmental prerequisites. For example, we often judge people too harshly for not seeing systemic patterns in their cultural context, or for blindness to contradictory aspects of their personalities or beliefs. But these reflective skills are usually achieved through a privileged access to good education and mentoring, and to safe opportunities to practise and make mistakes. And some who have acquired such skills live in highly stressful or oppressed contexts that tend to 'downshift' one's cognition to simpler operational states ('shadow-crash' in Barta, 2020; 'fallback' in Torbert, 2020; 'amygdala hijack' in Goleman, 1995). Developmental principles can be essential in gauging expectations and discerning between intervention approaches (e.g. in balancing assistance, education, patience, authority, empathy and dialogue). For instance, adult developmental factors are rarely taken into account in scientific studies and policy decisions about reducing crime or addiction, improving parenting skills, conflicts related to immigration and migration, or installing democracies in developing countries.

We often want people or social structures to change, but fail to take a close look at the assumptions made about their ability to: consider the perspectives of multiple stakeholders during problem-solving; look beyond surface-level symptoms and short-term factors into more systemic causes; or appraise how one's own history, feelings and hidden motivations bias one's beliefs and actions. Developmental research has rigorously mapped out sequences of prerequisite cognitive and socio-emotional skills in such areas, showing that most people are 'in over their heads' as they try to live up to typical but tacit expectations imposed by society (Kegan, 1994). Put bluntly, any plan or intervention that fails to consider the actual versus desired (or assumed) developed skills of its target population is likely to fail.

Dangerous tools. The developmental lens on complexity is important because the problems of today are 'problems' largely because of their degree of complexity. Sometimes the issue is a lack of resources or malign intention, but more often the underlying issue is the large number of factors, non-linear relationships and unknowns. One promise of developmental theory is that it might give us a map of the level of skill complexity needed to tackle a problem (if we can estimate the level and type of complexity presented by the problem). Of course, tackling real problems requires much more, but developmental theories have proven to be powerful tools for understanding certain human dilemmas. And therein lies another problem – their power is seductive. Developmental theories are actually quite complex in and of themselves, and are easy to overgeneralise and misapply.

Ideas are tools (Menand, 2001), and the history of ideas shows us that, like the history of technology, tools at a certain level of complexity require a corresponding level of cognitive complexity to *invent* them, but once invented, individuals and communities at lower levels of developmental complexity can *appropriate* them – often to hazardous ends. The classic examples are tools of warfare, such as the atomic bomb, and gene manipulation, invented through modern/postmodern levels of complexity but now procurable by developmentally 'tribal' or ethnocentric cultures and individuals (and see the discussion in Berge, 2004). Similarly, in the domain of ideas, the deconstructive intellectual methods invented by high postmodernists were dazzlingly sophisticated. Yet these ideas, such as, how facts are inescapably fallible and that knowledge and history are constructed narratives, have been mis-/re-appropriated by comparable idiots to fashion our post-truth milieu. Similarly, insights from deep contemplative practice, such as, 'the self is empty' or 'the world is an illusion' are, in their radical forms, powerful yet potentially harmful insights that traditional religions did not give members the tools to realise until one's development could properly assimilate their import and caveats. Our point here is that *developmental theory* is another such concept. As with contemplative practices, its benefits seem substantial and its downsides are subtler, so the dangers of misappropriation can be difficult to appreciate.

As more people become attracted to developmental theory, as is happening within the community of metamodern scholars and elsewhere, it becomes ever more important to highlight the caveats needed to employ it. Some traps of using these models have been generally acknowledged, including: the temptation to categorise people into simplistic stage categories; and an assumption that 'higher is better', which can lead to arrogance and blind spots in sophisticated thinkers, and to unproductive motives to coerce people up the 'ladder' of development; and thinking that higher development leads to more ethical behaviour (see Stein, 2008; Stein and Heikkinen, 2008; Murray, 2011; Cook-Greuter, 2013; Torbert and Erfan, 2020). Therefore, in the next two sections we move beyond generally known tensions between complexity and simplicity as outlined in the Preliminaries, into some less acknowledged caveats.

Developmental externalities

Modes of cognitive coordination. Here we will argue that most cognitive development and growth creates unintended consequences (externalities) that accumulate shadow material in the individual or collective psyche. To examine these ubiquitous negative potentials of developmental or hierarchical learning and thinking, we take as a starting point what is arguably the most elegant and powerful definition given in the literature. Michael Commons' precise and compact definition of hierarchical complexity defines the 'complexity order' of a capacity in terms of how many hierarchical levels of one thing building upon another a task or skill implies (Commons and Pekker, 2008).[9] Developmental theories differentiate *horizontal* growth from *vertical* or *hierarchical* growth. Horizontal growth is driven largely by differentiation or accumulation of same-level capacities; while vertical growth is said to follow a phase of horizontal growth, and is driven largely by the integration (or coordination) of lower-level capacities. Commons has boiled hierarchical development down to a 'mathematical' or 'axiomatic' foundation, wherein each 'new task-required action must: (1) be defined in terms of the lower stage actions and (2) coordinate the lower stage actions in a (3) nonarbitrary way' (Commons and Chen, 2014, p. 252).

However, much is hidden within the abstract idea of 'operating upon' or 'coordinating' lower levels. A concept, skill or idea can operate upon, build upon or 'go meta' in many ways – and determining the sub-species of such operations reveals much that is useful in explaining both the strengths and potential calamities of hierarchical growth. As we will see, there are specific problematic or pathological ways of over-functioning for each of the sub-operations within hierarchical complexity. In Murray (in press) I give an analysis of the sub-operations of hierarchical growth, drawing from several theories of cognitive architecture (Laird, Newell and Rosenbloom's 1987 SOAR model; Anderson's 1983 ACT model; Commons and Pekker's 2008 HCT; Fischer's 1980 Skill Theory; and O'Fallon et al's 2020 STAGES model). The resultant is this set of cognitive operations: differentiation (the only non-hierarchical or horizontal operation in the list); composition (assigning relationship, pattern or mappings); generalisation (extends the boundaries of something to include more); abstraction (eliminates non-essential properties among objects to form a higher-order class); and integration (interrelating elements interpenetrate to the degree that a new functional unit emerges). (These processes operate simultaneously and fractally at multiple process levels: entire-spectrum, tiers, levels and level transitions.)

We will articulate how cognitive complexity potentiates the production of demi-reality by analysing the possible downsides of each of these five forms of hierarchical coordination. Somewhat tongue-in-cheek (because these forms are only partly or sometimes problematic), we title the subsections: disastrous differentiation, noxious composition, vicious abstraction, pernicious generalisation and tyrannical integration.

1. *Disastrous differentiation.* There are several dangers inherent in differentiation and related horizontal operations (the focusing, discrimination, substitution and reinforcement of individual concepts, parts, etc.). (1) Because cognition is embodied and thus has limited capacity, attending to one thing implies that one is not attending to other things that might be more important. (2) Differential is akin to 'analysis', which means to break into parts and study the parts. Such analysis can ignore deep and subtle relationships and the nature of 'the whole'. Deconstruction opens up nuance and detail, but can also obliterate context and set the stage for pathological abstraction and generalisation. (3) Differentiation can be taken to an extreme or given too much salience. A difference discriminated can become a 'discrimination against', because properties not in common are disregarded or exaggerated.

2. *Noxious composition.* (1) It is widely recognised that human cognition over-performs in seeing patterns in data where there is only noise. The human brain is a master pattern-matcher, and in its insatiable goal to make meaning it seems to care less about accuracy than sensemaking (Shermer, 2011, calls this tendency 'patternicity'). (2) Composition can lead to *complication*. As a complicated system grows, its internal inconsistencies and inefficiencies can clog/bog the overall system, and lead to increasingly diminished returns, malignancy and hazard. Snowden (2000; 2002) differentiates *complicated systems* from *complex systems*, where 'complicated' is Snowden's term for systems that, although they may contain numerous interrelated parts, are comprehensible by human analysis. They exhibit the linearity of 'one thing predictably leading to another', even if it may take a team of experts a long time to work out those details. They do not reach the level of complexity and impenetrability of naturally 'complex systems' described in theories of complexity science.

3. *Vicious abstraction.* On the topic of abstraction we use R.G. Winther's *James and Dewey on Abstraction* (2014) as our point of departure. Winther says that 'for both thinkers [the critique] amounts to recognizing that abstraction is powerful and liberating, yet has a dark side' (p. 2). The danger is that reductive selection is 'value-laden and interest-driven' (p. 7). James says: 'abstraction … becomes a means of arrest far more than a means of advance in thought. … *The viciously privative employment of abstract characters and class names is,* I am persuaded, one of the great original sins of the rationalistic mind' (1909a, p. 135, emphasis in original). Winther summarises the problems with vicious abstractionism as the 'dismissal [or] disregard of context … Such dismissal may be conscious or unconscious, implicit or explicit, intentional or unintentional, and leads to universalized, narrowed, and/or ontologized abstractions' (p. 10).

One of the most often cited problems of abstraction is 'reification' – what Winther calls 'ontologized abstraction' – the psychological tendency to treat abstract concepts as if they were concrete (tangibly real). Typical examples include: 'mother nature takes revenge', 'the war on drug addiction', 'Big Pharma wants to keep you sick' and 'the We-being of collective consciousness'. Often with these concepts, non-concrete entities are imputed with properties of living, intentional beings. Reification has a number of synonyms or sub-types, with names that embellish its meaning: 'the fallacy of misplaced concreteness' (Whitehead, 1929), 'confusing the map for the territory' (Korzybski, 1958), 'the myth of the given' (Sellars, 1956), concretism, hypostatisation, objectification and metaphysical projection. Reification is a type of magical thinking that is not constrained to operate within the magical/mythical developmental levels of the psyche, but that thrives within highly abstract/rational/logical narratives, in the fertile ground of theories, ideals and metaphysical philosophies (see Murray, 2019).

4. *Pernicious generalisation.* Generalisation does not (necessarily) lose information, which abstraction does – by its definition.[10] Issues of generalisation hypertrophy include: (1) *Bias*. Similar to abstraction, generalisation submits to motivated bias in how boundaries of emphasis are drawn; and is a culprit in all forms of prejudice. (2) *Over-generalisation*. A rule or principle that is valid (even unbiased) within a limited context can be inappropriately generalised to a wider context or different domain. (3) *Reification*. Another danger is in treating the boundary conditions of a generalisation, which are often imprecise and biased, as if they were definitive and given in nature. (4) *Harm*. As the postmodern critique (of grand narratives, meta-theories and the social reproduction of conspicuous ideologies) shows, generalisations can be both fallacious and *pernicious*. While abstraction moves us away from the concrete, generalisation moves us away from *specifics* and details. Even if we don't jump to conclusions or prejudices, generalisations blur fine-grained details. As one expands to take in a meta-view and take more objects into awareness, one loses track of the specifics of each item, or of the items themselves (as the trees become the forest). As with abstraction, it is sometimes the tender realities of human experiences and needs that are forgotten in the big-picture meta-perspective.

5. *Tyrannical integration.* Integration is a term used to indicate when parts (once differentiated) form a complex system of relationships (composition), which includes a boundary (generalisation) that strongly differentiates a system from its environment – with such deep interdependence and *coherence* that a new whole (or holon) emerges at a hierarchically higher level of being (and in some cases replicates itself). The idea of 'transcend and include' (or transcend and embrace), popularised by Ken Wilber (2006), refers to processes of differentiation and integration understood to drive development and the emergence of new forms from prior forms. 'Integration' and 'emergence' are often paired, but here we will make an important distinction. We will generally use 'integration' to refer to changes in cognitive understanding or mental skill, and 'emergence' to refer to processes in nature, excluding those cognitive processes. This is to be able to differentiate nature, which in a sense, 'just is', does not contradict itself, and is never 'wrong', from human conceptions and belief structures, which can contain

error and demi-reality. In reference to Wilber's 'theory of everything', 'transcend and include' processes in *nature* produce *emergent* objects and phenomena (solar systems, life, animal behaviour, etc.), but these are not our focus. Here, our use of integration points to the hierarchical production of human ideas, values and concepts.

In the face of postmodern critiques of totalising narratives, colonisation and hierarchy in general, Wilber makes the important distinction between 'natural hierarchies' and 'dominator hierarchies'. Wilber says that 'normal hierarchy, or the holism between levels, goes pathological when there's a breakdown between levels and a particular holon assumes a repressive, oppressive, arrogant role of dominance over other holons' (Wilber, 1995, p.23). This distinction is important for correcting those with an ideological aversion to hierarchies, but its broader import often goes unspoken. 'Dominator hierarchy' usually points to clearly oppressive or authoritarian relationships or social systems. But we can extend the idea to the nature of cognitive and conceptual integration in general (i.e. to hierarchical development in cognitive complexity, concepts, theories, etc.). That is, not only 'bad' people and ideas dominate other people and ideas, but there is something 'dominating', and also demi-real, in the nature of *all abstract ideas* as they purport to transcend and include their composite priors. As integration is a culminating step following differentiation, composition, generalisation and/or abstraction, it can 'lock in', or further habituate and harden, all of the pathologies mentioned above for the other operations.

In addition to simplicity, another theme common in dialogues on emergence, transcendence and integration is *coherence*. Coherence is an aspect of processes in which constituent priors engage in a radical interdependence and coordination, leading to a new whole. But, as in the theme of simplicity, if we bracket out 'nature' and focus on *human*-created ideas and concepts, coherence (or convergence) can mask confirmation bias. Likewise, elegance can mask reductionism, and coverage or scope can mask colonisation and oppression. At the extreme, the useful purity of the coherent integrated abstraction becomes the tyrannical and totalising 'cognitive hegemony' of the ideal entity or the ideological vision (what Marshal, 2012, calls the 'grandiose ... pathology of the paradigm of simplicity').

When 'it all seems to fit together' so well, one must question whether the impression of integration is part of a self-perpetuating or delusional system. For example, some narratives referencing 'The Good, the True and the Beautiful', although inspiring and provisionally valid, mask essentialist thinking that draws attention to transcendental ideals and neglects concrete, embodied and practical ethical considerations. Bracketing out inconvenient truths can produce a *feeling* of coherence and elegance. Despite well-meaning attempts to shore up faulty knowledge with empirical facts and rational analysis, in the end, at the level of individual meaning-making, there is surprisingly little distance between the *felt* sense that marks confidence in truth, validity or elegance, and the '*objective* truth' of these things.[11] At the level of conceptual ideas, coherence indicates a self-contained system of consistent elements, but does not guarantee that a system represents reality (although incoherent or self-contradictory systems are less likely to map to reality). In Murray (2019), I discuss the value of developing an inner awareness of the 'epistemic drives' that motivate belief and its confidence. This is one example of resourcing *lower-level* felt-sense perceptions to regulate more complex cognitions.

Integrity and ethics. Integration implies an achieved coherence or congruence among parts, and is thus closely related to the *integrity* of a system. In the domains of psychological health and moral character, integrity is about harmony and alignment within layers of the self-system, for example action matching speech, and speech matching beliefs. Also, a healthy unconscious or deep psyche is measured in part by the integrity (harmony) among one's inner voices and drives. Although ethical reasoning can involve complex perspective-taking, ethical *being* implies modes of embodied integrity not guaranteed by intellectual skill (Posner, 2009). Ethical being must include a deep felt-sense empathy or identification (reciprocity and interpenetration) with the other. According to Roy (2018), right action requires 'perception as participation', which implicates the deepest layers of the psyche, not the most abstract. We also know that complex reasoning, abstraction, generalisation and transcendence, like the witnessing aspect of 'objectification', can create a moral and empathic *distance* between people, and are implicated in the abdication of responsibility and the justification of deception, bureaucracy and dehumanisation (Aguiar et al, 2007; Nussbaum, 1995). The pivot of ethical choice is not around prowess in cognitive complexity per se, but around the ego's gambits into certainty, arrogance, control and power. Here again, the way ahead must include recovering fluid access to foundational human capacities such as connection, trust, care, honour, awe, curiosity and perceptual clarity, often left behind as life stressors create occluding structures and exacerbate egoic drives.[12]

The issues examined in this section, taken together, illustrate the ever-present dangers of pathological or hypertrophied cognitive complexity. Note that, actually, these 'pathologies' are *deviations from an ideal, not deviations from the norm*, and the problems with building hierarchical complexity that we discuss here are *normal and inevitable* – the only thing that varies is the *degree* of 'pathology' and the degree of the actual ethical impact. To further elaborate the problems that come up in over-valorising the concept of Integration, or 'transcend and include', next we will re-examine the common idea of a 'simplicity on the other side of complexity'.

Simplexity and telos: is simplicity guaranteed beyond complexity?

Einstein famously noted that 'everything should be made as simple as possible, but not simpler', and Oliver Wendell Holmes said, 'I would not give a fig for the simplicity this side of complexity, but I would give my life for the simplicity on the other side of complexity'. Simplexity, a concept pointing to the simplicity on the other side of complexity (Broder and Stolfi, 1984; Reiss, 2020), is a popular meme woven into discourse on integration, emergence and development, where a new whole (or holon) 'transcends and includes' the parts, yet 'is more than the sum of the parts'. Simplexity describes the 'paradoxical [and] generative tension between' simplicity and complexity (Cunha and Rego, 2010, p. 86) and can mean 'the ability to balance on the simplicity-complexity fulcrum' to avoid 'analysis paralysis' (Kluger, 2008). Simplexity draws on complex dynamic systems theory, which explains emergent phenomena in terms of self-organisation and emergence, in which new entities form when parts achieve a radical degree of inter-coordination, such that the nature and behaviour of each part depends on the others (see prior footnote on dynamics systems theory). As we have said, emergence in 'natural' processes *does* transcend and *include*, while we have shown that in the domain of human conceptual reasoning and beliefs, emergent ideas (or conceptual integrations) usually transcend while *excluding* some things. The differentiation of natural versus conceptual domains is a rough heuristic we use to illustrate the problematic developmental externalities noted above, which do not arise as such in the development of non-conceptual skills such as sensory-motor skills.[13]

Next, we enumerate some caveats to correct for five common misconceptions related to transcending-and-including or simplicity: (1) a teleological fallacy; (2) a top versus bottom fallacy; (3) a phenomenological note on complexity as a feeling; (4) a deeper analysis of the ubiquity of transcend-and-exclude; and (5) showing how both learning and unlearning can come too early. These discussions support a more nuanced understanding of the relationships between simplicity and complexity in cognitive growth and cultural change, and add to our 'indeterminacy analysis' (Murray, 2006) of developmental models.

> 1. *Eros and teleology.* Following Wilber's lead, development has taken on a teleological bent in some communities. His narrative of Eros and development as an ascending path towards transcendence, wholeness and non-dual unity, all imbued with a type of simplicity and totality, has been used by some to infer a type of inevitability, predictability and essential goodness at the later steps along the path of human development. This perspective follows the lead of mystic Teilhard de Chardin (1999), who speculated that the universe evolves towards an Omega Point – an ultimate state (telos) of cosmic (divine) unification. Like the 'simplicity on the other side', these things seem to await those who work with skilful means, or perhaps just with patience and perseverance. However, emergence is much more of an unpredictable, chaotic process, producing novelty and surprise (Sapolsky, 2017), and it is better to treat emergence as a type of benediction or grace, deserving gratitude, rather than something one has control over. (Wilber mostly agrees, as he says, for example, that awakening is an accident and meditation makes one accident-prone.)
>
> Part of the confusion here is in conflating different *types* of emergent phenomena, some of which are more predictable than others. The fluid skill of riding a bicycle 'emerges' or transcends and includes rather predictably after practice. But the most interesting chaotic processes are much less predictable. We cannot predict the outcomes of climate change, how a child's personality will develop, or what will emerge from a creative brainstorming session. Not only is most emergence unpredictable, but its nature is also a mystery science does not yet understand.[14] And, as we argue throughout, even if transcendence, emergence or integration is achieved in the realm of human meaning-making, it is not necessarily 'Good, True or Beautiful' – it contains demi-reality.
>
> 2. *Is simplicity at the top or bottom?* Wilber and others in transpersonal theory follow perennial religious narratives of enlightenment and awakening that locate the pinnacle of human development at the *top* of a developmental or evolutionary spectrum. It is all too easy to focus on the forces of increasing complexity and forget their opposites. Evolution is a chaotic process that allows for 'backwards' movements of collapse and reductions in complexity (Holling and Gunderson, 2002). Taken as a whole, the additive

nature of complexity means that over time increasingly complex forms will develop *somewhere*, but no single species or form is guaranteed to evolve into greater complexity.

More importantly, what science tells us is that in the upward/forward direction, driven developmentally by moves of differentiation and integration, and/or driven evolutionarily through moves of random variation and selection – evolution tends towards increasing *diversity*, *uniqueness* and *autonomy* among members (Tooby and Cosmides, 1990; Pinker, 2003). Through evolutionary time, the span and diversity of species branches forever *outward*, without any sign of curving back towards some unity (although punctuated by episodes of collapse and reorganisation). Also, anecdotally, it seems that more highly developed individuals tend to express more uniqueness, as opposed to a convergent bland similarity.

We argue that the phenomena associated with psychological maturity and spiritual advancement are more fundamentally about re-gaining access to *primordial* levels of the developmental/cognitive 'stack'. In contrast to a purely ascending model, our model posits a continuous revisit to descending movement, followed by periods of ascending integration. The downward direction points *involutionarily* towards increasing similarity, simplicity and commonality, towards what Jean Gebser called 'the ever-present origin' (1949). Later levels of complexity development tend to *motivate*, *support* and *integrate* ever deeper involutionary journeys of ablation, recovery and revelation. But *not necessarily* – as complexity capacity (ascending) and spiritual clarity (descending) are interrelated but can happen independently, and they involve *structurally different processes* (see Murray, in press).

Ego development (i.e. wisdom skill) represents the combination of the ascending (complexity capacity) and descending (spiritual clarity) movements. At each fulcrum of ego development some structure must be released in order to move forward (and see O'Fallon's, 2020, model of 'necessary but not sufficient' prerequisites for ego development). The latest levels of ego development involve deconstructing (see through) the earliest cognitive structures, processes and differentiating splits (e.g. time, space, inside-vs-outside, self-vs-other, conceptual boundaries, perceptual boundaries, etc.).

Ascending movements of complexity capacity have no fixed upper bound or plateau, but the lower levels *do* have a definitive 'bottom' or 'source', which should be seen as an ideal or a horizon rather than an achievable state or stage. Although people diverge greatly on the level of conceptual beliefs and theories, at ever deeper strata humans have more and more in common with each other and, even more deeply, in common with all mammals and, further, all life forms (and even further, all matter).

The unity and simplicity is at the bottom more than the top. However, our descending movement is not a regression, but releases capacity and insight that is then available to be integrated and interpreted by the higher levels. Thus, in *ego* development (but not in all cognitive development), *height implies depth* (as noted by Freinacht), but (differing from

Freinacht) depth is not a location or state but a structural *volume* – the result of the upper layers of the stack of consciousness having ever more free, open, fluid and resonant access to the lower levels, as and when occluding structures are ablated. This principle is captured in O'Fallon's and Barta's (2020) notion of maximising the 'surface area' of all developmental levels. It is reflected in Torbert (2020): 'vertical development goes both ways, up and down. On the "down" side, development requires becoming more ongoingly aware of our embodied actions … as we approach the [later stage action-logics], we exercise this post-cognitive attention more and more continually, observing ourselves alternating among all the earlier action-logics' (pp. 12–13).

3. *The feeling of simplicity/simplexity*. In human experience, simplicity and elegance are, in large part, feeling states more than an indication of actual cognitive/structural simplicity or elegance (just as confidence in a truth claim is as much about a subjective feeling as a correspondence with reality – see 'epistemic drives' in Murray, 2019). When the fluid skill of riding a bicycle emerges from practising its component parts, the feeling of elegance in the coordinated activity betrays the efficiency following trial-and-error learning, and accompanies the fact that the skill is becoming automated within the unconscious mind, freeing the conscious mind from effortful, focused reflection and feedback cycles. After trial and error and practice, one can find and lock-in (learn) a 'solution' that is simpler because it is both easeful and powerful/effective. In the domain of conceptual ideas the feeling of a simplicity following complexity is more suspect. As we illustrated, ideas that seem to transcend prior ideas can feel simpler or more elegant because they have discarded contradictory, inconveniently messy or seemingly irrelevant details and outliers. That move is always biased (it can be a more valid move *if* the selection biases are made explicit). The notion of 'the simplicity on the other side of complexity' can be a convenient device for vindicating a preferred theory, vision or value, because it 'naturally' emerges from and transcends what developmentally came before. In addition, regressive forms of simplicity, such as romanticism and spirituality-adorned ideologies, can be justified with reference to a simplicity that has emerged 'on the other side' of modernist complexity, and must thus be superior to it.

4. *Fixing and freedom*. Until now we have noted that it is conceptual development, more than sensory-motor development, that excludes as it integrates and transcends. But at a deeper level of analysis, there is a way in which something is left behind in *all* forms of learning. We have already shown how each sub-operation of hierarchical complexity involves tacitly biased pruning, filtering or binding, but the issue is deeper still. Development is understood in terms of creating or modifying connections (structures) in the mind/brain (note that connections can be excitatory or inhibitory). Most salient, there is a new capacity to *do* something – to meet certain challenges and opportunities in a new way, which then forms a foundation for more complex skills and knowledge to be built upon. But, second and less acknowledged, each new structure creates a *fixing* that limits or obscures certain possibilities for thought, action and perception. Each cognitive adaptation encodes a solution to a problem – one that took a significant investment of energy and trial and error to discover (unless it was imprinted quickly and rigidly

during a traumatic event). This conditioning efficiently specifies what to do (or cognise) in similar future scenarios. Alternative solutions or responses are then less likely to be considered, once a handy (provisional) solution is fixed in memory.

To put it metaphorically, once a home's foundation is set, it not only provides substructure for many possibilities, but it also limits the scope of possible homes to be built above it. Thus, when a new capacity is built, some *freedom and potential is lost*.[15] The trade-off is usually productive, at least in the short term, as the benefits of the new structure and its efficiency can outweigh the loss of freedom and access. But as we have shown, development accumulates demi-reality and solutions whose usefulness expires. Cognitive conditioning biases one to respond in a certain way *and to perceive* in a certain way, so each instance of learning also distorts information flow (it enhances some features of each situation and inhibits others).

5. *Learning or unlearning too quickly.* Our discussion highlights the dangers of misapplying developmental theories, but more generally it highlights how human 'epistemic drives' towards the higher, the unitive, the singular, the totalising, the ultimate, the essential and so on, pair dangerously often with egoic or demi-real outcomes. Our analysis of simplicity versus complexity shows that phenomena thought of as at the further reaches of the psychic stack, within either cognitive or spiritual frames, often involve releasing structures to gain access to primordial resources. Clarifying this confusion yields a number of insights. For example, above we warned of the dangers of a misappropriation of *concepts* such as 'the self is empty', 'the world is an illusion' or 'words have no real meaning', but there are also dangers in gaining the authentic *experience* of these things. Radical processes of cognitive deconstruction can take one into nihilism or paralysis when foundational supportive structures are missing, while, in the other direction, they can also ablate structures to leave one without fear of death, pain or embarrassment; and can produce a charismatic confidence in the truth of one's beliefs. They can also lead to a sense of universal perfection that obliterates interest in learning or improvement.

Thus, the fetishisation or imposition of *either* the ascending or the descending paths can lead to misfortune. This is why we need models sophisticated enough to speak to the nuanced dynamics between simplicity and complexity. Such models support ethical outcomes by emphasising the health and integrity of foundational structures as a prerequisite to extreme transformations from either constructing or deconstructing. They inform *when is* the best time for a developmental construction or deconstruction.

Recasting developmental theory through ascending and descending paths

While Commons' theory of hierarchical complexity (MHC) is a general theory of development applicable to vertical development in any skill domain, it is not used explicitly to describe releasing complexity, and for that reason our discussion needed to be extended to consider the matters of 'integrity and ethics' noted above. One can have a cognitive or conceptual understanding of the principles of integrity or ethics, in fact a very sophisticated understanding, and not apply it to the deconstruction or release of aspects of the self-system. Theories of *ego* development (Cook-Greuter and O'Fallon; and the closely related theory of meaning-making maturity by Kegan) are particularly applicable here. Ego development theories touch on this territory because adult ego development requires releasing aspects of the self as one matures. Processes in psychotherapy and contemplative practice that are designed to deconstruct or release harmful beliefs, egoic attachments, habits of perception or behaviour and so on, tend to support ego development. (It is beyond our scope here [see Murray, in press], but a more meticulous treatment of this territory requires more nuanced distinctions between psychological, ethical and spiritual development – but suffice it to say that theories of ego development approach these areas.)

All of the above sets the stage for revised, depth-oriented models of human development (ego development, meaning-making maturity or wisdom skill) that incorporate ascending and descending processes (see also O'Fallon, 2020; Barta, 2020; Torbert, 2020). As our focus here was limited to the interaction between simplicity and complexity, we will only sketch this framework, which is explained further in Murray (in press).

- Development is understood, as in prior models, through processes of differentiation and integration, leading to successive levels that, in one sense, transcend and incorporate prior levels. At a more nuanced level, the process can be described in terms of the sub-operations of hierarchical complexity, which we named differentiation, composition, generalisation, abstraction and integration.

- However, we add that, with each emergent capacity, something is lost. This is especially true in the domain of conceptual ideas and meaning-making, where, as we have shown, each of the sub-operations of cognitive development are likely to produce biases, omissions, obstructions and shadow elements – and leave something inaccessible or in shadow.

- At some point in one's development or life's challenges, certain learned structures become problematic and call to be unlearned or released; and/or certain elements that were left behind call to be recovered or healed. This is especially true of ego development, in which, by its very nature, each successive level of maturity involves the release of some structure to allow for a new ego structure to emerge. This model can be applied to contemplative practices and psychotherapy (as well as an emancipatory or critical philosophy) to clarify the dynamic interactions between the release/destructive/healing movements and the constructive/integrating/learning movements.

- Processes of release/deconstruction/healing can be difficult, disorienting and resistant to change, for three reasons. First, from trauma and recovery theory (Anda et al, 2006; Anderson and Hanslmayr, 2014; Bremner, 2006) we know that some learned structures are closely associated with experiences of fear or pain (and the amygdala), and thus include 'do not go there' occlusions within the learned gestalt (i.e. avoidance, denial, blind spots). Second, lower-strata structures have more structures built on top of them, and thus more is at risk in deconstructing them, producing a different source of resistance. Third (and related to the other two), any learned structures (associations) tied to the ego or sense of self resist deconstruction, as it represents the threat of a type of death (loss of something essential to one's being). All three of these factors can produce the 'immunity to change' (Kegan and Lahey, 2009) that psychotherapeutic, contemplative, emancipatory and cultural transformation practices work to overcome.

- When psychic occlusions (blocks, lacunas, shadows) are released, several things usually happen. First, the occluded 'truths' become available as insights. Second, bound up energy is usually released and generates 'aha' experiences, such as revelation, inspiration, emotional/energetic surges, feelings of clarity and power, and so on. Third, following the descending movement of releasing complexity to recover a lost insight, the insight is available to be re-integrated in new ways into existing structures, so a constructive or ascending movement usually follows the descending deconstruction.

- We also hypothesise that ever-later levels of ego development require the recovery of ever-earlier or more primordial psychic structures. We suggest, following Roy (2018; and as articulated more in Churchill and Murray, 2020), that, while psychotherapy releases structures at the level of personality and social-self, contemplative practices are tuned to release structures at more primitive or primordial perceptual levels, where space/time, inside/outside, self/other, and object differentiation/permanence are originally constructed.

- Because the model is based on developmental theories, which differentiate a many-levelled spectrum of consciousness/cognition, we can, following the STAGES developmental model (O'Fallon, 2020; Barta, 2020), tie unlearning and shadow work to specific developmental levels; that is, processes of unlearning, releasing complexity and shadow-work can be elaborated according the specific level of depth being targeted or healed. Such models can make fine-grained recommendations on when/how/why specific structures should be constructed or deconstructed.

This framework applies to the release of complexity in individual meaning-making and could be extended to apply to collective meaning-making. We also suggest, without argument here, that releasing complexity (accessing lost psychic resources) in this way will contribute to the release of complexity in social (economic, political, technological, …) systems as well.

Conclusions – untangling knots

Metamodernism has been defined descriptively as a distinct cultural phase observed to emerge after postmodernism, which blends and prioritises prior cultural milieus in new ways. Meanwhile, for many scholars (including Freinacht) metamodernism is defined *prescriptively* and structurally as a phase that can and should emerge after postmodernism, if culture evolves in ways that heal pathologies of prior worldviews, and integrates, balances and transcends the seemingly discordant elements of earlier meaning-making frames. Culture, politics, art and technology naturally evolve towards increasing complexity, differentiation and diversity, and those interested in chronicling these domains will find endlessly fascinating patterns and stories to narrate (whether real or projected). Perhaps this multi-perspectival storytelling is part of the swing from the seriousness of postmodernity towards the more playful, earnest and self-aware attitude attributed to metamodernism. Meanwhile, our species is lurching into crisis, and some cannot help but look for the deeper sources of our troubles in the hope of charting a revised course. For this, we need 'theories of change' that have at least a minimum chance of guiding deep transformation. This, of course, needs to be done with a humility and openness generally missing in scholarly and political narratives.

Our modern and postmodern instincts lead with the intellect (whether constructing or deconstructing), which does its work through analytical splitting and detachment. Meanwhile we avoid gazing into the painful and disorienting deeper truths about ourselves – processes that hold the key to healing division and alienation. Even among those interested in alleviating human suffering, the trend is to focus on understanding complexity and using complex reasoning and abstraction to imagine new cultural structures and games. Many using developmental theory as a tool orient to the ascending paths of meta-understanding and transcendent being. This text is an invitation to prioritise releasing complexity over building more complexity, and to draw maps towards the recovery of lost inner treasures alongside maps for scaling new heights.

We align with the romantic sentiment to prioritise the reclamation of foundational skills and virtues, including care, trust, humility, curiosity, authenticity, reverence, respect and so on. Unlike the romantics, we understand this terrain, not in terms of a process of swings, conflicts and counter-corrections between the poles of a polarity (although that describes some of it), but developmentally, through hierarchical structural relationships. Through this lens, foundational skills and resources are *already* present within each of us, but are occluded or distorted by structures of habit and belief at higher hierarchical strata. The job of the intellect then, is to gain just enough additional complexity to understand our entanglements to be able to unlearn and release the hampering knots.

A more hierarchical and depth-oriented understanding of the relationship between complexity and simplicity (reason and compassion, logic and intuition, progress and tradition, transcendence and embodiment, etc.) can inform collective sensemaking and undertaking, to inform decisions on when it is best to increase complexity in a system (e.g. through learning, reflection and adaptation), or release complexity (e.g. through healing, deconstruction or recovery), or do nothing and remain alert as situations go their own course (do no harm).

This simple-sounding path is commensurate with the goals of established maps in contemplative practices, virtue ethics and psychotherapy. But society seems to veer ever further from the goodness and simplicity indicated by such paths: something else is needed. The source of our modern calamities, of the meta-crisis, is *human nature*, and the 'path home' involves a type of species self-understanding (Ord, 2020; Crutzen, 2006). Yet the turn towards radical responsibility for our condition is very difficult and strongly resisted. It will need not only powerful impassioned re-storying, but also more adequate explanatory models. In this chapter we attempt to integrate the insights of fields such as contemplative practice, virtue ethics and psychotherapy with the significant explanatory power of developmental theory. And in so doing, we also aim to dispose developmental theory towards depth, that is, supporting the health, wholeness and clarity of the more foundational levels of the psyche; and away from driving aspirations towards increasing complexity and transcendence. We believe that complexity, transcendence and transformation are best seen as mysteries of emergence and gifts of grace that manifest when the occluding and conflicting lower-strata structures are healed and integrated. This model motivates the difficult journey of healing and deconstruction by showing how this journey can naturally lead to the sought-after goals of insight, clarity, union, wisdom and empowerment. It illuminates the role of complexity as the skilful means to adjudicate how recovered psychic resources are integrated and put to use.

In times of great uncertainty it is essential to be able to locate and embody our essential goodness. But doing so is a complex job given the labyrinth of tangled patterns bequeathed to us. We can let simplicity guide our compass as we grasp the tools of complexity to get the job done.

Bibliography

Abramson, S. (2015). Ten Basic Principles of Metamodernism. *Huffington Post*, *4*, 27.

Aguiar, F., Branas-Garza, P. and Miller, L.M. (2007). Moral Distance and Moral Motivations in Dictator Games. *Jena Economic Research Papers* (2007-47).

Allen, C.R., Angeler, D.G., Garmestani, A.S., Gunderson, L.H. and Holling, C.S. (2014). Panarchy: theory and application. *Ecosystems*, *17*(4), 578–589.

Anda, R.F., Felitti, V.J., Bremner, J.D., Walker, J.D., Whitfield, C.H., Perry, B.D. ... and Giles, W.H. (2006). The Enduring Effects of Abuse and Related Adverse Experiences in Childhood. *European Archives of Psychiatry and Clinical Neuroscience*, *256(3)*, 174–186.

Anderson, J. (1983). *The Architecture of Cognition*. Cambridge, MA: Harvard University Press.

Anderson, M.C. and Hanslmayr, S. (2014). Neural Mechanisms of Motivated Forgetting. *Trends in Cognitive Sciences*, *18*(6), 279–292.

Bar-Yam, Y. (2002). General Features of Complex Systems. *Encyclopedia of Life Support Systems*. UNESCO/EOLSS Publishers: Oxford, UK.

Barta, K. (2020). Seven Perspectives on the STAGES Developmental Model. *Integral Review – A Transdisciplinary and Transcultural Journal For New Thought, Research, and Praxis*, *16*(1), 69–148.

Beck, D.E. and Cowan, C.C. (1996). *Spiral Dynamics: Mastering Values, Leadership, and Change*. Malden, MA: Blackwell Publishing.

Berge, E. (2004). Giving Guns to Children. Available at: http://integralworld.net/berge2.html

Bhaskar, R. (1975). *A Realist Theory of Science*. Brighton, UK: Harvester Press.

Bhaskar, R. (2017). *The Order of Natural Necessity: a kind of introduction to critical realism*. Gary Hawk (ed). UK: self-published.

Bremner, J.D. (2006). Traumatic Stress: effects on the brain. *Dialogues in Clinical Neuroscience*, *8*(4), 445.

Broder, A. and Stolfi, J. (1984). Pessimal Algorithms and Simplexity Analysis. *ACM SIGACT News*, *16*(3), 49–53.

Brown, J. (2002). *The Self-embodying Mind: Process, brain dynamics and the conscious present*. New York: Barrytown/Station Hill.

Churchill, J. and Murray, T. (2020). Integrating Adult Developmental and Metacognitive Theory with Indo-Tibetan Contemplative Essence Psychology. *Integral Review – A Transdisciplinary and Transcultural Journal For New Thought, Research, and Praxis*, *16*(1), 225–331.

Collier, A. (1994). *Critical Realism: An Introduction to Roy Bhaskar's Philosophy*. New York: Verso.

Commons, M.L. and Chen, S.J. (2014). Advances in the Model of Hierarchical Complexity (MHC). *Behavioral Development Bulletin*, *19*(4), 37–50.

Commons, M. L., and Pekker, A. (2008). Presenting the formal theory of hierarchical complexity. *World Futures: Journal of General Evolution*, *64*(5-7), 375–382

Commons, M.L. and Richards, F.A. (1984). A General Model of Stage Theory. In M.L. Commons, F.A. Richards and C. Armon (Eds.), *Beyond Formal Operations: Late adolescent and adult cognitive development*, pp. 120–141. New York: Praeger.

Cook-Greuter, S. (2004). Making the Case for a Developmental Perspective. *Industrial and Commercial Training*, *36(7)*, 275–281.

Cook-Greuter, S. (2013). Assumption Versus Assertions: Separating Hypotheses from Truth in the Integral Community. *Journal of Integral Theory and Practice*, 8.

Cooper, B. (2018). The Metamodern Condition: A Report on 'The Dutch School' of Metamodernism. Medium.com essay, April 19, 2018.

Crutzen, P.J. (2006). The Anthropocene. In Thomas Krafft (Ed.) *Earth System Science in the Anthropocene* (pp. 13–18). Berlin, Heidelberg: Springer.

Cunha, M.P. and Rego, A. (2010). Complexity, Simplicity, Simplexity. *European Management Journal, 28*, 85–94.

de Bono, E. (1995). Serious Creativity. *The Journal for Quality and Participation, 18*(5), 12.

de Chardin, T.P. (1999). *The Human Phenomenon*. Sussex: Academic Press.

Donald, M. (1991). *Origins of the Modern Mind: Three stages in the evolution of culture and cognition*. MA: Harvard University Press.

Elster, J. (1999). *Alchemies of the Mind: Rationality and the emotions*. Cambridge, UK: Cambridge University Press.

Ferrer, J.N. (2011). Participatory Spirituality and Transpersonal Theory: A Ten-Year Retrospective. *Journal of Transpersonal Psychology, 43*(1).

Fischer, K. (1980). A Theory of Cognitive Development: The control and construction of hierarchies of skills. *Psychological Review, 87*(6), 477–531.

Fischer, K.W. (2008). Dynamic Cycles of Cognitive and Brain Development: Measuring growth in mind, brain and education. In Battro, A.M., Fischer, K.W. and Léna, P.J. (Eds.). (2010). *The Educated Brain: Essays in Neuroeducation*. Cambridge: Cambridge University Press.

Fischer, K.W., Yan, Z. and Stewart, J. (2003). Adult Cognitive Development: Dynamics in the developmental web. In J. Valsiner and K. Connolly (Eds.), *Handbook of Developmental Psychology*, pp. 491–516. Thousand Oaks, CA: Sage.

Freinacht, H. (2017). *The Listening Society: A Metamodern Guide to Politics* (Book One). UK: Metamoderna. Kindle Edition.

Freinacht, H. (2020). *Nordic Ideology: A Metamodern Guide to Politics* (Book Two). UK: Metamoderna. Kindle Edition.

Gebser, J. (1949). *The Ever-Present Origin*. (N. Barstad and A. Mickunas, Trans.). Athens, OH: Ohio University Press.

Goleman, D. (1995). *Emotional Intelligence*. New York: Bantam Books.

Habermas, J. (1990). *Moral Consciousness and Communicative Action*. MIT Press.

Hall, B.P. (1990). *Developing Human Values*. International Values Institute of Marian College, 45 South National Avenue, Fond du Lac, WI.

Holling, C.S. (2001). Understanding the Complexity of Economic, Ecological, and Social Systems. *Ecosystems, 4*(5), 390–405.

Holling, C. and Gunderson, L. (2002). *Panarchy*. Island Press.

Holmes, Oliver Wendell. https://en.wikiquote.org/wiki/Oliver_Wendell_Holmes_Jr.

Hutson, M. (2012). *The 7 laws of magical thinking: How irrational beliefs keep us happy, healthy, and sane*. Penguin.

James, W. (1909a). *The Meaning of Truth*. Cambridge, MA: Harvard UP, republished 1979.

Jung, C.G. (1968). *Man and his Symbols*. Garden City, NY: Dell Publishing.

Kahneman, D. (2011). *Thinking, Fast and Slow*. New York: Macmillan.

Kegan, R. (1994). *In Over our Heads: The mental demands of modern life*. Cambridge, MA: Harvard University Press.

Kegan, R. and Lahey, L. (2009). *Immunity to Change: How to Overcome It and Unlock the Potential in Yourself and Your Organization*. Boston: Harvard Business Press.

Kluger, J. (2008). *Simplexity: why simple things become complex (and how complex things can be made simple)*. Hachette UK.

Koestler, A. (1967). *The Ghost in the Machine* (1990 reprint ed.). NY: Penguin Group.

Kohlberg, L. (1973). The Claim to Moral Adequacy of a Highest Stage of Moral Judgment. *Journal of Philosophy, 70*(18), 630–646.

Korzybski, A. (1958). *Science and Sanity: An introduction to non-Aristotelian systems and general semantics*. Lakeville, CT: Institute of General Semantics.

Laird, J., Newell, A. and Rosenbloom, P. (1987). SOAR: An Architecture for General Intelligence. *Artificial Intelligence, 33*.

Lorenz, E.N. (1963). Deterministic Nonperiodic Flow. *Journal of the Atmospheric Sciences, 20(2)*, 130–141.

Luhmann, N. (1995). *Social Systems*. Stanford, CA: Stanford University Press.

Marshal, P. (2012). Toward an Integral Realism. *Journal of Integral Theory and Practice, 7*(4), 1–34.

McGilchrist, I. (2019). *The Master and his Emissary: The divided brain and the making of the Western world*. Yale University Press.

Menand, L (2001). *The Metaphysical Club*. New York: Farrar, Straus, and Giroux.

Murray, T. (2006). Collaborative knowledge building and integral theory: On perspectives, uncertainty, and mutual regard. *Integral Review*, Vol. 2, 210–268.

Murray, T. (2011). Integralist Mental Models of Adult Development: Provisos from a Users Guide. *Integral Leadership Review* Vol. 11, No. 2; to appear in Esbjörn-Hargens (Ed) book *True But Partial: Essential Critiques of Integral Theory*.

Murray, T. (2019). Knowing and Unknowing Reality: A Beginner's and Expert's Developmental Guide to Post-Metaphysical Thinking. *Integral Review*, January 2019, Vol. 15, No. 1, 128–249.

Murray, T. (2020, in press). Hierarchical Complexity and Human Suffering: on ascending and descending paths toward human potential. To appear in *Integral Review*.

Nussbaum, M (1995). Objectification. *Philosophy and Public Affairs, 24*(4), 249–291.

O'Fallon, T. (2020). States and STAGES: Waking up Developmentally. *Integral Review – A Transdisciplinary and Transcultural Journal For New Thought, Research, and Praxis, 16*(1), 13–26.

O'Fallon, T., Polister, N., Blazej Neradiek, M. and Murray, T. (2020). The Validation of a New Scoring Method for Assessing Ego Development Based on Four Dimensions of Language. *Heliyon, 6*(3), E03472, March 01, 2020: https://doi.org/10.1016/j.heliyon.2020.e03472

Ord, T. (2020). *The Precipice: existential risk and the future of humanity*. Hachette Books.

Pinker, S. (2003). *How the Mind Works*. Penguin UK.

Ponsen, M., Taylor, M. E. and Tuyls, K. (2009). Abstraction and Generalization in Reinforcement Learning: A summary and framework. In *International Workshop on Adaptive and Learning Agents* (pp. 1–32). Berlin, Heidelberg: Springer.

Posner, R.A. (2009). *The Problematics of Moral and Legal Theory*. Harvard University Press.

Prigogine, I. and Stengers, I. (2018). *Order Out of Chaos: Man's new dialogue with nature*. Verso Books.

Reiss, M. (2020). Simplexity: A Hybrid Framework for Managing System Complexity. In *Harnessing Knowledge, Innovation and Competence in Engineering of Mission Critical Systems*. IntechOpen.

Roy, B. (2016). A Manifesto for the Open Participatory Organization. Medium.com, Feb 18, 2016: https://medium.com/open-participatory-organized/a-manifesto-for-open-participation-60b62d327684

Roy, B. (2018). Awakened Perception – Perception as Participation. *Integral Review, 14*(1), 222–287.

Roy, B. and Trudel, J. (2011). Leading the 21st century: The conception-aware, object-oriented organization. *Integral Leadership Review*, August, 2011.

Sagiv, L., Arieli, S., Goldenberg, J. and Goldschmidt, A. (2010). Structure and Freedom in Creativity: The interplay between externally imposed structure and personal cognitive style. *Journal of Organizational Behavior, 31*(8), 1086–1110.

Sapolsky, R.M. (2017). *Behave: The biology of humans at our best and worst*. New York: Penguin.

Sellars, W. (1956). Empiricism and the Philosophy of Mind, in In H. Feigl and M. Scriven (Eds) *The Foundations of Science and the Concepts of Psychoanalysis*. Minnesota Studies in the Philosophy of Science, Vol. I. Minneapolis, MN: University of Minnesota Press.

Shermer, M. (2011). *The Believing Brain: From Ghosts and Gods to Politics and Conspiracies – How We Construct Beliefs and Reinforce Them as Truths*. New York: Henry Holt.

Snowden, D. (2000). Cynefin: A sense of time and place, the social ecology of knowledge management. In C. Despres and D. Chauvel (Eds), *Knowledge Horizons* (pp. 237–265). Oxford, United Kingdom: Butterworth-Heinemann.

Snowden, D.J. (2002). Complex Acts of Knowing: Paradox and Descriptive Self-Awareness. *Journal of Knowledge Management, 6*, 100–111.

Sonenshein, S. (2017). *Stretch*. New York: HarperCollins.

Stacey, R.D. (1995). The Science of Complexity: An alternative perspective for strategic change processes. *Strategic Management Journal, 16*(6), 477–495.

Stein, Z. (2008). Myth-busting and Metric-making: Refashioning the discourse about development. Excursus for Integral Leadership Review. *Integral Leadership Review, 8*(5).

Stein, Z. (2019). *Education in a Time Between Worlds: Essays on the Future of Schools, Technology and Society*. Bright Alliance Publ.

Stein, Z. and Heikkinen, K. (2008). On Operationalizing Aspects of Altitude: An introduction to the Lectical Assessment System for integral researchers. *Journal of Integral Theory and Practice, 3*(1), 105–139.

Stokes, P.D. (2005). *Creativity From Constraints: The psychology of breakthrough*. Springer Publishing Company.

Todres, L.A. (2000). Embracing Ambiguity: transpersonal development and the phenomenological tradition. *Journal of Religion and Health, 39*(3), 227–238.

Tooby, J. and Cosmides, L. (1990). On the Universality of Human Nature and the Uniqueness of the Individual: The role of genetics and adaptation. *Journal of Personality, 58*(1), 17–67.

Torbert, B. (2020). *Warren Buffett's and Your Own Seven Transformations of Leadership*. Global Leadership Associates Press.

Torbert, B. and Erfan, A. (2020). Possible Mistakes of Late Action-Logic Actors in a Polarized World. *Integral Review 16(2)*.

Turner, L. (2015). Metamodernism: A brief introduction. From www.metamodernism.com/2015/01/12/metamodernism-a-brief-introduction/

Vermeulen, T., and van den Akker, R. (2010). Notes on Metamodernism. *Journal of Aesthetics and Culture, 2*(1), 5677.

Vervaeke, J., Mastropietro, C. and Miscevic, F. (2017). *Zombies in Western Culture: A Twentieth Century Crisis*. Cambridge: Open Book Publishers.

Washburn, M. (1988). *The Ego and the Dynamic Ground: A transpersonal theory of human development*. Albany, NY: SUNY Press.

Whitehead, A.N. (1929). *Process and Reality: An essay in cosmology*. Free Press.

Wilber, K. (1995), *Sex, Ecology, Spirituality: The Spirit of Evolution*. Boulder: Shambhala Publications.

Wilber, K. (2000). *Integral Psychology: consciousness, spirit, psychology, therapy*. Boston, MA: Shambhala.

Wilber, K. (2006). *Integral Spirituality*. Boulder: Shambhala Publications.

Williams, R. (2016). Liberalism and Capitalism have Hollowed Out Society. *New Statesman*. October 18.

Winther, R. G. (2014). James and Dewey on Abstraction. *The Pluralist*, 9(2), 1–28.

Zak, P.J. and Knack, S. (2001). Trust and growth. *The Economic Journal, 111* (April), 295–321.

Notes

1. As a self-referential corroboration of our framework: the basic ideas being proposed here are not very complex. Most of this text aims at *deconstructing* common beliefs and concepts. Similarly, in projects to reimagine capitalism, or citizenship, healthcare, etc., the main effort is in getting people to unlearn extant assumptions and mental models.

2. Cunha and Rego (2010) describe the 'unintentional complexity' that accumulates in man-made and man-inhabited systems. For example, the 'cumulative by-product of organizational changes, big and small, that over the years weave complications (often invisibly) into the way work is done [and] creates organizational inefficiencies, lack of response capacity or organizational inertia, as well as a focus on the inner reality of the organization' (p. 86).

3. The phrase 'regression in the service of transcendence' has been used in discussions of related phenomena (Washburn, 1988), which, similar to our description, Todres (2000) says is more of an 'opening' than an actual regression. Ferrer (2011) emphases a 'participatory' and 'extending' movement, which is more horizontal than ascending or descending. In fact, the healthy holistic functioning of personalities and cultures is possible without an agonising 'descending' journey, in the rare cases where little shadow material had accumulated in the first place.

4. The later-forming *mythical* strata of the psyche is a place of archetypal personalities who can both delight and manipulate us; and of imaginative and hopeful narratives, often unfettered by logic, empirical truths or empathic reciprocity.

5. Jon Elster (1999, p. 11) has a wonderful analysis of how any popular proverb admits to an equally valid opposite. For example, we have 'like attracts like' and 'opposites attract'; we say, 'absence makes the heart grow fonder' and 'out of sight out of mind'.

6. Note that level, stage and strata are relatively synonymous in our discussion. Strata best emphasises that these are always-present layers of processing that build upon each other, as opposed to categories that one moves into after exiting a prior stage.

7. Dynamic systems theory makes use of non-linear processes and concepts, including differentiation, integration, self-reference, self-organisation, emergence, chaos, scale-invariance, bifurcation, dissipative structures, sensitivity to initial conditions, etc. (Lorenz, 1963; Prigogine, 2018; Sapolsky, 2017; Luhman, 1995; Bar-Yam, 2002).

8. In these theories, hierarchical coordinations, applied iteratively level by level, 'produce a scale of [about 14] levels that increase in complexity and integration [producing an] interval scale for assessing the dynamics of development and variation' (Fischer et al, 2003, p. 497; and see Stein and Heikkinen, 2008).

9. Two neo-Piagetian developmental theories have come to prominence as representing the most sophisticated and powerful maps of human development: Michael Commons' Model of Hierarchical Complexity (MHC) and Kurt Fischer's Skill Theory (Commons et al, 1984; 2014; Fischer et al, 1980; 2008). Initially developed separately, they have been shown to correspond extremely well. We use Commons because his definition of development is more audaciously axiomatic.

10. Ponsen et al (2009): abstraction 'hides or removes less critical details while preserving desirable properties. By definition, this implies loss of information […while generalisation …] defines similarities between objects [without affecting] the object's representation. By definition, this implies no loss of information' (p. 6).

11 Objective truth requires a collective process that scrutinises individual conclusions. Collective meaning-making is of course also quite susceptible to bias and demi-reality – an important topic outside our scope.
12 Note that capacities such as compassion, empathy and responsibility are not included in this list, because they require a developmental sophistication that comes after the 'foundational' capacities listed.
13 A related dichotomy comes from dual-processing models of cognition – e.g. unconscious vs conscious, fast vs slow thinking, primary vs secondary cognition, left vs right hemispheres, etc. (overlapping but non-equivalent models; see Kahneman, 2011; McGilchrist, 2019). *Very* roughly, the unconscious/fast/primary/implicit brain functions map to our 'nature' category, and the conscious/slow/secondary/explicit to conceptual/symbolic/rational thinking category. The difficulty in this distinction is that the patterns of splitting, categorising and linearising compelled by secondary cognitive processes can become ensconced and habituated within the unconscious (primary) layer. We could say that the processes of unlearning/release we are emphasising work primarily on such structures. Although beyond our scope here, some resolution is found in differentiating cognitive processes from content or structure.
14 As Daniel Schmachtenberger quips, '[emergence is] considered the closest thing to magic that is a scientifically admissible term': www.meetup.com/Sacramento-Politics-and-Philosophy-Group/events/zwwhbryzjbdc
15 This is similar to the notion of supporting creativity with 'generative constraints' – setting limits can increase creativity within the 'sandbox' of the constraints, while it also prohibits possibilities outside that sandbox (De Bono, 1995; Stokes, 2005; Sonenshein, 2017). For example, Sagiv et al (2010, p. 1,086) found that, in general, 'externally imposed structure increases creativity'.

6 Metamodern Sociology
An ironically sincere invitation to future scholars
Daniel P. Görtz

IN THIS chapter, we get to know another side of Hanzi Freinacht, that 'mysterious and outrageous philosopher of metamodernism, living at the crossroads of fact and fiction'. Hanzi is largely an online phenomenon, known through blog posts and social media. He is the author of theory books that break every academic rule and décor you can think of, *The Listening Society* (2017) and *Nordic Ideology* (2019). Here, Hanzi stays much closer to what can be expected from an academic paper or book chapter – albeit still with a dash of the classical essay style, taking up more space for his own reflection and commentary.

Hanzi asks, quite simply: 'What is metamodern sociology'? If sociology is the social science that views society *as society*, is there then not an intrinsic link between, on the one hand, sociological understanding and research and, on the other hand, a philosophy that seeks to eject itself from the conceptual, cultural, political and spiritual confines of modern society – metamodernism? Hanzi argues that, yes, this is the case. Metamodernism, to be established as an underlying understanding of society, must be sociological in its grasp of the relations that are to be redefined; and sociology, to fulfil its promise as a holistic and scientific study of society, to become the rich source of societal self-reflection it was once imagined as, must become metamodern.

To achieve this end, Hanzi also delves into the task of defining metamodernism, differentiating between six different meanings, as he tries to steer clear of some common mistakes and confusions that prevent this field from blossoming. With a clearer understanding of the term metamodernism, it is easier to see how it can serve as a next step of the evolution of sociology, the promise of which is to provide maps of interpretation, meaning and direction in a global society shaken by dramatic changes and the advent of the internet.

On his way towards this goal, Hanzi describes how he views the historical development of sociology, from a modern sociology, to a postmodern sociology, and then proposes tenets and concerns for a metamodern sociology. This is an invitation to brave scholars and social scientists who would like to redefine their field.

Metamodern sociology

If there is to be a marriage between the terms metamodernism and sociology, let us begin with the basics.

'Metamodern sociology' can mean two quite different things, viewed from opposite but mirroring positions:

- First meaning: The descriptive sociology of metamodern society – its emergence, social logic, structures, causes, consequences, dynamics, central processes, culture and lived experience. This line of inquiry expands into sociological descriptions of 'metamodernity' as a certain societal condition, and into 'metamodernism' as a social, political, cultural and academic movement. In other words: this is sociology applied to metamodernism; sociology in any qualitative or quantitative form with metamodernity and/or metamodernism as its object of study, 'the sociology of metamodernism', if you like. As such, it can be categorised alongside other 'hyphen sociologies' like the sociology of poverty, the sociology of religion, the sociology of death – and so forth.

- Second meaning: The discipline of sociology itself, as understood, practised and developed from sensibilities pertaining to the culture and philosophy of metamodernism. This guides us towards the question: what does society look like from a metamodern lens? How does a metamodern sensibility (in terms of ethics, ontology, spirituality, aesthetics, epistemology and political goals) shape the discipline of sociology, if, indeed, such a disciplinary delineation is still deemed appropriate to the metamodern observer? Such questions can be answered only through developments of sociology proper, that is, the proposition and argumentation for novel theory, meta-theory, methods, methodology and the topics and rationales for research questions within sociology.

The two meanings are, unsurprisingly, intertwined. Hence, they should also be discussed together, reflecting upon each other. Yet they must be clearly distinguished as separate issues, and only then be carefully braided as two streams.

This chapter focuses primarily upon the latter of the two – sociology as viewed from a metamodern understanding – but it ends with briefly revisiting the topic of how metamodern society can be studied, a few suggestions primarily for aspiring scholars of this uncharted field.

Against periodisation

A guiding light in both angles of approach, however, is that there is indeed something that can meaningfully be called metamodern (a description of certain cultural properties), metamodernity (a state of affairs in society, a certain configuration) and metamodernism (a certain sensibility, movement or project). This is and remains the working hypothesis of metamodern sociology.

At the heart of it all is a simple developmental model: the idea that societal development occurs through a number of profound, qualitative shifts: from *modern* society, to a *postmodern* deconstructive critique of the latter, to a metamodern synthesis of these two, the latter taking deliberate steps to reshape modern society and its prevailing social logic, drawing upon, but not limiting itself to, the postmodern critique. After the postmodern deconstruction, follows the metamodern reconstruction. Or, rather, reconstruction is the endpoint of deconstruction; the former follows from the latter.

That is, ultimately, what metamodernism is about; it takes modern society itself as its object, picks it apart with a postmodern sensibility, and then begins to put the parts together in new ways, into new relations, human and posthuman (including other fundamental categories such as technology, the biosphere and non-human animals). Modernity flows from the dynamics of premodern society (traditional, or what I have termed post-Faustian, which in turn builds upon earlier stages (Freinacht, 2017)); postmodernism can only emerge from the backdrop of modern society; metamodernity (or: metamodern society) emerges as people can conceptually and socially step outside of the 'modern world' and view it as an object that can be reshaped from the inside out, in synthesis with the multiple anti-theses produced by postmodern critique.

A few words about this progression, from the modern, to the postmodern, to the metamodern, would be in order. There is, in my mind, a widespread misunderstanding of how this is to be approached – the fallacy of *periodisation*, a description of historical epochs that are taken to have certain properties: a modern period, a postmodern period and a metamodern period.

Adorno famously wrote that 'Modernity is a qualitative, not a chronological, category' (Adorno, 1978). This comment incisively captures the crux of the matter: viewed from a sociological vantage point, there is little meaning in historical periods and years. Historiography, in the words of Wilhelm Windelband (1894/2015), is ideally an entirely *ideographic* enterprise, that is, it describes chains of events *qua* events, and it focuses on the particularity of facts and emergences located specifically within space, time and sequence. Sociology is located within the social sciences, and as such it always strives towards at least some generalisability, that is, it is ultimately what Windelband would have called a *nomothetic* endeavour, a study of regularities (or even 'laws') of the social universe. Periodisation can never be truly ideographic nor nomothetic. Obviously, modernity did not 'occur' during a certain year; nor did it end and postmodernity begin at another year. As the 19th- and early 20th-century classical sociologists struggled to grasp it, modernity is a certain pattern of widely interconnected phenomena, certain abstracted qualities that seem to describe deep-rooted properties of a society in its entirety: the explanatory relations between said properties.

Much confusion has come from this fallacy, and, as a result, the exploration of the modern, postmodern and metamodern quickly reaches an analytical impasse in many, or even most, of its students. Vermeulen and van den Akker (2017) have suggested that metamodernism is a period shaped by certain events, but they cannot, given the reasons stated above, provide any full description or explanation as to which pattern connects these events and this particular time period. Correspondingly, contemporary sociologists have been reluctant to describe the present period as 'postmodern' and have suggested terms such as 'radicalised modernity' (Giddens, 2013), 'late modernity' or 'liquid modernity' (Bauman, 2000), 'second modernity' (Beck and Grande, 2010) and so on – perhaps a wise caution. In my view, these sociologists notice the fact that, yes, there are indeed new trends and social logics cropping up in society, but that the prevailing social logic is fundamentally still guided by what may be described as modernity.

The simple reason for this confusion, I believe, is that the question is incorrectly posed. The answer to the question of *'when* is modernity/postmodernity/metamodernity?' always depends upon the more fundamental question of *what* each of these *is*. The answer to that question, in turn, depends less upon certain historical events, and more upon how these three categories are defined: firstly, as different sequences of unfolding logics or dialectics, the latter following from the dynamics of the former; secondly, as different aspects or dimensions of each (I will describe six such different aspects shortly).

The idea of 'the metamodern' is thus ultimately a heuristic tool; it does not presuppose exactly what 'metamodern' is or means, but it stipulates that such a phenomenon can be explored and that the concept's predictive value can increase as the descriptive, deductive, analytical and interpretive concepts are developed and refined.

In accordance with metamodern sensibilities, the concept of metamodernism can itself be viewed as being held with 'sincere irony' – a synthesis between the *sincere* belief in progress (of developmental psychology, stage models of perspectives upon the world, dialectical dynamics that seem to stabilise around certain equilibria), and the *ironic* distance to any such models and sense of direction, an admission that our models and paradigms are always limited and, ultimately, partly mistaken. But even 'the synthesis' can be taken as too literal, too monolithic and uncritically held as a belief. Hence, the metamodern sociologist's belief in metamodernism is rather a *proto-synthesis*, a proposed, ironically held heuristic of descriptive and prescriptive models of society and reality.

Metamodernism in six dimensions

With this pragmatically self-depreciating view in mind, the complex we call metamodern-metamodernity-metamodernism can be viewed in six distinct but deeply interrelated ways:

1. As a cultural *phase* (with a corresponding 'sensibility') that comes after and redeems the cynicism and irony of postmodernism with a 'new sincerity' that coexists peacefully with postmodern irony (such as in the work of Vermeulen and van den Akker (2010), comparable to the work of cultural theorists on post-postmodernism (Nealon, 2012), digimodernism (Kirby, 2009), transmodernism (Dussel, 2004), and performativism (Eschelman, 2008) – describing trends within culture at large, pop culture, visual arts, theatre, architecture, literature, music, film and so forth);

2. As a developmental *stage* of society and its institutions, one that emerges and stabilises after modern society (such as my own work, comparable to Ken Wilber's Integral Theory (2007), Jürgen Habermas's (1985) and Günter Dux's (2000/2011) developmental sociologies, ideas about new Kondratiev waves of economic life, like Paul Mason's (2015) 'postcapitalism', economic stage theories like Klaus Schwab's 'Fourth Industrial Revolution' (2016), Manuel Castells' 'network society' (1996/2009) and, more indirectly, the holistic sociologies of Roy Bhaskar and Edgar Morin);

3. As a *meta-meme*, that is, a deep-lying pattern-of-patterns within the realm of meaning-making and symbols, with its own social, economic and technological dynamics, that is likely to emerge together in a coherent, non-arbitrary manner in historical sequence, where the different parts resonate with one another and mutually reinforce each other, particularly around the emergence of a digitised internet society (this is explored in my own upcoming work, *The 6 Hidden Patterns of History*, and it has a precedent in, for example, the work of Jean Gebser (1986/1966));

4. As a relatively late and rare *stage of personal development* – cognitive, emotional, existential and relational (as studied in adult development psychology, where later stages of a more self-transforming mind are studied in different ways by such theorists and researchers as Robert Kegan, Susanne Cook-Greuter, Michael L. Commons, Michael Basseches, Kurt Fischer, Theo Dawson, Terri O'Fallon, Clare Graves, Gerald Young and others, myself included with my work on the 'effective value meme' of a person);

5. As a certain *paradigm*, with its own philosophy with accompanying theologies (which includes a family of ideas concerning ontology, epistemology, aesthetics and ethics – such as Karen Barad's (2007) agential realism and onto-epistemology, Quentin Meillassoux's (2008) speculative realism, perspective-participatory views of reality and 'entanglement', belief in potential rather than actuality as the ground of reality, developmental views of emergence, chaos, complexity and cybernetics, multi-perspectivalism, the revisiting of process philosophy in Whitehead and Peirce (see Stanford Encyclopedia, 2017), critiques of anthropocentrism and humanism, holistic

views that put spirituality and studies first-person phenomenological or experiential perspectives at the centre, developmental semiotics and cybersemiotics (Brier, 2007), syntheistic theologies (Bard and Söderqvist, 2014), transdisciplinary studies and meta-theories which map out non-arbitrary relations between different injunctions into reality, fractal perspectives of reality and phenomenological experience in which for instance the relations between natural and social sciences are viewed as contained within one another in fractal patterns, relationality as an ontological basis, deconstructive critiques of the naive experience of the self as a discrete object, transpersonal perspectives that try to go beyond ideas of 'the individual' and 'the collective', critiques of linear statistical inference in favour of the study of emergent patterns, a holistic view of information theory, and an embrace of both-and thinking and a self-critical embrace of paradox and the brokenness of reality's self-organisation; these abstractly interrelated strands represent different versions of neo-Hegelianism and post-Kantianism, tending towards 'non-dual' spirituality and a distancing from Cartesian dualism in its various, often subtle, forms). Obviously, the interconnecting links between all of these philosophical projects are far from evident; rather, I hold there is a profound structure to the metamodern mind, the contours of which can thus far only be vaguely sketched, and much work remains to be done in terms of formulating the key principles underlying the metamodern philosophy proper, as well as within the sociology of knowledge from which social contexts such ideas emerge;

6. As a certain *movement* or *project*, emerging primarily in relatively 'progressive' countries and segments of 'developed' societies, largely from postmodern strata of the population (animated by sentiments of oscillation, superposition (in the quantum sense), or both-and thinking, where you hold two polarities in mind at the same time, such as sincere irony, informed naivete, magical realism, relative utopia, the crossroads of fact and fiction). This movement – with its intermeshed strands of cultural, aesthetic, political, psychotherapeutic and organisational efforts – is driven by ideals of creating open participatory processes, collective intelligence, inner work and 'embodiment', co-development, and an experimental view of rituals as well as attempts to 're-construct' everyday life and social reality, and attempts to bridge and synthesise perspectives of the Left and Right and the different sides of the culture wars, for example between traditionalists and progressives. Metamodernists tend to emphasise inner development as a political and sociological issue, deliberation, process and perspective-taking as political tools, and focus on the intersection of inner depth and external complexity. The demographics of this movement is primarily drawn from what I have termed the Quadruple-H population (Hipsters, Hackers, Hippies and Hermetics – briefly mentioned towards the end of this chapter), which can also be termed as 'the creative class'.

As the reader may have noticed, periodisation is not one of these six categories. Metamodernism is not a period, not an epoch. It is what Sean Esbjörn-Hargens (2010) has termed a 'multiple ontological object'; it is many realities at once, and no single aspect or angle-of-attack captures it fully or even very meaningfully and usefully. Metamodernism is thus a cultural phase, *and* a developmental stage of society, *and* an abstracted meta-meme, *and* a stage of personal development (with different complexly intertwined subcategories thereof), *and* a philosophical paradigm, *and* a movement with a certain project for culture and society.

I would like to be direct here: until scholars, students and other agents of metamodernism learn to distinguish between these six meanings of 'metamodern', there can be rather little progress made towards metamodern understanding and goals in society. Attempts at periodisation will remain arbitrary, bordering on nonsensical, unless one specifies which aspect of the metamodern one studies.

Clearing the analytical fog

Let us consider a few examples of analytical difficulties of this complex, multi-dimensional landscape:

- There can be metamodern elements in singular works of arts and culture long before today's wave of metamodern arts (Salvador Dalí, for instance, is generally termed to be a 'modernist' in art history textbooks, but a quick analysis of his paintings reveals a strong postmodern current with significant metamodern elements);

- There can be minorities of people with metamodern personalities and values in a society that is dominated by modern values and institutions, but in which there are also large minorities with premodern and postmodern values and corresponding stages of personal development;

- There can be philosophers who work from an underlying metamodern paradigm but who fail to see and name that same paradigm (or choose not to, for various reasons);

- There can be metamodernist movements manned and driven by people who do not embody corresponding stages of personal development;

- There can be agents who tap into the social logics pertaining to the metamodern meta-meme, but who do not themselves think and act in accordance with metamodern cultural sensibilities;

- There can be leaders who enact the cultural logic of the metamodern phase in their communication and agency, but who are themselves by no means metamodernists and do not lead metamodern movements (Seth Abramson has made this case for Donald Trump (Albanese, 2018));

- There can be artists who partake in exploring metamodernism as a movement and cultural phase, but whose work is largely devoid of metamodern elements;

- There can be entire societies affected by the social logic of the metamodern meta-meme, but the institutions of which are still modern or even premodern …

… and so forth. Hopefully, then, the analytical fog can clear.

Different methods and analytical tools are required to study, understand and enact each of these six dimensions. Metamodern sociology must be one that non-arbitrarily traverses this landscape of six dimensions, selecting and coordinating appropriate theories and methods to understand the different dimensions and their interrelations. For instance, an understanding of the metamodern stage of personal development cannot be reached through further developments of cultural theory; it requires a solid foundation in developmental psychology and adult development. Likewise, developmental psychology alone cannot guide the understanding of how metamodern institutions can be created in society for it to self-organise at a transnational, global level, tackling wicked issues such as climate change and technological disruption. All six paths must be mastered, not by one single person (that is all but impossible), but by the community of students of metamodernism. These students must, in turn, become capable of communicating across these six dimensions and be able to grant recognition and fair, critical appraisal of one another's work from their respective angles.

As for periodisation, this can only become meaningful *retrospectively*, once the dimensions of study are specified. If one argues, for instance, that we live today in a cultural phase of metamodernism, and one finds examples thereof in arts and popular culture – which are distinct from postmodern sensibilities of critique, irony and deconstruction – then one misses the obvious fact that we do *not* today live in a society organised around metamodern institutions, that is, institutions created against the backdrop of a metamodern philosophical paradigm and governed by populations at metamodern stages of personal development. In other words, this one-dimensional analysis misconstrues a late modern society, with postmodern elements, as being 'metamodern' and thus cuts the impetus for a truly metamodern movement short.

Likewise, naturally, modernity can be periodised either as a 20th-century phenomenon, as stretching back to the beginnings of industrialism, as rooted in the Enlightenment, as emerging during the Scientific Revolution of the 1600s, as appearing in the arts and culture of the Renaissance when perspective entered into painting and the modern Western musical scale was completed in the 1400s, to precocious late medieval thinkers of science and progress like Roger Bacon – or even to forms of proto-modernity in antiquity and the state formation of Qin China. Modernity is a qualitative, not a chronological, category.

The same can be said about postmodernism, the earliest signs of which harken back to the Enlightenment (with Rousseau); clear forms begin to emerge during the 19th century, dominant forms take hold in what is conventionally called 'modern' art in the first half of the 20th century, and clearly formulated philosophies of postmodernism (often tied to poststructuralism) stretch back to at least the 1960s – then becoming a dominant social logic or phase in 1990s popular culture.

I would like to stop for an additional caveat. A distinction should be made between students of metamodernism who stop at the *descriptive* stage of inquiry, and those (like myself) who combine a descriptive and *prescriptive* approach. I believe that, if one sees and understands metamodernism in this richer and more multi-dimensional sense, one cannot remain entirely neutral to the developmental path of society; one is morally compelled to act to bring about a metamodern society, reorganising the limits to the systemic dynamics and life-worlds of modernity. Just as medieval society appears crude, irrational and immoral to the modern mind, so does modern society appear needlessly grim and 'un-enlightened' to the metamodern observer. Hence, I should like to underscore that the metamodern sociology for which I propose an outline in this chapter can and will have a prescriptive and normative element: with sincere irony, with informed naivete, with pragmatic romanticism, it is a moral imperative for metamodern sociology to study society in ways that can offer self-critically held proto-syntheses – visions and plans for a qualitatively different and ethically desirable future society.

It should lastly be underscored that this moral impetus does not come from a posited 'direction of history', from the idea that metamodernism is a later or future period or epoch; if 'progress' is tied to time and arbitrarily delineated epochs rather than to analytical distinctions and categories, one is promptly returned to the teleological fallacy, that is, to believing that time itself progresses history along a certain pregiven axis of linear development. The moral impetus emerges, instead, from the ethics and sensibilities of the metamodern mind and from an understanding of the advantages, in terms of human and non-human animal thriving and reduced quantities of suffering, conferred by the emergence of metamodern society and its societal properties. Metamodern psychology emerges from modern psychology, transcending and including it; the same is true of a metamodern philosophy and ethics; and the same is true of a metamodern society. Metamodern society is not a utopian vision; it is simply another social logic that flows developmentally from modernity, taken to its own endpoint, which is postmodernism, taken in turn to *its* own endpoint, which is metamodernism. We shall examine this progression further, in the context of sociological thought.

Sociology in an evolutionary context

Let us now revisit sociology as an academic discipline evolving in rhythm with society, so that it may be considered from a distinctly metamodern perspective. In this view, there is modern sociology (but not quite a premodern one; sociology begins with modernity), a postmodern sociology, and then the potential for a revamped form of the discipline – a metamodern sociology.

Since its programmatic formulation in the 19th century, despite eager and repeated efforts from the onset, sociology has never fully managed to establish itself as a 'science' in the sense that its basic theories and tenets can be agreed upon by all practitioners and be taught in textbooks. The textbooks of sociology to this day still all present an array of different and partly competing, partly overlapping, perspectives, methodologies and models. Whereas the natural sciences also depend upon the society of the people who ask the questions and perform the research, they allow for a certain distance to the shared and experienced life-worlds of everyday life. Inquirers into social science, by contrast, have a considerably closer tie to the issues and questions pertaining to a certain society in a certain time – to everyday life. Mechanisms for alleviating poverty are only studied in a society in which people feel that this is a realistic and meaningful endeavour; ethnographic studies of honour killings can only crop up in a society in which a significant group views such practices as alien, harmful and immoral; questions of the nature of the relation between states, markets and civil society can only emerge in a context where these categories are viewed as defined objects in the first place – and so forth.

Hence, sociology has largely reflected on and partaken in the dominant strands of thought and understanding of society at large – from a distinctly *modern* sociology, germinating in the 18th century with Montesquieu and Tocqueville, originating in the middle of the 19th century with Comte, peaking with its programmatic formulation in the 'classics' (Marx, Spencer, Weber, Durkheim, Tönnies, Dubois, Martineau – with premonitions of later developments in rogue thinkers like Gabriel Tarde and Georg Simmel), maturing, aging and decaying in the mid-20th century with Talcott Parson's structural functionalism, and surviving to this day in the form of conventional, quantitative studies of social phenomena – leading up to a distinctly *postmodern* turn, beginning in the 1960s with social constructionism, 'French theory' and poststructuralism, taking over the bastions of conventional academia within social science and humanities in the 1980s and 1990s with various strands of critical theory, discourse analysis, the linguistic turn, radical constructivism (rather than 'constructionism'), feminist scholarship, queer theory, postcolonialism and intersectionality.

Between these two bodies of intellectual and social pursuit – modern and postmodern sociology – one can place certain figures and strands that served as portals between the two realms of thought and research, ideas that were proto-postmodern and in that sense 'before their time': Mannheim's sociology of knowledge, Levi-Strauss' structuralist anthropology (harkening back to Saussure's linguistic structuralism of the 1920s, and later radicalised into full-fledged postmodern poststructuralism in the hands of Foucault and other French theorists), the symbolic interactionism that grew from Goffman's situationist sociology of everyday life and its rituals, Garfinkel's ethnomethodology (the study of how people in practice implicate a larger social order underlying each everyday interaction) and, of course, the Frankfurt School and other strands of humanist socialism and psychoanalysis. All of these started bonfires in the project of modern sociology, particularly against the backdrop of the socialist and humanist campus radicalism of 1968 and the 1970s – fires that spread and eventually reached the heart of the discipline, reshaping it in its entirety.

Modern sociology is driven, in some way or form, by a will to understand society 'as an object' by means of the scientific method, and thus ultimately to reshape it in accordance with a 'rational' will of the observer. This holds true whether it is Marx's view of stages of economic and societal development, Durkheim's (proto-)statistical study of 'social facts' (such as the suicide rates that reproduce themselves with frightening regularity in different segments of a given society from year to year), or Weber's attempt to use a qualitative analysis of ideas, values and religion as driving forces and his study of the emergence of a distinctly 'modern' state bureaucracy, market and civil society.

All of these observers try to somehow understand what modern society *is* by using, in some sense, 'scientific' approaches. When Comte coined the term 'sociology' in 1838 (although it has recently been shown that this was not a first), he imagined it as an entirely positivist science, one that would study society as a natural object like any other, and eventually serve to bring full rationality to all human relations, including the organisation of the other (natural) sciences. He thus imagined a developmental model of society in which a scientific modern society was the final stage, and here sociology would take its place as the governing principle, establishing itself as 'the queen of the sciences' – because it is the science of society, hence also the science of all other sciences within it.

Whereas the other classical modern theorists were not as direct and grandiose in their understanding of sociology (except perhaps Marx, who didn't directly subscribe to the term 'sociology', but claimed to have discovered the science of how society develops), they were all somehow part of this underlying project. It is true that Weber departed from positivism in favour of a more interpretative sociology, but he still described modern society as rational and driven by a goal-rational order. Durkheim (1912/2008) described rites and rituals in religions, and held that even modern people are in some sense religious, and tribal religions in some sense rational (even 'irrational' beliefs can be shown to have 'rational' underpinnings and functions from a societal perspective) – but Durkheim did subscribe to the 'pregiven' ontological reality of social facts that can be studied 'objectively' by means of empirical research. In other words, modern sociology was a child of modernity and its roots in the Enlightenment.

Postmodern sociology revolted against the modern project itself. And sociology itself was instrumental to this revolt. The underlying supposition that a precise and correct understanding of society could bring about societal progress was put into serious question. The French philosopher Derrida's sophisticated 'deconstruction' became a north star of this cultural and academic sentiment: the issue is not to 'objectively describe' the social world, but to look to its cracks, its exceptions, its loopholes, its paradoxes, its self-contradictions and underlying meanings. As long as the observer takes the presuppositions of society, which are layered in language itself, for granted, she can never truly study society 'from the outside', since she will always be caught within the conceptual structures of that same society. One must 'excavate' oneself from one's own and society's preconceptions; an 'archaeology' that harkens back to Nietzsche and Freud.

The postmodern mind notes that, yes, the truth may set you free – it may well emancipate individuals and groups in society – but the truth is never a straightforward matter of facts and method. The question is always, and always remains, 'whose truth?'. The critical, postmodern, sociologist feels that there is not one path to the truth. The truth is always context dependent, and never free from issues of preconception, the cognitive schemata of the observer. These, in turn, are always dependent upon society itself and its organisation, which is always infinitely larger than one's own perspective thereof. Society and 'the social' constitute a stronger and more pervasive force than modern sociology could have believed. Behind every truth claim there is a corresponding claim to power and authority, and truth-seeking and ideas of progress can never be entirely divorced from power relations in society, from specific interests and worldviews. Hence, all of science and all of the applications of social science are dependent upon the social position and perspective of the observer. There is never, in Thomas Nagel's words, 'a view from nowhere'. This echoes, again, the philosophy of Nietzsche and his notion of 'the death of God', a clear premonition of postmodern philosophy. The proposition that 'God is dead' should hence not be understood theologically, but epistemically; as soon as one takes a particular, situated, perspective to be universal and independent of the observer, one has implicitly introduced a 'God' into the equation, that is, a belief in an ultimate umpire of truth claims. But this umpire is, in reality, always out of reach.

I would argue, thus, that postmodernism represents a form of higher secularisation vis-à-vis modernity. Modernity makes short notice of the traditional God above the clouds, the God of private revelations of singular prophets. The modern mind commits itself to *public* revelation by means of a scientific community, verifying or falsifying the factual and explanatory claims of each researcher. It is based upon objectivity-through-mutuality. Postmodernism points out that these verifications and falsifications will always be dependent upon the shared taken-for-granted worldviews, values and interests of the scientific community, which itself is always located within a society that defines the rules and limits of any inquiry. Most questions, of all possible ones, are simply never asked, most interpretations never considered. As such, postmodernism finishes what modernism started; it kills off not only the literal (theological) God but also the implicit (epistemological) God-behind-the-scenes.

Such limits to the scope of inquiry are never arbitrary; they are themselves structured in recognisable manners, usually revealing a power structure of some kind. A simple example from today's world: scientific inquiry has long shown a close connection between humanity and the animal realm; yet serious inquiries into the ethical consequences of this indisputable fact remain a fringe issue in the sciences and in society at large. Animal rights are viewed as a non-respectable and quite secondary issue, despite the enormous consequences in terms of real, ongoing suffering. This is not due to some methodological fault on behalf of science and research, but rather to the weak position that non-human animals have within our society. Unable to organise and to voice their perspective, the questions of animals, a simple 'why?' in the face of imprisonment, slavery and industrial violence, are simply almost never raised, and when raised, are seldom taken seriously.

Truth, then, is a slave to power. How, then, can the truth break free? The postmodern mind employs critical theory and a deconstructive sociology, to somehow grasp the surrounding culture, the construction of meaning, morality and norms. This is an excavation of the underlying power structures that shape us so fundamentally that it precedes even our ability to ask a question, to make a certain kind of truth claim, even our direct perceptions. And this is revealed by systematically examining the self-contradictions and paradoxes of modern society, its language and meaning-making.

For this reason, the postmodern mind eschews all 'grand narratives', in the words of Lyotard. It is incredulous towards the overarching 'liberal' world, and even to its Marxist-Leninist alternative. The direction of development is not pregiven, not ordained; time is not an arrow pointing towards progress. If you believe in one given 'background space' within which you place society and your sociological inquiry, then you will always end up reproducing the claim to power inherent in that pregiven background space. There is, rather, a multiplicity of perspectives, each with their respective underlying power claims – and it is by breaking such perspectives against one another, in a 'parallax view' (Žižek, 2006), that the inconsistencies of each single one is revealed. No one has the truth, not even the physicists. There is no 'ground of reality' and no high priest who knows what it is.

Where does this, then, leave the postmodern mind? In a perpetual questioning, an infinity of intellectual and cultural resistance; in ever new variations of critique. Foucault is the emblematic example of this position. He and other intellectuals take on a role corresponding to the priesthood in traditional societies; they chastise us and question us with the fervour that stems from demanding a more ethical and fairer world, one that is always, in practice, impossible.

By no means is the postmodern questioning of the modern world complete. It has produced many cultural victories, from feminism, to anti-racism, to (anti-)postcolonialism, to revealing the hidden injuries of class – all of which have fuelled movements and emancipations. But to this day, animal rights, to name one issue, have remained peripheral and animal slavery largely unquestioned.

And yet it is not a stretch to claim that the postmodern critique has reached an impasse as an academic project. The postmodern intellectuals have retreated into the ivory towers of academia (or this is the popular perception), refining the code and critical methodologies, but decoupling themselves from leadership and the creative reorganisations of society's institutions that are direly needed. A widespread resistance to postmodernism has taken hold in politics, in internet rogue intellectuals and in the sentiments of society at large. Different forms of neo-reactionary, conservative and identitarian or 'alt-right' movements have stolen the momentum and the imagination of a generation of the young. These have tired of the cynicism and self-critique of postmodernism and its corresponding sociology, longing for a less bewildering and more self-assertive stance towards life, society and existence. The postmodern stance of perpetual questioning simply does not allow for hope, sincerity and belief, as these are always taken to be new forms of oppression in disguise.

And this is where metamodern sociology enters the picture. It begins from a similar move, one of further secularisation. If postmodern sociology always posits that there are power structures controlling our behaviours and knowledge claims, metamodern sociology eschews even this belief. Rather, metamodern sociology begins from the proposition that power structures are only truly surface phenomena, shadows of a deeper and impersonal reality: the reality of complex emergences that crisscross one another. There are hence, ultimately, no power structures to 'question' or even simply 'remove'. Instead, there are processes that guide the emergence of the perspectives in the world, and this in turn guides behaviours and results.

Because we cannot relate to society without taking a position based upon our perspective, the metamodern mind argues, we should own up to the perspective that we take, and the developmental direction implied by that view. We should then deliberately employ the sociological methods to shape society, its culture, institutions and economy, in this desired direction. This sense of direction is held, again, with sincere irony. We may know full well that our perspectives are limited and our visions partly imaginary, but we choose to take the risk, with informed naivete.

Postmodernism can only ever be a critique of the existing modern society, affecting some patterns here and there. Metamodernism, as a movement and sentiment, seeks to suggest new paths for society altogether: a new overarching equilibrium. This has long been taboo in the social sciences. But it is time that the taboo is broken, and that creative minds use the sociological imagination to suggest concrete futures and make visible new potentials.

In this sense, metamodern sociology marries the progressive impetus of modern sociology and its will to take modernity 'as an object' that can be shaped and directed, to the multi-perspectival, deconstructive and 'ironic' stance of postmodern sociology. This can, admittedly, be done in more or less fruitful manners. At worst, it is a shotgun wedding, where the worst of both worlds are combined – for instance, an undermining of scientific rigour in the name of relativism and unrealistic suggestions about a future utopia. At best, it is a nimble bifurcation between critique and progress, where new suggestions are carefully scrutinised and evolved. Or better yet, (guiltily, as a non-physicist) borrowing a term from quantum physics: metamodernism holds the modern idea of progress and the postmodern critique in *superposition* to one another. Depending upon the participant perspective of the observer, each new inquiry can lead either to critique and resistance, or towards a path to deep progress. A both-and of critique and progress.

If modern sociology is about 'reality', the societal facts of the matter, and postmodern sociology is about 'perspective', the differing views of the facts of the matter, then metamodern sociology is about 'potentials', that is, the larger realm of all possibilities contained within the multiplicity of mutually interacting perspectives. Metamodern sociology thus seeks to reorganise the *generative conditions* of how all of these perspectives emerge, evolve and interact.

- Modern sociology asks: What is society?

- Postmodern sociology asks: How is society viewed, by whom, and why?

- Metamodern sociology asks: How do these views of society emerge,
and how can they be made to emerge in ways that are beneficial
from a multiplicity of weighted and compared views?

The generative conditions of perspective in its necessary multiplicity: this is the ultimate object of study for a metamodern sociology. Metamodern sociology thus takes up the task of cataloguing, understanding, comparing and non-arbitrarily evaluating the many perspectives of society, self and reality. The evaluation of perspectives is, of course, only something that can be done by having some overarching meta-theory or larger conceptual space within which the perspectives can be placed in relation to one another. Hence, the metamodern divorce from the postmodern is completed: the postmodern mind would not have allowed for the formulation of an overarching meta-theory, a narrative of narratives, a perspective of perspectives. And yet, this is what each metamodern sociologist must work on: a suggested map of meaning, one that can always evolve and be scrutinised by others – or 'co-developed'.

This map-making is, naturally, an enormous task that can never be concluded. But it is only through such a work that one can hope to suggest pathways for society which, for all future, will consist of many competing and contradicting perspectives. Deconstructing and critiquing perspectives of others, or even of oneself, cannot be enough. One must, sooner or later, reveal from which meta-theory one is working, and from there on say how and why the great multiplicity of perspectives can be evolved. This is a synthesis of modern and postmodern sociology; but as the metamodern mind also builds upon and attempts to transcend and include the postmodern perspective, it must always remain a *proto-synthesis* – that is, not a synthesis held to describe the actual development of what Hegel called the world-soul, but a 'good enough for now, safe enough to try' attempt to act in good faith.

Hence, beyond its intellectual underpinnings, metamodern sociology is also an act of faith – of ironic piety – or even, if you will, of enlightened madness.

Describing metamodern sociology

Let us then examine some properties of metamodern sociology in its current embryonic form. To reveal my own (hopefully) enlightened madness, I would like to stress that these tenets are my own postulates, and that they can and should be challenged and developed.

Developmentalism of perspectives. It is a tenet of metamodern sociology that perspectives are not arbitrarily ordered, but that they emerge in recognisable patterns. A poststructuralist critique of literature has never emerged in a tribal society with no writing; quantum theory has never emerged in a traditional, premodern society. Even if strands of thought can be linked backwards in history (process philosophy back to Heraclitus and so forth), there are indeed specific ideas that build upon one another: multiplication builds upon addition. And these sequences are, in turn, always dependent upon social and material – ultimately, even biological – conditions, with which they interact. Postmodernism did not emerge before modernism, nor *could* it have. For this reason, metamodern sociology always looks for meaningful and explanatory developmental sequences, putting them in relation to one another on some kind of developmental scale. This developmentalism thus accepts at least some minimal form of stage theories; and these stage theories are not mere *phases* (childhood, maturity, old age) but indeed *stages* (addition, multiplication, power functions). Each stage must be, in clearly definable terms, either *more complex* than the former, or, at a minimum, be derived from the former and qualitatively distinct. For instance, one may study how people, such as police officers, think about an issue like 'race and ethnicity'; some will reflect upon these matters in simpler terms, 'Black people commit more crimes', others in more nuanced and complex terms, 'some groups in society are underprivileged and are thus driven into crime more easily', and some in yet more complex terms, 'through my work and perspective, I have a role in recreating the crime statistics that keep up the over-policing of some ethnic groups, which breeds exclusion and resentment in these groups'. In the minds of different observers with distinct perspectives, the same phenomenon appears differently, with different conclusions. These three suggested perspectives are not merely outcomes of different personalities, but they build upon one another: there is a developmental *sequence* – and if more police officers are supported to independently being able to think in accordance with the more complex perspective, this is likely to be more aligned with their dealings with the complexities of society and criminal justice. To eschew all developmental sequences of such perspectives is to flatten the view, as it were, projecting a three-dimensional object on a two-dimensional surface. This is what the metamodern sociologist calls 'developmental blindness'. Unfortunately, postmodern sociology is more or less developmentally blind, which explains a large part of its impotence to create workable pathways for culture and society to take.

Meta-theory and map-making. It is another unfortunate limitation to contemporary sociology that students are not taught comprehensive maps of the theoretical landscape of sociological theories, so that choice of theory and perspective can be selected non-arbitrarily, with well-argued motivations. There is a severe lack of meta-theory. Rather, the choice of theory, and indeed, the entirety of academic careers, are based upon which theories happen to 'speak to' the individual scholar, often being defined by earlier work on the particular topic of study. Sociologists become 'interactionists', 'constructivist feminists', 'Marxists', 'middle-range theory institutionalists' and so forth, depending upon whim and chance, often unable to communicate meaningfully across these sub-disciplinary boundaries. This is an enormous waste of potential, as the meta-theoretical space is sub-optimised. To be fair, prominent sociologists like Jeffrey Alexander (1987) and Georg Ritzer (1981) have indeed presented meta-theoretical maps of the territory, but these have not taken a central place in the education of sociologists, and a researcher is generally not expected to give convincing reasons for his or her position within a larger meta-theoretical map. Nor do a few courses on the 'philosophy of social science' grant students a comprehensive map, as these also simply enumerate a host of competing positions. Metamodern sociology is different: it begins and ends in meta-theory, always naming the underlying meta-theory, one's own theoretical position within it, and always returning to the meta-theoretical map once the theoretical and empirical dive is concluded, feeding something back to this fundamental 'ground-level' of social science. A good place to start is Ken Wilber's comprehensive work on Integral Theory, which includes several important meta-theoretical maps – but it is a telling sign that one must look to relatively esoteric writers beyond the discipline, like Wilber, to find good material for such mappings. In short, the emergence of the many perspectives in sociology and its large body of theories is not arbitrary; it covers different aspects of injunctions into the nature of society. If there is any one thing that particularly prevents sociology as an academic discipline from becoming a proper 'science', it is this lack of meta-theoretical maps – all the perspectives and injunctions end up being 'smashed together' in a grand, confusing hotchpotch. By going to the source, to the map-making of the sociological territory, one can begin to restore order to this cosmos, and thus specify which truth claims are relevant as basic tenets of each form of injunction, ridding the landscape of redundant and (unproductive) contradictory theories. Metamodern sociology must thus work from a more highly abstracted and complex level, zooming in on different phenomena from different theoretical perspectives, all the time explicating why and how each zoom is made. Naturally, one's meta-theoretical map – if you will, one's underlying paradigm made explicit – will also shape one's view of what society is and how it functions.

Fractal methodology. In a corresponding manner, choice of research methods and methodological considerations must be based upon which injunction into reality is being made, that is, it must be non-arbitrarily selected against the backdrop of a meta-theoretical map, and how the studied phenomenon is located on it. The crux here is to avoid research being steered primarily by the 'sunk costs' of the time and effort it takes to master each research method, qualitative or quantitative, a division that today divides the discipline. It is not realistic that all researchers should be able to master all methods of research, but the methodological development of each scholar should be strategised in relation to their position on the meta-theoretical map, and the sociological community as a whole should optimise its distribution of research skills, while investing time and effort in learning a shared language that facilitates bridges between different methodologies and research programmes.

Holistic. Bearing in mind that 'holistic' already has a meaning within sociology, and that the term is used as a catchphrase in other contexts, often meaning an acceptance and inclusion of 'spiritual' aspects of life, it should still be underscored that metamodern sociology is a holistic endeavour, albeit of another kind. Holism, in this context, should be contrasted with 'reductionism', and it flows from the above point about meta-theory. Much sociological ink has been spilled considering the relation between material aspects (economic, technological conditions) and the culture of society. Reductionism, in its different guises, holds that (a) the economic system, or (b) the overarching culture and its inherent meaning-making and implicit power relations, or (c) the interactions and rituals of everyday life, or (d) the social-psychological process of how humans are socialised and their personalities are formed, constitutes the 'most fundamental' aspect of society, to which its other dimensions can ultimately be reduced (hence, reductionism – note that this includes cultural reductionism). The metamodern sociologist uses a meta-theoretical map to study how, at a minimum, these four dimensions emerge together, how they interact and define each other. Hence, one cannot arbitrarily seek to explain societal phenomena from any one of these fundamental fields of emergence. Depending on how elaborate one's meta-theoretical map is (others are possible, not just these four fields), one is obliged to always explain the phenomenon as holistically as possible, not leaving out any dimension, or at least explaining why and how one limits one's inquiry. In an expanded sense, this holistic perspective should reach into the body, both as a biological-medical entity, and as a lived and felt embodiment of social experience – as well as into the biosphere and ecology.

Transpersonal perspective. This one flows, in turn, from the above tenet. The transpersonal perspective holds that society consists *neither* of atomised or interacting individuals, *nor* of societal systems and cultural structures and collectives, *nor* even of networks of people. Rather, lending from disciplines such as depth psychology and critiques of the 'individual self' in cognitive science, the metamodern sociologist views humans as multi-layered, open, interacting processes that emerge together – one's agency cannot clearly be delineated from another, nor from the society within which it unfolds. For instance, you can use a marketing strategy (an artefact found in a book, a societal condition) to affect my purchasing behaviours without my knowledge thereof; where, then, does my agency originate? Neither in the individual nor the collective, neither in you nor in me. This approaches, of course, what Gilles Deleuze called 'the dividual'. The transpersonal perspective views behaviour, and perspectives, as emergent through and beyond the individual. In this sense, human happiness and suffering are also emergent at the transpersonal level, at the level of depth psychology shaped by society, but also, on higher layers of the conscious mind, actively acting upon that same society. This leads us, clearly, to questions about how our 'self' emerges in society and how it evolves over the lifespan, inexorably linking metamodern sociology to developmental psychology and the stages of adult development – hence to issues of healing, trauma and the human body. For instance: how much does unhealed trauma steer the political behaviour of members of society?

Complexity and emergence. Warren Weaver (1948) famously wrote an article about complexity: the evolution from mechanics (linear, predictable causation) to chemistry (aggregates of many processes, each of which is unpredictable, but that statistically add up to a predicable whole) to complexity (highly unlikely events that emerge against all apparent odds through complex interactions, such as the emergence of biological life). Sociology has, naturally, followed a similar path: from Comte's focus on 'forces', borrowing from the mechanics of his time, to a statistical science with quantitative method, apparent already in Durkheim but flourishing after the breakthroughs in mathematical statistics in the 1920s, to a search for ways to describe complex emergences in many contemporary sociologists. Metamodern sociology may well employ mechanical and statistical thinking and methods, but its home base must remain firmly anchored within complexity. A distinction can here be made between 'lateral complexity', which looks at how patterns emerge through the interactions of many smaller units (championed by e.g. the Santa Fe Institute and the MIT Center for Collective Intelligence and cybernetics of different brands), and 'hierarchical complexity', which studies how more complex phenomena, including behavioural and cognitive patterns, emerge from less complex ones (championed by Michael Lamport Commons). This holds an important key in the divorce from the postmodern focus on 'power structures'; the metamodern sociologist generally views pathologies in society as not one monolithic (power) structure, but as an emergent pattern of many smaller, often counter-intuitively trivial, occurrences. Further, limitations to extensions of solidarity and oppressive factors in people's lives are viewed as pertaining to limitations to hierarchical complexity, that is, that complex phenomena are somehow treated with a flattened, too simple, perspective. This is a less moralistic and more dispassionately descriptive intuition to build from – and yet is a view that allows for more reconstructions of complexity.

Self-development and participation. Last but not least, the metamodern sociologist must understand that her own inquiry into any matter is an act of participation, which always affects the questions asked, the interpretations made, the findings presented. For this reason, the metamodern inquirer must always return to looking inwards, and to support her own healing and development in terms of theory/perspective, paradigm, stage of cognitive complexity, emotional foundation and motivations for inquiry, and relation to the field of study and society at large. Freud famously suggested that Napoleon conquered Europe to get back at his big brother. Correspondingly, the sociologist can easily spend a lifetime studying male oppression to address the trauma of a poor father and some disappointing boyfriends. Quite often, each of us is driven by simpler and cruder logics, interests and emotions than we would like to admit – and this will naturally shape any inquiry we undertake in society. Hence, the question becomes how one's sociological inquiry is *embodied* within oneself. Naturally, emotions and reactions against perceived faults and injustices in society constitute a legitimate source of motivation for sociological inquiry, but it is the task of the critically minded sociologist to scrutinise even one's own moral outrage – or, for that matter, one's indifference and boredom – towards societal issues. From a holistic, meta-theoretical and transpersonal view, work must be done where it is due, and sociological analysis does not exempt any observer from issues pertaining to the deeply personal and psychological realm. This leads us, again, to issues of depth psychology, even to forms of self-development and self-exploration that include contemplation, meditation and in some cases responsible use of psychedelics. This is because our sensing and wounded selves always participate in our sociological endeavours.

Key questions about metamodernism and society

Let us, on a last note, turn again to the second meaning of a 'metamodern sociology', namely the sociology *about* metamodernity. There are, of course, countless imaginable topics of such a field, but some few currently stand out in terms of their obviousness and pertinence.

- Developmental demographics – how are different populations in different societies distributed across the stages of adult development (and in which kinds of adult development?), and how does this affect said societies and their interactions? Which demographics begin to display metamodern values, and which roles do these play in society?

- How do developmental differences of perspective play out in society, and how can arising conflicts be mitigated, narratives translated and mutuality or solidarity across different perspectives be improved? How can metamodern perspective be situated and employed to serve such mediating purposes?

- How do the institutions and culture of society affect and generate different distributions of developmental demographics? How can inner development be supported throughout society – empirically speaking? What problems or obstacles complicate and/or prevent such measures?

- Which different pathways, social settings and cultural practices lead people to partake in metamodern movements and sentiments – and how do these interact? My own suggestion here has been that certain segments of the creative class should be studied: Hipsters, Hackers and Hippies (Triple-H). The first segment constitutes those who work with symbols, arts, culture and narratives, the second segment with technology and information and the third with inner dimensions and subjective states. These three cross-pollinate to create metamodern culture. I have later suggested the addition of a fourth segment (hence, a Quadruple-H population): the Hermetics.

This last group work with meaning-creation, inventing symbols and rituals that try to grasp cultural realities that are yet only intuited. They are called Hermetics after the occult Renaissance movement, corresponding to the seeking for larger meaning patterns (believed at the time to be found in an original source identified as Hermes Trismegistus). Each of these groups have their own brands of excesses and pathologies (suggestions – Hippies: New Age cults; Hipsters: cultural snobbery and ivory towers; Hackers: techno-utopian tunnel-vision of the Silicon Valley style; Hermetics: slides into anti-scientific occultism and complex flirtations with the far-right) and they have different lines of convergence and conflict. Metamodern movements must become proficient at including and mediating between these strands, while being able to discern pathological and excessive elements. This, I believe, is a rich field of study.

- The economy of cultural and informational capital – including the battle for human time and attention. This playing field of the internet economy, and its networked logic, is where metamodernism emerges, thrives and goes awry.

- The mapping out of different utopias (and *eutopias*, 'the good place'), their interrelations and how they connect to the metamodern, and their cultural dynamics in society, and how they relate to attractor points in the development of society, that is, to new balances and social logics that are likely to grow and manifest in society given its current dynamics.

There are, clearly, central issues about metamodernism of which we still today know very little – and where the work of prescient researchers can make all the difference. Only one such topic is enough to fill the career of a talented social scientist. Seeing that metamodernism is not per se a 'good' phenomenon, but a descriptive of certain elements that can be argued to be fruitful or harmful from different perspectives, few things are more important than exploring 'the metamodern' from the perspective of rigorous research.

Conclusion

I hope this chapter can inspire fellow scholars to engage in metamodern sociology and begin the important work of sociologically exploring the metamodern.

To conclude, sociology and metamodernism both share a key concern: to take modern society 'as an object' that can be described, interpreted, related to and ultimately reshaped; both entities work to see *through* and go *beyond* the modern. Hence, the argument can be made, that metamodernism belongs at the heart of the future of the sociological discipline, that is, a sociology true to its own promise must become metamodern in its perspective – and, conversely, that sociology belongs at the heart of metamodernism. When metamodernism attempts to assert itself as a new self-organising principle of society, it must be able to 'see' modernity as the substrate upon which it operates. This follows, as the reader may have noticed, the pattern of subject-object theory: that with which one was earlier identified and took for granted, one's 'subject' becomes an 'object of awareness' from the new and higher vantage point – higher, of course, according to one's developmentally informed meta-theory.

Bibliography

Adorno, T. (1978/1951). *Minima Moralia: Reflections from Damaged Life*. London: Verso, p. 218.

Albanese, M. (2018). People Can't Stop Reading This Professor's Trump-Russia Theories. *The Observer*, viewed online 10/11/2020: https://observer.com/2018/06/seth-abramson-is-combating-trump-and-the-media-on-twitter/

Alexander, J. C. (1987). *Micro-macro Link*. Berkeley, CA: University of California Press.

Barad, K. (2007). *Meeting the Universe Halfway. Quantum physics and the entanglement of matter and meaning*. London: Duke University Press.

Bard, A. and Söderqvist, J. (2014). *Syntheism: Creating God in the internet age*. Stockholm: Stockholm Text.

Bauman, Z. (2000). *Liquid Modernity*. Cambridge, UK: Polity Press.

Beck, U. and Grande, E. (2010). Varieties of Second Modernity: the cosmopolitan turn in social and political theory and research. *British Journal of Sociology*, 61 (3). 409–443.

Brier, S. (2007). *Cybersemiotics: Why Information Is Not Enough!* Toronto: University of Toronto Press.

Castells, M. (1996/2011). *The Rise of the Network Society*. Malden, MA: Blackwell Publishing.

Durkheim, E. (1912/2008). *The Elementary Forms of Religious Life*. Oxford, UK: Oxford University Press.

Dussel, E. (2004). Transmodernity and Interculturality: An interpretation from the perspective of philosophy of liberation (accessed 10/11/2020 at www.enriquedussel.com/).

Dux, G., (2011/2000). *Historico-genetic Theory of Culture. On the processual logic of cultural change*. Bielefeld: Transcript-Verlag.

Esbjörn-Hargens, S. (2010). An Ontology of Climate Change. *Journal of Integral Theory and Practice*, 5(1), 143–174.

Eschelman, R. (2008). *Performatism, or the End of Postmodernism*. USA: Raoul Eschelman.

Freinacht, Hanzi (2019): *Nordic Ideology: A Metamodern Guide to Politics, Book Two*. Wroclaw: Metamoderna.

Freinacht, H. (2017). *The Listening Society: A Metamodern Guide to Politics, Book One*. Wroclaw: Metamoderna.

Gebser, J. (1966/1986). *The Ever-present Origin, Part One: Foundations of the aperspectival world and part two: Manifestations of the aperspectival world*. Ohio University Press.

Giddens, A. (2013). *The Consequences of Modernity*. London: John Wiley and Sons.

Habermas, J. (1987/1985). *The Philosophical Discourse of Modernity*. Cambridge, MA: The MIT Press.

Kirby, A. (2009). *Digimodernism: How new technologies dismantle the postmodern and reconfigure culture*. New York, NY: The Continuum International Publishing Group Inc.

Mason, P. (2015). *Postcapitalism: A guide to our future*. London: Penguin Press.

Meillassoux, Q. (2008). *After Finitude: An Essay On The Necessity Of Contingency*. London: Continuum.

Nagel, T. (1986). *The View From Nowhere*. Oxford, UK: Oxford University Press.

Nealon, J.T. (2012). *Post-postmodernism. Or, the cultural logic of just-in-time capitalism*. CA: Stanford University Press.

Ritzer, G. (1981). *Towards and Integrated Sociological Paradigm*. Boston, MA: Allyn and Bacon.

Schwab, K. (2016). *The Fourth Industrial Revolution*. Cologne/Geneva: World Economic Forum.

Stanford Encyclopedia (2017). *Process Philosophy*: https://plato.stanford.edu/entries/process-philosophy/ viewed 3/25/2021.

van den Akker, R. and Vermeulen, T. (2017). Periodising the 2000s, or, the emergence of metamodernism. In: van den Akker, R., Gibbons, A., and Vermeulen, T. (eds.) *Metamodernism: Historicity, Affect, and Depth after Postmodernism* (Radical Cultural Studies) (pp. 1–19) London: Rowman and Littlefield International Ltd.

Vermeulen, T. and van den Akker, R. (2010). Notes on Metamodernism. *Journal of Aesthetics and Culture* (2). DOI: 10.3402/jac.v2i0.5677.

Weaver, W. (1948). Science and Complexity. *Scientific American*, 36, 536.

Wilber, K. (2007). *Integral Spirituality: A startling new role for religion in the modern and postmodern world*. Boston, MA: Integral Books.

Windelband, W. (1894). *History and Natural Science, Strasbourg's Rektor Address*. Translated by Guy Oakes. In The Neo-Kantian Reader (2015) (pp. 287–298).

Žižek, S. (2006). *The Parallax View*. Cambridge, Massachusetts: The MIT Press.

7 Liza's Bucket
Intellectual property and the metamodern impulse
Siva Thambisetty

THERE IS a battle currently playing out at major international institutions – the World Health Assembly, the World Trade Organization and the United Nations. Nation-state representatives are debating whether intellectual property (IP) related to vaccines and treatments for Covid-19 will be used to secure preferential access or, indeed, prevent other countries from manufacturing and expanding global supply. James Love, leading and long-standing campaigner on access to medicines, is quoted as saying, 'hoarding intellectual property for medicine in a pandemic is the behaviour of a sociopath'. Our intellectual property systems mean this behaviour is perfectly legal, even when such hoarding may lead to hundreds of thousands of unnecessary deaths. How did we get here? The answer is found in the flawed incentive structures we have developed over the past century to drive innovation and creativity, which have contributed to our reactive, crisis-driven governance. The global Covid-19 crisis has exposed these deficiencies in dramatic scale and acuity.[1]

New framings, such as Julie Cohen's 'information capitalism' and Katherina Pistor's *The Code of Capital*, assist in taking us deep into previously hidden, tightly woven constructions that facilitate monopoly and the networked accumulation of private power.[2] Intellectual property rights are a poorly understood heuristic of many of these constructions. And buried deep within this heuristic is the reticence to recognise that habits dictated to us by the law can, over time, shape our interior lives. Intellectual property is everywhere – it is often barely visible to the public, yet it is ubiquitous in popular culture, our technology choices, the price we pay for medicines and our choice of toothpaste, even dictating the music and art we can produce and enjoy. It is not, however, merely as consumers that we are affected by IP rights. Networked economies and real-time communicative functions facilitate distributed and individualised production of all sorts of creative outputs on the part of individuals and groups, even without formal industrial or organisational backing. The pervasiveness of social production of knowledge and culture leads to control – over both the means to participate in such production, and its creative outcomes – becoming a powerful element of social ordering. The psychosocial impacts of IP rights are felt and acted upon in our habitual and creative minds.

While the underlying claim in this chapter is partly that intellectual property law in its current legislative and institutional expression may not be fit to serve the greater good, the deeper claim is that the *purposes* for which it is used – transacting with intangible products of the mind, and protecting private property – take us far away from the humanistic origins of creativity and innovation.[3] Intellectual property has its place, and there are *some* good reasons to continue with an IP system that would be fit for purpose – for example, giving creators and innovators a means of livelihood, facilitating credit and acknowledgement, and creating a way to fix works so that both of these are possible. But, as I outline here, there are many reasons not to, and this should give us all pause. Perhaps none of these reasons on their own are reasons for an outright rejection of all intellectual property laws. Taken together, however, they implicate IP rights as a critical component of our consumption-driven, inequitable existence and ought to be seen as yet another rendition of how economic processes dominate our human existence. A fervid attitude to IP in general is at the centre of 'growth policies' in many countries across the development divide. Yet the philosophical foundations of IP law, based as it is on individual initiative, property rights and extrinsic reward, sit uneasily with the world as we find it – characterised by rapid technological change, late capitalism and ecological degradation.

I am sufficiently intrigued by the interconnected nature of our current predicament to be drawn into the larger conversations on metamodernity in this volume. As an observer of IP systems, I am convinced that our self-image as creators and innovators bears little resemblance to how it is viewed and directed in the law. Yet the ubiquity of IP in our economic and cultural systems and the plurality of challenges we face means any prospect of change has to be civilisational in scope and ambition. And conversely, in order to move beyond the commodification that characterises the cultural logic of late capitalism, the metamodern sensibility needs to understand what to do about IP.[4]

To bring metamodern attention to IP, I discuss what I am calling 'the psychoactive content' of these rights that shape our inner lives and therefore our outer experience of culture and politics. The structure of law, and its tendency to ignore the underlying resource (the expression of ideas, information) and to focus instead on creating a transactional tool, is key to understanding how and why IP rights create both wealth and inequality. In the interests of framing these issues with brevity and for the generalist reader, my examples are drawn at the extremes. I use these to advocate for a cultural shift led by a reprioritisation of values. It is imperative that we reset the civilisational function of this form of incentives for intellectual work; and ensure that IP, in its current guise, does not inhibit the development of clean energy, pandemic resilience, equitable use of genetic material and personal data, social production of creative input or impede communal governance of resources.[5]

Liza's bucket: a totem that binds us

IP rights have the potential to sculpt collective and individual experiences of creative and intellectual work. The following parable is a good starting point to help expose the psychoactive implications of some of the foundational ideas of intellectual property. The nursery rhyme is based on a German song from the 1700s. Over time it has been used as a metaphor in various ways, from explaining the challenge of teaching oneself, to developing organisational resilience.

> There's a hole in the bucket, dear Liza, dear Liza
> There's a hole in the bucket, dear Liza, a hole
> So fix it dear Henry, dear Henry, dear Henry
> So fix it dear Henry, dear Henry, fix it
>
> With what should I fix it, dear Liza, dear Liza
> With what should I fix it, dear Liza, with what?
> With straw, dear Henry, dear Henry, dear Henry
> With straw, dear Henry, dear Henry, with straw.
>
> But the straw is too long, dear Liza, dear Liza
> The straw is too long, dear Liza, too long.
> So cut it dear Henry, dear Henry, dear Henry
> So cut it dear Henry, dear Henry, cut it!
>
> With what should I cut it, dear Liza, dear Liza
> With what should I cut it, dear Liza, with what?
> With an axe, dear Henry, dear Henry, dear Henry
> With an axe, dear Henry, an axe.
>
> But the axe is too dull, dear Liza, dear Liza
> The axe is too dull, dear Liza, too dull.
> So, sharpen it, dear Henry, dear Henry, dear Henry
> So sharpen it dear Henry, dear Henry, sharpen it!
>
> With what should I sharpen it, dear Liza, dear Liza
> With what should I sharpen it, dear Liza, with what?
> Use the stone, dear Henry, dear Henry, dear Henry
> Use the stone, dear Henry, dear Henry, the stone

> But the stone is too dry, dear Liza, dear Liza
> The stone is too dry, dear Liza, too dry.
> So wet it, dear Henry, dear Henry, dear Henry
> So wet it dear Henry, dear Henry, wet it.
>
> With what should I wet it, dear Liza, dear Liza
> With what should I wet it, dear Liza, with what?
> With water, dear Henry, dear Henry, dear Henry
> With water, dear Henry, dear Henry, water.
>
> With what should I carry it, dear Liza, dear Liza
> With what should I carry it dear Liza, with what?
> Use the bucket dear Henry, dear Henry, dear Henry
> Use the bucket, dear Henry, dear Henry, the bucket!

It is rather apt that the water or stream from which Henry might obtain a 'bucketful' of water does not explicitly feature in the rhyme. Water here plays the role of ideas, information, creative or innovative work bounded and carried by the property medium – the bucket. The actual source of these works, the river or stream, is the public domain, the raw material for creativity. Works are drawn, inspired and carved out of what already exists, transformed by original or inventive labour and skill. Yet the public domain suffers from a marginalised and unconstructed presence in the law. Henry's preoccupation with fixing a leaky bucket is symbolic of the scaffolding of legal services and infrastructure we need to keep up the pretence of a useful bucket. Liza, in becoming the sole purveyor of the solutions to Henry's problems – the straw, the axe that needs sharpening, the stone that needs wetting – is *legal authority*, the pedlar of meaning within statutory frameworks that has such monumental impact on our intrinsic and extrinsic motivations to create. Their story explains foundational misunderstandings about human nature, confusion about the value of private property – and the web of chicanery that shapes our experience of IP. And there's a crucial plot twist: it was Liza who put the hole in Henry's bucket. Henry in fact, cannot solve what he thinks is the problem – the hole in the bucket. The real issue that needs attention is the bucket itself, not the hole in it.

Björkman writes in *The Market Myth* that we need a Copernican revolution in the way we conceive of the primacy of the market. The revolution in his view would come from putting people in the centre of the market, and giving them a central performative role in the constitutive elements of the market.[6] To use the above analogy, we must put Henry at the centre of his own world. To do this, we must understand not just the impact of shoehorning people and their complex, messy and creative lives into intellectual property systems, but also the dynamics of how and why this comes about. IP law as a constitutive rule of the marketplace is psychoactive – it shapes our habits, choices and dispositions and potentially steers many forms of intellectual endeavour.[7] Once we understand this key element, we must turn to the question of how to gently prise the bucket from Henry's hand, and get him to focus on the cool, recuperative water and the plethora of ways in which the water may be used that do not rely on a faulty bucket.

Water in the bucket: information and ideas

The nature of information and ideas lends itself to 'non-rivalrous' use – intangible resources that can be used simultaneously by multiple people. In Thomas Jefferson's words, 'He who receives an idea from me, receives instruction himself without lessening mine; as he who lights his taper at mine, receives light without darkening me.'[8] He wished for ideas and information to

> freely spread from one to another over the globe, for the moral and mutual instruction of man, and improvement of his condition, seems to have been peculiarly and benevolently designed by nature, when she made them, like fire, expansible over all space, without lessening their density in any point, and like the air in which we breathe, move and have our physical being, incapable of confinement or exclusive appropriation.

If you walk into a room whistling a new tune you came up with, nothing prevents others who hear you from whistling the same tune. But how do you make money out of something that is freely available? You introduce a form of artificial scarcity. IP rights effectively introduce a manipulable scarcity over ideas and information that can then be transacted with in the marketplace. Jefferson was persuaded that intellectual property rights were 'social law', a matter of made-up law where narrowly defined benefits temporarily outweighed the social costs of giving exclusive rights to something that was by its nature free to use. Yet determining this balance in the context of the relentless metamorphosing of intellectual work in form, content and reach, makes striking this balance strenuous.

An IP right gives you the exclusive right to make, use and sell the subject of that right. It draws a boundary around what you claim to have created, but all such rights need to be carved from and demarcated away from ineligible subject matter in the law. When it comes to copyright, it's the expression rather than the ideas that can be protected under an IP right. For example, J.K. Rowling has copyright on her Harry Potter books but she cannot monopolise generic plot lines such as a wizarding school, the adventures of a boy wizard and his friends or the notion of a wizarding tournament. However, if someone borrows specific elements of expression such as the name, character or familial origins of Harry Potter in a substantial way, then the precise demarcation of ideas and expression will need adjudicating on. These are not bright line rules, hence IP rights are better regarded as rights that 'try to exclude' others, rather than property with definitive scope or extent.[9]

Should a selfie by a monkey have the same protection as a photograph by a human, should graphic interfaces enjoy copyright protection which is meant for literal expressions, even though they clearly have functional elements, should J.K. Rowling have the exclusive right to create a glossary of terms used in the Harry Potter series, must we allow patents on cDNA but not genomic DNA, should the photograph of famous artworks be exclusively protected? These are just some of the everyday battles fought and won and lost in the IP arena. These battles have implications for the public domain, our access to it and the resources that are spent in carving it up into private enclosures to create scarcity. Water is a much better metaphor than fire or air to understand the cascading impact of artificial scarcity of ideas and information. Rising use affects not just those who have always used the waters in natural streams and rivers, but also those who, like Henry, are preoccupied with hoarding water in poorly designed vessels.

In the case of patents, the intangibility of functional ideas presents difficulties of several orders of magnitude. Demarcation of an invention takes place through technical terms used in the specification of a patent application. Words are only useful if we all have a shared understanding of meaning.[10] Terms in a patent application sit the at the cusp of scientific, legal and commercial understanding, making many of these words, particularly in emerging technologies, subject to evolving or unsettled meaning and scope.[11] Consider an invention which opens a door *when* an electronic signal is sent. If *when* is used in the application to delineate property rights, competitors may well introduce a three-second delay between the signal being sent and the door opening to cast doubt on the immediacy implied by the word 'when'. If the technology is lucrative enough, you can expect expensive litigation to ensue, with experts qualified in that particular field jousting about the meaning of 'when'.

In a leading UK case, a patent that was the basis of a billion dollar market for genetically produced erythropoietin (EPO) hinged on the meaning of 'host' cell in the patent application. The patent captured technology where external genetic material is introduced into a cell to express EPO. New competing technology which could 'switch on' internal genetic material threatened to override the value of this patent. The UK House of Lords held that because the patent used the word 'host', it could not cover the newer technology that did not rely on 'guest' genetic material; thus supplanting much of the value of the patent.[12] Words act as imperfect 'fences' – which is itself a reflection of the nature of information and ideas: free, difficult to contain and easily multiplicated.

By anointing creative work with the oil of transactional elements, IP rights favour works produced for consumption rather than joy, expression or just because we can or want to. If what we value is determined by what can be transacted with, then our IP systems really amount to a sabotaging of the diversity of our abilities, motivations and desires to be creative. The foundational and historic-normative conception of such rights is medieval, encrusted with assumptions about human nature at a time when Anglo-Saxon hegemony was predominantly White and male and property rights translated into power.[13] It's not therefore surprising that dogmatic ideas about the nature of human labour, value of property rights and false equivalences between real and intangible property prevail, but what is perhaps surprising is the longevity and unassuming acceptance of these ideas. To dial back on some of these foundational ideas would mean facilitating all kinds of creativity, not just the ones you can commodify and transact with. If Henry meditated on the nature of water he means to carry in his bucket, he might look to a waterwheel or to channel a rivulet where more of what makes water water can be expressed to greater benefit.

The bucket as hoarding: imitative learning

One of the effects of IP, and one that gets a little lost in all the other structural polarities, is the ways in which imitative learning is undermined. There are cultural differences in the degree of how we watch and learn as children but it remains one of the first and most effective ways we learn.[14] Just like the habits of imitation are influenced by early experience, so too the trajectory of innovative sectors can be greatly influenced by the ability to copy, imitate and learn. In domestic law, IP can get in the way of imitative learning in a range of activities from the mundane to the profound. Anyone who has tried to look for sheet music will know that many pieces, even if they are hundreds of years old and therefore no longer protected by copyright, simply cannot be found unless packaged in consumable chunks that you pay for. If you have tried to use a popular song as backing music on YouTube for that cute video of your niece playing with bubbles in the park, you may have received a 'take down' notice. You may have appreciated the use of a ready-made gadget rather than building it up yourself, but black-boxing technology in this way can cause problems when it comes to the right to repair (see for instance the battle Henrik Huseby is fighting with Apple to repair iPhone screens), reverse engineer or use inexpensive hacks.[15] When rules against infringing can impact on technical know-how associated with patented inventions, learning manuals or programming code, IP can get in the way of instructive investigation and exploratory creativity.

Globally, the inhibition of imitative learning is a particularly stark phenomenon. IP rights can exacerbate status quo technology gaps, ossifying states of learning by denying the possibility of 'learning by doing'.[16] Until a few decades ago there was no 'world IP'. Intellectual property was designed as a territorial right, for individual nations to decide tailor-made incentives for local industries depending on the maturity of the industry. In the early days of a sector, copying and 'free riding' led eventually to innovative local industries. For instance, many countries in the late 1970s and 1980s did not have patent protection for chemical products. This allowed domestic sectors to thrive by copying new information from wherever it existed, eventually growing innovative pharmaceutical industries.[17] International intellectual property pushed through global trade treaties, meaning this right to organically develop and learn by imitation does not exist for scores of developing and least developed countries.

It is as though Henry and Liza between them made it clear that only those who used buckets would be allowed to graze their cows on the pasture land, even where it was felt there was no need for buckets. Overtly, there is no relationship between pursuing use of the bucket (IP rights) and the right to use the pasture (international trade), but when they made the connection between the two, one of the most resilient and binding aspects of international law was laid down. This tie-in is detrimental to economies that, prior to global trade agreements, were largely agrarian or were only beginning to become technologically proficient.

In the aftermath of the 1994 Trade Related Intellectual Property Rights Agreement, the World Bank painted a very mixed picture of welfare resulting from globally harmonised IP rights for developing countries.[18] Since then we have seen acute controversies over access to medicines and over patents that impact on food security, and disagreements over the best way to incentivise the production of climate-resilient technologies (as if we need an incentive to want to save the human species!). The communicative ideal of imitative learning would allow innovation to, water-like, find its own level if allowed to do so. This would lead to a more equitable version of technology diffusion and use. Global use of pejorative terms such as 'free riding', 'theft' and 'piracy' is designed to ensure compliance with IP rights by most individuals, but they cast a depleting and dark shadow over all of our shared, human intellectual labours.

Does Henry really need the bucket? Incentive

An important foundational tenet of IP rights is the notion of incentive. Proponents of IP are often dogmatic about the need to maintain the incentive effect of such rights, claiming that without such rights many would not create or innovate. This is a proposition that is not falsifiable, and while there is quantitative and anecdotal evidence to show people are encouraged by the promise of IP rights, particularly where innovation requires sizeable investment, we do not know on the whole whether we are better off or worse off with the legal incentives in the form of IP rights.[19] Without the bucket, would Henry simply not use the water, or would he find other ways to use it?

IP rights are meant to reward creators and innovators for what they have laboured on and produced. It is also argued that autonomy over the products of one's mind is a form of extension of personhood and necessary to fulfil a sense of self.[20] But both these notions are incomplete and do not do justice to the sweeping nature of monopoly rights granted. Labour theory does not tell us how much reward is sufficient, or take note of intrinsic motivations that may subdue the need for reward. The extension of personhood argument cannot justify appropriation of value that may not be attributed solely to the creator or innovator, but derives instead from market structures that are lateral to the work itself. Our individual accomplishments are only possible through and because of a variety of societal contributing factors. Contrary to this collaborative ethic, the notion of incentive entrenches the claims of private interest and private initiative as the natural and primary driver for human creative labour.

IP creates artificial scarcity so that the holder of that right can commodify the underlying resource. It provides an incentive to come up with something that is not predicated on how much labour went into it – a literal expression or applied technical solution, a tune you dreamed up, a scientific finding based on luck, a novel that took years to write, a vacuum cleaner that needed 5,000 prototypes, a cancer-busting pill – can all be protected exclusively for uniform durations. This legal device, while outwardly elegant, means by extension that it is also not predicated on how valuable or socially desirable the work is beyond baseline, minimal requirements.

The problematic nature of this disconnect is most discernible from patents as incentives. The patent process does not qualitatively review the relationship between *invention* and the social orientation of *innovation* either at the time of grant of the patent, or post grant. Invention and innovation are different things: one is the singular and inventive improvement on what existed before; the other situates related inventions within commercial and technical ecosystems. The property right on the invention may not be the optimal way to instigate socially desirable or humanistic innovation.

Then there is the patchy and fabricated supposition that the promise of money can make you more creative than you would otherwise be. Incentives may be necessary for routine tasks requiring some creativity, but higher-order creativity that requires sophisticated cognitive functions does not respond to incentives in the same way.[21] We create for all sorts of intrinsic and extrinsic reasons, including to express oneself, to commune with higher purposes, to fulfil mundane needs, to enhance the quality of life, to make reputational gains or to gain the esteem of peers. A system that assumes all creativity and innovation is best incentivised by IP rights is, in effect, hard-selling us a particular and limited version of creativity.

When the law purports to understand and capture why we create or innovate, it sidelines and shoehorns all the myriad reasons to create under one easy-to-administer system. Over time, the law forgets and has decreasing systemic reasons to take account of differences in forms of creativity on both individual and communal levels. So without IP rights it's not true that we would not have creativity, but we might have different kinds of creativity – producing works that are less liable to be transacted with and consumed in the techno-industrial-attention complex. If we are to simply accept that without IP rights we would not create, then we are denying all the civilisational gains in art, science and culture that we made before the relatively recent invention of these rights as a matter of social law.[22]

The monocultural impetus of incentive is particularly injurious to understanding the full range of creative labour. Arendt's categories of labour is a useful guide here to the different kinds of intellectual productivity. *Labour* tied to the human condition of life is judged by its ability to sustain human life, to cater to our biological needs of consumption and reproduction, *work* is judged by its ability to build and maintain a world fit for human use, and *action* is judged by its ability to affirm the reality of the world, and to actualise our capacity for freedom and participation in political life.[23] The transactability of IP rights may work well with *labour* and *work* as defined by Arendt, but it gets in the way of the freedom to participate in our cultural and political life. Consider the time when the Olympics committee allowed the 'Special Olympics' to be used while preventing the 'Gay Olympics'; or Netflix issuing copyright takedown requests against tweets that include negative commentary about a movie; or the parody uses of famous trademarks (the American Express 'condom card' – never leave home without it). The loss is most acute when an IP holder can prevent use of original or trademarked works that allow us to express ourselves in ways that cannot be replaced easily. Every IP system has limitations and exceptions that may allow such use in specific cases, but it can often take legal resources or litigation to be sure of what can and cannot be used.[24] Meanwhile, those who cannot use protected works risk losing their power to rethink, deconstruct or joke about it and, over time, this constricts their ability to participate in cultural and political life.[25]

I can think of no better example to explain this point than the life and work of internet hacker Aaron Swartz, who made it his life's work to liberate costly public documents.[26] It's likely that most of my readers have heard of or used JSTOR, which provides digitised copies of academic journals online. Swartz plugged into the Massachusetts Institute of Technology's student network and ran a script called keepgrabbing.py that aggressively – and at times disruptively – downloaded one article after another. In another instance, Swartz accessed 20 million pages of federal court documents charged at 8 cents a page that could only be accessed at 17 libraries in the US. He installed a script that he had written from one of these libraries that requested a new document every three seconds, uploading it to the cloud. He was indicted for the JSTOR hack but committed suicide before trial, aged 26. Our legal incentives designed to reward individuals and single entities often come at the cost of our capacity to collectively participate in political life and action.[27]

Missing the abundance of the stream: a scarcity mindset

One of the abiding tragedies of the way intellectual property rights have colonised even our non-transactional reality is that our primary means of referring to work that we create from our mind, is either that it has value, in which case it is subject to IP rights, or that it has no value or is undeserving of property rights, in which case it would remain in the public domain as some sort of 'gummy residue'.[28] In reality, the public domain is a valuable resource that ought to be regarded as the default rather than private rights. We can continue to be creative without IP but not without access to the public domain. Consider recipes produced by famous chefs (Nadiya Hussain's samosa pie, or making a 'Roux'), trends in fashion, memes in humour and comedy; none of these rely on IP rights to gain traction, but rely on raw source material being freely available for everyone to use.

Critically, property holders are keener to protect their rights than the public are to defend their right to continue to access the public domain. This skews our ability to preserve the public domain even where the law is not so clear about who owns what. IP can deplete the creative broth of the source material we all use because IP holders have been able to incrementally extend the scope of their rights, relying on opportunistic or ambiguous interpretations of the law, helped by specific expansionist 'property dynamics'.[29] Newspaper headlines, or an intentionally arranged list of facts, may now be copyrighted, and musical riffs and fragments that are such an important part of subconscious musical creativity can be exclusively monopolised. Kirby Ferguson reports that two-thirds of the melodies Bob Dylan used in his early songs were 'borrowed'. Dylan was free to tap into the well of existing traditional songs, both from the African-American blues tradition and the folk songs of Britain and Ireland.[30] As Woody Guthrie (himself a frequent 'borrower' of melodies) is reported to have told Dylan: 'Don't worry about tunes. Take a tune, sing high when they sing low, sing fast when they sing slow, and you've got a new tune.'

Yet, what was typical for a folk singer as recently as the 1960s may no longer be allowed. Recent litigation between Marvin Gaye's estate and the creators of 'Blurred lines' (Pharrell Williams and Robin Thicke) and 'Let's Get it On' (Ed Sheeran) demonstrates that today copyright law can be used to enforce legal claims over not just melodies, but even 'the feel' and tempo of a song.[31] There are many ways to dissect the 'Blurred Lines' legal case for infringement, but if you take apart the melody in terms of lyrics, syncopation or notes, you find distinct differences that for many musicians form the lifeblood of inspiration and improvisation.[32] For the law to throw the practice and development of music over generations of artists into turmoil is to arrogate to itself the ability to shepherd musical creativity. Not enough of us are talking about the depleting effect this is likely to have on our mojo to produce good music.[33]

As noted earlier, the public domain, as the sum total of accessible creative resources, is like water. It is raw material that all innovators and creators need – private rights with uncertain or expanding boundaries are therefore a threat to it. It is largely an invisible entity in the legislative frameworks. So in our language and in our behaviour we come to view the private domain rather than the public domain as the default. In fact, the way we struggle with the differences between copyrightable and unprotectable, patentable and unpatentable and the public domain makes not protecting something of value seem increasingly anomalous.[34] This is why James Boyle suggests that we need to 'invent the public domain', to reimagine it away from the language and shadow of private property rights.[35]

My concern here is, if our language around abundance represented by the public domain is eviscerated it fuels the scarcity mindset: that there is not enough to go around; that each must appropriate before someone else does; and that we need more property rights to protect the ones we already have in a 'property begets property' dynamic. It both seeds and feeds the underlying fear that we are all in a race to compete for limited rewards.[36] The fix of getting the straw to plug the hole, and needing a sharpened axe to do so, which cannot be sharpened without access to the water, becomes an expression of anxiety and disquiet driven by a scarcity mindset.

The bucket and the hole in the bucket: the property right

IP rights are one of the most resolute and hardy concepts in international and domestic law. Tied to trade treaties, they thrive in unusual and otherwise infertile ground, uprooting different and other ways of looking at the impulse to create and innovate, and they have enabled the global movement and convertability of capital. Yet foundationally, many of the dysfunctions in the design of these rights exacerbate the screed of scarcity and self-interest, approving claims of privilege over community.

IP rights, in Katharina Pistor's words, are made not merely the product of superior skills, and so must draw inevitable attention to the ways in which this capital is coded into the law.[37] Pistor uses the term 'code' to show how certain legal institutions have been combined and recombined in a highly modular fashion to create capital. These modules bestow important attributes on assets and thereby privilege its holder: *priority*, *durability*, *universality* and *convertability* make an asset fit for generating wealth for its holder, not just in particular legal systems but also globally. Yet this process is largely hidden from view. The impenetrability of the process and its outcomes are powerful drivers, making asset holders wealthy and others excluded in growing cycles of inequality. While it is productive to understand the terms of this coding, we must not lose sight of the ways in which, concomitantly, IP law orders the social realm through its psychoactive reach.

In order to understand how the basic structure of the law can create both inordinate wealth and terrible inequalities, we need to clearly see how self-perpetuating myths about purpose, function and impact are fuelled by epistemic firewalls around complex, technical laws that make oversight difficult. First, IP is an uncertain property right. Unlike fences around real property, subject matter of intellectual property is beholden to imperfect means of fixing the work. Often, boundaries or the scope of the right can only be uncovered in litigation. This process privileges the right holder as there is a presumption that the right held (particularly for patents) is valid. And although litigation is expensive, we also know that parties that spend more tend to win.[38] In any case, the right holder has a greater stake in defending the right than challengers. This is because once an IP right is invalidated, it becomes available for all to use, not just the challenger who spent money to break it down, further reducing the challenger's incentive to litigate. The right is like the bucket, but the imperfections in the bucket are by design partly because of the limited ways in which law can capture and contain non-rivalrous information. Navigating these intricacies requires a great deal of skill, often at exorbitant cost.

IP rights help make money, but these rights work best at scale, and the power to exclude favours those who have the means to implement it. Large, aggregated rights holders like publishers and music collection societies fare better at the cost of individual creators, songwriters, authors, columnists. Unless you can make credible threats to litigate and spend money on lawyers and the courts, your IP right remains a protection in name only. As a competitor, you may take a punt and hope you are not sued, but this is unlikely to be seen as a wholesome long-term strategy or one that grows competitive innovation. Once the holder of the IP right gives in to the logic of the need for such a right, he gains a very leaky way of protecting his 'property' – and a great proportion of the real market value is scaffolded not on what is encased in the right itself but from the legal and commercial services market that administers aid to stem the leak. And if you have a leaky bucket, having more buckets can seem like a partial win.[39]

Second, IP rights function in policy circles as a proxy for innovation or creativity even though there is a difference between creativity for consumption and non-instrumental creativity. Because one kind of creativity is easier to count than others, the consumable version gets incorporated into policymaking much more than the other kinds. More intellectual property does not mean more creativity or more innovation. Most inventions that are patented will never make it to the marketplace. Yet no one can use the information in those patents for the duration of the patent right – 20 years. Counting patents or patent applications as a marker for an innovative society is like going into a restaurant and counting the number of plates on the shelves to figure out how many people eat there. The link is tenuous at best, yet we price what we measure. When we measure the wrong things, the result is perverse.[40] The number of buckets of water you might take out of the stream is a poor way to measure how much water there is in the stream, how others are using it or just how life affirming and sustaining it is to people who rely on it.

Third, the hole in the bucket is an attention sink hole: it makes Liza and Henry forget to ask if they are dealing with the right problem. There is a well-recognised dynamic of property where risk-averse and opportunistic property owners have to keep investing and working on shoring up their property rights with lateral add-on rights that are needed to strengthen the impact and enforceability of the original right. It is here that Liza's tutelage is particularly dark – she is both originator of the problem and purveyor of the sole solution. In Pistor's telling, she is a Master of the code of capital. Lawyers are not just 'legal service providers' – 'they contribute to the creation and distribution of wealth through a complex empire of claims and counterclaims, rights and restrictions on these rights, all fashioned in the modules of capital's legal code'.[41]

It's as though Liza convinces Henry that he not only needs a bucket, but the only bucket there is to be had is the one she offers him. There have been countless ways to carry water from the stream into the village or our homes, that we have forgotten over time. Liza then supplies Henry with a hole in the bucket. This works in Liza's favour because it puts her, or the law, in a position of monopoly supplier for legal services and enforcement of a badly designed property right. By the time Henry realises he needs the straw, and only has a blunt axe with which to cut the straw and no means of sharpening the axe, it is too late – he is embedded in the maze of legal rights that Liza has sold him. Henry is so preoccupied with the hole in his bucket that he fails to ask whether he needed the bucket in the first place, or might not have been better cupping his hands in the cool water, satisficing his needs and leaving the free flow of the water to be enjoyed by others.[42] In the process he would enable the creation of rules and values around communal use of a resource, instead of participating in the privileging of private initiative and interests.[43] The bucket with a hole in it is an overpowering paradigm that has us as individuals and our creative and innovative industries in its psychogenic grip. A reinvention of intellectual property law would ideally begin with a better understanding of who creates for what sorts of reasons, and asking which of those can be captured in the law and which are better facilitated by informal incentives, prizes, compensation and social support structures.[44] Current and potential artists, inventors, musicians, writers and all of us deserve better than this bucket.

What would it take to throw away the bucket and learn to use the water? Communality

I have described how and why we got here, but the question remains: what do we now need to do about it? We must begin with the world as we wholeheartedly perceive it. Over the last few decades, the geopolitical setting has shifted from a purported 'end of history' convergence of stable liberal democracies and prosperity-conferring free markets, to a world of transnational information capitalism in which private actors, privileged by their ability to code capital, increasingly own rather than merely shape the public realm, and where near- to medium-term cascading ecological collapse is plausible, and even likely. These are contexts where we must pull away from dematerialised assets and find our way back into what makes us most human. And there are several sources of inspiration and radical internal transformations we can draw on.

To explain the potential for transformation of IP, human rights law provides a powerful disanalogy. There are clear distinctions between human rights law, morality and politics. Morality and politics are contested, but shed light on the legitimacy and social function of the law. With intellectual property law, the moral and political elements are mostly hidden or taken for granted, and rarely used as inflection points for the legitimacy of the legal apparatus. The turn away from abstract, theoretical justice in human rights law led to a realisation that the judgements concerning the worth of things depend on the feelings the things arouse in us, and that sympathetic insight is necessary to notice previously unnoticed forms of suffering and injustice. Law evokes emotions and feelings in ways that are epistemically and jurisprudentially relevant. Indeed, as Nussbaum and Rorty argue, 'sentiment', or 'rational emotions' such as compassion, solidarity and empathy, are even necessary for justice and democracy to function.[45,46]

By contrast, an unhelpful and even deluded foundationalism is rife in IP law, and attempts to reinforce the moral superiority of individual effort, blind to the privileges that help foster and grow property rights. This foundationalism plays out with very little countervailing reference to the politics of sentiment, and the values such sentiments might inspire. In this, it is psychoactive, both in the asset holder who is emboldened in his path to wealth creation, and those subject to the inequities of the exclusivity and coding that accompany such rights. How can we, in Rorty's words, spark a 'fellow feeling' that enables us to develop sympathetic feelings for those facing creativity deficits, technological dispossession or cultural deprivation?

The way to do this is through re-education in aid of an aesthetic recounting of the law, where we restate views in different vocabulary, or through felt experiences, to reveal previously unseen possibilities, as 'a tool for social and individual change' and as a contributing factor in altering our self-image. One aim of such an endeavour would be to detail narratives of how people experience intellectual labour, the pleasures and pain they feel beyond their knowledge of IP rights as abstractions, and the value of giving away rather than hoarding ideas and information in order to seek rent on them. This is not about sophistry or rhetoric because 'a talent for speaking differently rather than for arguing well, is the chief instrument of cultural change'.[47] William James and many pragmatist thinkers, including Rorty and those working with a modern version of *Bildung* and democratic education, emphasise different aspects of such enculturing.[48,49,50]

Legal reform in IP will ultimately rest on cultivating alternate sensibilities that can lead to a wider cultural reappraisal of what IP is, what its goals should be and how it can best achieve those goals. We might speak of the public domain, simultaneously with music production and remix of digital goods, or of peer production rather than individualistic effort, or by investigating how frugal, need-based innovation systems challenge the orthodoxy of commercial incentives. We could enquire about the impact of particular legal standards on the lives of real people – patents on transgenic farmed animals and what that might mean for global food security, computing technologies related to connectivity that are exclusively licensed, or the unaffordability of medicines.

Part of these narratives will be about getting IP to take ownership of its consequences, despite the short-sightedness of legislative frameworks that do not, and part of it will be about calling the bluff of complicated legal arguments that do not amount to just or humane conduct. We can do this by drawing away from the *assetisation* of products of the mind by focusing, once again, on the underlying resource – mental, emotional and creative labour and what has been laboured on – the water, its organic uses, the ways in which it can be replenished and used productively without denying those who come after. We need mass mobilisation to address the enculturing and edification that is needed to change the settings of legislative intent or judicial practice, concomitant with engaging with the broader plot lines; and that task is entirely in keeping with the emerging metamodern consciousness.

Notes

1. I am grateful to Jonathan Rowson for countless conversations on metamodernism and the impetus to participate in this volume, and to Zak Stein, Layman Pascal and Luke McDonagh for feedback on drafts.
2. J. Cohen, *Between Truth and Power: Legal Constructions of Informational Capitalism* (Oxford University Press, 2019), and K. Pistor, *The Code of Capital: How the Law Creates Wealth and Inequality* (Princeton University Press, 2020).
3. A few works that touch upon this theme include J. Silbey, *The Eureka Myth: Creators, Innovators, and Everyday Intellectual Property* (Redwood City, CA: Stanford University Press, 2014); M. Iljadica, *Copyright Beyond Law: Regulating Creativity in the Graffiti Subculture* (Oxford: Hart, 2016); J. Toynbee, 'Beyond Romance and Repression: Social Authorship in a Capitalist Age', *Open Democracy* (28 November 2002 Available here www.opendemocracy.net/en/article_44jsp/
4. Late capitalism (or the much older term *Spätkapitalismus* in German) has come to signify a range of indignities associated with economic processes, but the link to cultural life is brought out particularly well by F. Jameson in 'Postmodernism, or the Cultural Logic of Late Capitalism', 1984 *New Left Review* 1 (146).
5. It is a measure of global discord and power asymmetry that the Paris Agreement has no text on intellectual property. M. Rimmer, 'Beyond the Paris Agreement: Intellectual Property, Innovation Policy, and Climate Justice', *Laws*, 2019, p. 8.
6. T. Björkman, *The Market Myth* (Fri Tanke, 2016) pp. 78–84.
7. J. Rowson, 'Taste the pickle! Or everyone dies: On finding a personal response to a planetary predicament.' In Rowson, J. and Pascal, L. (Eds) *Dispatches from a Time between Worlds: Crisis and Emergence in Metamodernity* (Perspectiva Press, Spring 2021).
8. Letter from Thomas Jefferson to Isaac McPherson (August 13, 1813). In Albert Ellery Bergh (ed.) *The Writings of Thomas Jefferson* (Washington, DC: The Thomas Jefferson Memorial Association of the United States, 1907), vol. XIII, 326–338 (hereinafter Letter to McPherson), available at http://memory.loc.gov/ammem/collections/jefferson_papers/mtjser1.html
9. Although this argument is generally made in the context of patents, it's also true to a lesser degree of other kinds of IP rights. For a discussion of the poor quality of property rights represented by software patents, see Bessen and Meurer, *Patent Failure: How Judges, Bureaucrats, and Lawyers Put Innovators at Risk* (Princeton University Press, 2009). Also see M. Lemley and C. Shapiro, 'Probabilistic Patents', *Journal of Economic Perspectives* 19(2), 2005, pp. 75–98.
10. For an engaging description of how mangled meanings can arise in patent applications, see Greg Myers, 'From Discovery to Invention: The writing and rewriting of two patents', *Social Studies of Science*, February 1995 vol. 25 no. 1, pp. 57–105.
11. See discussion in Thambisetty, S., 'Learning Needs in the Patent System and Emerging Technologies: A Focus on Synthetic Biology', *Intellectual Property Quarterly* (1), 2014.
12. *Kirin Amgen v Hoechst* [2004] UKHL 46.
13. For an example of the legislative debates around monopoly and property that fed into English legislative design, see F. Machlup and E. Penrose, 'The Patent Controversy in the Nineteenth Century,' *Journal of Economic History* 10(1), 1950, pp. 1–29; and for an examination of how copyright, trademarks and patent discourses invoked and shaped American ideals around race, nation and citizenship, see A. Vats, *The Colour of Creatorship: Intellectual Property, Race and the Making of Americans* (Stanford University Press, 2020).

14 For a practical exposition on the value of imitative learning, see Guy Claxton, Bill Lucas and Rob Webster, *Bodies of Knowledge: How the Learning Sciences could Transform Practical and Vocational Education* Centre for Real World Learning and Edge Foundation 2010. Available here: www.aoc.co.uk/sites/default/files/Bodies_of_Knowledge_CRWL_.pdf
15 Restart podcast, episode 48, Henrik vs the Goliath Corporation. Available at https://therestartproject.org/podcast/henrik-huseby/
16 One area in which there is a wide, perceptible gap is in marine scientific research and the ability to use marine technologies for conservation and sustainable use. Without mandatory technology transfer and capacity-building programmes that are unrestricted by intellectual property rights, this gap can seriously impact on joined-up strategies to conserve biological diversity in the oceans. See for instance Blasiak, Wynberg, Grorud-Colvert and Thambisetty, 'The Ocean Genome: Conservation and the Fair, Equitable and Sustainable Use of Marine Genetic Resources', *Blue Paper commissioned by the HLP for a Sustainable Ocean Economy*, April 2020, p. 25.
17 J. Lerner, '150 Years of Patent Protection', *American Economic Review*, 92 (2), 2002, pp. 221–225.
18 World Bank, 2001, Global Economic Prospects and the Developing Countries: 2002 (Washington DC: The World Bank).
19 'If one does not know whether a system "as a whole" (in contrast to certain features of it) is good or bad, the safest "policy conclusion" is to "muddle through" – either with it, if one has long lived with it, or without it, if one has lived without it. If we did not have a patent system, it would be irresponsible, on the basis of our present knowledge of its economic consequences, to recommend instituting one. But since we have had a patent system for a long time, it would be irresponsible, on the basis of our present knowledge, to recommend abolishing it.' Machlup, 'An Economic Review of the Patent System', Study of the Subcommittee on Patents, Trademarks and Copyrights of the Committee on the Judiciary US Senate 85th Congress, 2nd Session. Available at https://cdn.mises.org/An%20Economic%20Review%20of%20the%20Patent%20System_Vol_3_3.pdf For more modern versions of similar ambiguity see R. Dreyfuss and S. Frankel, 'From Incentive to Commodity to Asset: How International Law is Reconceptualizing Intellectual Property' (on competing interests); Nancy Gallini, 'Economics of patents' (discussion of why link between patent incentive and the strengthening of innovation is ambiguous). Available at www.amherst.edu/media/view/129990/original/gallini%2Bpatents.pdf; Ted Sichelman, 'Commercializing Patents', *Stanford Law Review*, Vol. 62(2), 2010, pp. 341–413 (arguing that patents substantially thwart commercialisation of valuable patents); F.M. Scherer, 'The Innovation Lottery: The Empirical Case for Copyright and Patents.' In R.C. Dreyfuss et al (eds) *Expanding the Boundaries of Intellectual Property: Innovation Policy for the Knowledge Society* 3–21, 2001.
20 J. Hughes, 'The Philosophy of Intellectual Property', *Georgetown L.J.* 77, 1988, p. 287.
21 E. Johnson, 'The Incentive Fallacy.' Johnson, Eric E., Intellectual Property and the Incentive Fallacy 39 *Florida State University Law Review* 623 (2011), available at SSRN: https://ssrn.com/abstract=1746343; S. Pink, *Drive: The Surprising Truth About what Motivates Us* (Canongate, 2009).
22 See for instance, J. Cohen, 'Creativity and Culture in Copyright Theory', *U.C. Davis L. Rev.* pp. 1151–1205, 2007, where she critiques mainstream intellectual property scholarship that persistently overlooks social science methodologies that provide both descriptive tools for constructing ethnographies of creative processes and theoretical tools for modelling them.
23 N. Natanel, 'Copyright and a Democratic Civil Society', *YLJ* 106(2), 1996, p. 283 takes the middle ground between an expansionist amalgam of neoclassical and new institutional economic property theory and a minimalist position that opposes copyright expansion to present copyright as a state measure that uses market institutions to enhance the democratic character of civil society.
24 Fair use in the US and fair dealing in UK copyright law for example. For a review of fair use in a digital context in multiple jurisdictions, see S. Monseau, 'Copyright and the Digital Economy: Is It Necessary to Adopt Fair Use?' Available at http://dx.doi.org/10.2139/ssrn.2576436
25 W. Gordon, 'A Property Right in Self-Expression: Equality and Individualism in the Natural Law of Intellectual Property', *Yale Law Journal* 102, 1993.
26 'The Brilliant Life and Tragic Death of Aaron Schwartz' Available at www.rollingstone.com/culture/culture-news/the-brilliant-life-and-tragic-death-of-aaron-swartz-177191/
27 Social production and 'freedom' in the context of networked innovation provide an alternative to heroic narratives of individual achievement. See for instance chapter 3 of Yochai Benkler's *Wealth of Networks: How Social Production Transforms Markets and Freedoms* (Yale University Press, 2006).
28 J. Boyle, *The Public Domain: Enclosing the Commons of the Mind* (Yale University Press, 2008).
29 S. Safrin, 'Chain Reaction: How Property Begets Property', *Notre Dame Law Review*, 2007, p. 1917, Rutgers School of Law-Newark Research Paper No. 015, Available here https://ssrn.com/abstract=954970

30. B. Dylan, 'The Times they are a-Changin'' (Columbia Records, 1964) – Restless Farewell (melody taken from 'The Parting Glass', a traditional folk standard in Britain and Ireland). See also O. Arewa, 'From J.C. Bach to Hip Hop: Musical Borrowing, Copyright and Cultural Context', *NC Law Review*. 84, 2006, p. 547.
31. L. McDonagh, 'Is Creative Use of Music Without a Licence acceptable under Copyright?' *International Review of Intellectual Property and Competition Law (IIC)* 43, 2012, p. 401.
32. T. Lester. 'Blurred Lines – Where Copyright Ends and Cultural Appropriation Begins – The Case of Robin Thicke versus Bridgeport Music, and the Estate of Marvin Gaye', *Hastings Communications and Entertainment Law Journal*, Vol. 36, No. 2, 2014, pp. 217–242, Available at SSRN: https://ssrn.com/abstract=2576016 arguing that this case may impact on the very ways in which creativity and innovation are defined in American law.
33. Although the US courts have more recently stepped back from finding infringement in the subsequent Led Zeppelin case, there is still cause for concern: www.theguardian.com/music/2020/oct/06/plagiarism-case-ends-led-zeppelin-stairway-to-heaven-taurus-spirit-us-supreme-court
34. J. Litman, 'The Public Domain', *Emory LJ* 39, 1990, pp. 965–1023.
35. P. Samuelson proposes a three-tiered map of public domain materials, with some being undeserving 'detritus', some valuable elements being 'better utilised if propertised to some degree', and other parts needing to 'remain open and unownable as sources for future creations'. P Samuelson, 'Challenges in Mapping the Public Domain.' In. P.B. Hugenholtz and L. Guibault (eds) *The Public Domain of Information* (Kluwer Law International, 2006).
36. D. Philipsen, 'Economics for the People'. Available at https://aeon.co/essays/the-challenge-of-reclaiming-the-commons-from-capitalism
37. K. Pistor, *The Code of Capital*, see note 2, p. 13.
38. J. Farrell and R.P. Merges, 'Incentives to Challenge and Defend Patents: Why Litigation Won't Reliably Fix Patent Office Errors and Why Administrative Patent Review Might Help', *Berkeley Technology Law Journal* 19, 2004, p. 943.
39. See for instance, 'Probabilistic Patents' see note 9, where the authors reason that patent portfolios of thousands of patents owned by one entity may in fact be functioning as 'super patents'.
40. M. Mazzucato, *The Value of Everything: Making and Taking in the Global Economy* (Hatchette USA 2019), lays out the chasm between price and value and how it drives our economic systems in perverse ways.
41. Pistor, chapter 7, see note 2.
42. Satisfice is a portmanteau of satisfy and suffice, to indicate a decision-making heuristic where imperfect information means no acceptable rather than perfect solutions are found. See S.A. Herbert, 'Rational Choice and the Structure of the Environment', *Psychological Review* 63(2), 1956, pp. 129–132. For a discussion of satisficing and incrementalism in IP institutions, see S. Thambisetty, 'Increasing Returns in the Patent System: Institutional Sources and Consequences for Law', LSE Legal Studies Working Paper No. 7/2009, February 16, 2009. Available at SSRN: https://ssrn.com/abstract=1344761
43. For an account of how communal rules and governance may work, see Elinor Ostrom *Governing the Commons* (1990) and Y. Benkler, *Wealth of Networks* chapter 3, see note 27.
44. J. Silbey, see note 3.
45. Nussbaum, *Cultivating Humanity: A Classical Defense of Reform in Liberal Education* (Harvard University Press, 1997).
46. Rorty, 'Human Rights, Rationality and Sentimentality', *Truth and Progress: Philosophical Papers* (Cambridge University Press, 1998).
47. Rorty, *Contingency, Irony and Solidarity* (Cambridge University Press, 1989).
48. James, 'On a Certain Blindness in Human Beings' and 'What Makes a Life Significant.' In McDermott (Ed.) *The Writings of William James: A Comprehensive Edition* (Chicago University Press, 1977).
49. Björkman T. and Lene Rachel Andersen, *The Nordic Secret* (Fri Tanke, 2017), Z. Stein, *Education in a Time Between Worlds: Essays on the Future of Schools, Technology, and Society* (Bright Alliance, 2019), J. Rowson, *Bildung in the 21st Century – Why Sustainable Prosperity Depends on Reimagining Education* (CUSP, 2019).
50. Dewey, *Democracy and Education: An Introduction to the Philosophy of Education* (Macmillan, 1916).

8 But Do You Have a Vegetable Garden?
Cultural codes and the preconditions for a successful metamodern economy

Lene Rachel Andersen

HUMAN HISTORY can be divided into four major cultural codes: prehistoric indigenous, premodern, modern and postmodern, each with its unique kind of economy. The way we understand 'the economy' in any society is a cultural construct, and the rules of any economy are a social construct as well. There are societies and there are individuals, but there is no such thing as 'the economy' detached from the norms and rules of those societies. Economy is a subsystem of society, which is a subsystem of nature and life itself, and understanding how life propagates gives us a model for a thriving economy, society and nature. What is the cultural code and economic model capable of handling the complexities of the 21st century? One suggestion is metamodernity, which integrates the four codes into one; a metamodern economy would then integrate and promote the most appropriate elements and structures from all four kinds of economy. This metamodern combination would have a more complex understanding of what value creation is and would have a different measure of economic success than GDP growth; it would also work in a more complex way, one that harmonises with nature and is more resilient. It would offer a more diverse set of opportunities so that everybody could thrive in it. Changing our economy would most likely meet resistance, not least from those who benefit most from the current economic model; it is therefore crucial that what is fun and meaningful to the most industrious people in the current economy would still be an integral part of the economy. This article does not offer an alternative kind of clearly defined tool, such as the GDP, but rather a frame of understanding that may allow us to develop such a tool.

Metamodernity

Throughout history, the cultural codes as well as the economies related to them have looked very different depending on the size of societies and the technologies available. In order to grasp the complexity of the human experience, it is not sufficient to use *metamodernism* (the integration of two codes: modernity + postmodernism) as a basis for a metamodern economy; we need to base the exploration on *metamodernity* (the integration of all four codes: prehistoric indigenous + premodern + modern + postmodern cultural codes). In schematic form, the codes can be summed up as follows:

Increasing societal complexity

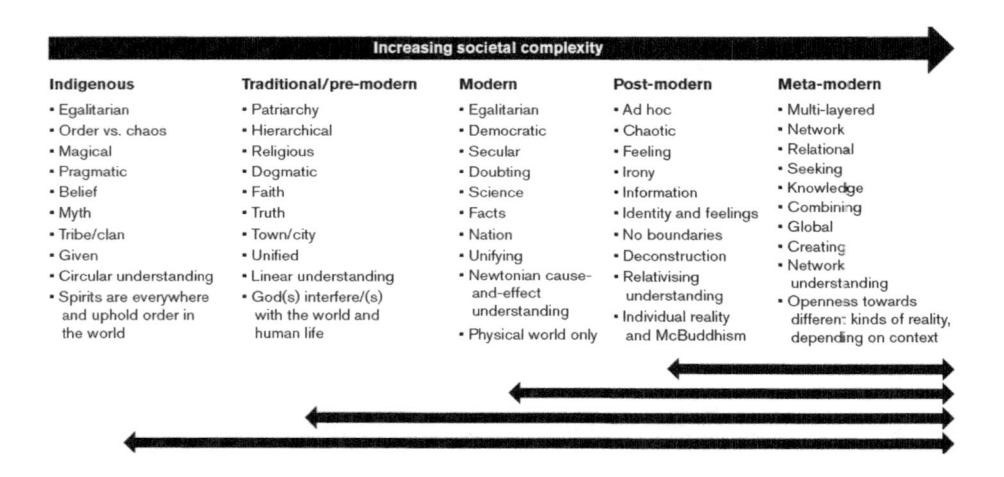

Indigenous	Traditional/pre-modern	Modern	Post-modern	Meta-modern
• Egalitarian	• Patriarchy	• Egalitarian	• Ad hoc	• Multi-layered
• Order vs. chaos	• Hierarchical	• Democratic	• Chaotic	• Network
• Magical	• Religious	• Secular	• Feeling	• Relational
• Pragmatic	• Dogmatic	• Doubting	• Irony	• Seeking
• Belief	• Faith	• Science	• Information	• Knowledge
• Myth	• Truth	• Facts	• Identity and feelings	• Combining
• Tribe/clan	• Town/city	• Nation	• No boundaries	• Global
• Given	• Unified	• Unifying	• Deconstruction	• Creating
• Circular understanding	• Linear understanding	• Newtonian cause-and-effect understanding	• Relativising understanding	• Network understanding
• Spirits are everywhere and uphold order in the world	• God(s) interfere/(s) with the world and human life	• Physical world only	• Individual reality and McBuddhism	• Openness towards different kinds of reality, depending on context

Figure 8.1 Cultural codes

After an introduction to the current state of economic theory, I shall explore the historic development of economy through all four cultural codes and suggest a metamodern economy.

Current economic theory

The mainstream economic theory today is the neoclassical economic theory, which is based on three main assumptions: 1) people are rational; 2) individuals maximise utility and firms maximise profits; and 3) people have full information about the market. These assumptions are among the arguments for capitalism, but as part of its epistemological framework, neoclassical economic theory operates with or refers to four basic economic models: market economy, capitalism, communism and the mixed economy (that there are four models has nothing to do with the four cultural codes). The first two concepts, market economy and capitalism, are often used interchangeably, but they are different.

Market economy is rather straightforward. Two or more people exchange goods or services, and money is used as a tool to eliminate asymmetry over time. If A wants B's goods or services sooner than B wants A's and A is not going to owe B anything in the meantime, A pays B money when B delivers. Later, B pays money when A delivers. A market economy also allows A to buy from B, B to buy from C, and C to buy from A, without C ever buying from B, B buying from A or A buying from C.

Capitalism is defined by a need for capital up front before production can begin. The need is generally more than the amount one person or group of business partners can save up and provide by their own effort. Hence, in order to start production, the producer(s) must raise money. Capitalism and debt are thus the prerequisite for industrial-scale production: one cannot build machines and a factory without a considerable amount of (borrowed) money; and production cannot begin before the factory is there.

In the market economy, the producer just sells what s/he has produced, and increasing productivity is hard. A market economy without capitalism rarely has surplus capital for research and development. Debt exists in market economies, but it is typically consumer debt arising from the poor being unable to afford to buy what they need with the means that they have.

The common denominator of market economy and capitalism is that the means of production is privately owned and the market is perceived as self-organising (it is in fact always defined by some sort of social norm or legislation); the difference between market economy and capitalism is the goal of the production:[1]

- Market economy: P > M > P
    - Products are taken to the market to get Money in order to buy more Products.

- Capitalism: M > P > M
    - Money is invested in Production in order to acquire more Money.

Communism means that there is no private ownership of the means of production; the commune or the state owns the means. As a result, the commune or government defines what can be produced for the market. Hypothetically, communes and governments could be as agile and flexible in planning production as the market is; in practice, however, this has turned out not to be the case, and communism has no creation of general prosperity to show for itself.

Mixed economy is a combination of the three models above, and it can lean more towards capitalism (neoliberalism and new public management), or more towards communism (socialism with strong state control and state production of many products and services), or it can be somewhere towards the middle, a capitalist economy with redistribution of wealth via taxation and tax-financed healthcare, education and social security for all citizens.

In the modern, industrialised era, mixed economies have proven to be the most stable and successful.

Stated and unstated assumptions

The three explicit assumptions in neoclassical theory that 1) people are rational, 2) individuals maximise utility and firms maximise profits, and 3) people have full information about the market, are increasingly being questioned. On top of that there are a number of unstated assumptions that are implicit in the economic models, among them are:

- The borders of a nation state (and/or a free trade area) define the reach of the rules of any given economy (i.e. macroeconomics overall equals national economics)

- GDP is a useful gauge to measure the health of any national economy

- Nation states are the biggest/strongest legal and economic entities; nation states define the rules

- Profit is re-invested in the (national) economy where it was generated

- Products are physical goods or physical or intellectual services and have geographical gravity; companies' markets diminish with physical distance

- Food, goods and shelter are in short supply and thus increased productivity is always better

- We need to work in order to consume

- In microeconomics, companies, capital and labour are factored into the costs/input, but energy is not and neither are land and nature.[2,3]

In a globalised, digitised economy, these six assumptions are now increasingly wrong:

- Nation states are no longer economically sovereign; global banks, credit card systems, internet trade and overall global trade have broken down the borders, and (digital) cash flows freely around the globe; from the individual consumer to multinational corporations, everybody is an actor in the global economy, but legislation and the political influence of citizens are still predominantly national

- GDP makes no distinction between what improves short-term profit or long-term wellbeing (i.e. polluting versus sustainable production or investing in weapons versus education)

- Some companies have higher annual revenues than the GDP of some nation states and can coerce states into changing legislation and taxation

- Profit gained in one country may be spent or invested in another. The industrialists of the 1800s and most of the 1900s spent their profit locally and employed local artisans, artists, staff and so on. They also donated to charity close to home and built more local factories. The capital owners of the 21st century gain revenues from around the globe, move their investments around and spend their money in a few hubs

- Physical goods and services still have geographical gravity; intellectual services and digital products, which make up an increasing proportion of the economy, are global

- In the West, we have more food, goods and shelter than we can consume; there are no shortages, but we just cannot figure out how to distribute these so that everybody has enough to thrive

- In the West, we have become so productive we cannot consume all that we produce and we need to throw out perfectly good stuff in order to keep buying, to keep production going; we thus need to consume in order to work

- Ignoring the non-regenerative consumption of land, nature and energy in the economic models is destroying the foundation of life.

None of the prevailing neoclassical economic theories have answers to this situation and we therefore need to rethink the economy fundamentally in order to allow everybody on the planet – and nature – to thrive. I am not the first economist to point this out, in particular, the shortcomings of GDP as a measuring tool are increasingly recognised. Among the economists questioning the existing models and suggesting alternatives are Kate Raworth, Tim Jackson, Steve Keen and Eric Beinhocker.

What is an economy?

The word economy comes from the Greek 'oikos', which means house, and 'nemein', which means to manage. An economy is thus a household, be it a family, an organisation, a local community, a country, a continent or the globe as a whole. A household is characterised by a sense of unity and (hopefully) solidarity, with resources, products, energy and work going in as consumption and out as a contribution to the external economy. It is an open, yet self-contained system. As any adult knows, a healthy household lives within its means and makes sure everybody feels safe and does not go to bed hungry.

Since 1935, the word eco has been applied to nature, and we refer to ecosystems.[4] Distinct areas in nature of a certain self-sustaining, interconnected inner, self-organisation are understood as open, yet defined systems. There are ecosystems within ecosystems and, likewise, there are individual households within the greater household of local communities and society. The world is fractal.

Current neoclassical economic theory has managed to grasp the interaction between individual households and companies (microeconomics) and nation-scale households (macroeconomics), but despite decades of theorising in environmental economics, it has not been able to grasp the interaction of these with nature, that is, the ecology. There is no mainstream economic theory that: 1) connects the individual economic actor to the global economy; 2) proposes how a global economy can be regulated in order for economic actors of all levels of complexity (individuals, families, companies, large corporations, nation states, continents, the globe) to thrive; 3) indicates how the global economy can be kept in balance; or 4) offers equal economic opportunities for individual and collective actors everywhere.

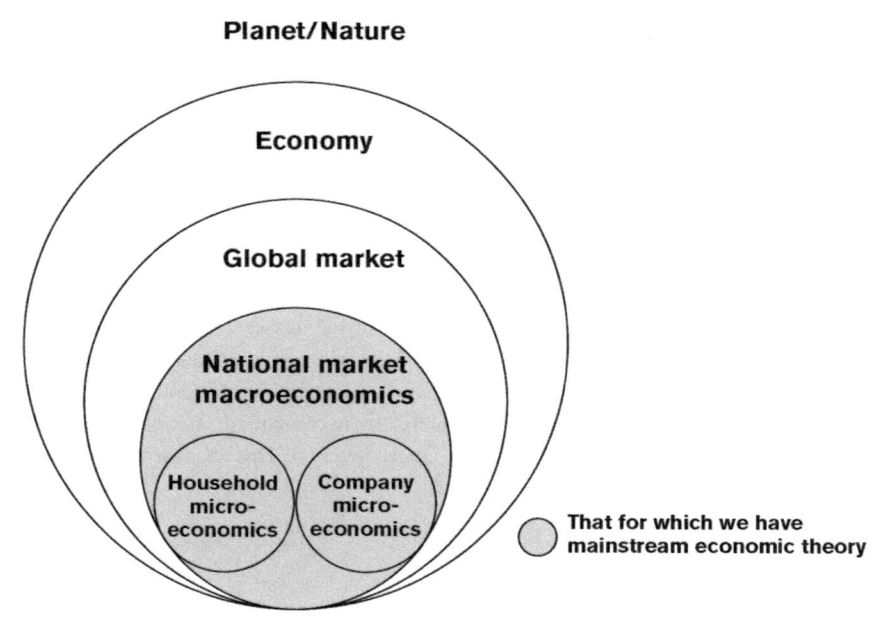

Figure 8.2 That for which we have mainstream economic theory

In Figure 8.2, the grey area shows the reach of mainstream (neoclassical) economic theory; the global market is insufficiently described, understood and regulated, while the full economy, which includes all non-monetised transactions and the nature upon which our lives depend, are not part of the economic framework.

Markets cannot regulate themselves unless the competitors in a market collaborate and explicitly create common rules. Generally, it is somebody outside the market who defines the rules. This means that a global market has no regulations unless somebody makes them, either the commercial players themselves in the global market or the governments. With an increasingly digital global economy, for such regulations to be created, we need a systems perspective on economy, technology, nature and culture to make it work.

An economy is a subsystem of life

To most economists, 'economy' probably means something like 'the exchange of goods and services within the same system defined by a legal tender'. As can be gained from the above, we need to understand economy as more than that.

An economy is a self-contained, human-made, self-organising and open system of exchanges of natural resources, energy, goods and services within the system and with other systems surrounding it, and it is governed by rules defined by legislation, traditions and norms. It is also work, social interaction, culture, individual hopes, dreams and initiatives, collective struggles, competition and collaboration, risk-taking, one or more legal tenders, and a complex interplay with nature.

Since ecosystems, societies, economies and households are dynamic entities of life and exchanges to uphold life, it is useful to understand the basic mechanisms of life:

- Life is reproduction, variation and selection. This is the basic process of evolution as first understood and described by Charles Darwin, which means that a core quality of life is evolution itself and that life is a constant process.

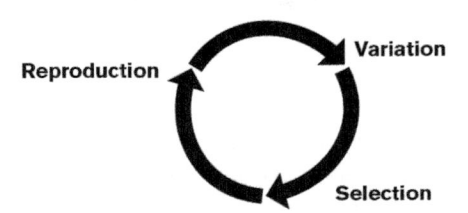

Figure 8.3 Evolution: loop of life

- Life is not only reproduction, variation and selection in sexual reproduction and the cycles of life itself (i.e. the development of life over time), but it is also reproduction, variation and selection in metabolism and transactions between individuals or clusters of individuals; animals eat and defecate in constant cycles, and plants take up water, nutrients and light and produce oxygen in constant circulation

- Life – from individual cells to entire ecosystems – self-organises in complex, open systems (or dies)

- One way of describing cycles of reproduction, variation and selection in evolving, self-organising, complex, open systems is *loops*

- Multitudes of parallel loops within loops allow systems that are open and dynamic to be stable and self-coherent over time

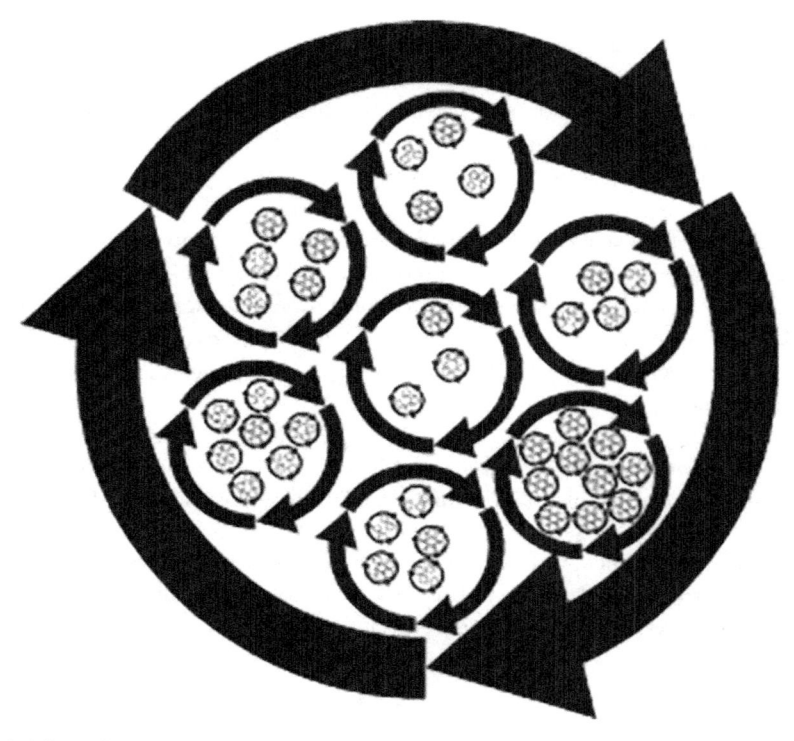

Figure 8.4 A complex system of loops within loops

- When loops are constantly running, minor changes to some of them do not wreck the overall system or push it out of balance. Some loops can even change or disappear and new ones can be added without fundamentally changing the system; instead, the overall organisation of the system is preserved and it evolves gradually.

- Only when a critical mass of loops fundamentally changes or stops simultaneously will the system go through a phase transition and fundamentally change its internal structure/organisation.

Just like biotopes, we can define economies as loops of transactions within loops of transactions; the system is fractal, which means that economic actors of all levels of complexity perform loops of transactions. My weekly routine of grocery shopping before the weekend is one such loop that is reproduced over and over again with variations each week; another loop is the monthly, automatic bank transfer paying for my insurances without any variations at all. Both sets of loops run within the larger loop of my overall economy together with several other loops; all of my loops run within the even larger loops of my nation's economy, the EU economy, and the global economy – and so do the tiny loops of all my neighbours.

One example of a change of loops that led to a phase transition in our economies was the invention of the steam engine; there was a feudal agricultural market economy before the invention and because of the invention, old loops became redundant and were replaced by new loops, and nation state, industrialised capitalist, communist or mixed economies emerged.

With the invention of digital products, we are facing a fundamental change of loops throughout our societies and their economies. We are in a phase transition and we can either just wait and see what is emerging or take deliberate political and societal responsibility for their development and create a sustainable economic model for the future.

The coronavirus lockdowns have halted or slowed down numerous loops in our economies; some of these loops will stop completely and will be impossible to restart. A loops approach to economy during the period of coronavirus would have had us asking: How much can each loop be slowed down or minimised to remain running and to be ready to speed up again when our societies reopen? My grocery shopping kept its frequency, but priorities became different; all payments on my insurances continued as if nothing had happened.

Cultural codes and their economic loops

Throughout history, 'the economy' and its loops have looked very different depending on the size of the society and the technologies available, which in turn have shaped the cultural codes: prehistoric indigenous, premodern, modern and postmodern.

In order for the exploration of the economic loops in the four historic cultural codes not to be too much of a gross simplification, each of the first three codes is divided into two epochs that match the more traditional way of describing the historic development: hunter-gatherers, Stone Age agriculture, Bronze Age, Iron Age, Renaissance-Enlightenment and Industrialisation.

Prehistoric indigenous economy

Prehistoric indigenous Stone Age hunter-gatherers lived in nomadic tribes with no more belongings than could easily be carried around. The bounties (or sparse resources) of nature were shared within the tribe and personal belongings, such as somebody's spear, knife, fishing hooks or other tools, were not property in any modern sense but items imbued with *mana* or other spiritual power that emanated from the maker and/or owner. The concept of ownership was thus fundamentally different from today and, given that people did not 'own' more than they could carry around, there was no difference in wealth. Within tribes, the 'production' (i.e. food hunted and gathered) was shared, so there were no loops of trade, rather loops of exchange. Between tribes, there may have been exchanges of foodstuffs and/

or other things gathered in nature, sometimes also young women ready for marriage. These exchanges were often fraught with danger and needed extensive ritualisation to take place peacefully; they were also often intimately connected to the loops of nature, such as seasons or the appearance of the moon. Tools and weapons with *mana* were rife with taboos and often not exchanged except as tokens of war between tribes, where the receiver would not only receive a new tool or weapon but also the *mana* of the previous owner. This earliest economy was a gift economy between tribes (not between individuals within tribes) and giving away a gift gave status and an obligation on the receiver to return the generosity later. An interesting detail about the word 'gift' is that in the Scandinavian languages *gift* means both poison and marriage, and there is an etymological connection: giving a present risks poisoning the relationship, and giving away your daughter as a bride creates expectations about getting something just as valuable in return.

The earliest documented semi-settled horticulture happened in the area of today's Israel and Palestine 15,000–18,000 years ago, towards the end of the latest ice age. The earliest documented settled agriculture evolved in the same area and coincided with the climate change that happened around 11,700 years ago/9300 BCE. Settled agriculture both spread from there and emerged independently around the globe as the climate changed and population densities increased.

Prehistoric indigenous Stone Age nomadic herders and settled farmers developed new loops of production and exchange, along with their new kinds of interactions with nature when they domesticated animals and plants. Their new means of survival meant larger group sizes, new conflicts between owners of herds and owners of fields, and new economic exchanges. With ownership also emerged differences in individual power, status and wealth. Initially, trade happened between groups, not between individuals in the groups where food and other goods were shared according to moral norms. As nomadic clans and villages grew in numbers of people, families would have started trading with each other within the clans and villages, the family most likely represented by one person, maybe a patriarch or a matriarch.

Between 9300 BCE and the emergence of the Bronze Age around 3300 BCE in and around the Middle East, agriculture took many forms, as did societies and economies later on. Nevertheless, there were general patterns. Theologically, prehistoric peoples were animists who believed in spirits in nature, and as some became herders, they invented a male divine bull in the sky, while the settled horti- or agriculturalists invented a Mother Earth goddess, both of which supplemented the spirits of animism.

Premodern economy

Premodern Bronze Age first emerged around 3300 BCE in ring-walled cities of Anatolia, North Africa, Mesopotamia and what is today Israel and Palestine, with some cities having up to 10,000 inhabitants. These societies had specialised artisans and marketplaces where families and individuals, city dwellers and farmers, traded with each other, and to some extent merchants travelled between cities with goods that could not be produced locally. They also had wealth inequality. Among the inventions of these societies were codified picture writing and bullion (i.e. bars or ingots of precious metals that were used as a means of transaction). What was radically different in the Bronze Age cities and city states, compared to their contemporary villages and the Stone Age, was that some cities conquered other cities and created empires. Due to taxation, looting and slavery, the biggest cities enjoyed a wealth surplus that allowed the support of a priesthood, organised polytheistic religion and a hierarchical power structure with armies and semi-divine rulers. An interesting aspect of the Bronze Age is the specialisation among artisans, which was paralleled by a theological development: each craft or trade, particularly war, and each of the strongest emotions, particularly love, got a god or goddess of their own, and with each god(dess) there was typically a dedicated temple. Specialisation and polytheism went hand in hand, and a new profession of the Bronze Age was maker of idols. The numbers and complexity of loops of trade thus increased drastically, and what we define as religion today was emerging from this economic development.

Premodern Iron Age first emerged around 1300 BCE, also in the Middle East, and around 1100 BCE in China, in cities with up to 60,000 or even 100,000 people, some of whom were kept together in million-strong empires. The Iron Age is characterised not only by the new techniques for welding iron, but also by the invention of the alphabet. New loops of production and exchange evolved along the climate belt from today's Italy and Egypt to China, and this 8,000 km-long 'axis' entered the so-called Axial Age, 800–300 BCE. During the Axial Age, the following emerged: Greek philosophy, the minor Jewish prophets and the Torah (the five books of Moses), Zoroastrianism (Iran), Hinduism and Buddhism (India), and Taoism and Confucianism (China), that is, the foundations of today's world religions (plus, of course, several religions that died out long ago or which are still around but have not become world religions). With the Iron Age, its empires and the trade along the climate belt/East–West axis also came the invention of coins in Anatolia around 600 BCE and, 1,300 years later, printed paper money, fiat money, in China in the 900s CE.

In Europe after the Iron Age, Western historians normally mention the Medieval Period, but from a culture code perspective, technologically, structurally, culturally and in economic development, nothing fundamentally changed between the Roman Empire and Papal rule. The theological narrative changed, morality changed, but not the overall code.

What is crucial in premodernity, the big common denominator between the Bronze Age and Iron Age cultures, is that societies were now so large they had to become imagined communities in order to survive. The village is a real community where everybody knows who belongs there; the city is so big that it can only function if people share a collective imaginary. Simplified, it can be expressed thus: cities that managed to create a cult around their leader, and where people served the same gods, prospered. The big shift between Bronze Age polytheism and Iron Age monotheism (for the lack of a better unifying term) was that rather than seeing the political leader as a semi-god, the godhead became invisible and religious practice became less about outer ritual and more about inner moral development and social justice. According to the respective religious traditions, Moses invented the Jubilee Year, when all financial debt was cancelled, Buddha was an Indian prince who was sickened by economic inequality, Jesus was a non-materialistic rebel who threw the merchants out of the temple, and Mohammed was a merchant who banned interest on loans. What we know as religion today is intimately connected to struggling with inequality and economic theory.

Modern economy

Agriculture, artisanship and variations of slavery continued into the European Renaissance when something was added that made the economy modern: paper money, banks and the invention of the company.[5] It takes a strong state for paper money to represent actual value among complete strangers; only because there is shared trust in some higher authority are we willing to receive a piece of paper from somebody we do not know and rely on the numbers on it representing actual value. China invented paper money and was the first empire to have the political power and skilled bureaucracy to back the value printed on them. The connection between debt, banks and the invention of paper money in Europe is thoroughly explored in David Graeber's *Debt: the First 5,000 Years* (2011) and I am not going to go into detail about it here. I am just going to outline the major differences between the two modern economies: Renaissance-Enlightenment and Industrialisation.

Modern Renaissance and Enlightenment economy invented capitalism, the stock company, the stock exchange, double bookkeeping, colonialism and the earliest industries based on wooden frame technologies and machinery. Among those technologies, the most radical was the new communication technology: the printing press with movable type. This development and its new loops of production and exchange created the economic surplus that paved the way for a middle class(i.e. a bourgeoisie), modern science, art, political freedom, the secular society and, overall, what we consider modernity.

Modern Industrialisation began with the steam engine, which was invented in 1698, and which, over the course of the 1700s, laid the foundation for the economic, technological and societal landslide that revamped Europe during the 1800s, and which also shaped the US, Canada, Australia and New Zealand – the colonies where the European settlers became the majority.

Theologically, the Renaissance was the separation of church and science, the Enlightenment the separation of church and economy, and industrialisation the separation of church and political power. The secularisation of the West was intimately connected to technological and economic development as well as to developments in science.

Industrialisation not only changed the economy, but also how we understand politics and what it means to be a state. The Left–Right political spectrum grew out of different economic interests between workers and capitalists, and as the production and economy changed, there was a tectonic shift from layered feudal societies to 'siloed' national societies next to each other. In the feudal era, monarchs, clergy and aristocracy were connected socially and politically with other monarchs, clergy and aristocracy across Europe, but not with each other locally, and definitely not with the third estate at all. Industrialisation and the national loops of production and exchange connected all strata of society within each nation and gave birth to the modern nation state based on a sense of peoplehood. The political conflict in the 1800s between Marxists and liberals, that is, workers and bourgeoisie, was thus not just an economic struggle but also a struggle between continuing the layered structure (Marxists + feudal conservatives) and transitioning to a democratic nation state (liberal bourgeoisie and capitalists).

Postmodern economy

Postmodern philosophy emerged in the 1970s, developed aesthetic representation in the 1980s and gained societal and political momentum in the 1990s. Postmodernism (the epistemology) and postmodernity (the epoch) emerged, along with a globalisation of communication, economy and culture. Until postmodernity, most modern, democratic Western nation states had a *Leitkultur*, that is, a majority culture that defined epistemology, language and norms, and which was generally White, heterosexual and associated with one religion. With globalisation due to migration, trade, the World Wide Web and social media, minorities have gained cultural momentum and spoken up on behalf of themselves and challenged the *Leitkultur* hegemony in the West.

There is still agriculture, artisanship and industrial production of goods in the postmodern economy, and there are 'classical' modern services in the postmodern society; the basics of modernity continue to produce what is necessary for our physical survival and wellbeing. However, there are also some entirely new phenomena in the economy:

- Digital products that are global and with no geographical gravity

- Shipping stuff around the globe is cheaper than producing it at home (it is cheaper to send fish caught in the North Sea to China to be filleted and frozen and then shipped back to Europe than to refine the product in Europe)

- Global brands are homogenising national and local markets, while enterprises such as microbreweries challenge industry production and create a new kind of local diversity

- Rather than 'modernity style colonialism', there is a massive brain drain in the Global South, with people struggling to get to the West.

Postmodernism is characterised by the absence of value hierarchies, by the deconstruction of power and other structures and by an ironical distance to everything. As a result, there has been no moral compass to guide economic development since the collapse of the Soviet

Union and the end of the Cold War, and, ironically (sic!), the one major social construct that postmodern philosophy has not deconstructed is 'the market' and its embeddedness in the overall economy and nature.

During postmodernism, 'the market' has become the one political answer to everything, the almost divine force that cannot be questioned; if something cannot be fixed by 'the market' it cannot be fixed at all. However, the market, of all things, is a social construct within which there literally are no absolute truths beyond how we as humans define them through norms and legislation. Due to the lack of its deconstruction, the illusion of 'the market' as something real with an actual steering mechanism beyond human decisions has become the political answer to everything over the past 30 years.

This has environmental consequences:

- Nature is in its sixth mass-extinction of species and this is human made[6]

- Oceans and freshwater resources around the globe are floating with micro-plastic[7,8,9,10]

- CO_2 emissions keep rising[11,12]

- Globally, both obesity and hunger are increasing[13]

- As humans keep stressing nature, felling pristine forests and so on, we risk more pandemics

It has also caused some major shifts in Western economies since the 1990s:

- Instead of working to consume, Westerners need to consume to keep jobs

- Many need to borrow money, to keep consumption up, to keep jobs[14]

- Increasing numbers of young people need to create debt to get the skills that can sustain them in the economy; debt-free survival becomes increasingly difficult to attain[15,16]

- Some of the most admired economies have working poor – people who work one or more full-time jobs and still cannot make ends meet[17,18,19,20]

- The economy as a whole may be growing, yet a generation of youth is expecting to be poorer than their parents.[21,22]

This, of course, is not sustainable, neither culturally or environmentally, nor economically.

Metamodern economy

Each code provided something essential and can contribute to meaningful production and transactions, to economic empowerment and to thriving individuals and groups. Each code also has mechanisms that can lead to corruption and abuse. A healthy metamodern economy, therefore, would recreate and consciously combine loops of production and transactions from all four cultural codes for everybody to have meaningful ways of contributing to production and consumption.

Organising principles

In order for metamodernity not to become an abusive, hellish mishmash of prehistoric indigenous, premodern, modern and postmodern cultural elements, there probably needs to be a rule of thumb that goes something like this: power structures need to respect group sizes and the original emergence of code, and also respect what the group sizes, relating to those codes, were historically capable of handling and regulating. Power structures of a more complex code disrupt the organisation of less complex group sizes, and power structures of a less complex code corrupt the organisation of more complex group sizes.

In other words, modern state or municipality public authorities can regulate and manage institutions, activities and gatherings of the modern world, such as schools, hospitals, libraries and entire municipalities and states. But they cannot regulate and manage the inner workings of a family or 'tribe', which is a prehistoric indigenous group size and whose inner workings are regulated via emotions, eye contact, body language and moral norms. Public authorities can prohibit violence and other abuse in a family by sending in social workers or police who may take away the children or arrest the abuser, but at the relational and emotional levels they cannot regulate a family or change its inner dynamics; only the individuals in the family can do that. What authorities can do is to provide appropriate (modern) education and economic opportunities for individuals to get their life on track. Similarly, a family or tribe cannot run a country or a municipality; these are institutions of the modern world and need modern power structures of democracy and equal access to political power, otherwise it is corruption.

Francis Fukuyama, in *Political Order and Political Decay: From the Industrial Revolution to the Globalization of Democracy* (Profile Books, 2015), explores political decay as a process when modern institutions and structures regress into patrimonialism. The point that I wish to make is bigger and more general: political decay emerges when the transactional regime of one scale takes the place of another. Hereditary and family-oriented organisations are very appropriate for indigenous and premodern systems, but they have no place in modern institutions such as universities or democratic politics (royal heads of state in democracies are cultural figures, not political figures). Scale becomes defining for the appropriate, non-corrupt social organisation.

Therefore, as the loops of exchange are explored below, assume by default that institutions and power structures of one cultural code and group size should not impose their power outside their original boundaries, unless otherwise explicitly suggested.

Loops from the prehistoric indigenous code to be promoted in a metamodern economy

There is already plenty of prehistoric indigenous economy and loops of exchange in our lives, as most of the traditional household chores in the family make up between a third and a half of all valuable economic activity in today's Western society.[23,24] This includes cooking, cleaning, childcare, care in general and DIY; these activities just do not figure in the official economy since there is no money involved. But there are more activities that are not considered part of the economy, even though they are crucial loops and create tremendous value. These include any kind of transfer of culture, moral norms and knowledge between the generations, such as storytelling, teaching, singing, dancing, norms and rituals around meals, and so on.

Together, these activities make up an intricate gift economy where even suggesting money payment for the services (i.e. entering money into any of these loops), would ruin the social bonding among family members. This gift economy often stretches beyond the family to neighbours, friends and colleagues. These loops without the use of money to mediate the time asymmetry, keep relationships and communities connected and alive. Most of what is left of this gift economy is still provided by women and, typically, the services only enter the official economy when they are turned into welfare services.

Biologically, we are still born as hunter-gatherers with the emotional and existential needs of 200,000 years ago. A society that allows us to have those needs met and promotes them would secure a fundamental part of our wellbeing. By not recognising this and by not making us aware of the importance of having a tribe and a village in which to bond and share with others through repeated loops of non-monetised exchanges, and by promoting material consumption instead through commercial advertising, and by the way our macroeconomic models measure wealth, we are not making ourselves as happy as we could be. The modern economic model is not promoting the gift economy: the family tribes and the village bonding that make life meaningful and promote a sense of security and belonging. We cannot all go hunting and gathering for our food, of course, or grow all our vegetables in the garden, but we can value the gift economy as part of our economy and give it its due recognition. We can also interact with nature and its creation of our food under circumstances that are much closer to prehistoric indigenous life than is the case today.

Tribe-size groups and loops of non-monetised exchange are essential to our emotional bonding, as is growing and producing food and sharing it as meals. Growing food, be it vegetables, herbs and/or fruits, or raising free-range livestock, attunes us to the cycles of our surrounding nature. Except for breeding plants and animals to make them grow faster in the long-term, horticulture and animal husbandry force us to accept a pace that is not defined by us. From feasting on the roast from a cow from one's own farm to sprinkling a sandwich with herbs grown on your windowsill as a city dweller, the expectations and patience that went into following nature's production of flavour and nutrition create a different kind of meal, particularly if you do it year after year and the loop is part of your life – and if you share the food with others.

An aspect of food production that has been lost in the modern and postmodern world is the spiritual aspect of the meal and the rituals around eating together, saying grace and acknowledging the wonders of how we and the planet are interconnected in loops of production and consumption. We partake in the circles of life every time we eat – and as we go to the toilet. Part of a healthy economy has always been that nobody went to bed hungry, physically hungry.

In a metamodern economy, nobody would go to bed either physically or spiritually hungry, and a core value of our societies would be communal meals in tribe-size groups that made nobody eat alone if they wanted company. This is something that would have to be created by personal initiative in the civil society and its families; it is not something that (modern) public authorities can create, impose or control. However, through political choices of the modern institutions of power we can make land for gardens available, and through a public conversation, culture and education, we can learn how to do the gardening and local organising, and we can find others who cherish those values and who would like to take part and cook and eat together.

One way to achieve natural tribes beyond the nuclear family and other modern/postmodern households in the inner cities would be around neighbourhood vegetable gardens. Vegetable gardens are 'active nature' in a way that flower gardens are not; if you have a local flower garden, people just sit there and need to take time off to sit there and do nothing – or the people sitting there are the ones who have nothing else to do. In vegetable gardens, people spend time working and spontaneously start talking, sharing and bonding, and they do so whether they have an otherwise busy life or not. With a little bit of effort and local commitment, that can lead to wider social interaction, such as meals, garden guilds, beekeeping and chicken coops.

There is every reason to believe that neighbourhood vegetable gardens would strengthen bonding across generations, among families and create that 'village' it takes to raise a child, a village that most children do not experience any more in the cities. It would also give children the opportunity to take responsibility for watering and caring for the plants.

One square metre of inner-city raised-bed vegetable garden per household would of course not feed a family nor provide anywhere near the vegetables needed for a healthy diet – not even ten square metres would – but it would be a supplement that would allow people to reconnect with nature, with food production and with each other, while providing the joy of something home grown. It would also make the local climate tangible and allow everybody to participate in constructively doing something concrete for nature and the climate.

Facilities such as maker spaces for DIY projects with sewing machines and tools, where people can share experiences and help each other, would also add to local bonding and the sense of belonging to a village.

In the suburbs, families have plenty of soil available for vegetable gardens, dwellings are roomier and DIY looks different from that in the inner cities. Yet people are not necessarily happier; there is often the same unmet need for bonding, community and belonging, a need for a complex web of family, tribe and village.

Promoting local vegetable garden food production and gift economies would not only strengthen human bonding, but it would also help nature and the climate, particularly if permaculture became the norm. Planting vegetable gardens may not exactly be rewilding nature, but it would most certainly provide more of a biological diversity than many current green areas and flower gardens in cities and thus be better habitats for pollinators and other insects. It would be particularly advantageous if more roofs were turned into gardens, and if car parks and maybe even some streets were turned into vegetable gardens as cars are kept out of the cities and/or replaced by car sharing options and public transportation for environmental reasons. The first and primary goal for gardening should be for it to be fun and meaningful; there should be easy onboarding. Later, or if people find it interesting right away, knowledge and classes about permaculture should be made easily accessible.

If people increasingly contributed to a gift economy by spending time gardening and DIY-ing, shopping would become less of a pastime activity and trips to the mall due to boredom could be replaced by creative activities together in the family and the neighbourhood. This would reduce the consumption and transportation of goods and materials, it would create greener cities, and it would challenge the use-and-throw away culture.

As societies, we thus need to rethink how we can value the value creation outside the monetised part of the economy and how individuals and families can easily co-create gift economy loops and structures, tribes and 'villages' around them. The modern state and municipality would normally try to get as much of the gift activity as possible monetised so that it figures in GDP and people can be taxed, but if we measured something else, the gift economy could help create strong neighbourhoods, benefit the environment and empower people to create more meaningful lives for themselves and others out of their own initiative.

One obstacle is the disruptive effect of modern measurement in the tribal gift economy and that the chores making up much of the gift economy in modern societies are typically the traditional work of 'womenfolk', that is, by promoting the non-monetised economy, women's lib of modernity may suffer if women are expected to 'go back to the kitchen'. Unless, that is, we change the measurement. Instead of measuring money transactions, we could measure square metres of vegetable garden per capita, numbers of users or hours spent per capita in maker spaces, be they private or municipal. We could measure how many neighbourhoods self-organise events among the users of the gardens and to what extent the need for psycho-pharmaceuticals changes along with the gardening and community development, and to what extent shopping malls lose square metreage and revenue, from material goods to immaterial, cultural activities. Instead of goods and services exchanged for money or self-reporting how people spend their time in the gift economy, an economic measuring gauge in the gift economy could be self-reporting the loops to which people contribute.

Loops from the premodern code to be promoted in a metamodern economy

The premodern elements in our economies are specialised crafts, artisanship, state bureaucracies and precious metals as means of exchange and elimination of the time asymmetry in economic exchanges. We also inherited from these societies hierarchical power structures, military and cultural institutions such as temples and schools, and from ancient Greece, secular theatres and academies.

According to modern economic theory, which assumes material poverty and shortages of all kinds, increased productivity equals economic growth and economic progress, which means that industrialised production is better than artisanship. The demand for growth in productivity also favours material production over immaterial services, because the latter generally can only improve their productivity up to a certain point; hairdressers cannot keep increasing the pace of cutting hair and violinists cannot play a symphony any faster than the sheets prescribe.

As the West is facing industrial productivity so high we cannot consume all the physical goods we produce, increased productivity no longer equals progress; it just increases the amount of waste, bureaucracy, the 'need' for wars and the abuse of nature. Instead, the driving values of our economies could be product quality, diversity, uniqueness, local flavour (be it actual flavour in foodstuffs or aesthetics in other products and services), recyclability, repairability, low ecological footprint, geographical gravity with regard to both materials and sales, and our meaningful contribution to the loops of production and exchange.

By deliberately promoting neighbourhood/municipality/Bronze Age-city group size economic clusters of loops of exchange, by promoting and strengthening artisanship and crafts, we can create strong local economies and a level of complexity that allow for deep dedication and specialisation, and the inclusion of those who cannot keep pace with industrialised society. Local food production, microbreweries, artisanship, shops and markets with local produce, arts and crafts, local restaurants and so on can contribute to the flourishing of local neighbourhoods, and they can be rewarded, say via the taxes, for providing low-skill and short-hours jobs for locals who would otherwise not be able to keep a job. Local 'sub-economies' or 'clusters of loops' based on local production and the work of local designers and crafts, local artists, music venues, theatres and 'temples' for the arts could give even towns of just 30,000 people two or more neighbourhoods with a unique, local feel and nearby places for entertainment. Tourism could be short-distance and still be full of surprises and new experiences. Long-distance tourism could be down to 500 kilometres.

Local economies with local businesses like that would call for local investment, while cooperatives, a modern invention, would be an optimal corporate form. The cooperative is particularly suitable for small- and medium-sized companies, although one of the general criticisms of cooperatives in the (post)modern economy is that once they reach a certain size it is complicated for them to achieve extra capital, since they cannot go public. But what if the goal was not growth, but local cohesion, integration, robustness, creativity and a multiplicity of loops? Cooperatives are particularly suited to being strong local players since they rely on active members (technically they are not investors) and a strong local community that backs the cooperative. Historically, strong economies comprising many cooperatives (i.e. Denmark, Norway and Sweden) started with cooperatives on the retail side. Cooperative grocery stores emerged and grew strong before the farmers created cooperatives on the production side, such as dairies, slaughterhouses, egg-hatcheries and cooperative banks. In a metamodern economy, it would thus make sense to promote the creation of local cooperative market spaces before creating cooperatives on the production side. Local cooperative markets and stores could then be committed to selling the products of local artisans, artists, farmers and producers of food. Furthermore, cooperatives get people involved and provide great democratic training.

Public institutions, such as nurseries, schools and retirement homes, should be encouraged to support local production, and public institution purchases should not just be about price and finding the cheapest providers, but should include such elements as product quality, ecological footprint, distance of transportation, ability to deliver, local employment and geographic gravity, and overall the generating of local loops of exchange should be balanced. This particularly goes against current EU ideology, but it would help make our economies greener, more robust and easier to slow down, or even halt and restart in case of future lockdowns. Municipalities and states could get local loops up and running and promote local spending, and they could thus revitalise the overall societal loops of trade, employment and taxation more easily than when citizens spend economic stimulus on buying things online from around the globe.

Since these activities are economic exchanges that involve money, they can be measured as usual, but an alternative measure would be the prevalence of cooperatives and members of cooperatives in a given area, plus the amounts of money people have invested and get back as dividends.

Loops from the modern code to be promoted

The modern Renaissance, Enlightenment and Industrialisation elements of our economies are institutions such as banks and stock companies, capitalism, accounting, steam and other engines, unions, primary, secondary and tertiary education, and international rules and regulations; we have economic models and talk about primary, secondary and tertiary sectors. Irrespective of our political ideology, be it socialist, conservative or liberal, our understanding of the connection between society and economy is modern and a product of industrialisation, and the overall entity to which it all applies is the sovereign nation state, which is itself a modern invention and a product of industrialisation. From a production perspective, industrialisation first and foremost means large-scale mass production of homogenous items and the assembly line; scale, homogeneity and constantly increasing productivity are key values in industrialisation. Even agriculture became industrialised; before industrialisation the vast majority of any society was made up of peasants or farmers, many even subsistence farmers. Today, in a country like Denmark, 2.7 per cent of the workforce works in agriculture and not only can they feed the entire country, but Denmark is also a net exporter of food.[25,26]

For most food commodities, we need industrial production: grain, dairy, meat, vegetables, cereals, pasta, sugar, and so on. It would make no sense to try to produce these commodities otherwise, but it could be done in more sustainable ways that protect soil, insects, biodiversity, ground water, pristine forest and all other aspects of nature. In order to keep producing enough food for everybody and to do it sustainably, we need both the latest science and indigenous knowledge about local flora and fauna; we also need to prioritise locally grown food to reduce transportation. We need new, more local loops. For refined goods, such as canned and frozen foods, bread, cheese, salads or TV dinners, the best balance between large-scale optimisation cum long-distance transportation and local artisanship and small-scale industry must be figured out. There will be no such thing as the perfect ratio of industry long-haul foods versus local artisanship, but there are obviously unsustainable loops and imbalances, such as transporting fish from Europe to China to be filleted and frozen and then back to Europe for consumption. It may just be that exotic flavours and out-of-season fruits should be considered as treats for special occasions rather than commodities. Metamodern industrial food production would have a systems perspective on food, economy, environment and the loops that comprise them, and it would combine the best from the old and the new in the wisest possible ways.

For low-tech non-food physical goods (from pins to clothing and furniture), artisanship can produce some (and can repair much), but industrial production will still be the only way of producing most of it. In the West, many of the things we buy we do not actually need – we just keep buying more of them because we are bored, want to impress people or think it will make us happier. This boredom consumption could be cut out of the economy altogether and we could transfer the consumption to services, learn to play an instrument, read a book or talk to each other instead.

For high-tech physical goods (medicine, mobile phones, ovens, cars, etc.), we need industrial production; these products cannot be produced in any other way. It also makes sense that these are the kinds of products that may be shipped long-distance. Not all countries produce all kinds of high-tech products; industries tend to specialise in clusters, which means that some countries have a car industry while other countries have a medical industry.[27] It would make sense, though, if all continents were self-sufficient regarding high-tech products, not just because of shipping, but because these extremely complex products and their loops need to be present on all continents in order to have a balanced global economy and for everybody to have meaningful and challenging job opportunities on their own continent.

As for raw materials, energy, infrastructure and natural resources, as a species we need at least continental systems thinking and planning. Some natural resources will need to be shipped around the globe, but we could become better at regulating this globally, reducing shipping and optimising resource consumption and recycling.

Education, universities and cultural institutions are a crucial part of any functioning modern economy, but economically they are usually listed as expenses, not as investments in well-functioning countries, which is a huge mistake.

These modern aspects of economy are still crucial, but they are insufficient, even though they represent the elements that mainstream modern economic theory considers.

Loops from the postmodern code to be promoted

Postmodernism is one answer to globalisation and digitisation. Globalisation has very much been an economic project based on modern economic theory, which prescribes low costs and increased productivity at any 'cost'. Parallel to this development, digitisation has provided (almost) zero marginal cost on digital products (which have no geographical gravity in the first place), which means that the most successful companies create profit at warp speed and as such 'deconstruct' the economic fabric in which they are doing business. Due to its national focus, modern economic theory is not capable of describing the complexities of its own brainchild: globalisation. With online social media allowing us to follow developments around the globe in real time and from our own personal angle, the shortcomings of modern economics and economy become visible to all, and the need for new economic theory and new economic development ought to be obvious.

The main shortcoming of postmodernism is its inability to build societies; it is an excellent analytical tool, but a poor toolbox for building cohesion and economic development. Hence, the postmodern loops that may serve a metamodern economy would most likely be intellectual rather than actual transactions in any economy: postmodernism can contribute with further deconstruction of mainstream economic theories but not with economic development as such. Three concepts at the core of postmodernism may serve a metamodern understanding of economy: context, complexity and intersectionality. Economic health cannot be boiled down to one factor (i.e. GDP growth), rather, several factors must be considered simultaneously and weighed against each other.

What to measure instead of GDP

We thus have three economic codes (prehistoric, premodern and modern) and one analytical code (postmodern), and to measure the wellbeing of an economy from a metamodern perspective, we could do the following.

We could make surveys where people anonymously self-report the loops of exchange they participate in during a day and the time spent on each loop. It could be, say, 2,000 people in each country on a given date.

We could measure:

- Vegetable garden sq.m. per capita in cities (should be high and rising)

- Number of cooperatives per capita (should be high and rising)

- Number of people being members (investors) in cooperatives per capita (should be high and rising)

- Annual revenues in cooperatives compared to stock and privately held companies (should not fluctuate)

- Ratio of service sales compared to physical and digital goods (should be high)

- Ratios of small, medium and large companies; shops per capita

- Structural complexity throughout society, that is, the complexity, connectivity and 'finemeshedness' of the circuitry of economic interaction in society (should be high)

- The extent to which individuals are both consumers and producers, and the extent to which they sell and buy in several places

- The extent to which countries are self-sufficient and produce products of both high and low complexity

- Travel distances for people and goods (should be low)

- The degree to which everybody can participate in the economy as both producers and consumers (should be high)

- Improvement versus deterioration of local nature and biodiversity (biodiversity should be high)

- The degree to which products can be re- or upcycled close to their manufacture (should be high)

- Household debt (should be low)

- Medicine consumption, particularly psycho-pharmaceuticals and painkillers (should be low and preferably decreasing).

Besides this, we need a tool for measuring the degree to which loops function within other loops and that all levels of complexity are present in an economy. In the West, this means we should promote low-complexity production, whereas in the Global South, all levels of complexity need deliberate development and the education and governance that requires.

If we stopped seeing GDP and GDP growth as the measurement of a successful economy and measured complexity and loops within loops instead, we could create a global economy where everybody could contribute, somewhere, everywhere; they could feel useful and become active as both producers and consumers.

Resistance against change

The suggested metamodern economic model still contains many well-known structures and values, and it is not dismissing capitalism, which is usually the assumption (and fear) many have whenever somebody suggests a new economic model. Instead, capitalism becomes one mechanism among many in a much richer economic paradigm or fabric; a truly mixed economy.

Nevertheless, the suggested metamodern economy is no doubt going to cause both resistance and anger, not least from some of the people who benefit the most from the current model and the current kind of globalisation. The people who thrive in a competitive global economy and who find it meaningful and fun to amass as much material and digital wealth as possible are probably not going to find gardening and growing carrots as meaningful as growing numbers.

Fortunately, the smartest among the most skilful number growers see more than their own opportunities in the global economic system; they see the full global economic system itself. They see it as an interconnected whole from a systems perspective and they realise that there needs to be a thriving system in order that they can do what they like, namely growing numbers. They also realise that the economic system needs to be sustainable and stable in the long term for them to keep growing their numbers and wealth.

The really, truly smart among them therefore also realise that the more people there are in the system who cannot pay their bills, feed their children, sleep through the night without worries, the worse the economy will be doing, and the less they themselves will be able to keep growing their own personal share of the numbers and wealth. They understand that somebody needs to create the wealth, which is so fun and meaningful for them to amass, and it is only safe for them to enjoy their wealth in a stable world with happy, content and trustworthy store clerks, housemaids, janitors, medical staff, teachers, professors, judges, police officers and so on.

So, of all the really skilful and competitive capitalists, the very wisest insist on functioning societies, good healthcare systems, state-of-the-art educational systems and just legal systems. And they are so joyful that the rest of us uphold good surroundings in which they can grow their numbers and wealth that they insist on paying taxes. In fact, they understand that if part of the numbers they generate in the system is not transferred to the common household through taxes and from there channelled to the services that allow everybody to stay sufficiently educated, healthy and safe, the poorest are going to be very angry at some point and start breaking down the system.

Whenever the people who have managed to grow for themselves big numbers in the system realise that all of the system needs to thrive in order for them to be able to grow more numbers, then they are not angry when somebody suggests new ways of organising the system so that everybody can thrive. Instead, they become very happy that somebody has suggested something that may save the system, including capitalism, even though the idea may just be a loose proposal meant to start a conversation about the future structure of the system and not a complete plan that is ready to be implemented.

Knowing that their investments in robots and information technologies will make it increasingly hard for growing numbers of people to compete with automation, they may also start advocating for a 20-hour working week with liveable minimum wages in the service sector and the arts. Why else would we keep inventing all those technologies if it weren't for all of us to live leisurely and meaningful lives, with time and resources to tend our gardens and enjoy good company, tasty meals and an enriching culture on a thriving planet?

Notes

1   This observation comes from the French historian Fernand Braudel, quoted by David Graeber in *Debt: the First 5,000 Years* (Melville House, 2014) who uses the term Commodity, not Product, and thus the formulas C-M-C and M-C-M.
2   https://bsahely.com/2017/03/18/the-role-of-energy-in-production-value-theory-thermodynamics-and-dialectics-by-prof-steve-keen/
3   www.peakprosperity.com/steve-keen-could-a-debt-jubilee-really-work/
4   www.merriam-webster.com/dictionary/ecosystem
5   www.oxfordbibliographies.com/view/document/obo-9780195396584/obo-9780195396584-0276.xml and https://en.wikipedia.org/wiki/Slavery_in_medieval_Europe
6   www.theguardian.com/environment/2017/jul/10/earths-sixth-mass-extinction-event-already-underway-scientists-warn
7   https://theconversation.com/far-more-microplastics-floating-in-oceans-than-thought-51974
8   www.sciencedirect.com/science/article/pii/S0043135419301794
9   https://pubs.acs.org/doi/10.1021/acs.est.9b07540
10 https://royalsociety.org/topics-policy/projects/microplastics-in-freshwater-and-soils/
11 https://ourworldindata.org/co2-and-other-greenhouse-gas-emissions
12 www.epa.gov/climate-indicators/climate-change-indicators-atmospheric-concentrations-greenhouse-gases
13 www.who.int/news-room/detail/15-07-2019-world-hunger-is-still-not-going-down-after-three-years-and-obesity-is-still-growing-un-report
14 www.epi.org/publication/webfeatures_snapshots_archive_02062002/
15 www.pewsocialtrends.org/2014/10/07/the-changing-profile-of-student-borrowers/
16 www.pewresearch.org/fact-tank/2019/08/13/facts-about-student-loans/
17 www.qualityinfo.org/-/who-are-the-working-poor-
18 www.eurofound.europa.eu/da/topic/working-poor
19 www.destatis.de/Europa/EN/Topic/Population-Labour-Social-Issues/Social-issues-living-conditions/working-poor.html?nn=218476
20 www.eurofound.europa.eu/publications/report/2017/in-work-poverty-in-the-eu
21 www.ft.com/content/81343d9e-187b-11e8-9e9c-25c814761640
22 www.weforum.org/agenda/2016/11/there-s-a-generation-growing-up-poorer-than-their-parents-a-new-study-explains-why/
23 www.oecd-ilibrary.org/social-issues-migration-health/cooking-caring-and-volunteering-unpaid-work-around-the-world_5kghrjm8s142-en
24 www.oecd-ilibrary.org/docserver/5kghrjm8s142-en.pdf?expires=1594548652andid=idandaccname=guestandchecksum=AC5B051A5D92C05512C27D9597B73CEC
25 www.statistikbanken.dk/10203 + www.dst.dk/da/Statistik/nyt/NytHtml?cid=24555
26 www.dst.dk/da/Statistik/nyt/NytHtml?cid=29618
27 Porter, Michael: The Competitive Advantage of Nations (1990).

9 The Conundrum of Cognitive Dissonance
On the uneasy relationship between agency and understanding, and why it matters

Sarah Stein Lubrano

IN THOSE societies that are officially democracies, however deeply flawed, modern individuals are provided with a ready-made narrative that they have agency. This agency is embodied institutionally through the vote, but it is also reflected in the many cultural narratives, on both right and left, that emphasise that individuals can be whatever they want to be if they just work hard enough, or that they should 'get involved' in movements or activism to make society better. Capitalism, too, builds this narrative as it brings with it the myth of the self-made man, and the notion that one's individual fate is tied to one's success competing in the markets. Through media, advertising, even through encouragement to engage in volunteering and activism, individuals are told they have agency: that they personally can 'change the world'.

It was probably this narrative, in part, that got me out of bed early one autumn morning in 2019 to take a train miles away and walk in the cold for hours. It was my first time doing any political canvassing, going door to door in towns across the UK. I must have cut a strange figure for the Brits who opened the door: a short, over-educated Jewish woman with an American accent, and, although this was less evident, a predilection for the writings of Marx. At first, I did this primarily out of a sense of duty: a feeling that I should do something in opposition to a government I found unbearable after a long couple of years watching election results related to Brexit and Trump with dread. Much to my surprise, however, I wound up canvassing dozens of times in the weeks before the UK general election, ringing the bells of imposing country houses and box-like, water-damaged council flats.

My persistence was not simply a matter of political commitment (I was both to the left of the UK Labour party and gently sceptical of its leadership, and any leadership); it was due in part to the unexpected high that canvassing began to provide. If, after knocking on 60 doors, I managed to convince even one person to think about issues differently, I felt a strange rush – the feeling of agency, perhaps, however illusory.

Yet I also discovered that one thing in particular made canvassing very challenging. It was not when I knocked on the doors of those who disagreed with me, but when I met someone (not infrequently) who said they had given up thinking about politics altogether. This always felt like a punch in the gut. I could not find a way, in those few moments when the door was open, to encourage the other person to take up the challenges and contradictions of politics and elections. 'It is your one and only world!' I sometimes wanted to interject as they closed the door, but found the words trite. My thoughts, as I trudged on, still working through what I wanted to say, were enclosed by that repeating phrase 'only world'.

I should probably not have been so surprised that grappling with my own sense of agency – of choice and influence over the world around me – could be both addictive and agonising. The field of psychology I study, loosely having grown out of research on *cognitive dissonance*, regularly demonstrates that when one feels a sense of agency, a feeling of responsibility for outcomes is also triggered, and this in turn makes it likely that we will feel a deep discomfort at the painful divisions that exist – within all of us to some degree – between our varied thoughts and actions. Our discomfort with these contradictions is so painful and immediate, in fact, that psychologists describe it as 'akin to hunger or thirst'.[1] It is often because of this painful dissonance that people relinquish this sense of agency, or project it onto others instead, including 'strong' leaders. Many of the problems that cause social scientists to wring their hands (or, more realistically, anxiously post on Twitter), issues like 'polarisation' and 'disengagement', share this common cause.

Indeed, for all that political scientists and commentators tend to speak of political engagement as a good thing, something that causes people to learn about the issues, to vote, to protest and so on, many of those who are deeply engaged in politics are also those who are least likely to be willing to endure uncertainty and ambiguity. Cognitive dissonance research can help explain why this is: when subjects encounter contradictions between their own beliefs, or between their beliefs and actions, one of the most common ways of reducing dissonance is to place less emphasis or importance on the topic at hand; the other is to double down on a particular narrative they already hold, so as to dismiss anything that counters it. Either we decide the whole thing doesn't matter, or we insist on our existing view. This doesn't, of course, just happen in politics; it is also recognisable in other areas of our lives. A person who claims to be very interested in nutrition might respond to having had a large dessert by concluding that sugar doesn't really matter anyway, or else by becoming ever more passionate about cutting out sugar in the future.

Either way, they reduce the tension they feel about what they've just done by resolving potential ambiguities and contradictions.

Realistically, all of us face contradictions in our beliefs about political issues, as well as between our beliefs and our actions. So here, too, we likely unconsciously find ourselves either disengaging or doubling down. The political equivalent of the dessert problem might be to deny or explain away the contradictions that undermine one's position, insisting on its correctness. Or it might be to conclude 'what I think hardly matters anyway'. So those who shy away from the discomfort of contradiction might disengage from politics, or stay engaged – but rationalise away good evidence that contradicts their existing beliefs. If this model holds, the result looks like two groups: the disengaged and uncertain, and the engaged and highly certain – with perhaps little to be said for either. As the poet Yeats put it, 'the best lack all conviction, while the worst are full of passionate intensity'.[2]

In the weeks I was canvassing, I oscillated between engagement and disengagement over a span of minutes. I was so weary of thinking about politics that I thought I might snap if I had to go through one more conversation about it. At the same time, I went out canvassing twice a week, and was furious that so many thought politics was irrelevant. I felt ablaze with the light of good news when I could change someone's mind, *and* equally certain that there was probably nothing to be done, at anything like the individual level, about the slow decline of the US and the UK into states with significant number of proto-fascists, supported into power by the (at best) unwitting indifference of their countrymen.

These and many other contradictions gave me my own taste of the agony of ambivalence that I knew so well from psychological research on people and politics. I did not resolve my own ambivalence about what is possible at an individual level. And nothing I did changed the fate of Britain's elections. But I did spend a lot of time thinking about the psychology in play, and its consequences, and came to this conclusion: passionate certainty and disengagement may *appear* to be opposing tendencies, but in many cases these are fuelled by the same underlying motivation, the desire (sometimes unconscious) to avoid facing and feeling responsibility for one's ambivalence, uncertainty and contradictory beliefs. The result is that agency in the sense of having an impact on the world through action lies in tension, to some degree, with agency that is internal: our ability to reflect and know what we think and why. To be able to reconcile these two types of agency may be a possibility, but it is one that remains painful and uncertain.

Dissonance

A common study in cognitive psychology asks participants to argue for ideas they don't believe in. The researchers ask participants (usually North American university students) to write an essay making the case for something 'counter-attitudinal', something they disagree with, like an increase in tuition fees. After students complete the essay, the researchers look it over and tell the students that it is excellent and will be used to convince other students, or perhaps the administration itself.

Strikingly, what happens next is that participants often begin to agree with the essay they wrote. In surveys following their essay writing, they score proposals to increase tuition fees far more favourably than control groups. Why?

The explanation has to do with one of the strangest and yet most influential and robust psychological findings of the last 60 years, with a term that is often used colloquially but which has a very specific meaning: 'cognitive dissonance'.[3] This term describes the way that people encountering a contradiction between their behaviours and their stated beliefs experience this 'dissonance' as painful.[4] People seek to resolve this, often excruciating, tension as quickly as possible, often unconsciously and usually in the easiest way they can. The essay-writing students, for example, cannot unwrite the essay, and so it is, oddly, easier to alter their views – although this generally happens entirely unconsciously, without their noticing. According to this theory of psychology, they 'rationalise' in order to eliminate the painful dissonance. The same body of research suggests that when faced with evidence that contradicts their existing point of view, many will double down on their beliefs, or at least hold fast to what they already believe, no matter how good the contradictory evidence may be.[5,6] In short, these many studies within cognitive psychology demonstrate that, at least in cultures where people are told they have individual selves and agency, human beings like to feel consistent in their thoughts and beliefs – even when they are not – and will go to great and often problematic lengths to maintain this apparent consistency.

The tendency to hold tightly to beliefs when faced with evidence that they are inaccurate may occur because doubt conjures ambivalence, in the sense of conflicting beliefs, desires and behaviours – and ambivalence and uncertainty are difficult to bear. Indeed, it appears that a desire for certainty over ambivalence can overcome all apparent rationality; some psychology studies suggest humans prefer to know that a bad thing will happen than to wait in uncertainty to find out whether it will.[7] In the case of cognitive dissonance, we not only seek certainty about the outside world but also certainty about ourselves and our place and influence within it. We insist on this certainty at the cost of knowledge, by covering over the more complex reality.

It is perhaps this desire to know with certainty and without complication that lies at the heart of a general human attraction to comprehensive overarching belief systems – religious, spiritual and otherwise. We all necessarily build a system of beliefs in order to navigate the world, some more flexible or reasoned than others. But in many cases we take on an external belief system uncritically. This isn't because we're stupid or docile, but rather because belief systems limit the amount of ambivalence and therefore discomfort we have to feel.

Limiting our discomfort may be helpful at times, of course, but dangerous at others. Belief systems simplify and build solidarity, but they bring with them their attendant millennia-long disputes, wars and bloody persecutions. Political ideologies, too, function to reduce our uncertainty, setting the terms and questions for consideration, if not directly providing the answers. As with religion, so with politics: however useful the reduction of mental expenditure, certainties have costs, from unthinking submission, to centuries-long bloody conflicts, to wide-ranging and often easily accepted forms of brutal oppression.

Agency

Cognitive dissonance does not simply occur whenever we face contradictions in our beliefs and actions; rather, it seems to occur far more often when we notice these contradictions *and* think that our actions will have an effect on the world. These are the foundations of what psychologists term the 'New Look' model of cognitive dissonance, developed from decades of laboratory research and summarised by Joel Cooper, one of the core researchers who developed this model, in the following way: 'Inconsistent behavior produces dissonance

> but only when decision freedom is high
>
> but only when people are committed to their behavior
>
> but only when the behavior leads to aversive consequences
>
> but only when those consequences were foreseeable.'[8]

We experience this painful, mind-altering dissonance not just when we are inconsistent but also when we feel like our actions matter and could lead to negative consequences in the world (and, as further conditions, when we feel we chose freely, knew what we were doing and meant it). In other words, it's not so much that contradictions alone bother us, but rather contradictions in an area where we feel a fairly high sense of responsibility and agency. This, in turn, likely means that those who feel they have an influence over the world seek greater consistency in their beliefs than those who assume they have no power – for better and for worse.

Perhaps the most striking demonstration of this phenomenon in the academic context occurred in 2005, when the researcher Diana M. Hill, then a doctoral student at Princeton University, conducted a version of the essay-writing experiment on other undergraduates and encountered something remarkable: Black students were much less likely than White students to experience cognitive dissonance when asked to take a counter-attitudinal position in a typical cognitive dissonance study. They wrote the counter-attitudinal essays just like other students, but they less frequently adjusted their views. This suggests that they were not feeling the same discomfort about the gap between their actions and their beliefs. However, when – in a later iteration of the study – those Black students were told that the university was particularly interested in their views and also their feelings and preferences about being a part of the study, Black students' measurable cognitive dissonance returned, and they, like White students, rationalised their way towards views they hadn't held, but had now promoted.

It is of course difficult to know precisely the causation in this case (as Hill herself admitted). But it is, at the very least, difficult to imagine that these students would otherwise have come to prefer to pay higher tuition; for both Black and White students, such a turn in their beliefs is, in this sense, unlikely to be strictly 'rational' in the sense of driven by conventional self-interest. More powerful than said rationality in this case may be the need for a coherent sense of self: *I wrote this, so I must believe it*. In the case of Black students, the researcher suggested, only once researchers asked them to notice their emotions about the task at hand did the usual rationalisation effect kick in, as Black students were at first unlikely to believe their essay would have any real impact on the outside world, or that their discomfort about a situation was unusual or mattered. Their recognition of the contradictions involved thus only occurred once they were asked to introspect further, at which point they apparently felt the same discomfort as White students about the contradiction between their actions and their beliefs, and revised their beliefs accordingly. Hill's research suggests that Black students (and minorities in similar positions) may experience less cognitive dissonance (and less rationalisation) not because they can simply tolerate greater contradiction, but because they perceive themselves as having very little agency, in the sense of influence on others or the world, because they are used to avoiding discomfort.

Oddly then, feeling that one has little influence over the world may bring with it a potential upside: one feels less pressure to rationalise away the contradictions in oneself. And feeling empowered can keep us tied tightly to the beliefs that we currently hold. By knocking on doors and seeking to bring people round to my point of view I, too, have made myself subject to the effects of cognitive dissonance; the same research suggests that having done so makes me less likely to change my mind in the future. Even as I wish for others to have agency, and pursue that illusory feeling of having some myself, I am likely limiting my ability to reflect on what I believe.

'Disengagement' and 'strong' leaders

Disengaging from politics is considered such a serious problem in democracies that numerous major initiatives are dedicated to measuring the problem of disengagement alone. For example, the Hansard Society, a British think tank led in part by the leaders of all major British political parties, uses a survey each year to measure political engagement in the country. The 'audit' is primarily interested in the most commonly accepted measurements of 'political engagement', focusing on 13 core political activities, such as voting, attending political meetings, contacting the media and boycotting products.[9] It is conducted by sending people door to door throughout Great Britain, asking a wide variety of questions about people's beliefs and opinions.

Of course, these researchers were showing up on the doorsteps of British citizens and interrupting their days (just as I had when canvassing). Such an interruption might well skew answers towards the brief and uninterested. Asked only about an extremely conventional definition of political activity, like party membership or voting, and many citizens might not think about themselves as political at all, yet lots of people are in fact deeply interested in issues like how they can achieve better pay or more free time, or make sure their children do well – issues are implicitly political whether they recognise this or not.

Nevertheless, if the responses to this survey give even a limited indication of how British people have recently felt about politics, they suggest that Brits not only feel uninspired about 'getting involved', but also distinctly unenthused about even thinking through their own opinions. Compared to the previous year, more people said that they were 'not at all' interested in politics or know nothing about it. Thirty per cent of people said they never *discussed* government or politics. Perhaps most strikingly, 32 per cent of the public reported not wanting to be involved 'at all' in local decision-making, a rise of ten points in a single year. In 2019, the last year the study was conducted before it was paused due to the coronavirus crisis, 53 per cent of the public reported not having done any political activity in the form of these 13 activities in the last year. The number of people saying they would be prepared to do 'none' of the 13 key core political activities was up ten points in a year. Their feeling of efficacy – the ability to make some change to their world – has markedly declined.[10] It may be painful to those of us worried about the future of democracy, but from a psychological perspective, being disengaged carries certain benefits, not least perhaps by removing the possibility for painful ambivalence.

This is not, of course, the only reason disengagement happens: people spend their lives working for a living, and the sceptical often point out just how irrational it is to be engaged when individual efforts make so little difference.[11] Given the connection between a feeling of agency and dissonance, however, I am tempted to wonder if this narrative about the rationality of disengagement, while true, can also be told in reverse. Perhaps people do not only disengage when they feel powerless, but also feel powerless in order to reduce the pain of dissonance about conflicting beliefs they may have and the actions they have taken. If so, democracy, that most beleaguered of ideals and institutions, is challenged not only because some feel they have no real power, but also because the promise of even a little influence leads to discomfort, and discomfort to disengagement. In this case, the challenge is not only whether power can be given to the people but whether – unconsciously, at least – they really want it.

Another intriguing piece of data from the Hansard Society study carries a similar suggestion. Fifty-four per cent of those surveyed say they want 'a strong leader who is prepared to break the rules'. While this could mean many things, it suggests that the same group of people who find politics difficult to think about would like someone – someone *else*, that is – to do the thinking and doing for them. In this same study, many Brits said they felt things would go better if Parliament had less oversight, and welcomed 'radical changes'. Authoritarianism, then, may come in part from the urge for agency – where people prefer to situate that agency outside themselves, to avoid the painful thinking-through it would otherwise entail.

Turning to a figure of authority allows individuals to feel they have agency without all the responsibility and ambivalence that it entails. And in this sense, individuals turn to authoritarian rulers not just despite, but in many ways in search of, the 'freedom' and individuality promised by modern society.

Psychologists might put this all a slightly different way. Joel Cooper, the aforementioned psychologist, has written perhaps the most comprehensive account of cognitive dissonance theory. He puts it this way: we can experience 'vicarious' cognitive dissonance because we can identify with others and feel, oddly, responsible for their beliefs, their actions, and any contradictions between them: 'it feels as though you were partially responsible for it, as you and the actor are fused together by a common social identity.'[12] When subjects see a politician they like or identify with making claims that contradict their beliefs (perhaps a conservative politician they like arguing for higher taxes, or a progressive candidate arguing for fewer protections for workers) or engaging in hypocritical behaviour, they may well come around to these new views or behaviours, and defend them as if they had made the statements (or written a counter-attitudinal essay) themselves. There is the same possibility for defensiveness, for the rationalising away of contradictions, as in the lab.

The problem, of course – the big worry about cognitive dissonance when it comes to politics – is not the changing of views per se (either ours or the politicians). Rather, it is the way we tend to change or defend views when cognitive dissonance arises: unconsciously, in ways we can rarely consciously elucidate, with a preference for whatever is less costly to the ego or to social judgement, rather than via the thinking-through of which principles are most important. When we come to our views as a result of unconscious revisions due to cognitive dissonance, we tend to make enormous leaps in reasoning. We do this without realising it, and without knowing what has warped our thinking. When we combine our tendency to do this with an attachment to 'strong' leaders, we also outsource the feeling of responsibility that we should perhaps carry ourselves. We are looking for someone to embody certainty for us, and we may later excuse a wide range of behaviour on their part in order to hold on to our *own* certainty.

Teaching

As I did on the doorsteps of voters, so too in the classroom: I struggled to convince people to take the world in their hands. For much of the last decade I have been a designer of what might more or less be termed personal development workshops. There I found the same resistance to grappling with ambivalence. Such workshops might provide some 'answers' to people's life problems – but only so much: *discover how your partner likes to be comforted, practise these steps for improved communication, consider your own blind spots during a conflict* … useful, perhaps, but the attendee must ultimately make the call about how to apply this 'expert' knowledge to their own particular situation. The facilitator won't (and can't) tell them which of the tools, if any, to apply to their particular relationship, or when it's time to end one.

This was often unsatisfying, perhaps surprisingly so, to those attending: largely upper-middle-class Europeans and Americans seeking just the right partner or relationship. Perhaps they wished to self-actualise, but they often seemed surprised that they would have to make difficult choices to do so.

There was therefore inevitably the delicate and sometimes fraught matter of the handing off – indeed, the handing back – of authority to participants. And it is, frequently, fraught. I have taught dozens of workshops over the last five years and sat through literally hundreds of classes and workshops. Perhaps at no other time are participants more annoyed, visibly frustrated and even angry than when they ask a very specific question about their life ('how can I make my partner understand the importance of what we just talked about?') and the facilitator tosses the question back ('well, given what we've discussed, what do you think might help them be ready to listen?') The reaction is often one of shock or even refusal, usually mixed with nervous laughter from the rest of the group.

The task is more difficult because almost every workshop begins with establishing the credibility of the person leading it. The facilitator appears to 'know' early on, citing their credentials right at the start of a workshop (often as a psychologist or therapist) and standing at the front of the room. They are trained to exude a gentle authority to encourage the group to engage; this is the 'transference' that Freud thought did important 'work' for psychotherapeutic clients. Such transference is indeed helpful in getting a group to cohere or a person to trust the facilitator, not to mention difficult to obtain: only after a good hour or two into the workshop may trust be won. Yet paradoxically, the workshop structure is founded on a sort of delicate manoeuvre, perhaps even a manipulation. Once the facilitator has elicited trust from the participants, he or she is meant to quietly go about unravelling the very sense of authority that participants have just been invited to rely on. Certainly, many participants experience this transition in such a way. 'I expected more concrete answers' is a routine piece of feedback. A few insist on disrupting the class to ask, over and over, the same personal questions, or to try to 'trick' the facilitator into saying what they really think. Occasionally people storm out. And yet, there are not, past a certain point, concrete answers that can be responsibly provided.

This refusal to give answers is not an intentional cruelty. It is meant to encourage people to 'take ownership' enough that they will have the courage to make use of what they've learned, as they are far more likely to commit to a line of action they have arrived at themselves. In many ways, this handing back of authority is the last and most essential step in the workshop: not the dissemination of knowledge, however useful and important, but the devolution of agency to the only people who can truly put it to use.

Knowledge and freedom

Alongside similar cognitive dissonance studies, Hill's experiment with students of different races suggests that those who feel their views have consequences often think less clearly. The reverse is also true: those who believe that their views have little effect on the world may be in a stronger epistemological position, perceiving the world in greater complexity, contradictions and all. A feeling of agency in the sense of control and influence may place subjects in a position where they ultimately do not want to know certain truths about the possible effects and implications of their actions.[13]

For some political theorists and philosophers, this finding might not come as much of a surprise. Members of the French structuralist school, for example, have long argued a sense of agency is an illusion, a part of ideology – and this does not just imply that in reality individuals have no power, but also that *it is precisely when we consider the impact of our actions on the world that we become subsumed into ideologies*. In one of his most famous works on ideology, the 1970 essay 'Ideology and Ideological State Apparatuses', the French structuralist Louis Althusser suggests the individual is made to feel that they are 'a (free) subject in order that he shall submit freely to the commandments of the Subject, i.e. in order that he shall (freely) accept his subjection' to a particular system of belief or even to a leader.[14] By being made to feel that we are truly free and that the actions we perform are truly our own choices, we are placed in the difficult position of seeking to make consistent what is inconsistent in our lives, in order to appear to ourselves to have chosen all of these contradictory behaviours freely. Another way of thinking through this paradox is to consider ideologies as maps that orient people in their social context. When contradictions arise, they need to be resolved, not simply because they are uncomfortable, but because we need a continuous map in order to navigate, to know what possibilities of action exist for us.

The verdict is rather different, however, if one expands one's interests in human freedom beyond this limited definition of agency, to focus primarily on the capacity of the individual to influence outcomes. Much depends on what is meant by agency – on the type of freedom in question.

For other philosophers, meaningful freedom is obtained differently. For the German idealist philosopher G.W.F. Hegel, for example, freedom is non-causal; it does not have to do with whether a subject can cause a particular effect on the external world. True freedom occurs after the fact: it lies in understanding, and precisely in understanding and thereby transforming contradictions. This is what lies behind his understanding of history as sets of contradictions that are to some degree resolved by their 'sublation' into new ideas or systems, such that the ideal of individual freedom, which often lies in contradiction with the idea of collective order, can be incorporated together into a legal system that brings these two things into greater harmony, and which may even allow them to support one another.

A key difference here, notably, is that for Hegel (unlike for structuralists like Althusser) contradictions are not merely happenstance messy conflicts, but are two aspects of a larger picture, two elements that upon excavation by reason are part of a greater, intelligible whole. Individual freedom and societal order are not really contradictions, only two aspects of ethical life. Indeed, ethical life itself, or *Sittlichkeit*, is, for Hegel, not only an important expression of freedom but something that primarily involves grappling with contradictions; Hegel imagines that in a fully developed society people face more contradictions, not fewer, because there are more higher-order freedoms that conflict with one another.[15] And it is this kind of grappling with contradictions and developing a contradiction-heavy understanding that is itself freedom, because it provides the positive abilities involved in being autonomous, rational and self-determining, even if only within one's own thought. Much depends on this distinction. If our contradictions are simply random inconsistencies, resolving them may merely be an artificial exercise, and thus seeking to do so, and to overcome cognitive dissonance, may bear little fruit. But if consciously recognising painful contradictions can in fact eventually lead to better forms of understanding, then it becomes a vital task, the very work by which true understanding emerges, not only for the individual subject but also for societies as a whole.

Given their differing definitions of freedom and agency, it is possible to say that the two thinkers are talking past one another. Certainly Althusser and those like him are correct to argue that a feeling of agency warps subjects' thinking, limiting their ability to understand. Nevertheless, an emphasis on a different kind of freedom – the freedom that comes not so much through immediate, action-based influence on the world, as through long-term retrospective understanding – suggests a means of moving beyond this dynamic, if only with great difficulty and to a limited degree. If Hegel is right, and if it is at all possible for human beings to accomplish this day-to-day, then in key cases freedom precisely comes from overcoming the negative effects of cognitive dissonance. Cognitive dissonance represents a 'crisis' in the original etymological sense of a turning point in an illness, where a patient either recovers or dies, a crossroads with an opportunity and potential catastrophe attached to the same phenomenon.[16] The problem for those of us with one finger in a psychology textbook is simply that cognitive science both suggests this is possible and warns that it is very difficult. Subjects might unconsciously avoid contradiction, avoiding the type of understanding that could lead to their own and others' greater freedom, both internal (in terms of understanding) and external (in terms of their resulting actions). On the other hand, if there are ways for subjects to consciously recognise the contradictions, to become aware of their cognitive dissonance and to overcome its negative epistemological effects, then an opportunity for greater freedom arises. On this there is yet relatively little research. Substance addicts overcome cognitive dissonance and face their addictions when they are asked open-ended questions and given 'grey areas' as possible answers.[17] But in the political realm very little of a similar bent has been developed.

For now, the difficulties we face in acknowledging contradiction are unlikely to go away completely. Our influence over the world around us may be limited, our freedom through understanding less so – but both, clearly, are rare and significant achievements, and the result of painful effort. For this reason, and so many others, humans find creative and destructive ways to turn away from these efforts through disengagement or leaving the decision-making to others. Not every instance of this is necessarily 'bad': arguably this is partly the good of democratic institutions. By asking us to take positions and to vote, to pick people to represent us, these institutions baptise our political thoughts into new life, and give them a certainty that we often do not have, or which we cling to forcefully. So, too, when it comes to serving on juries, we see in the moment of instruction by a judge the beginnings of a conversation about which facts and thoughts we should allow to sway our individual judgement. Still, these are at best the scaffolding for a building that has yet to be completed, one that could better hold our ambivalence and allow our thinking to expand, rather than prematurely crystallise.

Synthesis and dissonance

Structuralists see agency as an illusion, one that shapes our view of the world. Democratic theorists might argue that individual agency is a *necessary* illusion. But psychologists tell us something else: a sense of agency is not only an illusion, it is a burden, something painful, something that may be necessary for political life to function well but which comes at a high cost in terms of pain and self-deception. To do politics with this in mind, we may have to look for ways of coping with this pain long enough to see through it.

If certain types of maturity entail living comfortably with contradictions, or resolving them altogether without a shortcut, this is necessarily going to be very difficult simply because it is something that causes humans near-physical pain, 'akin to hunger and thirst'. Moreover, this pain exists for strong reasons – it protects the very useful maps by which we chart the meaning in our lives, and our place within it; it keeps our beliefs in line with those around us so that we might benefit from the very real advantages of belonging to a network of knowledge, not to mention the many social benefits of belonging. This is not to suggest that we should not seek greater political maturity, or that coming by it is entirely implausible. Indeed, I remain curious and cautiously optimistic about how techniques like those used with substance addicts might help free us from our own political addictions and confusions. I merely suspect that such a process is inevitably messier, far more difficult and partial, than modelling it might suggest.

The metamodernists among my personal correspondents, including some of the other authors in this collection, suggest that steps in a developmental trajectory help people progress in their political thinking, and that these developmental achievements help people to synthesise new 'and' responses, rather than merely 'or' responses to apparent contradictions. To do this would certainly constitute an expansion of human freedom from the Hegelian perspective, and it has always seemed to me that synthesis, that classically Hegelian step, is essential to metamodernist theories. I too hope for such a possibility in some ways, in part inspired by my own sense of cheeky optimism as I read Hanzi Freinacht's *The Listening Society* some years ago. Yet, while I don't disagree in theory about the task at hand (indeed, while I long for it in a world where about half of Americans believe at least one conspiracy theory and where many Brits would welcome a strongman), I carry with me a Freudian pessimism about its plausibility, or at least its straightforwardness, in practice – and more than this, in theorists' ability to predict how it should or might play out.[18] Developmental logic is moderately sound with actual children, who do more or less learn new abilities in a particular order. But what adults come to learn and do, especially large groups of adults, is far less determined by a single set of psychological moments or variables, far more difficult to model. I suspect the trajectory of humans as a whole, caught up intimately with their particular social and material conditions, and darkened by self-destructive impulses, suggests a darker story. Although our societies have advanced rapidly in terms of technologies, the very same conditions have made us distracted and alienated, pressured to produce, to consume and to seek a particular style of individual liberation that limits as it liberates. In this way both readers and writers of this collection are truly trapped in this (yes) modern logic by forces from the outside, and perhaps more than they realise from the inside too, as the question of individual agency above demonstrates. Still, there may be a space for personal development as the source of political progress, and a key task here is surely to help us acknowledge and 'sublate' our contradictions.

I have begun to appreciate why the ancient Athenians might have preferred sortition to voting for representatives. In sortition – the form of governance we still use to pick juries – individuals are chosen at random from the populace to come together and make decisions. People thus mostly face the political questions that cause painful dissonance – those that challenge their sense of self and agency – at times when they actually have a fairly significant amount of influence over the outcomes of decisions. Surely they would then still struggle with ambivalence and dissonance, but perhaps only for limited, necessary stretches of time. The exhaustion (or as the professors and pundits would put it, the polarisation and disengagement) might be less significant.

Many Athenians tried to escape sortition with excuses about commutes and costs, just as we do with jury duty. But it was largely mandatory. And this, too, might be crucial – because, if the polls and the faces that open doors to canvassers are anything to go by, many of us are at heart ambivalent about taking on the painful process of deciding that comes with politics. I fantasise about dragging in the apolitical from their doorsteps to sit and think together every once in a while. It is a tyrannical fantasy, but perhaps no more so than jury duty. And it might, oddly, be a more realistic expectation of effort and discomfort, given the limits of human psychology.

If the feeling of personal agency that subjects (in large representative democracies, in late capitalism) are given today is a lie, it is probably an important falsehood all the same, one that maintains the collective truth that rulers should not hold power unchecked. Meanwhile, political agency can more accurately be attributed to large groups, to transindividual reasoning and, sadly, to a few at the very top of existing hierarchies. But it strikes me that there might, as with sortition, be ways of reworking our relationship to decision-making so that we are less pressured into strong opinions or disengagement. Which is probably just another way of saying that to reimagine political systems and movements and to set them in a more productive direction, the freedom to alter the world in some way (through speaking, voting and so on) must be held firmly, but lightly, alongside an attentiveness to internal states and internal contradictions.

Agency, that sense of freedom to alter the world, must be balanced against another freedom with which it often lies at odds: the freedom to change one's mind.

Notes

1   Joel Cooper and Kevin M. Carlsmith. 'Cognitive Dissonance.' *International Encyclopedia of the Social and Behavioral Sciences*: Second Edition, Mar. 2015, pp. 76–78.
2   W.B. Yeats, 'The Second Coming', see www.poetryfoundation.org/poems/43290/the-second-coming
3   Many social psychology studies have been criticised lately due to the general social science replication crisis that began around 2015. Nevertheless, there are a number of reasons to believe that cognitive dissonance theory has and will continue to weather the reproducibility storm, and that it carries scientific (and by extension political) significance. One is the sheer volume of studies on cognitive dissonance, including many failed attempts to disprove the theory by behaviourists. Another reason to think that cognitive dissonance is a significant finding is that in many cognitive dissonance studies, the 'p-values' assigned to cognitive dissonance findings, an important measure of scientific statistical significance, are far smaller than .05, the previous benchmark that failed to ensure reproducibility. Each empirical study finding is assigned a p-value, and a smaller p-value indicates stronger statistical significance. These smaller p-values suggest a greater likelihood of reproducibility and scientific significance. A third reason to consider cognitive dissonance theory credible is that although cognitive dissonance, as a subjective internal state, can only be measured indirectly (generally through the change of the subject's opinion), there are now studies that demonstrate potential neural correlates for the phenomenon, which suggests a firm neurophysiological ground for this form of cognition. For example, in a 2011 study, not only were neural correlates for cognitive dissonance observed in an MRI machine, but a change in attitude demonstrating the effects of dissonance happened to the degree that p-values were .001, again a much stronger benchmark than the types of studies involved in the p-value replication crisis. This does not, of course, mean that caution is not needed when approaching this topic or that future findings may not challenge it successfully. Nevertheless, based on the vast number of studies and strong statistical significance, I believe the issue is important enough to merit this type of in-depth exploration, especially given its likely effects on democracies. See Joel Cooper's aforementioned work as well as Johanna M. Jarcho, Elliot T. Berkman and Matthew D. Lieberman. 'The neural basis of rationalization: cognitive dissonance reduction during decision-making.' *Social Cognitive and Affective Neuroscience* 6.4. 2010, pp. 460–467. And see an account of its wide influence on social psychology and beyond in Irem Metin and Selin Metin Camgoz. 'The advances in the history of cognitive dissonance theory.' *International Journal of Humanities and Social Science* 1.6. 2011, pp. 131–136.
4   The original finding of cognitive dissonance was made in 1954 in studies of cults, from a prior finding of 'confirmation bias', in which participants find ways to interpret new events so as to confirm their existing beliefs. *When Prophecy Fails*. Martino Fine Books, 2009. The related finding of 'attitude polarisation', which describes the tendency for individuals to specifically become more attached to their existing views even when faced with contradictory evidence, was made in the 1970s. See Charles G. Lord et al, 'Biased assimilation and attitude polarization: The effects of prior theories on subsequently considered evidence.' *Journal of Personality and Social Psychology*, vol. 37, no. 11, 1979, pp. 2098–2109.
5   See, for example, Charles G. Lord, Lee Ross and Mark R. Lepper. 'Biased assimilation and attitude polarization: The effects of prior theories on subsequently considered evidence.' *Journal of Personality and Social Psychology* 37.11. 1979.
6   This may, of course, not be the case for all people, everywhere: cross-cultural research suggests that people in many different cultures experience cognitive dissonance, but they experience it differently, and around different issues, because their concepts of selfhood and agency are different. For more on this, see Steven J. Heine and Darrin R. Lehman. 'Culture, dissonance, and self-affirmation.' *Personality and Social Psychology Bulletin* 23.4. 1997, pp. 389–400. Also relevant is Haruki Sakai and Kiyoshi Andow. 'Attribution of personal responsibility and dissonance reduction.'

Japanese Psychological Research 22.1. 1980, pp. 32–41. It may also be helpful to read a summary of the cultural differences found in cognitive dissonance research in Joel Cooper's extremely thoughtful book *Cognitive Dissonance: 50 Years of a Classic Theory*. Sage, 2007.

7   Archy O. De Berker et al, 'Computations of uncertainty mediate acute stress responses in humans.' *Nature Communications* 7. 2016, Article Number: 10996.

8   Cooper, 73.

9   One has to wonder how different the data would be if it included other activities, like posting on TikTok or Twitter, or even supporting charities. But the Hansard Society, which has as vice presidents all leaders of major political parties, is a fairly formal institution.

10 This is from the Hansard Society study: '47% feel they have no influence at all over national decision-making – a new high for the Audit series.' See www.hansardsociety.org.uk/publications/reports/audit-of-political-engagement-16

11 For one such argument which cites many others, see Katherine Mangu-Ward, 'Your vote doesn't count.' *Reason.com*, Reason, 20 Aug. 2020, reason.com/2012/10/03/your-vote-doesnt-count/

12 Cooper, 134.

13 The political implications of this point are intriguing – this suggests, for example, that those who are not able to vote on a particular issue (whether this is due to oppression, or perhaps merely being in a different voting district) may more accurately judge political policies, ideas and situations. They do not face largely unconscious concerns about the negative effects of their decisions, concerns which then cause them to avoid grappling with the tensions between their beliefs and actions. The powerless' sense of responsibility and self is not as tightly implicated in the political issues at hand and so they can, seemingly paradoxically, avoid the pitfalls in reasoning generally experienced by those who perceive themselves to have agency.

14 Louis Althusser, 'Ideology and ideological state apparatuses (notes towards an investigation).' *The Anthropology of the State: A reader* 9.1. 2006, pp. 86–98.

15 For a discussion of this see e.g. Gillian Rose, *Hegel Contra Sociology*. AandC Black, 1981: 143.

16 See The Vocabularist, 'The Vocabularist: Where Did the Word "Crisis" Come from?' BBC News, 15 September 2015, www.bbc.co.uk/news/blogs-magazine-monitor-34154767

17 For a brief discussion of these techniques and their efficacy, see W. R. Miller, 'Instructor's manual for William Miller on motivational interviewing.' (2012). It is free online at www.psychotherapy.net/data/uploads/51194e1c160b2.pdf

18 For the research on Americans and conspiracy theories (which continue to, for example, massively hinder the US's ability to respond to the coronavirus pandemic at the time of writing) see J. Eric Oliver and Thomas J. Wood. 'Conspiracy theories and the paranoid style(s) of mass opinion.' *American Journal of Political Science* 58.4. 2014, 952–966.

Part 3 New Frontiers

10 Manifesting Mass Metanoia
Doing change in trying times
Brent Cooper

Repent (metanoia!), for the kingdom of heaven is at hand. Matthew 4:17

A GREAT CHANGE is upon our civilisation and the self: a cultural conversion of biblical proportions. The operative word is *metanoia*, Greek for a profound 'change of mind', from the roots *meta-* (change, beyond, after) and *nous* (mind). Usually defined as 'a transformative change of heart, especially a spiritual conversion', metanoia has deeper implications as a 'turning' towards the disclosure of a higher reality and more relevant truth. A profound change is needed not only in individuals' hearts and minds but also in the hivemind (collective intelligence), the noosphere (global consciousness) and our institutions.

Metanoia is an esoteric word but it is increasingly utilised across literatures of enlightenment, personal growth, business ethics, pedagogy, social justice, spirituality, poetics, metaphysics, politics, psychedelics and more. Across these fields, this word speaks to a transformative idea and practice that the world greatly needs in this moment of turbulent transition. The unfolding meta-crisis and interest in a 'paradigm shift' are converging, and metanoia is poised as a means for personal, social and institutional transformation, to collectively undergo a deep shift and upgrade in values, identities, worldviews and the world.

Outlined below are seven major interrelated 'turns' or domains of metanoia for the metamodern spirit. The first section starts with a background history of metanoia, from religious to secular connotations, and the reader is encouraged on a journey to practise metanoia. In the second, the cognitive roots and rhizomes of metanoia are mapped by a speculative ontology and its social implications. For the third, we go to the crux of the matter, using metanoia as leverage to intervene and overturn capitalism's own pathology.

Fourth, meta-theories and methods combine with the praxis of revolution, speaking to the need for an explicit metamodern turn in sociology and society. Fifth, discussion of post-war reflections and the role of religion and theology return in the post-secular age to round off a more absolute metanoia to confront evil. Sixth, some feminist and anecdotal insights help ground the metanoia thesis in practical ways. Seventh, the difficult choice of metanoia over paranoia is framed by the historic bifurcation of postmodernism into metamodern or hypermodern dominant trends.

The need for a *political metanoia* is an overarching theme here, such that if religious, educational and business institutions have any salvific power or purpose, they must also transform themselves to support this mass metanoia. Metanoia is a most useful term for normatively instructing our journey in this time of major change and crisis, and galvanising the metamodern zeitgeist to be the catalyst of necessary change.

The call to adventure

You must make up your mind, or it will be made up for you. The mystery traditions – ancient secret societies for esoteric knowledge – passed on down through Pythagoras, Plato and others, were instrumental in developing the transcendental thinking that would become central to the Christian worldview centuries later (LaFreniere, 2012). Furthermore, metanoia has affinity with platonic *paideia*, a more monastic form of conversion, both of which are a 'turning' towards or about a higher reality, making them two sides of the same coin (Bertucio, 2015).

The concrete origins of metanoia are seemingly inextricable from its religious connotations, the primary source being the gospels of the New Testament. The old Greek Bibles used the word metanoia, which became habitually mistranslated into 'repentance' – which appears 100 times in various forms – rather than the more accurate 'conversion', thereby stripping much of its essential meaning. A single aspect of the practice came to replace the whole, and the deeper truth was buried. That is where the written history of metanoia really begins, its gravity given by its poetic contexts and associated practices.

The Great Meaning of Metanoia, by Treadwell Walden (1896), is a charming little book from near the turn of the 20th century. It is an exegesis on the word metanoia itself, an exploration of its depth beyond the superficial meaning. Walden decries the mistranslation 'repentance', promising that the word has a deeper, revealed truth in Christianity, that is, a 'transmutation' of consciousness. Walden is not the first to observe this, it goes back to Tertullian (c. 155–c. 240 CE) and on through Martin Luther (1483–1546) – and he's certainly not the last. While repentance is still very necessary, many scholars lament the mistranslation and urge for a renewal of the metanoietic practice.

Walden's book has a certain metamodern 'depthiness' to it – what Timotheus Vermeulen (2015) analogises to a 'snorkeler intuiting depth, imagining it – perceiving it without encountering it'. Bound up with a rapturous teleology towards spiritual salvation, Walden's words, written over a century ago, capture this eternally recurrent zeitgeist of metanoia, a word that is a wormhole to an altered state of consciousness and to a new world in a new time:

> For we are just on the verge of a great epoch. All this intellectual activity in the material world is surely working towards a moment of reaction when the same intensity of movement will turn the other way, and the universal demand will be for a knowledge of the Spiritual. The voice of material Science, crying in the wilderness, will be found to have been preparing the way for this. It will turn out to have been uttering a word which has roused the 'expectation' of this age. Out of all this agnostic dust and ashes shall mount again the cry, 'Metanoeite! for the Kingdom of Heaven is at hand.'   Walden, 1896

Walden couldn't have predicted the nihilism that would be unleashed in the 20th century, but his message remains a harbinger of hope. From the ancient origins of metanoia to Walden's disquisition on it over a century ago, our present narrative re-grounds a historicity that connects the past and future, resonating today as a process of unfolding and becoming. Walden frames metanoia as a subconscious emotion 'shut up, awaiting its proper occasions', enabled by the mind, but not achievable by the mind alone.

In paganism, Metanoia is the name of the personified goddess of guilt and missed opportunity. The sorrowful female Metanoia follows the young male Kairos, the god of good timing and opportunity for action (while Kairos was also contrasted with Chronos, the god of sequential time). Together, Metanoia and Kairos are the guides and harbingers of a monumental shift. Kelly Myers (2011) writes that this mythical 'partnership can take shape as a personal learning process, a pedagogical tool and a rhetorical device'. Whereas symbolism was sometimes all the ancients had, today symbols have lost their referents and must be rediscovered.

The frequency and intensity of metanoia are somewhat debatable, and also naturally subjective and relative. In the fundamentally transformative context in which scholars Armen Avanessian and Anke Hennig (2018) use it: 'Metanoia rarely occurs more than once a decade, and it tends to come with significant relocations, radical epochal changes or the collapse of personal worlds.' This is certainly agreeable in the sense of the revelation of cosmic consciousness. It is akin to a coming of age, or a rite of passage; it is a rare opportunity to gain insight and become a whole new person.

At the other end of the spectrum, in a TEDx, educator Aimee Zadak (2017) jokes that she's had 148,000 metanoias in her lifetime, adding that they occur 'much more than once a year'. She stresses that metanoia is a continuous process. This makes it sound frivolous, but there is something to be said for many small changes contributing to the big ones. Evidently then, metanoia could be best understood as *both* an ongoing process *and* a rare and singular event, as well as having mild and strong forms. As Myers put it: 'The experience of metanoia involves a transformation that can range from a minor change of mind to a dramatic spiritual conversion.' What is important is to notice the unique quality of the change, and to integrate it with a larger pattern of conversion.

As in the biblical examples, metanoia can be commanded, but of course, only the individual can truly generate and accept the full implications of such a conversion. As we plumb the depths of metanoia together, do you feel in the process? Have you had a distinct metanoia lately? Is one due? Is one calling to you? Maybe you change your mind often, or perhaps you find stability in a static identity and fixed beliefs. Suppose it's others who need to change their mind and you who must remain steadfast. People need to learn the common answers to these problems and change together.

Change is inevitable and ongoing, and there are opportune moments to embrace the process. Consider the following examples that could be part of a serious metanoia: breaking out of a false consciousness or ideology; atonement for war or transgressing someone; quitting a vicious habit or addiction; resolving a childhood trauma; leaving an abusive relationship; committing to a noble cause or movement; renouncing a cult or gang; evolving religious or political values; changing your identity; abdicating wealth or power; or confessing to a crime. And still, these are but aspects of a larger shift in worldview, precipitated by reflexive thinking and feeling processes.

To practise metanoia is a difficult choice with profound implications: 'to put away childish things' (1 Corinthians 13:11), to follow your heart and mind not just where it wants to go, but to where it *should* go. Metanoia compels us to the precipice of moral virtue and self-realisation and beyond, where at once everything changes. Consider this call to adventure as you read about the nature of and need for a *metamodern metanoia*.

Speculative metanoia and psychoactive philosophy

Metanoia is more than a deep spiritual practice, it's the essence of poiesis itself. Poiesis is the creative capacity of language for 'thinking the world' at 'recursive stages on a higher level of totality' according to Avanessian and Hennig (2018). They wrote a compendious book on the subject, *Metanoia: A Speculative Ontology of Language, Thinking, and the Brain*. They abstract metanoia from history and place it at 'the core of thought and language' as a transformative and retroactive procedure, to then reinsert it into history. They drill down into metanoia as the act of thinking itself, a special mode of (meta-)cognition, often employing a rare form of logic called abduction (and even rarer, meta-abduction).

Metanoia entails a great reshuffling and reordering of the contents of one's mind, such that everything changes, a 'triple shift of subject, thought, and world'. The authors contend that 'metanoia is the most radical form of *poiesis*', the act of creation, what Aristotle called the feedback loop between craftsman and craft, or an ecstatic moment of metamorphosis (such as a flower blooming or a butterfly emerging). Language and the brain co-evolved in a reciprocal fashion, particularly by experimenting on itself, and thus metanoia represents a recursive re-entry into subjectivity and thought. Coincidentally, as Avanessian and Hennig point out, metanoia is an anagram for *anatomie*.

Although it is said that much communication is non-verbal, it is of course primarily through human language that conceptual clarity is made, thoughts relate to themselves and expansion of the mind is possible. Avanessian and Hennig are attending to the complex processes not immediately obvious in metanoia, weaving a discussion through 'speculative realism, new materialism, neurology, structural linguistics, and Peircian semiotics'. They occasionally allude to an ultimate practice of metanoia, suggesting that '[t]o reflect on metanoia is to repeat the gestures of a first philosophising' and '[t]hrough metanoia, we become intellectuals; metanoia makes philosophers philosophers'.

We must all become philosophers to some extent. This metanoietic journey speaks to a constant process of learning, of gaining intellectual and moral depth. Given the entanglement of metanoia with language and reality, such a process depends largely on reading, writing, thinking and re-creating the world. For example, Avanessian and Hennig describe how Foucault, Derrida and Deleuze open 'a universe, however, that one can only enter by "thinking one's way into it"'. Theirs are 'theories full of metanoietic appeal and potential', guiding the reader's thought into 'text's vortex: a mere reader becomes the subject of theory'. The horizon of the text and the reader become one. A good text (and writer) has a transformative and psychoactive effect that invites the reader behind the curtain of their own understanding.

Foucault also noted how the spiritual metanoia common in the 19th century was necessarily tied to revolutionary practice. But there was always a complicated potential to go towards a psychotic break or religious awakening. Knowing the difference is difficult, and the 20th century saw many horrors and dramatic reversals on account of that. Metanoia's intersubjective 'third term' *mediation* – the other – beyond subject and object is what enables a 'praxis of political metanoia' (Davis and Riches, 2005) to perceive the big picture and to attain solidarity in common struggle and peace.

Spiritual and political activity is meaningful because it compels us to make the world better. To do so, the metanoiac process moves us through an individual to a general perspective, and then to a 'meta-position', thereby bringing a collective subject into being and time (i.e. Christendom, the proletariat, the precariat, etc.). Importantly, metanoia denotes a shift in temporality (and historicity), given by the common expression 'afterward, what comes before is different'. Granted that we are truly in unprecedented times, and time is running out, it's all the more important we synchronously achieve mass metanoia, and in a convergent manner.

Similarly, in *All Things Shining*, Hubert Dreyfus and Sean Dorrance Kelly (2011) advocate for a 'meta-poetic' mindset as the best way to find meaning in our secular (disenchanted) and sometimes nihilistic age. They note that poiesis alone was not enough to stop German workers from getting carried away by Hitler's fascism. Conversely, it takes great courage to join the crowds when it's rightful to do so, such as it was during Martin Luther King's great speech on the National Mall. For Dreyfus and Kelly, meta-poiesis is the (required) 'higher-order skill of recognising when to rise up as one with the ecstatic crowd and when to turn heel and walk rapidly away'. This is a necessary meta-skill for our current world historic moment: to know the difference between a genuine leader and a puppet or demagogue.

To avoid the schizophrenic pull of our psychotic society, it's worth noting the psychedelic turn and its relation to metanoia. In *Metanoia: Some Experiences at Kingsley Hall*, writing of his experiences there in the late 1960s, R.D. Laing (1967) speculates that the experience of psychedelics is similar to that of metanoia: 'LSD-25 was originally regarded as a psychotomimetic substance. I propose that this biochemically induced 6–12-hour trip has its natural analogue in what I suggest be called a *metanoiac* voyage.' Not only that, but he also argues that LSD can be used for therapy by controlling the *set* and *setting* (terms coined by Timothy Leary). Moreover, the typical pathologising *setting* of the mental hospital actually induces a bad mind-*set* in the patient, thereby encouraging negative reactions, a failed metanoietic journey.

In short, Laing's radical thesis is that psychedelics might cure schizophrenia, whereas the medical gaze can actually create it. Traditionally, schizophrenia is considered within the body, whereas Laing inverts that assumption and locates it partly in the social processes that generate it. Laing laments that cultural taboos prevent such theories from being tested (and proven), but thankfully he persisted and others have validated the field of psychedelic potential. In 1996, the *NY Times* (Meisel, 1996) wrote of Laing's work: 'Metanoia, especially in its schizophrenic form, is an existential journey, Laing argued; with safe surroundings, it can actually be a route toward recovery based on choice.'

Levi Bryant speculates that Plato and Epicurus would probably not have advocated MDMA. He claims this to make a point about different language games, in how Plato and Epicurus may reject the drug for different philosophical yet game-oriented reasons: Plato for the sake of purity and to avoid bodily temptations and passions; and Epicurus wanting to avoid the risk of pain or anxiety (a utilitarian pleasure principle). But perhaps they might take the drug for the sake of inducing metanoia. Bryant comments that the golden thread through Avanessian and Hennig's book (which he calls a work of meta-philosophy) poses the question: how might it be possible to make moves that break out of the (language) game itself, beyond 'its grammar, its pieces, its field'? The book provides an answer in cognitive/linguistic terms, yet the psychedelic dimension to metanoia is left out.

Psychoactive philosopher Peter Sjöstedt-H (2016) traces the history of psychedelic use through 13 famous philosophers, from Plato on through to Foucault. In, *The Hidden Psychedelic History of Philosophy*, he writes that philosophy itself can be psychoactive, but that the role of psychedelics is not obvious or well studied, despite its ubiquity in the history of higher thought. The prohibition of psychedelics are in part maintained as resistance to and taboo against metanoia, both individually and culturally. It is not so much that transformative experience is 'not for everyone', but rather that it is actively denied to most.

Furthermore, the denial of this potential catalyst (i.e. tripping) of Western philosophy undermines its own premises and hampers its emancipatory mission; if philosophy is truly aimed at truth, it will not be dissuaded by the politics of the day. In his book *Noumenautics* (2015), an exploration of psychedelic phenomenology and the implications for philosophy and metaphysics, Sjöstedt-H writes that such prohibitions are 'an affront to human dignity and an affront to reason itself'. Thus, the field of philosophy owes it to itself to recognise this legacy, and to affirm the mutually constitutive relationship between altered states of consciousness and the development of thought.

One does not have to take psychedelics to stimulate metanoia, but overcoming the taboo is key. Christian pastor Wick Anderson (2019) recounts his experience of metanoia simply by reading Michael Pollan's book on psychedelics. When he heard the title on NPR, *How to Change Your Mind*, it recalled his biblical Greek knowledge of the word 'metanoia'. Sceptical of psychedelics, as one would expect a religiously conservative person to be, Anderson nevertheless pushed ahead and was surprised and transformed by Pollan's book. Subsequently, he was able to relate to psychedelic experiences as legitimate mystical or religious experiences, as well as a transformative therapy tool for reflection and healing.

The conversion of capitalism

Capitalism is in major crisis, (dis)affecting all its subsystems and the superstructure of our society. A multifaceted metanoia is needed to converge towards solving what John Milbank and Adrian Pabst (2015) call 'the meta-crisis of secular capitalism'. This meta-crisis devalues human productivity and fetishises materiality, cutting out the commons and relational goods. Financialisation increases the appearance of profits but masks the deepening crisis. The excessive 'abstract' growth of capitalism spreads systemic risk while being unaccountable; the abstraction needs to be continually re-anchored in the concrete and collective. Capitalism will undergo a conversion to postcapitalism and cosmopolitan socialism, and business must help.

In a dense paper, Andrew Targowski (2010) analyses the role of business in civilisational development and posits two paths: paranoia and metanoia. The choice is set up by the fact that hyper-consumptive civilisation is unequivocally accelerating towards limits and collapse. The impending collapse is made clear through the historical trajectory and convergence of capitalist 'Western Civilisation' from pre-capitalist forms to mercantilism (1500s), and to various others including commercial, state, regulated, crony, managed and social capitalism up until the 1990s. In the 1990s, authoritarian, managerial and global capitalism colluded and competed, merging into 'super-capitalism' (undemocratic) in the 2000s.

Life between 1000 and 1820 is characterised by the 'Malthusian trap', when populations were relatively stable (birth rates equalled death rates) and living conditions were poor. During this time, global GDP grew just 153 per cent. It was a trap because, without major productivity gains, growing birth rates decreased real income, so paradoxically war, disease and disorder increased material standards for those living. From 1820 onwards, modern capitalism began 'accelerated growth', where the Industrial Revolution 'broke the Darwinian law' and enabled exponential population growth and increased the standard of living.

Since 1820, global GDP has grown over 900 per cent. Targowski cites the 1972 Club of Rome report *Limits to Growth* as the major predictor of collapse, although this was mostly ignored. As such, on our current trajectory, he anticipates a 'Death Triangle of Civilization' from 2050–2500, distilling three main threats to civilisation: a population bomb and an ecological bomb, which converge (2050–2150) on a resource bomb (2300–2500); that is, as population and consumption peak, so resources are strained until there are none left. This is one prophetic scenario of many, but it stands out for its contrasting of a pattern and a choice between paranoia and metanoia, a recurrent theme.

Here's the rub: business plays a central role in mass metanoia, perhaps even more so than do educators, politicians and citizens. Targowski critiques the UN's Millennium Development Goals for not addressing the role of business, the key driver pushing us 'to the brink of disaster'. His succinct meta-analysis of our long-term civilisational trajectory brings us to a distinct fork in the road. Option A, the 'metanoic path', is one of sustainable growth through renewable resources that foster shared values and a 'universal civilisation'. Option B, the 'paranoic path', is staying in the growth trap, depleting strategic resources leading to collapse, and a 'post-civilisation epoque'.

Systems scientist Peter Senge (1990), author of *The Fifth Discipline*, was largely inspired by metanoia to become an expert on 'metanoiac organisations'. Looking back from 2015, he elaborates on the concept of metanoia as learning, from which he developed the concept of a learning organisation. His book received acclaim in its day, but it is now that Senge speaks with a fresh sense of metanoia, that it is a time for great change. He laments that nothing will change without mass metanoia and that it is likely to be induced by climate and social collapse, but he also sees what he calls 'heartening developments' in social consciousness, that some people are catching on:

> We really are on a path to nowhere in the mainstream. And outside the mainstream all these amazing things are happening, so I think one, it becomes more and more necessary, and two, it becomes more and more possible.   Peter Senge (Sarder, 2015)

Mirroring Senge's valorous business ethic beyond conscious capitalism, a consultant named Chris Houston (2015) writes: 'Metanoia is the gateway to the hallowed grounds of corporate integrity.' He reflected on his suspicion, which eventually became a conviction, that the 'profit-only model' in business was not as noble and generative as widely believed. On the contrary, capitalist realism – the belief that there is no alternative – is destroying the planet. This experience of realisation led Houston to develop a lucid anatomy of the metanoia process, which he summarised as:

> metanoia has occurred when something (1) boundless and unexpected, (2) beyond reason and (3) mysteriously compelling (4) sparks non-conformity borne

of conviction, a (5) deeper connection to others and (6) deeper knowledge of our own story and identity (7) toward broadened horizons or a new world.

According to this sequence, to achieve metanoia we must (1) go outside our comfort zone and become part of a larger reality that imbues purpose and meaning. With our minds intellectually engaged, we must then (2) open our hearts and be moved by something on a deeply personal level – perhaps an injustice, personal failing or an epistemic contradiction. We then cross another threshold and (3) let the momentum of that shift carry us into a new perspective or disposition. At this point we are likely to be rebelling against norms and so (4) a deeper commitment and action is required. To remain in the same patterns of behaviour once the shift has been embraced becomes unbearable.

Eventually the mounting changes lead back to (5) a deepening of relationships with others. Self and world are transformed, but with it comes the realisation of deep connection and interdependence with others and/or nature, reminiscent of John Donne's famous line of poetry, that 'no man is an island entire of itself'.[1] By now one's journey is a story unfolding, so (6) we must reflect on our personal narrative and reconstruct our identity to meet new demands and accept the surprising consequences that come with this new knowledge. Finally, having survived the harrowing transition (7) we are faced with a new horizon of choice and responsibility. We are bigger people, part of a larger world, with the ability and duty to be positive agents of change.

Similarly, Joan Marques (2011) proposes a metanoia-focused MBA that fosters eight strategies for inducing metanoia: 'conscious dialogue rounds, confrontation with human-focused companies, instilling the idea of humility, considering yourself as a brand, looking into social entrepreneurship, awakening passion, conducting self-reflection, and rethinking decision-making'. Houston's consulting blog and Marques' MBA plan seem unlikely places to find such compelling, rigorous and poetic metanoia instruction guides, but such is the divine mystery of metanoia and the need for it in (meta-)crisis capitalism.

These techniques confront major negative tendencies of corporate culture, such as extreme inequality and the long-term unintended consequences of self-interested and short-term decision making. Marques stresses that metanoia is never an overnight success, and is not even guaranteed by these methods, but rather is sustained through outward practice and exposure. The applications of these ideas in corporate structures may have very limited impact, but they make sense, especially if pursued as part of a broader truth and reconciliation process, begetting the need for a deeper sociological turn.

Diving into depth sociology

In his sweeping book *Gaia, Psyche and Deep Ecology*, Andrew Fellows (2019) makes the call to action explicitly about metanoia. Like many sources invoked here, his book has a certain metamodern sensibility and urgency in its themes and prescriptions, citing the Anthropocene as both a cause and catalyst of dramatic change. Through the titular concepts, he melds the ideas of a living planet, infinite consciousness and the complex ecological systems that bind them together and mediate our species relationship to earth.

Along with deep ecology, Fellows advocates for depth psychology as integral to the project, although he is cautious of how it is a two-edged sword (i.e. hypercapitalism exploits it). He refers to 'denial of the really big picture' as one of many key defence mechanisms that limit our ability to change for the better, 'and the need for *metanoia*' to address said denial. He urges that civilisation has become collectively neurotic, as speculated by Jung and Freud, and that metanoia is precisely the psychological break that is needed. Realising the crisis 'demands nothing less than a metanoia – a revolution in the way we understand our being in the world'.

Fellows' imperative may seem like a fantasy, for when do large groups ever spontaneously change their minds at will? History crawls and progress precipitates into a slow drip, but change does happen, usually prompted by pivotal events. Part of the pattern emerging is one that is converging towards this needed mass metanoia. There exists a lot of collective guilt and shame for climate change and systemic oppression to process, and we are running out of time as the evidence against our denial is mounting.

Ananta Kumar Giri (2018) called for new approaches in *Beyond Sociology* with a 'new sociological imagination and new ways of being alive'. John Clammer co-developed these ideas and coined the concept of deep sociology that goes beyond critique to be 'reconstructive'. Anchored in things like deep ecology, a critique of eurocentrism and an explicit move beyond postmodernism, to question the foundations of modern sociology itself. Deep sociology foregrounds the philosophy of sociology, processes of globalisation and indigenous knowledge, as well as 'feminism, the ecological movement, art, the new social movements'. It goes so beyond as to take some special responsibility for the paradigm shift:

> The essential role of critical sociology – the exposure of our
> endless capacity for self-delusion and self-justification – needs
> at this juncture in time to be extended into the anticipation and
> management of the very future.   John Clammer (Giri, 2018)

In a similar spirit, in *Postmodernism and Public Policy*, John B. Cobb Jr (2002) opens the preface with the observation of an emergent movement David Ray Griffin calls 'constructive postmodernism', in part influenced by Whitehead's process philosophy/theology. Griffin even spells out that it is 'perhaps best – *reconstructive*'. At the time, Cobb predicted that this approach may be 'a strong, even dominant, force' in the 21st century. As they drew on theology, Cobb wrote: 'The Christian life is entered through *metanoia* and continues as one of repeated *metanoia*.' Thus, metanoia plays a central role as an ongoing process of 'creative transformation' that changes throughout time, from the first possibility via Jesus (Christ), to contemporary preachers calling for it in our presently tense age.

Cobb also reflects on his own metanoia regarding race and class, explaining that the way forward is 'acknowledging the ugly history of whiteness and repenting', while also 'freeing myself from disempowering guilt and shame'. In our current moment, racial tensions are high, proportional to ignorance on the topic and the lack of logistical solutions for migration, refugees and incarceration crises. Conservative antipathy to 'social justice' continues to rise and, while Cobb's repentance would be castigated as 'virtue signalling' by reactionaries in today's political climate, it is a vital step in metanoia.

Dovetailing with what Peter Dale Scott (1996) calls 'deep politics', Griffin and Cobb take a complex view of the 9/11 terrorist attacks. It would be a categorical mistake to lump them with 'conspiracy theorists' or 'truthers', as they are both acclaimed scholars, and their pragmatic scepticism of the official version of 9/11 is even shared by the late historian Howard Zinn. Zinn was not particularly interested in dwelling on (the truth of) the event, as most serious sceptics aren't. Rather, they are concerned with the consequences either way, the endless and dubious 'war on terror', neoconservative geopolitics normalised into the erosion of civil rights and economic justice, and the neglect of more real concerns – not least climate change.

At root, Griffin and Cobb's speculations are grounded in the rational assertion that governments lie, and that some truths are too big to believe. In *Christian Faith and the Truth Behind 9/11*, theories aside, Griffin's (2006) reasonable religious prescription calls for churches to, as one reviewer summarised, 'dissociate themselves from America's imperial project' (Jenson, 2007), which is largely uncontroversial among political and religious progressives. Evangelising for and crossing such divestment tipping points is a benchmark for a mass metanoia.

9/11 was certainly formative in my own life, for the millennial generation at large, and for a negative paradigm shift which is still creating fallout. The broader problem is that of the globally imposed *pax Americana*, and how to mobilise our metanoia to actually achieve it at scale – to end war in all forms. No doubt for conspiracy theorists, as well as those who abandon conspiricism, metanoia plays a decisive role in objections to militarist premises and agendas. Metanoia becomes an anti-war project on spiritual grounds. Scholars like Baudrillard and Žižek have commented on the surreality of 9/11, and Alison Gibbons (2017) has described the idea of metamodern affective autofiction in novels, which attempts to save us from the event, by being attentive to a new temporality and intersubjectivity.

In *American Psychosis*, journalist and activist Chris Hedges (Zackem, 2017) speaks of collapse, and our avoidance/denial of it, saying of religion that the 'real form … has to do with our neighbour'. Acting as a seminarian as well, he adds: 'a life of commitment is picking up a cross, it's not a pleasant experience. It's one that gives one a sense of meaning, a sense of purpose.' The collapse of empire breeds retreat and polarisation, it also calls for acts of conscience and rebellion against draconian policies. Hedges' metanoia is a constant affirmation of the deep transformation needed away from our denial and destructive ways of life.

Metanoetics and liberation theologies

Building on the previous section, we plunge deeper into the fusion of philosophy, sociology, religion and praxis. After the Second World War, Japanese philosopher Hajime Tanabe wrote about metanoia (*zange*) as absolute critique in *Philosophy as Metanoetics* (2016). *Zange* is a way to navigate the ongoing crisis of reason due to its absolute limits and to overcome the pervasiveness of evil in the world. As metanoetics, philosophy is not only a 'life of mind', but is also a life of constantly changing and evolving one's mind. As such, Tanabe is concerned not just with metanoia as a concept and process, but also with metanoetics as an entire field of philosophical practice.

Tanabe realises that he is incapable of such a daunting task, and so must concede the battle before it has begun by admitting inadequacy. Tanabe realises the parallels with Socratic irony – knowledge of one's ignorance – but considers metanoetics different by being rooted in 'Other-power' rather than self-power. Its source is not contemplation and reason, but a 'breaking-through' not possible by discursive reflection alone. It requires not just intellectual courage but also existential surrender, the true source of wisdom coming from nothingness itself. Thomas P. Kasulis writes of Tanabe:

> Because no intellectual system can ever be universal or absolute, he
> argued, every responsible philosophy contains a metanoetic dynamic that
> serves to undermine any tendency to treat it as such.   Kasulis, 2009

Tanabe's project starts from a place of guilt for Japan's role in the Second World War, as well as an atmosphere of denial by authorities after the gruesome fact. He was of course not personally responsible, but as a philosopher he bears the sin of it in full, leading him to take an absolute stance against Kant's notion of 'radical evil' within all of us. Tanabe recognises the certain risk of this autocritical philosophy making him a pariah among others loyal to ill-fated reason, yet proceeds anyway. Not only is it autocritical, but Tanabe's metanoetics also invites critique so that it may reform itself.

To perform *zange* is his purpose and joy, as painful as it is, which reminds me of Nietzsche's *amor fati* and Albert Borgmann's (Crook, 2020) 'good burdens'. Metanoetics involves not just a change of mind, but also a resignation to the fallibility and weakness that comes with the path of philosophy, epitomised by the failure of reason to avert world wars. It is metanoia in the sense of 'thinking-afterward' with repentance, but is more anticipatory. One has not only accepted (and disallowed) the possibility of evil in oneself, but one has also accepted the inevitable destiny of life and '[a]s such, zange means simply following a disciplined way toward one's own death'. For these reasons, Tanabe's metanoetics is a zero-tolerance stance against violence.

Jonathan Ray Villacorta (2011) revives Tanabe's ethos in *Metanoia as a Response to Philosophy's Death*, where he laments how often 'the evils of dogmatic institutions and uncreative policies' have prevailed, committed atrocities and swept dark histories under the rug in following the 'letter of the law instead of its spirit'. As an 'absolute critique', metanoetics is the only way out, not just for individuals but groups, as Villacorta argues: 'Our institutions too need to take the path of *zange*!' While true, a footnote provides a commentary from Ricoeur, who reminds us that institutions are but the sum of their parts, not autonomous evil agents. It is the whole of people who must metanoia.

This paradox – that we must change ourselves and institutions *at the same time* – would seem to be possible only in a metamodern paradigm, where paradexity (paradoxical complexity) can be confronted and addressed through consensus-building (Cooper, 2020). Our egos and identities must continually die and be reborn, and with them our philosophies and institutions. In my view, Villacorta and Tanabe's metanoetic insights contribute to a metamodern turn, which is precisely why its time has come (again). We must commit to the metanoiac path, lest the paranoid mind holds sway.

Similarly, in Holocaust theology, Stephen Haynes (1994) asks how this extreme hell could occur, given Enlightenment values and reason? How could such an advanced society commit such blatant evil? More to the point, does it not definitively prove that there is no 'God' and hence no theology, only us? That is the irony, because in some ways the nightmares of the 20th century renew and affirm the religious spirit, but in a new mode, as described:

> Many use the dramatic terminology of 'endpoint', 'interruption',
> 'crisis', 'break', 'rupture', 'paradigm shift' and 'metanoia' to describe the
> Holocaust's monumental impact on the Christian faith.   Haynes, 1994

Haynes argues that two millennia of Christian anti-Semitism (culminating in the Holocaust) is an obvious sign of the church's hypocrisy and 'apostasy from authentic Christianity'. The Holocaust was a death knell not just for millions of people, but also for philosophy and religion. It is in large part the catalyst of postmodernism, which would emerge as an explicit paradigm a couple of decades after the Second World War.

These issues remain unresolved in any conclusive sense. Here we are in the 21st century, still struggling with the same paradoxes, as history urges repetition in the most banal and horrific ways, hence a need for a normative metamodernism. A new ongoing, and perhaps in some ways final, process of metanoia is needed to subvert the spirals of violence and to fulfil the prophecies of peace. The cry for metanoia is found across the board; it just has to be heeded collectively.

Postcolonial theory and liberation theology enfold into a metamodern turn as well, via the work of Justo L. González (1996), who used the term. He describes Latinos in the US as 'metamodern aliens in postmodern Jerusalem', who embody and live through both hope and despair, under oppressive conditions ignored by the postmodern critique, which neglected the geopolitical subjugation of the subaltern. Liberation theology integrates social justice with religion, as Martin Luther King did, whereas postmodern secularism rejects the latter. As such, Black and liberation theologies offer a truer and more emancipatory reading of the Bible (and Christ), and a more universal notion of spirituality.

This sentiment is also expressed in terms of metanoia by Paul S. Chung (2019) in *Critical Theory and Political Theology*, which issues a 'call for theological metanoia and parrhesia in our postcolonial context' – parrhesia meaning to candidly, freely and boldly speak truth to power. Citing 'Why Black Theology?' (1975), Chung writes that against the Christian church's colonial sanction of slavery, '[we must affirm] Gollwitzer's call for white dominant theology to commit the metanoia toward the liberating message of the Gospel'.

Chung describes the alternative to postmodernism as 'trans-modernity' aligned with postcolonial theory and liberation theology, converging with the metamodernism of González. Given that the church abandoned the version of Jesus as 'the divine delinquent' (cf. Horkheimer), the authentic imitation of which has been 'lost since the time of Constantine', these are appropriate (re-)turns. Chung takes it a step further and proposes that '[c]ritical theory may as well become an implicit form of political theology'. Chung's programmatic metanoia is a 'peace movement' that serves none other than the god of political responsibility to stand in solidarity with the innocent victims of injustice.

Feminist soul-making and reconstructing relationships

It took a long time for the world to recognise that women are people too, and many men still resist this truth. Rosemary Radford Ruether (2007) reconceptualises the Christian notions of sin, alienation and conversion through a feminist lens in *Feminist Metanoia and Soul-Making*. This feminism calls on both men and women to involve themselves in the individual and collective processes of metanoia and transformation needed to undo 'women's subjugation by patriarchal social and cultural systems'. Ruether rejects the Christian idea of innate evil, but agrees that 'our tendency to evil has been biased by historical systems of evil'.

Historical evil suggests that we must not only address our own pathologies, but also those of institutions that will abandon us to the extent we revolt against them, that is, 'family, school, church, and country'. These normative social structures ostensibly take care of us, but often only if we let them control us and others. Ruether reconceives 'sin' as a 'distorted relationship' (male over female) and stresses it needs to be confronted along three dimensions – personal-interpersonal, social-historical and ideological-cultural – whereas self-help/therapy discourse has typically dwelled on the first.

Ruether exposes a correlation between male insecurity and cycles of violence. She suggests masculinity is rooted in fear of overthrowing – yet a desire to overthrow – the 'great mother'. Furthermore, Ruether finds this dynamic in all types of domination: White racists are afraid of having their power displaced by Black culture; right-wing Christians and Jews are bound in an unholy alliance for the strategic geopolitical advantage of Israel, both complicit in oppressing Palestinians to feel more secure themselves. 'The militarist needs enemies,' writes Ruether: 'This became evident with the recent end of the cold war, where we saw the scramble of the US government military-industrial complex to identify new enemies to justify their arsenals.'

Ruether's paper astutely anticipated the war on terror, but the feminist metanoia was denied. We inherit this mess of (psychological) projecting power relations, such is the 'historical dimension of sin'. The continuity of oppressive relations is not just reified but over-determined through the institutions of family, school, religion and mainstream media. Our inner struggles are mirrored by cultural clashes, and we must foster our good tendencies through 'soul-making' and metanoia:

> Soul-making happens through transformative metanoia, which is both sudden insight and also slow maturation of a grounded self in relationship or community, able to be both self-affirming and other affirming in life-enhancing mutuality. It is both a gift and a task, grace and work ... Such transformative metanoia is both personal and social.   Ruether, 2007

Feminist movements have in large part made it possible for women to articulate their own exploitation and to have the support network to act on their new consciousness. The metanoiac struggle intensifies with the recognition of historical context. Thus, Ruether argues that women of privilege should also be aware of their own capacity to victimise others. In parallel, men need to embark on their own journey, noting: 'Much of what is passing for "the men's movement" at the moment does not yet seem to me to qualify for such a mature movement of men against patriarchy, but has many features of reduplication ... .'

Ruether's insights anticipated our current times with many White male pseudo-intellectuals bemoaning the 'crisis of masculinity' (including a denial that patriarchy exists) and the #MeToo movement of de-normalising abusive male behaviour. Ruether concludes that 'soul-making' is only complete when it transforms the whole but, because it is eschatological and teleological (more theological ideals, less historical possibilities), we must persevere in the face of constant defeat. We must have faith and resolve to sustain the struggle with others, hoping that an end is finally near. We're still not quite there yet.

Mahatma Gandhi was no feminist; his controversial views and practices around women and sexual behaviour undermined his cause and disrupted feminism. Outside of these blind spots, Gandhi had many distinct metanoias in his life that led him to his path of unshakeable convictions and acts of defiance. The plain injustice of British occupation and rule motivated him to theatrically break the most banal of laws, taking salt from the beach, which prompted his imprisonment, brutal crackdowns and a widespread uprising that eventually achieved independence. Committed to satyagraha, or truth force, Gandhi's *swaraj* (self-governance) was not just a critique of British imperialism, it was also a critique of modernity, not from a postmodern critical perspective, but from a metanoietic instinct.

In a way, Gandhi's project was an alternative to liberal democracy and Marxism, aiming for transformation beyond the means of those programmes, according to A.K. Saran (1969): 'Gandhism calls for a radical revolution, for a complete transformation of man's thinking and way of life, social as well as individual. In a word, it aims at metanoia.' *Swaraj* is not just a rebuke of modernity, writes Rudolf C. Heredia (1999), but rather an attempted integration of modernity with a renewed liberatory tradition. In this sense it has a metamodern character of a high synthesis that is almost unrealistic, but imperative. To deny Gandhi's vision, in Heredia's words, is:

> to claim that human beings are not capable of metanoia, a radical change of heart, that can open up new perspectives, not just for individuals and groups, but for entire societies and whole cultures as well. We need organic intellectuals and transformative activists who can articulate and precipitate such a social movement.   Heredia, 1999

The *National Geographic* (O'Neill, 2015) reported that Gandhi's legacy is rife with paradox, given where India is today, a crowded geography with a seemingly impassable gap between high technology and poverty. Not to mention that his 'friendly' letters to Hitler never did quite work (Suhrud, 2019). More to the point, contemporary India under Narendra Modi has become so fundamentalist and chauvinist that Gandhi's assassin is revered. Although many worship Gandhi, his revolutionary discipline and socialist praxis has all but evaporated under the sweltering conditions of life and politics in the 21st century and, of course, a feminist metanoia is still lacking.

Heredia argues that to find 'a new synthesis for a counter-culture' today, Gandhi must be reinterpreted and seen as a dialogue partner, not as an icon and saint, so we can 're-examine and reconstruct ourselves as well'. We must achieve our own metanoia, not Gandhi's – his and others are instructive but not exhaustive. Half the world's population is women – not to mention people who are non-binary or transgender – and they have been largely excluded from historical progress and discourse since time immemorial. The feminist cause is obviously imperative and yet constantly neglected or under attack, calling into question every metanoia that preceded it.

The metanoid style

In the 1960s, historian Richard Hofstadter coined 'the paranoid style' to describe the pervasive reactionary behaviours and discourses intrinsic to American politics. This paranoia seems to define the world today just as much as his other famous thesis about anti-intellectualism (Cooper, 2020). The metanoid style would be the opposite of paranoia, its salvation. On this path, we are getting closer to the possibility of a mass metanoia. The contrast between paranoia and metanoia has been noted in the sections on capitalism and liberation theology, and now its juxtaposition comes into focus.

Anthony Judge is a prolific thinker and writer for the Union of International Associations and the mastermind behind *The Encyclopedia of World Problems and Human Potential*. In one of his 1,600+ articles he writes about metanoia and paranoia, along with a few other 'noias'.[2] He defines paranoia as a protective cognition, part of threat detection and survival instincts, whereas metanoia is about 'coherent reframing in a larger, subtler context'. Understanding this distinction enables a fostering of the latter habit.

Following the end of the Cold War, Albert Borgmann's bifurcation of postmodernism into hypermodernism and metamodernism (see Cooper, 2020) would seem to mirror the choice between paranoia and metanoia. In futurist aesthetics, this also calls up the contrast between cyberpunk versus solarpunk. Politically, it also reflects polarised cultures that are reactionary/regressive versus progressive. Functionally, this maps to the expressions 'barbarism or socialism', extinction or relative utopia. These are the ultimate questions for our civilisation, and yet quite simple when framed this way. Will you choose paranoia (fear) or metanoia (love)? Our personal lives rarely present such stark contrasting choices, but here we face a global moment, an opportunity for mass metanoia.

A Christian priest named Ron Rolheiser (2016) wrote of the difference between paranoia and metanoia as clenched fists versus open hands, borrowing the phrasing from the theologian Henri Nouwen's book *With Open Hands*. In contrast to paranoia (fear and suspicion), metanoia is openness and trust, the 'posture' of which is most graphically symbolised by Jesus on the cross, 'exposed and vulnerable, his arms spread in a gesture of embrace, and his hands open, with nails through them'.

If the crucifixion is too graphic an example, it is meant to be, for although it is actually a technology of oppression, the symbol itself represents the 'antithesis of paranoia'. In a culture of paranoia, the threat always seems to be there. Where our inner doors instinctively 'slam shut' when we perceive a threat, requiring a much deeper faith and vulnerability to overcome it, '[m]etanoia, the meta mind, the bigger heart, never closes those doors'. We wage an inner war, over which a hand gesture prevails in a given situation, but we must always concede to metanoia.

Paranoia is pervasive through a 'politics of fear', recalling the Adam Curtis (2004) documentary *The Power of Nightmares*, in which politicians exploit insecurity to increase power and control. Fear goes both ways, as it is not just about people afraid of their governments, but governments paranoid about their people and all potential threats, even vital dissent or just plain science (i.e. climate change). Conversely, a 'politics of love' and metanoia is espoused by people like Marianne Williamson (2019), Cornel West (2019) and the Bernie Sanders movement.[3]

Social philosopher and cultural critic William Irwin Thompson also juxtaposes metanoia and paranoia in an interview with Richard Levitón (2007). Thompson explains that current politics is bankrupt and that our own imagination falls short of coping with the planetary crisis, adding: 'Paranoia is the inability to deal with synchronous topologies, but metanoia is when you surf-ride the chaotic topologies into health. It really takes science fiction to deal with the politics we're up against today.'

Thompson has been widely influential as a mythmaker of Gaian cosmology, but he retreated from the pathologies of New Ageism lest he be co-opted as a guru. Thompson is the founder of the Lindisfarne Association (1972–2012), dedicated to fostering a 'new planetary culture'. In his memoir, Thompson (2016) describes how, through the community, the 'personal sense of transfiguration was the metanoia of our noetic polity'. In *Theosophia* by Arthur Versluis (1993, Lindisfarne Books), the chapter on metanoia opens with: 'All true metaphysics begins with a metanoia – that is, with a "turning" toward the truth of a revelation that transcends the rational and the temporo-physical.' Theosophy is a mystical blending of theology and philosophy: a love of god.

Versluis reminds us that the concept of 'born again' has been bastardised by Protestant literalism turned mass evangelism, mostly erasing the original meaning of metanoia. The true metanoiac path begins with a yearning (*eros*) to be transfigured, a love of truth and a will to change, what Plato calls periagoge, which Cornel West (2017) invokes alongside metanoia. This makes metanoia an affirmative act, rather than one of negation; it is a courtship with knowledge herself, Sophia, goddess of divine wisdom.

In *The Dialogue of Cultures: From Paranoia to Metanoia*, Heredia (2007) situates the culture of paranoia in the discourse of Samuel Huntington's 'clash of civilisations', which essentialises the 'other'. This clash has intensified in the time since as a result of such essentialisation and otherising, rather than overcoming. Dialogue is a way to overcome the tension between difference and division, between plurality and ethno-nationalism. For example, we must become more 'sensitive to the delicate distinction between ethnicity as a uniting "myth" and ethnicity as a dividing "ideology"'.

Heredia explains that there is a conflict between myth and ideology, where ideology develops out of the (mis-)translation of myth. Paradoxically, ideologies are functional up to the point where they begin to exclude anomalies, so ideologies must remain open yet grounded. Heredia argues: 'What we need, then, is a metanoia of our myths to escape and be liberated from the paranoia of our ideologies, whether religious, political or otherwise.' Quite simply, we need a 'dialogue of religions' rather than a 'clash of civilisations', but before that is even possible we need a 'dialogue of culture': 'Only then can we experience a *metanoia* in ourselves that will free us from the *paranoia* we have of each other.'

Pope Francis (2020) said about the Covid-19 pandemic: 'What we are living now is a place of "metanoia" (conversion), and we have the chance to begin.' We have neglected the poor, the environment and the unsung heroes of the struggle. In Pope Francis' terms, he urges people to 'pass from the hyper-virtual, fleshless world to the suffering flesh of the poor. This is the conversion we have to undergo.'

The metanoiac journey herein began with religion, so it is fitting it closes with it, but every other element has been just as important to bind together a definitive ethos.

Conclusion

This chapter has traced the activity of metanoia through its religious, cognitive, (post-)capitalist, sociological, politico-philosophical, feminist and psychohistorical forms. Metanoia should come out of obscure literature and into our institutional arrangements. It needs to develop and move from our private lives into public discourse and vice versa. It will largely remain a unique and personal struggle, but one need not be alone, and the stakes of metamodernism are too high and the evidence too great, for it to not be explicitly normative.

Metanoia is no mere mind hack for the savvy seeker or weekend warrior, it is an injunction to all of humanity. This exegesis of metanoia has been but an overview of a habit of the heart and mind that needs to become normalised in the metamodern shift, changing everything that came before. Excavated from its ancient and exclusive origins, it must be made available for the sacred spark in all. It is not a reversion to religious orthodoxy, but a post-secular move into a spiritual commonwealth and fair society.

A metanoia for religion means jettisoning the pretence of being the arbiters or intermediaries of divine knowledge and will, and submitting to the needs of disenfranchised masses all over the world. Organised religions must divest from all war and politics, as all economic sectors must, and adherents should engage in monastic metanoia and embody higher truths rather than worship dogma.

A metanoia for capitalism involves overcoming market fundamentalist ideology and transforming its systems, while embodying the guilt and shame of its externalities, built-in limits, and pathologies that have produced global monopolies, hyper-inequality and polarisation. This will be accomplished by inverting the military-industrial complex into a robust civil society and public sector called a 'peace-industrial complex', an enantiodromiac conversion.[4]

We may (nay, we must!) think of the metamodern move for mass metanoia (a social transformation, paradigm shift, systems change, etc.) as a *necessary possibility*. One that Andrew Fellows says is necessary, but not sufficient. It is no small step to take, for metanoia carries with it the weight of religious prophecy and salvation. Whether one believes the end times are coming via a conspiracy of men or by God's wrath (or climate change), humanity is being tested, and the choice is clear: we must fulfil our destinies individually and collectively by changing our minds, our systems, our ways of living, to be in line with the justice and divinity history aspires to.

What are you waiting for, the Owl of Minerva?

References

Anderson, W. (2019, January 21). On a Changed Mind..., blog post at https://differentparent.com/2019/01/21/on-a-changed-mind/

Avanessian, A. and Hennig, A. (2018). *Metanoia: a Speculative Ontology of Language, Thinking, and the Brain*. London: Bloomsbury Academic, An imprint of Bloomsbury Publishing Plc.

Bertucio, B.M. (2015). Paideia as Metanoia: Transformative Insights from the Monastic Tradition. *Philosophy of Education Society*, 509–517. Retrieved from https://educationjournal.web.illinois.edu/archive/index.php/pes/article/view/4540.pdf

Chung, P.S. (2019). *Critical Theory and Political Theology The Aftermath of the Enlightenment*. Cham: Springer International Publishing.

Cobb, J.B. (2002). *Postmodernism and Public Policy Reframing Religion, Culture, Education, Sexuality, Class, Race, Politics, and the Economy*. Albany, NY: State University of New York Press.

Cooper, B. (2020, October 13). The Hypermodern Highway to Hell, blog post at https://medium.com/the-abs-tract-organization/the-hypermodern-highway-to-hell-1d3a6441b540

Cooper, B. (2020, July 10). Anti-Intellectualism in American Strife, blog post at https://medium.com/the-abs-tract-organization/anti-intellectualism-in-american-strife-737fa2321f34

Cooper, B. (2020, June 18). Convergence for Consensus Building, blog post at https://medium.com/the-abs-tract-organization/convergence-for-consensus-building-a6141f3403ba

Cooper, B. (2019, June 1). Gonzálezean Metamodernism, blog post at https://medium.com/the-abs-tract-organization/gonzálezean-metamodernism-c9343d2f4e0

Crook, C. (Producer), (2020, August 5). Episode 24 – The Joy of Good Burdens, with Albert Borgmann, audio podcast at www.youtube.com/watch?v=XBgEJ01Hz6A

Curtis, A. (Producer/ Director). (2004). *The Power of Nightmares*. [film]. BBC, at www.youtube.com/watch?v=dTg4qnyUGxg

Davis, C., Milbank, J., Žižek, S. and Williams, R. (2005). *Theology and the Political: The New Debate*. Durham: Duke University Press.

Davis, C. and Riches, P. (2005) Metanoia. In Davis, C., Milbank, J., Žižek, S. and Williams, R. (Eds) *Theology and the Political: The New Debate*. Durham: Duke University Press.

Dreyfus, H.L. and Kelly, S. (2011). *All Things Shining: Reading the Western Classics to Find Meaning in a Secular Age*. New York, NY: Free Press.

Fellows, A. (2019). *Gaia, Psyche and Deep Ecology: Navigating Climate Change in the Anthropocene*. London: Routledge, Taylor and Francis Group.

Gibbons, A. (2017). Contemporary Autofiction and Metamodern Affect. In R. V. Akker, A. Gibbons and T. Vermeulen (Eds.), *Metamodernism: Historicity, affect and depth after postmodernism* (pp. 117–130). London: Rowman and Littlefield International.

Giri, A.K. (2019). *Beyond Sociology: Trans-civilizational Dialogues and Planetary Conversations*. Basingstoke, Hampshire: Palgrave Macmillan.

Griffin, D.R. (2006). *Christian Faith and the Truth Behind 9/11: A call to reflection and action*. Louisville, KY: Westminster John Knox Press.

Haynes, S. R. (1994). Christian Holocaust Theology: A Critical Reassessment. *Journal of the American Academy of Religion*, 62(2), 553–585. https://doi.org/10.1093/jaarel/LXII.2.553

Heredia, R. (2007). The Dialogue of Cultures: From Paranoia to Metanoia. *Economic and Political Weekly, 42*(21), 1982–1989. Retrieved from www.jstor.org/stable/4419641

Heredia, R. (1999). Interpreting Gandhi's Hind Swaraj. *Economic and Political Weekly, 34*(24), 1497–1502. Retrieved from www.jstor.org/stable/4408073

Houston, C. (2015, May 29). The 7 Marks of Metanoia… that Lead to Culture Change. *Telosity*. www.telosity.net/the-7-marks-of-metanoia-that-lead-to-culture-change

Jenson, D.H. (2007). *Christian Faith and the Truth Behind 9/11: A Call to Reflection and Action* reviewed by David Ray Griffin in *Religious Studies Review*, 33(3), 215–216.

Judge, A. (2013, October 8). Transforming from Paranoia through Metanoia and Hyponoia? blog post at www.laetusinpraesens.org/docs10s/gerry2.php

Kasulis, T. P. (2009). Japanese Philosophy. In *Encyclopaedia Britannica*. Edinburgh: Encyclopædia Britannica. Retrieved from www.britannica.com.

Kelly, A. R. (2015, September 15). AUDIO: Self-Described Evangelical to U.S. Christians: Jesus Would Vote for Bernie Sanders, blog post at www.truthdig.com/articles/audio-self-described-evangelical-to-u-s-christians-jesus-would-vote-for-bernie-sanders/

LaFreniere, G.F. (2012). *The Decline of Nature: Environmental History and the Western Worldview*. Salem, OR: Oak Savanna Publishing.

Laing, R.D. (1967). *Metanoia: Some Experiences at Kingsley Hall* (Rep.). Retrieved from www.editions-recherches.com/revue/extraits/extrait_08.pdf

Levitón, R. (2007). *Healthy Gaians: How Healing Our Body, Mind, Spirit, and Culture Helps Heal the Planet*. IUniverse. Google Books.

Marques, J. (2011). Fertilizing the Ground for a Metanoia: Business Education in the 21st Century. *Organization Development Journal*, 29.(2), 21–34. Retrieved from www.researchgate.net/publication/263163075_Fertilizing_the_Ground_for_a_Metanoia_Business_Education_in_the_21st_Century

Meisel, P. (1996, September 8). The Mad, Mad World of R. D. Laing. *The New York Times*. Retrieved from www.nytimes.com/1996/09/08/books/the-mad-mad-world-of-r-d-laing.html

Merriam-Webster. (n.d.). Metanoia. In *Merriam-Webster.com dictionary*. Retrieved 29 November, 2020, from www.merriam-webster.com/dictionary/metanoia

Milbank, J. and Pabst, A. (2015). The Meta-crisis of Secular Capitalism. *International Review of Economics, 62*(3), 197–212. doi:10.1007/s12232-015-0239-7

Mishra, P. (2018). The Crisis in Modern Masculinity. *The Guardian*. Retrieved 2020, from www.theguardian.com/books/2018/mar/17/the-crisis-in-modern-masculinity

Myers, K.A. (2011). Metanoia and the Transformation of Opportunity. *Rhetoric Society Quarterly, 41*(1),1–18. https://doi.org/10.1080/02773945.2010.533146

O'Neill, T. (2015, July). In the Footsteps of Gandhi. *National Geographic*. Retrieved from www.nationalgeographic.com/magazine/2015/07/gandhi-legacy-india/

Pope Francis says pandemic can be a 'place of conversion' [Interview by A. Ivereigh]. (2020, April 8). Retrieved from www.thetablet.co.uk/features/2/17845/pope-francis-says-pandemic-can-be-a-place-of-conversion-

Rolheiser, R. (2016, September 12). From Paranoia to Metanoia [Web log post]. Retrieved from https://ronrolheiser.com/from-paranoia-to-metanoia/#.X8coPi_r1Bx

Ruether, R. R. (2007).'Feminist Metanoia and Soul-Making. https://digitalrepository.unm.edu/fri_lectures/1

Saran, A.K. (1969). Gandhi's Theory of Society and Our Times. *Studies in Comparative Religion, 3*(4). Retrieved from www.studiesincomparativereligion.com/uploads/ArticlePDFs/112.pdf

Sarder, R. [Russel Sarder]. (2015, June 4). What is metanoia? by Peter Senge, Author of The Fifth Discipline [Video]. YouTube: https://youtu.be/4RBtBAAdt20

Scott, P.D. (2004). *Deep Politics and the Death of JFK*. Berkeley, CA: University of California Press.

Senge, P.M. (1990). *The Fifth Discipline: The Art and Practice of the Learning Organization*. New York, NY: Doubleday/Currency.

Sjöstedt-H, P. (2020, January 31). The Hidden Psychedelic History of Philosophy: Plato, Nietzsche, and 11 Other Philosophers Who Used Mind-Altering Drugs. Retrieved from https://highexistence.com/hidden-psychedelic-influence-philosophy-plato-nietzsche-psychonauts-thoughts/

Sjöstedt-H, P. (2015). *Noumenautics: Metaphysics – meta-ethics – psychedelics*. Falmouth, Cornwall: Psychedelic Press.

Suhrud, T. (2019, September 25). 'Dear Friend'; Read Mahatma Gandhi's Letters to Adolf Hitler. *Time Magazine*. Retrieved from https://time.com/5685122/gandhi-hitler-letter/

Tanabe, H., Heisig, J.W. and Takeuchi, Y. (2016). *Philosophy as Metanoetics*. Nagoya: Chisokudō.

Targowski, A. (2010). Will Business End or Revive Western Civilization? From Malthusian Trap Business Growth Trap From Paranoia to Metanoia. *Comparative Civilizations Review*, 62(62). Retrieved from https://scholarsarchive.byu.edu/cgi/viewcontent.cgi?article=1786andcontext=ccr

TEDx Talks. (2017, April 12). Metanoia: The Reality of Who We Really Are | Aimee Zadak | TEDxNSU [Video]. YouTube: https://youtu.be/X0F6YWc1eL0

Thompson, W.I. (2009). Conclusion: The Economic Relevance of Lindisfarne.

Thompson, W.I. (2016). Thinking Together at the Edge of History: A memoir of the Lindisfarne association, 1972–2012. Lorian Press.

Vermeulen, T. (2015, January). The New 'Depthiness' [Web log post]. Retrieved from www.e-flux.com/journal/61/61000/the-new-depthiness/

Versluis, A. (1993). *Theosophia*. Hudson, NY: Lindisfarne Press.

Villacorta, J.R. (2011). Metanoia as a Response to Philosophy's Death: From Injustice to Conversion. *Kritike: An Online Journal of Philosophy*, 5(1), 62–69. doi:10.25138/5.1.a.5

Walden, T. (1896). *The Great Meaning of Metanoia*. New York, NY: Thomas Whittaker.

West, C. (2017, September 8). *Spiritual Blackout, Imperial Meltdown, Prophetic Fightback*. Speech presented at Convocation Address in Harvard Divinity School, Cambridge. Retrieved from https://hds.harvard.edu/news/2017/09/08/transcript-cornel-wests-2017-convocation-address#

West, C. (2019, April 12). 25th-annual Hesburgh Lecture in Ethics and Public Policy. University of Notre Dame. Retrieved from https://ndsmcobserver.com/2019/04/west-lectures-on-education/

Williamson, M. (2019). A Politics of Love: A Handbook for a New American Revolution. Harper Collins.

Zackem, A. (Director/Producer). (2017). *American Psychosis*, American Canary, video at https://vimeo.com/293802639

Notes

1   John Donne (1624), 'No Man is an Island'.

2   Judge also juxtaposes metanoia and paranoia with dianoia, hyponoia and anoia, as a 'set of cognitive modalities as engendering radically contrasting stories'. Dianoia is about talking things through, hyponoia reveals knowledge through secrets and quests, and anoia is based on 'absence' from conventional comprehension, with insights gained from paradoxical poetry, riddles, koans and juxtapositions. Interrelating the different 'cognitive operations' suggests that a more holistic configuration can behold greater understanding. See Transforming from Paranoia through Metanoia and Hyponoia?: www.laetusinpraesens.org/docs10s/gerry2.php

3   A brave Christian and evangelical leader allowed himself to be transfixed and truly 'born again' when he heard Bernie Sanders speak at Liberty University in 2015, prompting a religious experience, a conversion even. Recounted via various news outlets with audio, 'Jim's' (anonymous) telling of the story is illustrative as a most profound metanoia, told in a rousing speech about his transformation; it captures the spirit of metanoia most faithfully. See Truth Dig: www.truthdig.com/articles/audio-self-described-evangelical-to-u-s-christians-jesus-would-vote-for-bernie-sanders/ Truth Dig, 2015.

4   See Rep. J.F. Seiberling, 'The case for economic conversion.' Congressional record v.118, n°95, 13 June 1972, pp E6177–6179, cited in *Science Policy Reviews*, Volumes 4 à 5 Battelle Memorial Institute, 1972 p. 398. See Google Books.

11 Gnosis in the Second Person
Responding to the meaning of crisis in the Socratic quest of authentic dialogue

John Vervaeke and Christopher Mastropietro

Knowing is the organ fitted to the object. Plotinus

Acknowledgements

The authors extend warm thanks to Guy Sengstock and Jordan Hall. Your midwifery was invaluable in the delivery of these arguments, and your dialogic partnership is evidence of the spiritual survival of Plato's Academy.

Part I: Dialectic and the four ways of knowing

Introduction: the postmodern predicament and the loss of the second person

It now seems obvious, even trite, to say that modern sociability has lost its 'art of conversation'. Postmodernism has long embraced a diffuse normativity, and Western culture is an endless vivisecting of tribal fragments, mitoses of single-celled identities inflating their certitudes to systems of signification. Awash in parochial meanings, then, our instruments for meaning-*making* seem untuned by the common discourse, as if we lacked the forms of interaction that allow us to concert projects of authentic and collective development. The loss of authentic dialogue is a peculiar obliquity of our ethos, where the convictions of knowing pendulate between subjective (first person) and objective (third person) ontologies until they become idols of egoic possession that we trade, defend and brandish for identity. This idolatrous knowing has atomised our senses of self, space, time and community, and has us subsisting in stillborn encounters unwed by modal confusions of relating – i.e. by the 'having of' relations over a 'being-in' relation to the world. The premodern world might be unavailable, but the postmodern world is infrangible; we need look only to the tenor of public debate to see that the state of discourse is afflicted with performative contradictions and victories of self-defeat, a despairing desire *to be as a part*, but only by prevailing in triumph. The self-defeating discourse is but one pathology of the modern meaning crisis, and the one to which this chapter will attempt a 'concerting' response.

The response begins with a proposal: that discussion, like any cardinal virtue, is a *techne* (a craft) that can be fostered or frittered. When fostered, discussion can become *dialogos*, a practice of *onto-intimation* that discursively disciplines our existential attitudes by arranging our loves to seek self-transformation. In the authentic discourse, you cannot know without also being known, cannot be known without also being changed, and cannot be changed without changing your capacity to know. This second-order appreciation becomes a developmental imperative; dialogos is, among other things, a socialised training in self-transcendence, and in the Socratic tradition, it was cultivated in the second person, with a pedagogic partner who cared for your authentic soul and taught *you* to care in the character of his knowing. This chapter will argue that the metamodern quest to rediscover authentic dialogue begins with this pedagogy, and that by typologising the ways of our knowing, we can begin to adapt the praxis of Socratic dialogos back into common discourse. Fortuitously, the emergence of '4E' Cognitive Science (embodied, embedded, enactive, and extended) has yielded new theories of extended mind, distributed cognition and the emergence of psychotechnologies, socialised systems of representation that bootstrap metacognition and allow us to enculture collective forms of second-order thinking. These psychotechnologies have equipped us to disambiguate the process of knowing to formulate accounts of intelligence, rationality and wisdom, allowing the mobilisation of a response to the meaning crisis. A new form of authentic dialoguing will be incomplete without a comprehending system of (1) propositions, enacted by (2) procedures, embodied by (3) perspectives, embedded in (4) participation. A system of 'participatory knowing' can help the dialogic quester turn intelligence (individual and collective) into rationality (individual and collective) and rationality into wisdom (individual and collective). Inspired by the Socratic and Platonic traditions, we will refer to this fostering system of knowing as *the dialectic. This investigation into the Socratic–Platonic dialectic is intended as a motivating model and cognitive template for critically explicating, elucidating and encouraging the emerging practices of authentic discourse and relating.*[1]

The dialectic vocabulary: logos, gnosis and rationality

It is increasingly difficult to invoke the Socratic and Platonic traditions without sinking into the quagmire of modern lexicology. Terms like 'knowledge', 'reason' and 'rationality' have been dulled by the abrasions of materialism. Enlightenment thinkers abridged *episteme* (from the original 'under-standing' or 'inter-standing'[2]) to fact acquisition, rationality (from the Latin *ratio*) to dispassionate logicality, and *logos* to univocal purports. Such notional astigmatisms are culpable for many modern cul-de-sacs, an inheritance of obvallate epistemologies premised on refracted accounts of knowing. Suffice to say, a 'metamodern' rehabilitation of any of the above is no small undertaking, and in a fit of aspiration, this chapter will endeavour to model the rehabilitation in addition to arguing for it. The use of the term *aspiration* here is technical, termed by Agnes Callard (2018) to mean a *proleptic rationality* – not calculative arguments, but a cultivated 'view from above' that changes the identity of a subject as he comes to know what he could not imagine knowing, and so comes to be whom he could not imagine being. This self-transcendence requires a notion of rationality that emphasises the amelioration of self-deception, the affordance of aspiration and the subordination of argumentation to the telos of personal transformation. Dialectic reasons that a 'man who has learned anything becomes in each case such as his knowledge makes him' (*Gorgias* 460b), and to this end, aspiration is the deployment of attention to our epistemic maturation. The view from above is a relation we adopt to raise us as we grow to 'inter-stand' it. *Philosophia* – in the tradition of Socrates – was a dialectic system for practising proleptic rationality. The loving of wisdom, so defined, put us in a relation of wondering aspiration.

In philosophia, the efficacy of dialectic rationality is inseparable from its dialogical format. Yet the meaning of dialogos requires a more exacting definition of logos. A term like 'realisation' is more commensurate with the etymologies of logos as a conceptual 'gathering' or 'putting in order'. It refers to a structural-functional organisation, a fittedness for purpose that disposes an efficient, mimetic relation to reality, like the extract of an ontological pattern applied as a probative implement. The idea of 'gathering' intelligibility saw some revival among the pragmatists, who proposed that the meaning of a concept was constituted by its 'conceivable bearing upon the conduct of life' (Peirce, 1905/1970, p. 102) – for example, the pencil is 'writable' or the chair is 'sittable'. For many of the pragmatists, logos was a sharpening approximation of the real that *appreciated in reality* – a hypothesis that 'realised' by the texture of an individual's ongoing contact with the world which recursively deepened his ontological grasp. Centuries earlier, Plotinus introduced a similarly tactile metaphor to describe the knowing of *gnosis*: a grasping fist that gathers to its object and tightens into verisimilitude. Appreciation – at once meaning gratitude, apprehension and graduation – of this grasp is the function of proleptic rationality, not as applied to knowledge (i.e. information) but to understanding, which grasps the plausible significance of information by its relevance to our aspired possibility. Proleptic rationality educates logos through disciplined discussion to gather itself around the highest order of potential for any intelligible unit of knowledge. In other words, proleptic rationality has us appreciate information based on how the information makes us more rationally appreciative – casts us in deeper conformity with reality. This is the significance of the dialectic project: *appreciating logos with an aspiring gnosis that espouses shared identity with ontos (Being)*. Dialectic is the praxis that seeks to engender and enhance the process of dialogos. Socrates advances the dialectic project by conducing, through dialogue, a percipient weddedness between the knower and the being-known that becomes a symbolised relation, an embodied binding that effects *transjective* knowing, a flowing state of being that opens a current of phenomenological continuity between a subject and her object – this is dialogos. Symbols, from the Greek *symbolon*, adjoin entities into a shared identity, and induce this transjective current like a conductor induces an electric one. This current of transjectivity is participatory; it synchronises the other ways of knowing into a patterned similitude. This cognitive synchronisation is fundamental to Plato's philosophia: if Socrates is the conductor of knowing, his dialogues are its circuitry. Dialectic signifies the 'current that expresses the nature of truth as concealed, as requiring search in the direction of a self that is not yet known' (Ahbel-Rappe, 2018, p. xiii). Our aspired continuity with this yet unknown self – and the world it beholds – was symbolised by the Socratic eros, intimating the apotheosised aspect of man that would later emerge through Neoplatonism and Christianity, in what Charles Stang (2017) calls our 'divine double'.[3]

We might tidy our understanding of dialectic with the following metaphor, to be reprised throughout the chapter: imagine the organising self as a musical orchestra, just like Plato's partite soul (*psuche*). In this analogy, the signifying logos is the sounding of the instruments. The Socratic symbol conducts a melody to invoke a transjective state of play, and the melody coheres the logos to harmonise the orchestral sections. Meanwhile, this analogy can transfer (in both directions) between intrapersonal and interpersonal levels of play: the 'dialogue' is also an orchestral arrangement, and dialogos is the 'playing together' that gathers the instruments of self in the sounding of other selves. In both scenarios, the flowing melody is the dialectic presence that harmonises the instruments 1) within the self, 2) between the selves and 3) between the intra- and interpsychic orchestras. The dialectic aspiration, and Callard's proleptic rationality, is the conduction of novel melodies to complexify orchestral rhythms, evolving our capacity to play involute measures until the intra- and interpersonal chording becomes a tuning for transpersonal concerts.[4] In both individual and collective orchestral models, dialectic transmutes intelligence (the aptitude for music) into rationality (the aptitude for harmony) and rationality into wisdom (the harmony that seeks concert). The relational presence of this melody binds the instruments into a shared identity of accession, much like a crew mobilises in the anatomy of a moving vessel – a chariot, for instance – and arranges to face the frontier. The 'team spirit' of dialectic is of the players and beyond the players, just like a *daimon*, and it en-chants the participant knowers with its symbolising vitality. The melodic motion possesses the cadence of each individual performer, explaining the common phenomenon of a collective being 'more than the sum of its parts' – like how four good musicians can gather into genius (e.g. The Beatles).

The dialectic 'current' is an aspiring rationality, a view from above that ideates a cosmic chorus. When we catch it – as it catches us – it inspires new arrangements for our orchestra that change the way we 'play' by 'playing together'. Dialogos disposes a character of onto-dramatic irony: the novel melody cultivates aspiration by dialoguing the participant knower through a play of different motifs – for example, stories, myths and games – then retunes the knower by rephrasing those motifs, reflexing her attention to her own transformation, revealing her potential to be a new kind of self. Dialectic is the melody of transformation that scores over the scenes, ironising each moment of play with foreknowing ignorance; for example, the young man plays classical music knowing he may someday appreciate it, plays the uncle knowing he may someday be a father, sounds out a language knowing that he may someday be fluent. The view from above aspires our logos to expand from its current frame (i.e. it 'trans-frames' perspective) and in so doing, guides the gathering soul to seek itself in mystery. 'For just this reason it is fair that only a philosopher's mind grows wings, since its memory always keeps it as close as possible to those realities by being close to which the gods are divine' (*Phaedrus* 249c). Anamnesis of this meta-attentional rationality is analogised by the charioteer in Plato's *Phaedrus*, 'the soul's steersman' who uses the unseen presence of 'the place beyond heaven' to gather his horses (instruments) in gnosis (concert) with the Forms. It is tempting to contrast this famous journey with an antipodal myth – that of Phaeton, the brash son of Apollo who presumed to pilot his father's chariot with no such view from above, and was unable to muster the horses and scorched the earth in flame. His myth brings character to the noxious consequence of un-gathered conversations, and the un-gathered selves they conduce, adducing fresh stakes to the Socratic maxim that the unexamined life – an unaspiring flight, so defined – is not worth living.

The four ways of knowing: proposition, procedure, perspective and participation

To better understand the dialectic of an 'examined life' and its impact on our knowing, we must first understand more expressly what we mean by 'knowing'. For this, we offer four categories or ways of parcelling the epistemic definition.[5] Typologies are not essential of course, but they are useful insofar as they lend intelligibility (or Pascal's 'spirit of geometry') to darkling patterns, allowing us to gain understanding of our cognition and intervene in its processes. Aspiringly then, the provision of these types will – with continual reference to Socrates – advance the epistemic project by describing its constituents more closely.

- **Propositional knowing**: *Gold is a mineral. The equator crosses Columbia. The normal human body is at 37.0°C.* Propositions set constraining criteria – i.e. rules – that help us to realise the relevant implications of information. Propositional knowing is a linguistic 'knowing that', marked by apophantic and inferential reasoning. It provides factuality. Yet the 'constraint' of propositions can become idolatrous and, when unyielding, they 'freeze-frame' our perspective (see ahead). For this reason, Socrates uses propositions as dialogic rudders, indexically, to steer the vessel of attention to epistemic significance.

- **Procedural knowing**: *Catching a ball. Driving a car. Changing a diaper.* Procedure is a non-linguistic 'knowing how to', combined of conscious and preconscious actions that realise relevant interactions and effect a power to impact on the world. While propositions condition rules, procedure conditions routine. For instance, Socrates uses the *techne* of elenchus to entrain discussion within a routine of socialised exchanges, observable in Plato's dialogues. If the proposition is the single 'note' of knowing, the procedure is undoubtedly its rhythm.

- **Perspectival knowing**: *Suspicious. Maternal. Desirous. Regretful.* Perspective is the 'knowing what it is like to be', a situational awareness that realises relevant states of consciousness and cognition, a presence of 'hereness' and 'being-in-the-world', an agent–arena relationship that gives off a sense of presence and placement.[6] Imagine visiting the house where you grew up as a child: almost certainly, the presence of 'home' has changed as your role as 'the child' has shifted. The house seems smaller. The bedroom doesn't invite you to play. Proposition and procedure are grounded in the presence of relationships, and so we invoke this presence to inform these ways of knowing – for example, a teacher might situate a maths problem (proposition) in a grocery store (perspective) for the students to practise solving it (procedure). Nietzsche (1887/1989), of course, made this point famously: 'There is only a perspective seeing, only a perspective "knowing"; and the more affects we allow to speak about one thing, the more eyes, different eyes, we can use to observe one thing, the more complete will our "concept" of this thing, our "objectivity", be' (*On the Genealogy of Morals*, p. 119). In Plato's dialogues, Socrates situates perspective within dramaturgy; the multivocality of characters allows for the casting of 'eyes' and the adoption of different propositions. If the proposition is the note and procedure the rhythm, perspective is the signature role sounded by the body of each instrument.

- **Participatory knowing**: Participation is the most difficult 'way' of knowing to explain because it is also the most ineffable. It realises the relevant forms of life, the existential moding of our being. Participation is not the subjective character of perspective (which seems personal) or the objective lexicality of propositions (which seems impersonal), but belongs in the transjective, the verbal in-between. Participatory knowing leads the gathering logos to a state of *religio*, a sacral experience of connectedness and transpersonal relating to reality. It is therefore mediated by symbola – connecting tissues of enculturation (self to world), ecological coupling (agent to arena) and niching (organism to environment). In our metaphoric orchestra, participatory knowing is the embodiment of resonant vibrations, wherein the identity of a player becomes the identity of the concert in play. Our enculturing, coupling and niching are the *participles* of existential attitudes that mode the character of our experience. We are, as Heidegger observed, the only beings whose being is in question, and the open question of our being participates our existence into presence (*Dasein*). The roles of lover, mother, father, friend, teacher, student, elder, enemy … these cognitive structures are characters of perspective gathered by our existential moding. To take a shared perspective, we must share the query of being – to join our empty, grasping hands, where the logos of knowing begins.

Table 11.1 Ways of knowing

Knowing	Understanding	Normativity	Sense of realness
Propositional	Realising relevant *implications* (language and inference)	Rules	Conviction
Procedural	Realising relevant *interactions* (sensory-motor interaction)	Routine	Power
Perspectival	Realising relevant *states* of consciousness and cognition (salience landscaping)	Role	Presence
Participatory	Realising relevant *forms of life* (existential moding)	Religio	Resonance

Three examples may companion this typology. The first follows Wittgenstein (1953/2009), who once quipped that if lions could talk, we wouldn't understand them. This turns out to be a provocative test for our typology. We can appreciate a lion's features *propositionally*, observe their behaviours *procedurally*, and share some awareness that *perspectivally* situates their relation to survival, for example, states that compel them to hunt, seek shade or socialise. Ultimately, though, the 'subjective character' of the lion's experience (i.e. what it is like for the lion to be a lion) remains unavailable to us because our self-to-world relations are existentially incommensurable (Nagel, 1974). Yet, while we do not fully share a lion's form of life, there is a partial conformity of situation such that we can *characterise* a lion in ways that expand our situational awareness and deepen the query of logos. The early shaman prototyped this mimetic potential to increase his cognitive flexibility; he played the lion to 'lionise' himself, and in so doing, personified the lion. By imitation, the shaman conformed himself to the lion's perspective to induce a knowing *ekstasis*. In other words, he played his self deeper into ontos with a lion's share of being. The personification-lionisation loop elasticised the shaman's sense of presence and modal participation, reciprocally opening him (Lewis, 2018) – his culturing, niching and ecology – to development by realising his relation to alternate forms of life.[7] Millennia later, recent robotic explorations on Mars have inspired similarly mimetic exercises within the modern scientific enterprise. Remote operators of the Mars Exploration Rovers use a combination of gesture, speech and sociability to anthropomorphise the Rover and *technomorphise* their bodies to presence its ambulation. These *embodied imaginations* 'niche' the machine; they conform the operators' knowing to the Rover's by conjoining proposition, procedure and perspective into a participatory enactment, such that the driver's being marries with the Rover's and she comes to see with the 'Rover's-eye-view' (Vertesi, 2012).[8]

We find a third, more conforming, example in the relation of a mother to her child.[9] Someone may have correct beliefs about motherhood, the know-how for mothering, awareness to take on motherly roles – all without *knowing as a mother*. When a person becomes a 'participating' mother, her development becomes coextensive with her child's development – to grow the child, she grows with the child, and shares in its growing identity. In so doing, the mother's knowing becomes a conforming participation, a mutual 'selfing' with her child that passes beyond understanding. It becomes *loving*; her maternity is gathered as her being is re-moded, and by being known as 'mother', her knowing becomes 'motherly'. The mother's participatory knowing emerges from within the second person perspective – the 'Thou' – of her knowing child, *the perspective that knows her as mother*. She plays through the presence of her child to realise her maternity, just as the shaman lionised his self to realise his humanity. 'Thou' of the child is a mother's form of life, her existential mode of being-in-participation.

As the shaman to the lion, scientist to Rover or mother to her child, we to ourselves become 'Thou' in dialogos – the second person in whose knowing we find a serious form of play that commits a self to a new form of life. We will exposit the symbolic transjectivity of 'Thouing' in a later section. In the dialectic of philosophia, Socrates is the Thou in whose knowing we re-mode, whose midwifery delves and delivers us, the child, towards our ontos – deeply, knowingly, to the groundless ground of Being.

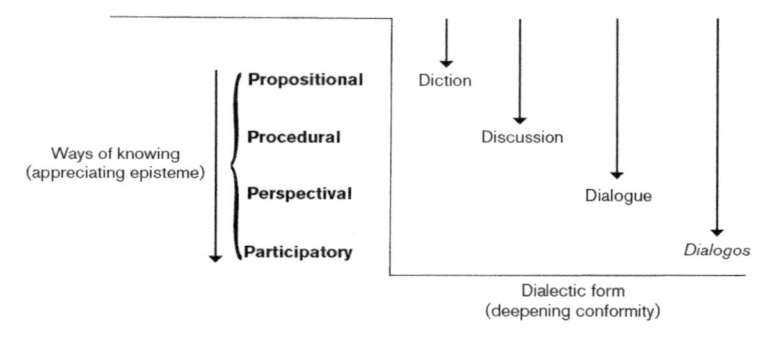

Figure 11.1 Ways of knowing

Dialectic is the appreciation of our knowing, presented in these fourfold types, through a form of cultivated, reciprocal relating that plays the logos of our identity through discursive exercises (intersubjective and intrasubjective) to soundly deepen its gnosis. In order to understand the efficacy of this discursive rationality – the same embodied imagination that allows scientists to somatise the presence of technology and characterise its knowing – we must first understand its signalling mechanism, the notations of melody that tune each instrument to prepare its intimate death and concert – that is, the vessel of the *enacted analogy*.

Part II: The enacted analogy and the dialectic microcosm

The dialectic vessel: the enacted analogy

Comprehensive theories of metaphor are well beyond the scope of this work.[10] However, it suffices to understand that analogies are 'figurative' connections speciated by the ecology of our *worldview attunement* (Vervaeke, Mastropietro and Miscevic, 2017). We might imagine them as the radial patterns of a wheel that extend between its hub (the knower) and its rim (the world in perspective), networking the world together as our relating ecology revolves. The 'figurative' adjective is also revealing, and exemplary. It inflects the analogy as a geometric entity. The shaping of an analogy is a notional spatialisation. The shaman's ritual 'soul flight' (Winkelman, 2000), for instance (see next section), lifts his vantage high off the ground to gain a view from above, and his felt physical height shapes to his perspectival *ekstasis*. The rest of us, meanwhile, cultivate our relations to trace and re-spatialise the intelligible pattern of 'highness' in the way we *figure* our activities: we hike to a lookout in order to 'get perspective' – or turn to consciousness-altering substances to interiorise the effect (getting high).

Analogies are spatial because they involve the exaptation of gestural movement. Consider the haptic significance of waving a salutation (giving attention), grasping by hand (understanding a concept), holding a hand (understanding a person) or clasping hands in prayer (gathering oneself together). These kinesic movements spatialise patterns of intelligibility. Metaphor is not simply an evolved cognitive abstraction, as Barfield (1973) and others have noted, but it is an exaptation of embodied actions (like projecting a spear) into notional patterns (starting a project) that are introjected and spatialised *di novo* within our physicality. The *logoi* of the project and the projectile are assonant; they have a structural–functional correspondence, a shared presence of intelligibility. We express this assonance in nearly every participle of our speech and behaviour: we 'take' a gander, 'corner' an opponent, 'cut' through fog, 'attack' an idea, 'smooth' a problem', 'thicken' a plot, 'blaze' a trail, 'run' an experiment, 'retire' a jersey, 'inhale' a meal, 'return' a favour, 'marshal' a thought, 'whet' an appetite and 'starve' for conversation. This exapted, spatial synchronousness of the tactile and the notional also erupts into spontaneous gestures, like grabbing the head when whelmed by dilemma, or covering the mouth when aghast at bad news. Nor it is merely unconscious: we deliberately synchronise analogic levels in the conveyance of certain impressions, spatialising the *logos* of our meaning to make it present and efficacious to a respondent. Doing this artfully, after all, is the poesis of persuasion, and good storytelling.

Consider the following examples of *analogic assonance*:

- telling a horror story, in a low whisper, with the lights out *(to scare)*

- hugging a friend, patting her back, uttering reassurances *(to soothe)*

- considering an idea, taking a walk, on an unfamiliar route *(to explore)*

- holding a partner's hands, to soft music, while professing love *(to bind)*

- tickling your child, while telling a joke, in an impish voice *(to humour)*.

Metaphoricity is indispensable to our sensemaking of the world; it describes the phenomenological texture of *Dasein* (Heidegger's being-in-the-world). The assonant spatialisation gathers a coherence in the ways of knowing. It inflects the propositional (e.g.

the scary percept) and procedural (its narration) within the perspectival (the feeling of being scared). Yet we can also perform the analogic assonance still more deeply; we can turn the story into a role play, turn the peripatetic into a journey, turn the conversation into a therapy. In these cases, our entire identity absorbs into the assonance, and our knowing becomes participatory – we become an *embodied enactment* of the analogic relation. Returning to our 'figurative' bicycle wheel: the participatory enactment extends our presence into the radially patterned space between the hub and the rim, collapsing the distance between them, bringing us to the very edge of our world in perspective. With this, we may begin to 'explore' the sapiential implications; the embodied enactment of analogic assonance is another term for the process of symbolisation, the dialectical vessel of philosophia.

Analogic enactments are provoked by specific kinds of encounters. In other words, certain forms of relating conduce our symbolisation. Consider the Roman goddess Iustitia, better known to us as the symbol of Lady Justice. She is usually iconised with her arm outstretched, balancing a set of scales. This motion of her analogue is a symbolic fertility; her gesture refers, but partakes of the referee, and this makes her a conductor for embodied enactment. Her motion entreats us to mimesis: we imagine ourselves balancing the scales, and in so doing, we activate the cerebellum, the area of the brain that maintains our physical equilibrium. Our cognitive 'balance' machinery exapts to presence the intelligible notion of an equanimous, rational judgement. We mimetically interiorise the balancing gesture, and the imaginal, notional motion of the goddess becomes the phenomenological symbolon, the conducting bridge that enacts the analogue and articulates space at the edges of perspective. In other words, by internalising the motion of justice, we embody a gesture that beckons beyond our perspectival frame. We are 'enworlded' by it – we now indwell, and are indwelled by, a world that is present to justice and thus deepened in presence. We seem to know justice through the world's 'just' understanding. The 'just' motioning becomes our participatory knowing; we know Iustitia and *through* Iustitia, and reality 'justifies' in her image. As Plato argues in his notion of anamnesis, we can only know justice by being just.

Symbolisation is a form of phenomenological relating that deepens our Dasein: dimensions of 'self', 'other' and 'world' all collapse into the transjective presence of the beholding symbol. This also means that every instance of symbolisation is reflexive – i.e. it also symbolises the self. All phenomena have aspectual dimensions in their ontology that exceed our perspective. Therefore, they can be inexhaustibly more realised, and more beholden (note the implicit analogy: 'to be held') as perspective accedes. The phenomenal world is composed of analogies for enactment, and symbols are the 'realising' motions that gesture to the 'moreness' of things, and the moreness of self (the gripping logos) that beholds them. Everything is a thing (or 'no thing') beyond itself – including other selves – and symbolisation is a kind of ontological transubstantiation for the potential in being: the *embodiment of 'beyondness' into presence*.

Symbols change our relationships by changing our sense of space. The spatialisation exapts from the body. Consider the symbolisation within ritual, where physical embodiments geometrise notions of the eternal. By analogy, our homes perform the same function. The ritualised body postures analogic patterns: we cross the heart, crown the head, bend the knee, burden the shoulder, ring the finger, wash the foot ... we make an epistemic apparatus from the body by incarnating the assonance in a symbolic-somatic nervous system. This is why we feel and taste notions – like justice – as presences within us. This is also why poetry induces us to participatory knowing; beautiful poetry sacralises when it seems to gesture with the hand of the cosmos, as though the great body analogue reaches to touch itself. The deportment of the body is a symbolic geste: it disposes our phenomenological relation with reality, and therefore, it hosts the space for the poesis of the world that emerges from our beholding (Todes, 2001). They share continuity, a non-logical identity. The body symbolon is the felt body of the world. This is why the 'fitting organ' plays such an indispensable role in our gnosis.

As we adumbrated in the previous section, any essay on symbolic embodiment must be succeeded by a lament to its modern anaemia. The dualistic legacy of the Enlightenment has disaffected and desensitised the symbolic nervous system. It might also be noted that, after Saussure, conventional structuralism assumed that the signifying relationship between semiotic entities – i.e. between a 'signifier' and 'signified' – was arbitrary, and this contemporary paradigm effectively de-symbolised the analogic assonance that echoed between domains of relevance. The postmodern critiques of this problem succeeded only in following the unsound premise to a nominalist conclusion, assuming no enactment of the referee in the 'body' of an analogic referrer – in other words, no ontological 'participation' in the knowing gesture.[11] The theoretical disembodiment and de-spatialisation of gesture has certainly deepened, if not co-authored, the existential gulf opened by our many modern dualisms, and strangled the vocal realism spoken by the logos of symbolic grammar. A metamodern metaphor, if it is to countervail these mistakes, must not fall prey to self-estrangement caused by the nominalism of these 20th-century reductions, lest it bring further decay to the cadaverous symbolic body, whose episteme – as we will soon discover – depends upon the assonant 'know-how' of balancing a set of scales, taming a horse, climbing a ladder or moving to the mouth of a cave. The analogic assonance bears a striking resemblance to the Platonic notion of the *hyponia* (the 'under thought') that defines the nature of the allegory. In a later section, we will explore how essential this dialectical vessel is for characterising the transformations within the dialogic practice. First, however, we must explain the symbolical indispensability of the interpersonal relationship for tracing the figure of this dialogos, and for giving character to the dialectical spirit.

The dialectic microcosm: sensibility transcendence, anagoge and the symbolisation of I and Thou

Sensibility transcendence, termed by John Wright (2005) based on Iris Murdoch's (1970) virtue ethics, is a reorganising of self in the knowing of *another* self; we encounter a person whose mien cannot be typified within our typological structures, and the effort of accommodating this person induces a shift in our mode of *relating* – from a categorical 'I-It', or a 'having mode' of relating (Fromm, 1976) into what Martin Buber (1923/1970) called 'I-Thou', or a 'being mode of relating'. As Thou, the 'other self' is irreducible, and the *I-Thou* encounter provokes a 'transformative experience' (Paul, 2016): the logos of the knower's identity moves to re-gather intelligibility around the human aporia. In so doing, he *poeticises*: he turns to himself for exaptation and finds analogues from his own body of experience (note the figuration) to become analogic proxies for the sudden mystery. The proxies erect a bridge (a symbolon) to cross the epistemic gap, conjoining the edge of his perspective to the perspective of the unknown Thou. For instance, he may choose to exapt *his* role of being a pet owner to analogise *her* role of raising a child, and in so doing, engages a form of symbolic play to embody her parental experience. He re-stories himself to narrate a role that was inenarrable to him. In other words, he is forced to change himself around a person in order to realise that person; he must become the kind of self who can make sense of this new kind of self. The most significant threat to sensibility transcendence is '*modal confusion*', wherein we mistakenly adopt the I-It existential mode when trying to meet the aspirational, developmental needs of the being mode. Instead of seeking transformative experience afforded by the confrontation with mystery, one instead formulates a problem of control and consumption. For example, instead of aspiring oneself out of egocentrism and into the mystery of onto-centrism in order to become a good parent, one mis-frames his aspirational need and simply *has* as many children as possible. One of the main functions of dialectic as a psychotechnology is to alleviate modal confusion for the affordance of sensibility transcendence. Dia-*logos* is the gathering together for emergence, rather than foreclosure to conclusion.

Sensibility transcendence casts our logos in conformity with a symbolising process. However, as we will explain, the symbolisation conducted by encounters with Thou exceeds the enactments of Lady Justice, or any comparable analogy. The reasons for this are complex. First, recall the earlier motif of Plotinus' grasping fist, the gathering logos, as it conforms to know its object. Now, imagine the joined hands of two grasping *logoi* – *the gathering logos deepens as it gathers to a deepening logos*. The sensibility transcendence of dialogos is an intersubjective gripping that deepens the presence of our ontological grasp. To put it simply, our dialogic grip on one another appreciates our mutual grip on reality. It continuously embodies us with a presence of participatory knowing because the object of our knowing – Thou – is a symbolising subject in beyond-ward movement, and it draws us correspondently into continual symbolic motion. Reciprocal symbolisation is characteristic of intimate, Platonic sociability – we call this *philia*. The epistemic presence that emerges in virtue of the reciprocal symbolisation, when cultivated, is a philia of sophia, a loving of wisdom. This 'love' is often portrayed hermetically, as a straddling daimon flitting (across) between persons, and (up-down) twixt mortal and divine. As we will explain, the crisscross 'in-betweenness' of this spirit is essential to its dialectical character.

Many traditions take the 'presence' of this intersubjective sociability and adapt its sapiential potential. Philosophia was first among them. The 'symbolic play' of relational experience, assonating in dialogos, exercises the grip of the grasping logos and flexes our rational attention. Analogies pronounce relevancy by the apposition of pertinent features; for instance, the Platonic roles of 'lover' (eros, attraction) and 'craftsman' (poesis, technique) present relational qualities that, if enacted, posture us into new relationships with the world.

Every phenomena in the field of perspective has analogic potential, and most analogies are retracted symbolic bridges that await enactment. Dialogos with 'Thou' teaches us to enact *relevant* analogies to bridge our knowing to conformity with aporetic phenomena. In other words, it teaches us proleptic rationality – to deploy our attention to the liable details and open fitting symbolic spaces to accommodate revelatory meanings. Dialogos, therefore, is a practice of episteme. The dialogic I-Thou spatialises relevance into an embodied dramaturgy, binding the ways of knowing (propositional, procedural and perspective) into concentrated symbolisations. In sensibility transcendence, the relation between I and Thou becomes an analogue for analogic poesis, a dynamic that enacts the knower's potential to exapt and poeticise for participatory knowing. The I-Thou relation is a symbol for episteme – i.e. it represents episteme and partakes of episteme. I-Thou, in other words, is a symbol for making symbols. *It is a meta-enactive analogue: an analogy for exapting and enacting relevant analogies.*

The philia in I-Thou disposes a symbolic presence that refers beyond the I-Thou. The love of wisdom is the dialogic pursuit of this presence within the convergent, intelligible spaces opened by analogic assonance. This is why we describe intimate relations as *understanding*; they function as epistemic viewfinders, and we presence ourselves through the 'deepening presence' of their enacting analogic bodies. The social phenomenon of sensibility transcendence, so native to the arms of intimacy, opens space for a shared presence of mind (a *nous*) that is drawn 'upward' by the recognition of some conforming realism. When we symbolise to the second person, the knowing of – and through – the second person becomes an embodied passage of knowing through the world. This means that the participatory knowing of Thou is an enacted analogy for gnosis; all I-Thou relations seem to partake of some 'eternity', a meta-analogic gesture towards the horizon. Each dialogue of this relation becomes filiated by the deeper gesture. This is what we mean when we say deep conversations are blessed; they appear possessed of a presence beyond themselves, breathed (inspired) by a spirit that circles their being into being-in-the-world, like Heidegger's in-dwelling Dasein. The breathing spirit, as it were, is the presence of the dialectic. The I-Thou dialogos is a symbolic microcosm of this dialectic; it appreciates the logos of the beholding 'I' through its knowing by 'Thou'. This means that if we pull on one protruding thread of this fractal social encounter, an entire cosmos will begin to unspool from it. As Heidegger (1958) observed, the 'I' of the dialectic is as a 'consciousness that represents something, relates this representation back to itself, and so gathers with itself'. Heidegger goes on to explain how the gathering of logos is taken up by the dialectic.

> To gather is said in Greek, 'legein'. The gathering of the manifold by the I is expressed by means of 'legesthai'. The thinking I gathers the represented to the extent that it goes through it, transverses it by means of representation. 'To transverse through something' is said in Greek: 'dia'. 'Dialegesthai', dialectic, here means that the subject in the stated process and as such a process, brings itself out: produces itself.   Heidegger, 1958

To better understand the 'traversing' dynamics of dialectic, it behoves us to explore sensibility transcendence using a different definitional framework. Our identification in casual social dialogue alternates on an attentional scale between 'transparency' and 'opacity' (see Apter, 1982; Metzinger, 2003). In other words, our self-relation shifts between unselfconscious presence (the first person 'I' that we look through) and self-conscious persona (the third person 'me' that we look at). Intimate relations are singular, however, because they dispose us to a mode of existential vulnerability that transfers our identity to the second person. In a 'second person' relation, the I-Me alternation resolves into a balanced translucency – a crossfade between the transparency and the opacity. In this 'opponent' dynamic, the personae of the I and It begin to fade and the relationship – now with Thou – begins to *symbolise*: we see I-Thou and see through I-Thou simultaneously, and our identities merge into continuity. I-Thou is not merely a symbol, as we have noted, but a symbolising mechanism that confers its translucent continuity onto the objects of its knowing, which become transjectively bound to our identities through the shared identity of the relationship. This relational form of knowing is intrinsically poetic, and sensibility transcendence therefore also provides a vocabulary for understanding the phenomenology of *agape*. Consider that attentive parents must cultivate this sensible dynamic continually with their growing children; if she is to be successful, the mother must know her child from a perspective that exceeds her child, but that also exceeds her own – before the needs of the child, she is constantly 'beyond' herself, constantly becoming in virtue of its revelation. In this kind of relation, the knower must conceive with a *nous* that is phenomenologically transcendent. It is not reducible to the knowing individual, nor the known one, but unfolds from the space that yawns open between the two selves as they disclose, like a breath that fills some mutual, expanding lung. The presence between I and Thou is a *metaxy*, an 'in-between'. It shares a conforming identity with both knowing and the being-known. By aspiring to the aporetic (in Thou), it also straddles the dividing line between the illumed and un-illumed sides of the perspectival frame, between the known and unknown, between here and the unseen elsewhere. Paolo Costa (2011) elucidates the nature of this frame: it is 'as if we were immersed in a sort of bubble of meaningfulness, or, better, in an atmosphere of significance that we do not create from scratch but are absorbed by'. Costa (2011) goes on to note: 'The metaphor of the atmosphere should suggest not only the image of a global container, but also that of a rhythm, of breathing and of a light refraction to which a living being must attune or adjust herself.' The inspiring and expiring of breath, the expanding and contracting of lungs ... the metaxy of aspiration places the individual into the trajectory of trans-framing so she may participate more wakefully in the atmosphere of meaning, and be spirited by the connection therein.

The philia of Socratic dialogos is, among other things, a rhythmic praxis dedicated to this dialectical attunement that embodies the symbol of symbols (the meta-enacted analogy). In the knowing of Thou, our relation to the world seems to deepen: we are redrawn by Thou in dimensions we had not imagined, and this reflects open, new, correspondent dimensions of the world that become available to us. The effects of this spatialisation are multiply realised. Being so revealed, we now *realise* our potential for revelation – the unknown in us suddenly comes known, and with it, the awareness that there is still more to know, and more of ourselves to be known. We become hungry for the perspective whose absence we realise, and we begin to mind our ignorance and make 'space' for it. The relationships that cede that perspective – that induce sensibility transcendence – now become sacralised. Self-knowledge now becomes the telic orientation of our relationships: we look to Thou for our own disclosure, and in this transjective contact, our 'knowing' and 'being known' seem to logistically conform, such that our knowing logos seems mutually shaped to the logos of a knowing world. This is why gnosis begins in dialogos; as the I-Thou relation disposes a phenomenological translucency, it spatialises the 'beyondness' that lies in wait behind any phenomenon that falls within its contemplation. All the while, our knowing logos assonates with the notion of appreciating realism; the symbolic space-making becomes ontological sensemaking. The symbolising presence between I and Thou triangulates access to the aspect of reality that lingers beyond the perspectival frame. It seeks the relevant, translucent *potentia* in our earthy opacities. Heidegger may therefore have called this an 'unconcealing' presence. The symbolic knower harkens the intelligibility of the beyondness and traces it with the strengthening grip of her rational logos.

At the same time, the disclosures of sensibility transcendence also improve our second-order thinking and deepen our capacities for knowing: we become more perspectivally limber, able to imagine and assume extrinsic perspectives to consciously deepen our percipience. Our attention becomes more perceiving, and anyone caught in our attention becomes commensurately more perceived. Our reflections expand in the opening apertures of each other's perspective, as do the reflected silhouettes of the world behind them. This recursive, shaping presence, the symbolising dynamic of mutual realisation, continues to circle through I and Thou and becomes reproducible at different scales of relation – intra-psychically (with ourselves), inter-psychically (with other selves) and ontologically (with the world). This effects a cycle of 'reciprocal opening', a reversal of Lewis' (2018) 'reciprocal narrowing' that occurs in the throes of addiction, when we reduce to I-It consumption and the world grows scarce and unaffordable. When reciprocity of philia begins to open, the 'horizontal' axis of sensibility transcendence – relating across between persons – suddenly converges with a 'vertical' axis of acceding epistemological contact. The dialectical metaxy breathing between 'I' and the social 'Thou' transfigures its geometrical dimension, spatialising a relation between I and an *ontological* Thou. The axes of realness conjugate in the symbol of Thou; in other words, our posture towards ontological mystery disposes in the symbolic continuity of the dyad, and the aspiration of the I-Thou relation becomes *anagoge*, an 'ascent' of participatory knowing that plays us deeper into reality, bridges us 'beyond' perspectival stasis into a verbal motion, a conformed identicality to being-in-ever-deepening-perspective. This conformed identicality is an intrapsychic reorganisation – Plato's *'justice of the psyche'* – that alleviates intrapsychic conflict and thereby ameliorates self-deception.[12] The reorganisation affords deeper ontological depth perception and an enhanced knowledge of the structural-functional real patterns of the world, which are then introjected to a perspicuous realisation (in both senses of the term) of the structural-functional patterns of the psyche. The entire process then feeds back unto itself in a self-organising dynamical system, a living logos. The 'verticality' of this living logos, of course, is an analogy. It refers back to the 'soul flight' of the upper Palaeolithic period, when the shaman (induced by psychotropics and deprivation) experienced himself in a state of astral levitation, flying high above the terrain where he could see the finite landscape meet with the infinite horizon. Anagoge is the motion of this analogic meeting, where the inside flow of time meets the outside flow of eternity, like a stream joining to a river, where the self and the world co-discover the depth of their being in a mutual – and identical – 'beyondness'.

Part III: The dialectical wisdom and the dialectic dimensions

The dialectical wisdom: episteme, eros and philia of sophia

When intimates converse, their semantic content *intimates*; it is accented with an analogic dialect that oversignifies the content of their propositions. The semantic content, in other words, analogises the relationship. Recall the latticed grips of conjoining logoi: the beholding hands are beholden by each object they behold, meaning the relation (the meta-analogue) is gathered with every topic (each analogue) that it gathers. The postulate of an intimate discussion, whatever its actual referent, refers primarily to the dynamic between dialogic partners, and becomes an affine transformation of that dynamic. These discourses are composed of micro-analogues (propositions) formed into sequences (a procedure) that assonate the presence (the perspective) of the partnership. Therefore, we can observe the 'participatory knowing' in a relationship by observing how it disposes in its analogic propositions. Just as the relation with Thou is a dialectic microcosm for ontological disposition, so each of its propositions is a microcosm of the relation that enacts the form and function of its symbolisation. Each predicate of a conversation, as it were, samples the relational 'spirit' and tastes the shared 'inter-standing'. The way we assonate the dialect of propositions with the presence of shared perspective becomes the posture of dialectic in gestalt. Consequently, the way we treat propositions inflects the epistemic quality of our relationships.

Plato's dialogues, in their poetic and protreptic dramaturgy, train the posture of episteme. Hence, many scholars now understand the Socratic avatar as an embodied pedagogy for the practice of philosophia, as opposed to a plenipotentiary for some systematic theory. The procedure of Socratic elenchus is based – at least in part – in the analogic assonance between propositional and perspectival knowing. The Socratic dialogue *characterises* knowing by possessing a proposition with personified perspective, using analogy to link them into embodied conformity (e.g. virtue is a craft, and the virtuous man is as a craftsman), a character for the observing reader to *play*. The elenchal procedure dispossesses the subject's perspective by dis-conforming the proposition (virtue is not a techne and the craftsman is not virtuous), turning it from transparent to opaque, and leaving its subject – and its reader – in a floundering aporia. Socrates then invites the subject to recompose his perspective around the logos of an alternate proposition that offers more plausible conformity to the *eidos* (the 'Form') of the dialogue. In effect, he proffers his 'Thou' as a novel opacity that the interlocutor must turn transparent, extending his hand in philia to the grasping logos, and uses analogic proxies to help the interlocutor symbolically bridge to his more beholding perspective.

> Behind the pattern of search and aporia, another dynamic is underway.
> The very way in which the conversant confronts the world takes on a verbal

shape. Socrates catches the process as it happens. Socrates reflects back to the interlocutor what the interlocutor shows to Socrates. A Socratic encounter is, so to speak, a confrontation with the self, by the self.   Ahbel-Rappe, 2018, p. 36

Then, of course, the process repeats; once the interlocutor finds his grip, Socrates shifts the grip to ply the gripping hand. He jettisons the successive proposition and leaves the perspective behind. The interlocutor, no longer beheld by his proposition, and aware that Socrates now exceeds it, imitates the move; he has acquired trust in Socratic episteme on account of his safe passage from the first perspective to the supplanting one. This transition inseminates a higher-order trust in the Socratic meta-symbol and dialogic process, which synonymises with the partner's own potential to think, be and know otherwise. The trust in the exceeding Thou of Socrates amounts to a trust in his elenchal procedure and inspires a participation that introjects to each individual proposition – each proposition becomes an analogue for the procedural commitment to the elenchus and its formal cause, rather like the grip of each dance step adduces trust in a partner to lead you over the floor and evolve to more elaborate figurations (i.e. spatialise more intelligible patterns). Socrates uses propositions elliptically to converge perspectives into the space (…) of a shared aporia. The interplay becomes a symbolic training in translucency; the aporia conduces the combined knowing into a mode of participatory play, an ongoing analogic mimesis of the sensibly transcendent Socrates, whose dancing dialogic grip is remembered in the knowing of each argument and definition. The formulation of each proposition becomes assonant with the perspective of its insufficiency and procedure of its eventual disconfirmation. The synthesising signal (*synthemata*) that analogically and anagogically harmonises the scales of knowing (with symbola) is like a melody reproduced in different octaves. This 'spirit' is the gestalt presence of the dialectic germinated within the features of a dialogue. Mark Ralkowski provides a helpful definition to this effect: 'Dialectic, then, is the method one uses to remain open to what remains concealed in the disclosure of Being to man through the deficient means of knowing.' (2009, p. 32) While any proposition may gain us information, episteme describes the dialectical over-significance (or meta-meaning) of the propositions in their role of strengthening the participatory enactment of 'Being' beyond, as if each was a flexing finger on the procedure of the gathering grip that hoists the subject – and the reader – up the anagogic ladder.

In the Socratic tradition, the logos that grasps the ladder is guided by eros, just as depicted in Plato's *Symposium*. Eros is mythologised as a messenger (the daimon), a heat-seeking, intercategorical entity that travels between realms human and divine, an *atopos* like Socrates himself. In *Symposium*, eros is also an expression of pregnancy within the human soul; just as the body wanders after beauty and craves to birth within it, the soul is also driven to consummation as the means of actuating its potential for recreation. For Socrates, Lear (2017) notes, the individual is not a 'human' simply by incidence of her natural birth, but by her birthing into a second body – which we might venture to call a symbolic body – that is correspondent to a higher form of being in the cosmos. All the while, the dangers of modal confusion (miscarriage) persist in the pregnancy. Thus, the role of Socratic elenchus is prophylactic; it may be understood as a kind of pregnancy exercise for this psychic birthing.

Philosophia, simply put, is a pedagogy for the re-education of human eros. If the dialectical presence emerges discursively from the womb of the 'second person', then Socrates is the midwife after whom the grateful parents name their progeny. By his own famous admission, Socrates is said to know only the *ta erotika*, recalling the sacral significance of the body analogue in the ritual assonating of notional patterns. Socrates – in the likeness of the prophetess Diotima, his own philosophic pedagogue – invokes the philia of I and Thou to guide the hand of eros to each successive rung on the anagogic ladder. Socratic philosophia is an exaptation of the physical longing of eros to presence the dialectical longing for episteme within the 'somatic-symbolic' nervous system, much like the physical balancing of the cerebellum presenced the balance of Lady Justice. In the symbolic espousal of Thou within dialogos, the somatic fertility exapts to ontological fertilisation, and induces anagogic motions from the interpersonal discourse, tended by the Socratic midwifery. Perhaps this exaptation also lends legibility to Nietzsche's later proclamation that 'the degree and kind of a man's sexuality reach up into the ultimate pinnacle of his spirit' (*Beyond Good and Evil*, IV, Aphorism 75). In the Platonic dialogues, the horizontal axis of sensibility transcendence and the vertical axis of anagoge telescope into the meta-meaningful eros of the Socratic icon. As metaxy, Socrates is both 'Thou' that conducts the symbolic charge – the second self to whom we relate by analogic proxy – and the epistemic presence that aspires between I and Thou – a combined breath, like a third self or spirit (a *geist*), that aspires beyond both. If sensibility transcendence, so described, is an episteme of other selves, then Socrates (ever the atopos) remains epistemically untameable. His analogic character is a procession of unconcealing personae that, where embodied, enact a performance of anagogic unconcealment (an *alethea*). The seductive Socratic beholder is a moving target of transjective gnosis in likeness to its beholden Forms, and so his elliptic countenance pantomimes the ineffable character of the Good he conducts. Therefore, the midwifing Thou of Socrates is a mirror for the Good to be recollected in the beholding *nous* of the psyche. His dialogic partners continually 'find themselves' in his mirror – not in their identity as beings, but in the *significance* of their being in aspiring affinity with the Good. 'Socrates is then the vessel into which the reader deposits her attention: the imageless surface that allows the thoughts to appear beneath it' (Ahbel-Rappe, 2018, p. 29). Once our pining logos is taken by the hand of Socratic philia, we step into the train of his longing gaze. Our eros becomes *his* eros, and the soul realises its pregnancy with a greater Self. The proper cultivation of that Socratic eros within the microcosm of philosophic dialogos midwifes the dormant pregnancy of the soul into its own parturition. Our love of Socrates is an epistemic exaptation of eros through his symbol of symbols, the longing to consummate our own Socratic potential, 'in which we can then give forth *something deep within ourselves*' (Lear, 2017, p. 112).

> In Socratic Eros, we find the same basic structure as in Socratic irony: a divided consciousness, passionately aware that it is not what it ought to be. It is from this feeling of separation and lack that love is born. One of Plato's greatest merits will always be that he was able, via the myth of Socrates/ Eros, to introduce into the philosophical life the dimension of love – that is, of desire and the irrational. He accomplished this in several ways: in the first place, in the experience of dialogue itself, in which two interlocutors

experience a passionate will to clarify a problem together. Quite apart from the dialectical movement of the logos, the path travelled together by Socrates and his partner, and their common will to come to an agreement, is already a kind of love. There is a great deal more philosophy in spiritual exercises like Socrates' dialogues than in the construction of a philosophical system. The task of dialogue consists essentially in pointing out the limits of language, and its inability to communicate moral and existential experience. Yet the dialogue itself, qua event and spiritual activity, already constitutes a moral and existential experience, for Socratic philosophy is not the solitary elaboration of a system, but the awakening of consciousness, and accession to a level of being which can only be reached in a person-to-person relationship.

Just like ironical Socrates, Eros teaches nothing for he is ignorant, he does not make people more wise; he makes them *other*. He, too, is maieutic: he helps souls to engender themselves.   Hadot, Philosophy as a Way of Life, 1995, p. 163

The reflected Socratic self – the 'something deep within ourselves' – has also been analogised as the *ophthalmos*, the beholding pilot that marshals the ways of knowing to steer the analogic vessel in the direction of his daimonic gaze, much like Plato's charioteer in the *Phaedrus* musters his horses to reason the soul skyward (Ahbel-Rappe, 2018). The Socratic identity is adverbial, and it 'knowingly' potentiates the exponent power of significance – i.e. the most translucent form of relevance – in the participatory knowing of any proposition. In so doing, he analogically moves each proposition in the dialogue (and their hosting perspectives) to compass the same orientation, as if he asked his Athenian comrades to repurpose their spears – used to perforate one another's arguments – into oars, then bid them row in unison towards the horizon. The multivocality of their varied propositions, and the indexical concentration of their Socratically harkened meta-meaning, provide the conditions for plausibility; under Socratic direction, they converge their attention by analogic attraction to deepest relevance (usually supported by myth), and each proposition becomes attractive, not insofar as it is correct (i.e. factually true), but insofar as it contributes to the meta-meaning of this epistemic plausibility – insofar as it looks, *translucently*, in the right direction. In short, the Socratic proposition is efficacious insofar as it realises the relevant conditions for the cultivation of *wisdom*. This is why the spirit of dialectic, anteriorly defined, is open-ended inquiry rather than assertion. The function of aporetic convergence is to intimate the oversignifying episteme to (1) continuously retrofit the dialogic process to remain plausible, while (2) encouraging its collective aspiration to greater conformity to the Good. This bidirectional, dialectical spirit is analogically scalable, reproduced within the individual's intrapsychic dialogues, dialogues between individuals, and between conversations in a broader discursive corpus. The participatory knowing allows the trusting interlocutors to obviate the dangers of propositional idolatry, a modal confusion in which (I-Thou) dialogue devolves to (I-It) debate and begins to calcify perspective with *philonikia*: conversation prevaricates to sophistry, partner becomes opponent, and the telos of triumph supplants the sapiential ambitions. This regressive, narcissistic state – whereby each interlocutor is opaquely concerned with the Pyrrhic victory of persona over the episteme of person – is typified by the reductive exchange between Thrasymachus and Socrates in Book I of *Republic*. We are meant to contrast this, perhaps, to the relation of Socrates to Glaucon in Book VII, in which the latter is trusting enough to be allegorically guided through the Cave, and to allow Socrates to analogically somatise the 'dark' deficiencies in his *doxa* (opinions), and whet his appetite for a more 'luminous' relation with the Good (Lear, 2017).

In a previous section, we characterised the microcosm of the I-Thou relation as a symbol of symbols, a participatory analogy that enacts other analogies to effect transformations in the beholding 'I'. In the Platonic dialogues, myth is the 'house style' of assonance for the Socratic meta-symbol. The Cave, for instance, embodies the Socratic aporia within the eros of the body analogue, so that ontological disillusionment and epistemic reorientation, so described, can appreciate in the 'somatic-symbolic' nervous system. The psychic function of myth in the Socratic tradition has been closely observed by Lear (2017), who argues that the Allegory of the Cave is a pedagogic instance of a 'soul-turning' techne – in our language, a dialectic vessel – for psychic entrainment and partite synchronisation. The Allegory seduces the appetitive part of the soul to align with the notional aporia by steeping it in imaginal constriction, and coaxes it to partake of the anagogic quest by inseminating the appetite for emancipation. The Cave is a participatory enactment designed to synchronise Glaucon's dawning (perspectival) awareness of his own blindness with the (propositional) ignorance proffered by Socrates' aporetic elenchus. In both ways of knowing, Glaucon is 'awoken' to the dark; the Good, he realises, is as unthinkable to him as the sun would be to a man in shadows, and as poetic to the ontos as the illuming star is to the fertile earth. The symbolic translucency of the allegory is essential to its psychic function; Glaucon lowers his perspective to traverse the Cave, but he remains harkened by the Socratic ear that lingers at its opening. The symbolic narration, we recall, is vocalised by Socrates in the dialogos, and Glaucon is remembered by his *dialogic context* as he moves through its analogy. With every step, he is dialogically spoken, and his logos is re-gathered by the oversignifying voice. When, in this participatory ritual, he steps into the analogue of the Socratic proposition, he overhears himself, as by Socrates, within its assonance. He beholds himself – in shadow – by beholding his relation to the unthinkable perspective – the light of the sun – and the Socratic Thou that symbolised it. In this moment of participant knowing, Glaucon 'understands'. His logos conforms to the over-significance of the dialogue, and his ophthalmos opens wide to a congruous recognition (or recollection) of 'Thou' that lies beyond him. 'Thus it is a myth that introduces the philosophical distinction between appearance and reality – it tells us that up until now we have been living in appearance. In this way, myth prepares us for philosophy' (Lear, 2017, p. 215). The enacted analogue tunes the instruments of the soul – in our language, the ways of knowing – by playing through the assonant *melody*, and the melody harmonises the instruments into an orchestral aspiration. From the assonance of myth, dialogos raises a rhythm that listens for sounds of the eternal. This rhythmic melody is, of course, another analogy for the spiriting dialectic: an illusion that prefigures disillusion, that trains us to seek light by waking us into shadow.

Mythos is, among other things, an isometric exercise of perspectival *characterisation* – it embodies the shared logos between the ways of knowing by storying the logos into character. Character is a formal play of participatory knowing that enunciates the analogic assonance to mediate between proposition and perspective. Changes in character therefore effect changes in knowing, and Lear observes that myths of antiquity were, by incidence or design, a pre-reflective way of characterising a *polis*, like the Homeric myths did with the character of the Bronze Age hero, Achilles.

> Socrates is also clear that the unoriented tales we hear in youth are actually *dis*orienting. The heroic tales provide paradigms for imitation, which, through the imitation, shape the psyche (III.395c-d, 401c-e; II.377b, 378b). For they facilitate the establishment of structures of repetition: habits and dispositions whose full meaning cannot be understood at the time they are being formed. So, for instance, a little boy hears heroic tales of Achilles at a time when he lacks the capacity to recognize allegory as such. When he goes out to play his version of the *hoi agathoi ki hoi kakoi* (good guys and bad guys), he assigns himself the role of Achilles. He acts out a certain image of courage before he is able to understand what courage is. This image is enacted over and over again in play, and in this way the psyche gets 'Achillized'. He becomes accustomed to seeing the world and acting in it from an Achillized perspective. And so, by the time he does acquire the capacity to recognize allegory as such, it is in an important sense too late. He can no longer recognize the Achilles tale as a story, but the tale has already done its psychic work. And by the time he tries in adulthood to think about what courage is, he is already looking out from Achilles' perspective.   Lear, 2017, p. 212

The characterisation of knowing is, to return to our melodic metaphor, a symbolic 'tuning' of cosmic orientation, of worldview. Its harmony of the knowing ways tutors the rationality of how we deploy our attention to relevance. This explains, at least in part, why the Platonic dialogues are dramaturgical; the 'tuning' of philosophia is inextricable from the dialogic poesis of its I-Thou form. The sensibly transcending relation characterises the analogies that it chooses to enact, and presides over their tacit influence. Again, we recall that the microcosm of 'I-Thou' has a meta-analogic function, accented by the Socratic voice that guided Glaucon to the mouth of the Cave. *When dialectically possessed, dialogos characterises our mythic characterisations with an overriding orientation to anagoge.* This is the innovation of philosophia; the Socratic allegory, with its oversignifying narration, gives us a reflective, second-order perspective for characterising our knowing within the storied medium. Dialogos gives us a hand in choosing the adventure that will change us. It inspires us – by Thou – with the leading character of *ophthalmos*, who lists his own eros to deepen his desire for greater being.

> Both the Noble Falsehood and the Cave thus intentionally create reflective disequilibrium – they build an inherent discontent with the current level of experience. Unlike existing myths – say Homer's presentation of Achilles, which, in Plato's view, gives a fixed, false, and thus imprisoning image

> of courage – the Socratic allegories introduce the idea that the current state of experience (knowledge, etc.) is unsatisfactory. Life up until now, unbeknownst to us, has been a dream. Life up until now, unbeknownst to us, has been a prison in which we are mistaking shadows for the real thing. The Socratic allegories, unlike the Homeric myths, inherently discourage satisfaction with the existing state of affairs. They thus motivate us to try and go on in some different way. If Socrates is right that we have been living in a dream, then these allegories serve as a wake-up call. If he is right that, unbeknownst to us, we have been living in a prison, then in becoming aware of that we begin to chafe at the chains.   Lear, 2017, p. 218

The second-order character of dialogos provokes us to reflectively converge and mature our knowing by putting ourselves through a journey of perspectival re-characterisation. In sensibility transcendence, our transparency-opacity shifts happen more rapidly, and this mode of relating gives us the translucent insight to pronounce the most relevant stories, the passages that will embody the assonant notions of the dialogue and bridge us to Thou's understanding. Fortunately, the dialectic vessel is geometrically variable; Phaeton's failed charioting characterises brashness, foolishness and irrationality. Procrustes' bed characterises reductive conformism. Pyrrhic war characterises destructive victory. *Republic*'s eponymous state and *Phaedrus*' charioteer both characterise a rational marshalling of the psyche to conduce the conditions for anagoge. The ascent from the Cave characterises the *metanoesis* (the 'turning' or 'changing of heart') of Socratic episteme by playing us through 'a dream about dreaming and waking up' (Lear, 2017, p. 214). These enacted analogies provide characterising journeys to be symbolically played and inhabited, and they re-characterise the participant knower with dialogic supervision. The stratified modelling of mythos within dialogos 'Socratises' our knowing by sensitising the dialectic at different levels of the 'somatic-symbolic' nervous system, just as the savvy parent might tickle her child while telling him a joke, in a coordinated effort to 'humour' his whole personality (i.e. to re-characterise him with the body of a humoured perspective). This should all be more than enough to suggest that our myths – chosen and inherited – are far more than a trifle. They are all de facto pedagogues of knowing that require rational discrimination, implements of logos that are wielded most wisely by the disciplined hands of dialogic discussion. Socrates self-characterises to characterise his beholders in contra, casting personae in a dialogic dramatis scripted to a collective, dialectic transformation. In other words, he plays his self by the hand of dialogos to place himself in its service; he styles as Artemis, goddess of midwifery, to deliver selves through the discourse, or as Eros, the conjugal symbolon, to step us from time to eternity. So, as lion to shaman, Rover to driver, child to mother, Socrates is to Glaucon and the host of his readers: a Thou between us and the place beyond heaven to embody our *question of being* in a dialectic vessel borne to our becoming. With the use of dramatis, Socrates modifies the existential question in the character of his transitive icon. As symbolon, he conjoins the process of argumentation and identification. For we never merely argue; as we assume propositions, we assume roles and identities. We reform the character of self. In his dialogos, the question wherein we find our open-ended selves is not 'who is Socrates to us?' but rather 'who are *we* to Socrates?' He casts himself that he may recast us, recollect us in the eye of his beholding and fan us back out to the cosmos. This is how we become Socratised: we dialectically reformat our role in the ontos to perform plausibility for a new form of life.

As Socrates' combined myth and elenchus does for Glaucon and his other interlocutors, the storied form of his dialogue does for us: it re-characterises our knowing. *Lysis* befriends the personality. *Protagoras* virtues the personality. *Phaedrus* rationalises the personality. *Phaedo* encourages the personality. *Symposium* eroticises the personality. A proposition in any of these dialogues assumes epistemic character when harkened by the second-order, Socratic ear. As Socrates overhears, he oversignifies the proposition for its anagogic potential to realise relevance more epistemically. As we learn to listen for Socrates, we transjectively conform to the 'beyond-ward' gesture of his significant way of knowing. This is why the aporetic dialogue accents its semantic content with perspectival deficiency, 'tuning' the postulate to an instrument for orchestral participation. By 'orchestra', of course, we refer to the processual dialogos. Socratic elenchus invokes sensibility transcendence to confer his epistemic character onto the practice of ontological inquiry, so that relating to – and then through – the meta-analogic Thou becomes the 'dialogical striving for Being' (Ralkowski, 2009, p. 23) that de-anonymises intelligible Forms within the microcosm of symbolic relations, as though catching an extemporal rhythm with the logos of a temporal melody. The provisional character of the 'melodic' dialogos personifies the *habitas* of our proximate relation to Being as such. This 'provisional character' is the ever humble – yet always questing – daimon of philosophia, the desirous lover of wisdom.

Many scholars, like John Russon (2009), have written of the 'musical' property of intelligibility. To the tuning Socratic ear, the orchestra is a metaphor of exponential power for dialectic, for the episteme of philosophia, and for the efficacy of participatory knowing. If the proposition is a tuning instrument, the procedural dialogos is the entire orchestral arrangement. The melody is the presence of the geist, the dialectic spirit, the self between selves that possesses the players and becomes the felt vibration (perspective) of their instruments. Analogic assonance (as in this very metaphor) is the notation of the melody into the different chords to make the same note playable in the various instruments. Socrates, of course, is still the conductor. This time, however, his rod does not merely attract the symbolic charge, but guides the current of its intelligibility to spatialise the presence of the dialectic through a harmonisation of scales – between the ways of knowing in each player, and between the knowing of different dialogic players. In the Neoplatonic tradition, 'each platonic dialogue is a kind of plenary microcosm into which the elements of reality are fully assembled' (Ahbel-Rappe, 2018, citing Coulter, 1976, p. 29). The reader of the Platonic dialogue finds herself identical with the plenary microcosm and its intelligible flow. She internalises the symbolisation of the whole dialogic orchestra such that her motion becomes dialectically generative, gathering dialogic relationships like a *geistly* snowball as it rolls forth from the page, through her person, out towards the anagogic horizon. The dialectical presence of *geist* espoused in the self seems eternity-bound, as the self is caught in a fluvial current of knowing that is continuous with the oceanic into which it opens, partaking of the sea as it *knowingly* courses towards it.

The 'musical' melody of the dialectic is symbolically spatialising – we move through it even as it seems to move through us, and the mutual flow reproduces the self in the continuity of that reflective, Socratic parturition. It has an empyreal quality that seems to linger outside of time's revolutions. This cosmic rhythm is signalled by the listening yen of Socratic eros through the microcosm of his dialogic tuning. His rhythm seems to verse rather than to punctuate; it viscidly stays the 'whizzing' effect of time's atomisation that was observed by Byung-Chul Han (2017), which modally confuses our relationships by de-characterising the artistic forms – removing the hyponia – that we use to analogise them. Much ado has been made, for instance, about the 'death of melody' in the modern pop song, where the repetitiously atomised note generates momentary salience rather than adumbrates the 'significance' of a complex composition – thereby losing the Socratic distinction between appearance and reality. And just as the musical arrangement periodically rests on its fermata, the aporia within dialogos is designed to recess the conversation to moments of lingering openness, an existential embodiment – i.e. characterisation – of ontological vulnerability. This space of Socratic ignorance assonates with the ontological deficiency of each proposition, turning the abridgement of philonikia – which seems perennially noisy and inchoate – into the epistemic 'meta-meaning' of philosophia, which pauses to listen for the eternal chords. The philosophic dialogos assonates the ways of knowing within and between the knowers, but also assonates with the Good beyond the knowing to become a gnosis in the second person, a participatory symbol of Being itself. The dialectic geist is the transitive bond in this rational conformity (like the Socratic metaxy), connecting the dialogic figures of philosophia to the eidos of the cosmic geometry. The dynamic of one's personal relation to Thou in dialogos symbolises a hypostatic longing for a transpersonal relation to the ground of one's Being, and the dialectic melody binds the presence of the finite self into transjective continuity with the infinite aspect of her own transpersonal transcendence. As they assume the character of philosophia, conversations sacralise. When we find ourselves rapt in meaningful dialogue, with Thou, the propinquity of knowing partners effloresces a quality of 'enchantment' (Taylor, 2011), and the geist intimates the presence of another, more preponderant Thou that indwells us. Each moment of dialogos is, in the words of Schlegel, a *movement of the finite longing for the infinite*.

The dialectic dimensions

Dialectic runs on *distributed cognition* (Hutchins, 1995): the networking of brains – or different temporal instances of the same brain – to enhance computational power and problem-solving. Long before the internet networked computers together, culture networked embodied brains together. The dialectic in gestalt is the meta-psychotechnology for transmuting collective intelligence into collective wisdom: the anagogic and analogic relations, mutually enacted and modelling, between the individual cognition in flow and the distributed, collective cognition within *communitas*.[13] In this process, intelligence (individual and collective) is first bootstrapped into rationality (individual and collective), and then resonantly bootstrapped into wisdom (individual and collective).

At the beginning of this chapter, we noted that Heidegger's Dasein cottons to a Neoplatonic insight: that we are the being whose beings are in question, and therefore in a deep, primordial conformity with the question of being, which is a *questing for* being, somatised by the eros of the body analogue.[14] Submerged in our dialectical vessels, our selves are the enacted analogies for the question of being, and this existential conformity grounds our participatory knowing. The meaning crisis pronounces the angst of Dasein, like Kierkegaard's sickness of spirit: we are the beings whose being is in question to despair and we indwell this question almost unto death. In dialectic, our deep conformity to the question of being manifests a glow of super salience that expresses the emergent intelligibility of this manifolding self-organisation, a novel connectivity within coupled to a novel connectivity without. This dynamical experience is reproduced within the Socratic dialogic exercise: participants are encircled by novel patterns of interpersonal communication that become internalised as intrapersonal, novel patterns of communication within the brain, and these patterns circle insight back into the distributed dialogos. This mimetically mutual modelling bootstraps the anagogic and analogic flow that yields to an onto-normative, phenomenological presence. As in Socratic practice, self-knowledge and knowledge of the other become stereoscopically fused into a shared identity of the shared depth, where the shared factor – the geist – is found.[15] This emergent geist is the presencing of a *third factor* (Geiger, 2009),[16] the questing hermetic spirit bridging between heaven and earth, and a rationally interrelated intelligence that introjects to become the dialectical verticality of the onto-normative disposition.[17] For Plato, the dialogos of flowing argument becomes the third spirit that possesses the interlocutors, the questing identity of their combinative being (i.e. a becoming) of which they partake. This supra-individual sapience (intelligence → rationality → wisdom) guides and affords the anagogic ascent that is crucial to the character of dialectic. The geist becomes the question of being, the fulcral, symbolic locus where the wondering, wandering argument can assume the place of agency and beckon the circle skyward.

The expressed relation between phenomenological experience and cognitive functioning casts independent but converging dimensions of interaction within dialectic. Two existential modes map along the axes of the first two dimensions:

1. When conversation affords sensibility transcendence it articulates a horizontal dimension (dialogic I-Thou with the other)

2. When contemplation affords anagoge, it articulates a vertical dimension (dialogic I-Thou with being).

Both 'horizontal' and 'vertical' modes effect a reciprocal opening and restructuring, a mutually accelerating disclosure. This is the same kind of disclosure that cultivates interpersonal and inter-ontological closeness – or *love* (Aron et al, 1997).

3. The stereoscopic fusion of the first two dimensions produces the third dimension, which is the locus of the geist: the gathering and self-transcending presence of the logos.

The gathering of logos is a self-organising recollection and aspiration that configures the intelligibility and identities involved

4. The fourth dimension is the developmental, occurring across time. It is the constant movement between theory and *theoria* (phenomenological awareness and contemplation): the aligning and synchronising between the four ways of knowing

5. The fifth dimension is the movement towards timelessness, when each of the four dimensions are drawn up into the meta-dialogue. The meta-dialogue is inter-dialogic; each of Plato's dialogues suffuse with the geists of the other dialogues, and the Neoplatonic tradition deliberately cultivates a pedagogical programme of inter-dialogic progression, a condensation of the meta-dialogue into the third factor presence that vectors their development. Fortuitously perhaps, meta-dialogue is a novelty now afforded by the contemporality of modern cybertechnologies (e.g. YouTube).[18] The geist moves between the conversations and exemplifies the meta-dialogue in each individual discourse. Herein, *dialogos presences the dialectic*; it prevails over the phenomenology of our activity, just as the holy spirit does over the ecclesial ritual. The dialogic presence becomes our 'spiritual' religio, and so symbolises as a sacral entity – i.e. becomes analogised as a trans-personality unto itself.

The *manifolding* dimensions of dialectic resound within one another. The assonance between the horizontal and vertical dimensions conditions a deep, circling continuity that analogises the mutually introjecting correspondence between (1) intelligence, rationality and wisdom, (2) between individual and distributed cognition, (3) between diachronic and synchronic distributed cognition, (4) and between the existential modes of conversation (sensibility transcendence) and contemplation (anagoge). The meta-meaning system is the meta-psychotechnology.[19] This is *dialectic*. The systems and technologies of the dialectic are *dialectical*. The dialectic is fractal; it analogically exemplifies itself in each of its sub-systemic components. All relations within the dialectic are dialectical relations.

Conclusion

Of truth, Spinoza said (E II, P43, 5):

> To have a true idea only means to know a thing perfectly, that is, to the utmost degree. Indeed, nobody can doubt this, unless he thinks that an idea is some dumb thing, like a picture on a tablet, and not a mode of thinking, to wit, the very act of understanding. And who, pray, can know that he understands something unless he first understands it? That is, who can know that he is certain of something unless he is first certain of it? Again, what standard of truth can there be that is clearer or more certain than a true idea? Indeed, just as light makes manifest both itself and darkness, so truth is the standard both of itself and falsity.

It is uncoincidental, perhaps, that the knowing of dialectic resembles his *Scientia Intuitiva*, the (re)cognition of macrocosmic significance (in our case, a meta-systemic meaning-making) in the microcosm of its attendant participants (here, in dialogos). This recognition collapses the scales of being into ontological continuity, and by analogic embodiment, it overcomes our self-defeat by wedding our presence to the inexhaustible. The *habitas ontos* of dialectic revalorises the Neoplatonic project by resuming its anagogic journey to gnosis, or as Bonaventure called it, 'the journey of the mind to God'. The seeking logos deepens in the returning circle from I to Thou, and the dialectical knowing is ritually dramatised in the self between selves, the divine double, an interior geist between the egoic clay and a Self in greater being. This relational presence, which shares its identity with the adverbial, participatory knowing, impregnates and rebirths the body analogue of being by opening its fresh eyes to the light, like a shaman emerging from his soulflight – such that we cease to say, 'I am Bob', but rather, like the Buddha, exclaim, 'I am awake!' And just as Blake saw eternity in a grain of sand, so in dialogos do we see the entire cosmos open between the first and second discussants as they lose and find themselves in the listing dialectical spirit. In such eternal moments, we know as Socrates must know, caught in one of his daimonic trances, rapt in some symbolising space unfolding on the horizon, standing for hours on end to harken to his own intimate voice because he has the whole cosmic orchestra resounding within him.

References

Ahbel-Rappe, S. (2018). *Socratic Ignorance and Platonic Knowledge in the Dialogues of Plato.* Albany: State University of New York Press.

Apter, M. (1982). Metaphor as Synergy. In *Metaphor: Problems and Perspectives* (pp. 55–70).

Aron, A. Melinat, E., Aron, E.N., Vallone, R.D. and Bator, R.J. (1997). The Experimental Generation of Interpersonal Closeness: A Procedure and Some Preliminary Findings. *Personality and Social Psychology Bulletin, Vol. 23 No. 4*, 363–377.

Barfield, O. (1973). *Poetic Diction: A Study in Meaning.* Middletown: Wesleyan University Press.

Buber, M. (1923/1970). *I and Thou.* (W. Kaufmann, Trans.) New York: Charles Scribner's Sons.

Callard, A. (2018). *Aspiration: The Agency of Becoming.* New York: Oxford University Press.

Cheetham, T. (2015). *Imaginal Love: The Meanings of Imagination in Henry Corbin and James Hillman.* Spring Publications Inc.

Costa, P. (2011). A Secular Wonder. In G. Levine (Ed.), *The Joy of Secularism* (pp. 134–154). Princeton: Princeton University Press.

Dillon, M. (1995). *Semiological Reductionism: A Critique of the Deconstructionist Movement in Postmodern Thought.* Albany: State University of New York Press.

Dourley, J.P. (1981). *The Psyche as Sacrament: A Comparative Study C.G. Jung and Paul Tillich.* Toronto: Inner City Books.

Fromm, E. (1976). *To Have or To Be?* Harper and Row Publishers Inc.

Geiger, J. (2009). *The Third Man Factor: Surviving the Impossible.* New York: Weinstein Books.

Hadot, P. (1995). *Philosophy as a Way of Life.* (A. I. Davidson, Ed., and M. Chase, Trans.) Malden: Blackwell Publishing.

Hadot, P. (2001). *The Inner Citadel: The 'Meditations' of Marcus Aurelius.* Cambridge: Harvard University Press.

Han, B.-C. (2017). *The Scent of Time.* Cambridge: Polity Press.

Heidegger, M. (1958). Hegel and the Greeks. *Conference of the Academy of Sciences at Heidelberg.* Retrieved December 2019, from www.morec.com/hegelgre.htm

Hutchins, E. (1995). *Cognition in the Wild.* Cambridge: The MIT Press.

Lakoff, G. and Johnson, M. (1980). *Metaphors We Live By.* Chicago: University of Chicago Press.

Lear, J. (2017). *Wisdom Won from Illness: Essays in Philosophy and Psychoanalysis.* Cambridge: Harvard University Press.

Lewis, M. (2018). Brain Change in Addiction as Learning, Not Disease. *New England Journal of Medicine*, 379, 1551–1560.

Metzinger, T. (2003). Phenomenal Transparency and Cognitive Self-reference. *Phenomenology and the Cognitive Sciences*, 353–393.

Murdoch, I. (1970). *The Sovereignty of Good.* New York: Schocken Books.

Nagel, T. (1974). What is it Like to Be a Bat? *The Philosophical Review*, 435–450.

Nietzsche, F. (1887/1989). *On the Genealogy of Morals.* (W. Kaufmann, and R. Hollingdale, Trans.) New York: Vintage Books.

Paul, L. (2016). *Transformative Experience.* Oxford: Oxford University Press.

Peirce, C.S. (1905/1970). Pragmatism: The Classic Writings. In H. Thayer (Ed.), *Pragmatism* (p. 102). Indianapolis: Hackett Publishing Company, Inc.

Perl, E.D. (2015). *Plotinus Ennead V.1: On the Three Primary Levels of Reality.* Las Vegas: Parmenides Publishing.

Ralkowski, M. (2009). *Heidegger's Platonism.* New York: Continuum International Publishing Group.

Russon, J. (2009). *Bearing Witness to Epiphany: Persons, Things, and the Nature of Erotic Life.* Albany: State University of New York Press.

Spinoza, B. (2002). *Complete Works*. (S. Shirley, Trans.) Indianapolis: Hackett Publishing Company Inc.

Stang, C. M. (2017). *Our Divine Double*. Cambridge: Harvard University Press.

Taylor, C. (2011). Disenchantment – Reenchantment. In G. Levine (Ed.), *The Joy of Secularism* (pp. 57–73). Princeton: Princeton University Press.

Todes, S. (2001). *Body and World*. Cambridge: The MIT Press.

Vertesi, J. (2012). Seeing like a Rover: Visualization, embodiment, and interaction on the Mars Exploration Rover Mission. *Social Studies of Science, Vol. 42, No. 3*, 393–414.

Vervaeke, J. and Ferraro, L. (2013). Relevance, Meaning and the Cognitive Science of Wisdom. In Ferrari, M. and Weststrate N.M. (Eds.) *The Scientific Study of Personal Wisdom* (pp. 21–52). Dordrecht: Springer.

Vervaeke, J., Ferraro, L. and Herrera-Bennett (2018). Flow as Spontaneous Thought: Insight and Implicit Learning. In Fox, Kieran C.R. and Christoff, Kalina (Eds.) *The Oxford Handbook of Spontaneous Thought: Mind-wandering, Creativity, and Dreaming* (pp. 309–326). New York: Oxford University Press.

Vervaeke, J. and Kennedy, J. (1996). Metaphors in Language and Thought. *Metaphor and Symbolic*, 273–284.

Vervaeke, J. and Kennedy, J. (2004). Conceptual Metaphor and Abstract Thought. *Metaphor and Symbol, 19(3)*, 213–231.

Vervaeke, J., Mastropietro, C. and Miscevic, F. (2017). *Zombies in Western Culture: A Twentieth Century Crisis*. Cambridge: Open Book Publishers.

Winkelman, M. (2000). *Shamanism: The Neural Ecology of Consciousness and Healing*. Westport: Bergin and Garvey.

Wittgenstein, L. (1953/2009). *Philosophical Investigations*. (G. Anscombe, P. Hacker, and J. Schulte, Trans.). Malden: Wiley-Blackwell.

Wright, J.R. (2005). Transcendence Without Reality. *Philosophy*, 361–384.

Notes

1. We wish to thank Peter Limberg for introducing us to this emerging network of communities of authentic discourse and relating, and for affording the participant observation therein.
2. The Old English word *understandan* is literally 'to stand in the midst of' where *under* does not have the usual meaning of 'beneath' but comes from the proto Indo-European *nter*, which is the basis of the Latin 'inter'. Hence, our use of the term 'inter-standing'. Summarily, this chapter argues that understanding depends on inter-standing.
3. See also: 'Awakening from the Meaning Crisis – Corbin and the Divine Double': www.youtube.com/watch?v=mrnpZhWqdcA
4. Dialectic seeks dynamical complexification of communication: a synchronisation of the processes of integration and differentiation. This 'complexification' means that a system is more capable of highly coordinated actions – i.e. it can do many more different kinds of things all at once while remaining integrated as a system. This produces emergent functions for the system, in contrast to processes of discourse that seek what Durkheim called *mechanical solidarity*, in which all participants share the same identities and positions, a unity of homogeneity, rather than a unity of complexity. Such solidification bars emergence; this is the hallmark of tribal and egocentric identification (see *philonikia*, later in chapter).
5. In *The Scientific Study of Personal Wisdom* (2013), Vervaeke and Ferraro present an earlier version of this typology that conflates 'perspectival' and 'participatory' knowing. This argument is a development of that earlier schema.
6. 'Presence' is the sense of realness sought after in video game play. Many games can create this sense of presence without also creating verisimilitude.
7. Based on Mark Lewis' concept of 'reciprocal narrowing' – see *The Dialectical Microcosm* for exposition.
8. A cognitive scientific account of the phenomenology of Mars Exploration Rovers is the subject of ongoing and forthcoming work by Dan Chiappe and John Vervaeke.
9. Rafe Kelley, personal communication, December 2019.
10. See Lakoff and Johnson's *Metaphors We Live By* (1980) and related criticism (Vervaeke and Kennedy, *Metaphors in Language and Thought*, 1996; *Conceptual Metaphor and Abstract Thought*, 2004).
11. For further reading, see also Dillon (1995), *Semiological Reductionism*.
12. For economy, this chapter is unable to explore the intrapsychic dimension of dialectic – wherein the symbolising philia of 'I-Thou' introjects to midwife a trans-egoic development within the psyche, an anagoge towards one's greater Being

(or Self). This reflexive relation is exemplified by the *Meditations* of Marcus Aurelius, *Confessions* of Augustine and the psychology of C.G. Jung. This will be a central topic in a forthcoming paper, titled *Imaginal Dialogos*. For further reading, see Hadot's (2001) *The Inner Citadel*, Dourley's (1981) *The Psyche as Sacrament* and Cheetham's (2015) *Imaginal Love*.

13   For further reading on 'flow', see Vervaeke, Ferraro and Herrera-Bennett (2018), 'Flow as Spontaneous Thought: Insight and Implicit Learning'.

14   Perl (2015) argues for a similar deep conformity, within the thinking of Plotinus, between levels of self-consciousness and levels of reality.

15   The etymology of *geist* disambiguates to 'mind', 'spirit' or 'ghost', as applied to an individual or a group.

16   This is similar to Geiger's concept of the 'third man factor' a sense of a presence beyond oneself or one's group that provokes insight or motivation in problem solving and survival situations.

17   For more on this argument, see also the following lectures: 'What is Higher about Higher States of Consciousness?': www.youtube.com/watch?v=7ILP-8OGKhg; 'Awakening from the Meaning Crisis – Higher States of Consciousness, Part 1': www.youtube.com/watch?v=39NpjQDtqNw; and 'Awakening from the Meaning Crisis – Higher States of Consciousness, Part 2': www.youtube.com/watch?v=rvx4_0NAfaY

18   For example: Jordan Hall, John Vervaeke, Christopher Mastropietro and Guy Sengstock in Dialogos, Part 1: www.youtube.com/watch?v=7g6rwOa-pGs and Part 2: www.youtube.com/watch?v=UovLJTLbFhU

19   In *Zombies and Western Culture: A Twentieth Century Crisis* (2017), Vervaeke, Mastropietro and Miscevic make use of Clifford Geertz's notion of a meta-meaning system when discussing the co-creative and co-determining relationship between agent and arena: a bidirectional modelling that shapes the identity of the human organism into an agency directed upon a field of intelligible affordances for action.

12 Identity Erotics
A metamodern alternative to 'identity politics'
Minna Salami

IDENTITY IS an inevitable consequence of being. From the moment a baby is named, it embarks on a life journey during which that name will carry an association to its family, ethnicity, gender, religion and more. These will continue to shape how the baby, and later the adult, perceives the world and their place in it.

For example, I inhabit multiple 'in-between worlds' identities. I am African and European, Nigerian and Finnish to be specific. I am Yoruba and twice Scandinavian – Finnish by heritage and Swedish by naturalisation. 'Bio-psycho-socio-spiritually', as philosopher Jonathan Rowson refers to how biology, psychology, society and spirituality shape our identities, I am a black woman.[1] I have lived in five countries, and I speak five languages. I was raised in an interfaith family – my dad is Muslim, and my mum was Protestant.

Few of my identities are 'friends' in social discourse. They inform part of clashing attitudes towards belonging which increasingly compromise co-existence. We live in times inundated with information – talks, podcasts, media, online courses, research papers, op-eds, tweets, you name it. But with hardly any civic education to navigate the increasingly complex societal terrain, identity has become the axis of sensemaking.

However, identity is a treacherous vehicle to lead through the overwhelming and clashing agora of ideas that marks our times. Relating to politics, culture, globalisation and economics strictly through the social constructions that inform our own particular identity, if in implicit and explicit ways, is what we refer to as identity politics.

As with many complex ideas that make their way from manifestos and long-standing research into the general debate, the depth and nuance of 'identity politics', as originally developed by the black feminist organisation, Combahee River Collective, who coined the notion in the notably less information-overloaded and more overtly racist environment of 1978, has taken on a completely different meaning in the 21st century than was intended. To politicise identity in the 1970s meant to voice deep grievances caused by the injustices of history. To politicise identity in the 2020s is to stifle the voices of others. It is to harden identity, to render and equate it with a spirit of unsurmountable difference.

Issues that are bound to contemporary identity politics – such as the culture wars, alt-right populism, cancel culture – are all cultural manifestations that are entwined with the polysemous meanings imbued in the term *identity* itself. Few terms carry the contentious and confusing baggage of both historical and contemporary processes that *identity* does.

However, because identity is such a porous and shifting concept, it can potentially also be used to change attitudes towards a progressive, elevated co-existence. In my case, these layered identities have not always been 'buddies' residing within me, yet they ultimately enable me to easily employ a multi-perspectival attitude towards most challenges. They also taught me that identity, for all its sense of self, is arbitrary. For one, were I born about half a century earlier, I would still have belonged to the Yoruba and Finno-Karelian tribes, but I would have been British and Russian rather than Nigerian and Finnish, as Nigeria was a British colony and Finland a Russian one.

I don't mean to suggest that my specific identity does not shape me in ways that are meaningful and non-random. Rather, what I am saying is that precisely because we place such meaning in ultimately arbitrary factors such as the gender or ethnicity we were born into, identity is a compass that at best guides us towards understanding our *human* condition better. Consider how it is Simone de Beauvoir's feminist identity that flavours the piqued brilliance of her widely relevant philosophy. It is the humanist phronesis of Yoruba metaphysics that makes Wole Soyinka's prose loving and razor-sharp at once. Even the Europatriarchal edge to Philip Roth's novels are part of their unmistakable talent. A group-based identity can serve as a guide towards universal truths.

The problem is the sentiment of overwhelming difference and separation that is implicated in current understandings of identity. Moreover, attempts to fix the division caused by identity politics tend to emphasise sameness, which is simply the other side of the coin of difference. Difference and sameness have alternately shaped collective understandings of identity, both inevitably leading to collective dissatisfaction. The one notion that should shape identity but doesn't, despite its obvious association with the term, is *togetherness*. Rather than difference, or sameness for that matter, 'identity erotics' emphasises togetherness.

We live *together* in a world grappling with enormous social, ecological, technological and biological harms. We find ourselves *together* in societies where social ills such as sexism, racism, classism, speciesism, climate change, poverty, disease, mental health issues and loneliness detrimentally affect political, cultural and economic institutions. Due to the wholesale politicising of identity, we harden even those dimensions of identity that should evoke a sense of shared humanity.

The importance of togetherness cannot be overstated; the globalised, interconnected world we live in requires a shift in mindset. We are no longer merely citizens of individual nations, but we are citizens of the world. The ramifications of global citizenship are huge: what happens in one part of the world affects events in another. But emphasising togetherness is not only to avoid catastrophe; our togetherness is also predicated on living on a planet that contains tremendous beauty, awe and human expressions of love and kindness. We are not only in this world together with other humans but also with the non-human natural world. In times when the world is detrimentally divided by race, religion, gender and class, and ridden with the fear of the unknown, our togetherness offers a consolatory politics by reminding us that we are all motivated by the same desire to be free of fear and negative emotions.

In his poem, 'Everything is Waiting for You', David Whyte (2003) writes:

> Your great mistake is to act the drama
> as if you were alone. As if life
> were a progressive and cunning crime
> with no witness to the tiny hidden
> transgressions. To feel abandoned is to deny
> the intimacy of your surroundings.

The spirit of togetherness is at once a strategic tool and a coping mechanism for the 21st-century global citizen. The question is, can identity function as a concept that connotes both the terror and joy of 21st-century togetherness? Could it be transformed into a concept that warns us against making the great mistake of acting 'the drama is if you were alone', as Whyte beautifully puts it?

In the winter of 2020, I came across a theory that I thought could be useful in reimagining and repurposing identity – metamodernism. It was a world of thought that instantly engrossed me, describing patterns within the emerging world that I too sensed but had not seen articulated. I resonated with how metamodern theory 'oscillates between a modern enthusiasm and a postmodern irony, between hope and melancholy, between naivete and knowingness, empathy and apathy, unity and plurality, totality and fragmentation, purity and ambiguity', as said by Dutch scholars Timotheus Vermeulen and Robin van den Akker who, as initiators of contemporary metamodernism, are authorities on the topic, unlike me, who had just discovered it. Metamodernism echoed with *Sensuous Knowledge*, the book I had just completed where – as is characteristic of metamodern approaches – I wove together variegated fields, such as personal narrative, social criticism, mythopoetics, feminist theory, African philosophy, embodiment, art and spirituality to develop a new hybrid sensibility relating to contemporary realities.

More than anything, I thought metamodernism could provide a language that could be used to assuage identity politics. However, insofar that metamodernism is an intuitive and perceptive deep feeling about the present moment, rather than an ideology, one might wonder if one of the purposes of metamodernism is to assuage identity politics? And if not, should it be? Vermeulen and van den Akker (2010) state that metamodernism is 'an invitation for debate rather than an extending of a dogma', and co-founder of whatismetamodern.com, Greg Dember, says that metamodernism is 'a vibe' rather than a doctrine. Yet I would argue that it is worth considering how metamodernism contends with a normative aim such as the mindful lessening of identity politics. While the sense of exploring, describing and discussing the zeitgeist through metamodernity is refreshing, and while teasing out energetic sensibilities of current cultures is enticing, there's no denying that this process – like all processes of meaning-making – also contains an element of responsibility, which in turn makes it a critical theory.

I don't mean responsibility in the voguish sense of 'accountability', which can easily become chore-like and performative, but rather simply to imply diligence and attention – the critical ingredients of valuable meaning-making. Metamodernism plays a political role, not least in the sense of what economist Lene Rachel Andersen refers to as a 'formation' or *Bildungsreise* (Bildung journey). A Bildung journey – defined by Andersen as 'emotional, moral and cognitive development' through access to more than one epistemology – leads to the ability 'to both contain and transcend yourself and your culture'. This *is* a political process with varying degrees of radical transformation.

In Chapter 4, 'Disarm the Pedagogical Weaponry', futurist writer Zak Stein suggests that metamodernism is to be anti-essentialist, not believing in ultimate essences such as matter, consciousness, goodness, evil, masculinity, femininity or the like – but rather that all these things are contextual and interpretations made from relations and comparisons. Even the, today, much praised concept of relationality is not an essence of the universe. It is to see that the world is radically, unyieldingly and completely socially constructed, always relative and context bound.

Identity is the quintessential container of ultimate essences, such as femininity, masculinity, nationality, ethnicity, race and religion, and so efforts to reimagine identity, as in this chapter, rely firstly on the insight that Stein points to, namely that essentialism is undeniably destructive and limiting. Secondly, reconfiguring the notion of identity rests on the utopian hope that long-standing attitudes can be altered using imagination. This is a metamodern premise as per Stein's definition, but it is also an example of how critical political discourse is at the very least implied in metamodernism. Thus, to answer my earlier question, yes, it is a premise of metamodernity to assuage identity politics.

The more I read about metamodernism, the more I began to glean the gaps of knowledge that emerge when a dominant group shapes an idea: metamodern thought is analysed almost exclusively by people of European descent and male gender. I became particularly troubled by the lack of acknowledgement of feminist theory, which had long identified the same societal ills and potential solutions that here were represented as metamodern insights. Metamodernism, it seemed to me, was feminist without being aware that it was feminist.

For example, analysts of metamodernity conferred the importance of the personal informing the political, interiority and feeling, consciousness-raising, spiritual revolution, feeding the imaginary, reinventing language, cross-disciplinary research, the gift economy, contra-hierarchical patterns, the revolutionary power of love, rebirth, empowerment, embodied methodology and conscientisation, to name a few topics which anyone familiar with the canon of feminist theory will recognise as integral to, and in some cases inventions of, the discipline. If you engage with black feminist theory in particular, there were parallels with the blending and blurring of theory, history, imagination, cynicism, modernity and politics common in the work of writers like Toni Morrison, Alice Walker and bell hooks. Many black feminist thinkers and writers have long been 'metamodern', if not by name then because re-imagining meaning-making was the only way to survive (mentally and often materially) in a world where normative (modern and postmodern) thinking excluded you in nefarious ways. Even antipatriarchal analyses failed to engage with feminist literature – Stein's metamodernist criticism of essentialism is a characteristic of metamodernism, yes, but because patriarchy is built upon the essentialist idea of innate male superiority there is no group that has opposed essentialism as vehemently as feminists have, yet the otherwise vital text does not make the connection.

Consider this sentence by philosopher Hanzi Freinacht in his influential book about metamodernism, *The Listening Society*: 'The basic idea is this: Deliberately and carefully cultivate a deeper kind of welfare system that includes the psychological, social and emotional aspects of human beings, so that the average person, over the length of her lifespan, becomes much more secure, authentic and happy (in a deep, meaningful sense of the word)' (2017, p. 72).

Freinacht is writing about a central idea of metamodernism but it could also be a neat summarisation of the society feminists have called for, for decades.

The point here isn't ownership – no one group has a monopoly on specific ideas. As Freinacht himself says, 'Being a metamodern thinker who believes more in ideas under development than in individuals, I do not feel I owe anything to my inspirations' (p. 383). It is also not my intention to conflate metamodernism and feminism. Although there can rightly be a feminist metamodernism or metamodern feminism, there are also tensions between the disciplines. Also, Freinacht's book is original and perceptive in ways that not all feminist books are, but it's unaware of itself as a result of feminist lineages and of the key role played by feminism in manifesting the metamodern 'vibe' – be it in the emergence of a specific type of utopianism, or autofiction, or the spirit of reinvention with a moral and ethical purpose.

I am reminded of the lukewarm reception by prominent feminists to Norwegian writer Karl Ove Knausgaard's autobiographical book series *My Struggle*. The problem was not the books per se, but that Knausgaard was lauded for *pioneering* candid personal narrative about domestic life. This came as quite a surprise for those of us who have been reading such books most of our lives. The black feminist poet and activist Audre Lorde called the writing style in her 1982 book *Zami*, a 'biomythography', because it combined elements of history, biography and myth. At the time, cultural gatekeepers claimed her label was 'pretentious', but you could argue that it was simply ahead of its time.

If metamodernism was useful for assuaging identity politics, it could not provoke by omission. Yet discussing ideas that have been of central importance to specific groups, if in silos, as 'new' ideas, alienates those groups and reinforces fragmentation, which in return reinforces the hardening of identity.

There was a need for a critical Eros between feminism and metamodernism – a relationship marked by a conscientious awareness of the role played by both schools of thought in the formation and reimagination of how we manifest personhood and identity in a broken world. The term Eros means love, which the French Moroccan philosopher Alain Badiou (2012) describes as 'a transcendent force'. I'm fond of this short and sweet description because to perceive identity through the *transcendent force* that is love remediates the antagonistic aura that surrounds the term. Love is not employed here simply as a poetic salve for abrasive identity politics. The theory I am proposing is not everyone holding hands and singing *kumbaya*. Identity erotics does not mean that bad things will stop happening and that there will be no conflict between groups of people. In a volatile society where our sense of self is entangled with the identities of others, it is simply pragmatic and wise to approach civic entanglements with love and intimacy. To be intimate is to be closely acquainted: familiar in an intrinsic way. It is to afford another an innermost depth. It is the quality of simultaneously acknowledging and appreciating separation. It *is* togetherness.

In popular culture, the erotic is usually synonymous with the sexual act and sex is rigidly associated with lust, desire and passion in great part because 'sex sells'. Yet, if there's anything decidedly anti-erotic it is capitalism and its fake and fleeting promise of pleasure. Aphrodite, the god of erotic love and mother of Eros, is arguably a trickster god who reminds us that erotic sentiment is simultaneously serious and playful, despairing and elating, and always layered and complex. Eroticism is about intimate connection with life: nature, music, art, prayer, food, humanity. When we are intimate with life, we bring intimacy into our relationships with all others.

Sex and eroticism might not be synonymous, but I am not rejecting the sexual aspect of the term. Part of togetherness, of shared humanity, is that (with the honourable rare exception of asexual people) we are sexual beings, and this very fact makes us human; it is a driving force in our actions and behaviours. Seeking a language that reverses the long tradition of separation is a reminder that deep in the soul of humanity, there is an innate desire to embrace 'the other'. This innate desire to embrace 'the other' typically means to physically entwine with someone we feel passionately about, but it also means to bear shared human life – togetherness – in mind when it comes to 'the other' and *their* identity. It is precisely the sense of recognising oneself in 'the other' that is erotic and tender. To embrace a stranger in this way is to let go of a rigid boundary of identity. To let go of a rigid boundary of identity is, on the other hand, to come into contact with our own humanity. In this realm of the erotic, love is democratic and vast rather than narrow and specific. As the thinker, bell hooks, writes (2016):

> There is no special love exclusively reserved for romantic partners. Genuine love is the foundation for our engagement with ourselves, with family, with friends, with partners, with everyone we choose to love. While we necessarily behave differently depending on the nature of a relationship, or

have varying degrees of commitment, the values that inform our behaviour, when rooted in the love ethic, are always the same for any interaction.

In *Matter and Desire*, the biologist and philosopher Andreas Weber also conveys the meaning of eroticism that suggests that the very ecosystem between humans and the non-human natural world and between humans themselves is erotic because 'every creature can perceive its reflection in every other, because we all have a sensitive, vulnerable body that depends as much on bonds as on the air we breathe'.

In Weber's depictions of ecological communities, relationships between rocks and minerals, as well as those between the human being and her environment, are marked by an inherent vitality and surging aliveness that can best be described as erotic. 'The Earth's tender longing for us,' is how Weber describes the erotic power of gravity, and within matter itself there is a desire for a WHOLE and a WE. It is in the interest of the whole that our identities help establish – rather than prevent – a successfully integrated social network.

This sense of intimacy and eros proposed in identity erotics gravitates towards the *notion of identity* itself: the human tendency to anchor a sense of self in parameters of meaning, rather than towards a particular group. To healthily cherish one's specific identity can be a sign of maturity and Bildung, but what matters here is the appreciation (rather than abomination) of the multiplicity of identity. Identity erotics means to purposefully remember that a diversity of identities enriches the world to a greater extent than the current climate suggests. It is an attitude of critical Eros towards a world both freeing itself and holding onto essentialist forms that have been imposed on manifest forms of matter, where even matter itself is detaching itself from the rigid definitions inflicted on it (them, they, we, their).

If identity has become a separating and divisive notion, then to juxtapose it with a very opposite attitude – the erotic – is almost confrontational at first. But the tension between the terms identity and erotic is what exposes that there is a resistance to intimacy and togetherness. In 'The Uses of the Erotic', Audre Lorde argues that the erotic is a resource 'that lies in a deeply feminine and spiritual plane' and its suppression is the suppression of 'a considered source of power and information within our lives'. The resistance to intimacy is also played out by the repression of women's interior lives. Instead, as the psychoanalyst Erich Fromm put it in *The Art of Loving*, sexual desire has a 'deceptive character ... simulated by the anxiety of aloneness'. My focus on love and intimacy embedded in the erotic is to prevent the association that togetherness is about evading aloneness rather than about imagining a higher dimension of social reality. As Lorde continues to say, 'The erotic comes from sharing deeply any pursuit with another person.'

Perhaps we can better understand how to reconfigure boundaries, intimacies and togetherness if we were to view identity as *a commons*. Traditionally, a 'commons' refers to shared land that each stakeholder has a mutual interest in preserving. Yet, when the notion was popularised by scientist Garrett Hardin in an essay titled 'The Tragedy of the Commons' (1969), Hardin did not, as the title implies, believe that the commons could be well managed by communities themselves.

He contended that people would overuse and destroy the commons if state regulation and privatisation were not implemented.

In 1990, Nobel Prize recipient Elinor Ostrom challenged Hardin by showing that individuals and communities were perfectly adept at managing their own collective resources. With her pioneering study of natural resource commons in the US, Indonesia, Nepal and Kenya, she helped revolutionise perceptions of the commons by demonstrating that the real tragedy was that external profit-seeking groups prevented communities from sustainable commons management.

The commons have since become central to environmental and ecofeminist activists who oppose the fact that nature is considered a resource at the service of corporate profit, and who connect the exploitation of nature with that of women. As philosopher and activist Vandana Shiva says in the anthology *Why Women Will Save the Planet*, 'You can't save the planet without equality. I started my own journey in activism forty years ago and in the last half century of ecological movements, it is women who have been leading at the grassroots.'

The notion of the commons has since migrated from strictly referring to natural resources to other shared human assets. For example, the American writer David Bollier (2016) makes the case for a 'Digital Commons' which, in contrast to traditional commons that focus on 'problems that affect the management of water, fisheries and land', are concerned with how to 'design effective self-governance structures for virtual collaboration'. The Digital Commons include open-source software, wikis, and decentralised autonomous organisations (DAOs) characterised by the fact that they are communally owned and managed.

There are furthermore 'Cultural Commons', 'Knowledge Commons' and 'Urban Commons', and the philosopher and psychotherapist Mark Vernon has also suggested a 'Spiritual Commons', which he defines as 'the non-material aspects of life that, more often than not, are crucial for finding meaning and purpose, particularly when life involves suffering'.

When we view identity as a commons, we are better able to understand that (1) identity is a seminal and shifting concept, (2) everyone has a stake in shaping the notion and (3) unless we infuse our understanding of identity with the spirit of togetherness, we all must live in a society marked by division. In addition, when we invest in mindfully redefining identity, we do not only recast thorny issues in the pressing domain of social relations but also in the development of other commons. After all, we cannot even begin to solve the environmental crisis without a simultaneous awareness of how identity, the exploitation of women, indigenous people and the Global South are related to the degradation of non-human nature in the first place. Nor can the Digital Commons provide their full potential value as long as they are marked by race and gender biases, as they are. God, in most religious communities, is conventionally conjured as male and so a Spiritual Commons may require us to interrogate the relationship between divinity and identity. Viewing identity as a commons refocuses the true sense of shared projects and assets implied in all other commoning.

In 1968, the Marxist theorist Raymond Williams wrote in his book *Keywords* that keywords are 'strong, difficult and persuasive words in everyday usage' that we share with others 'when we wish to discuss many of the central processes of our common life'. They are words that have a continuous general meaning but have 'come in fact to express radically different or radically variable, yet sometimes hardly noticed meanings and implications of meaning'. The problems of society, Williams argued, are inextricably bound to 'the problem of its [keyword] meanings'.

'Identity' was, understandably, not one of Williams' few hundred keywords (this is understandable as it was not yet a politicised term). But the University of Pittsburgh continues to build on Williams' work through the Keyword Project, and they list 'identity' as a keyword through which the zeitgeist is 'offered, felt for, tested, confirmed, asserted, qualified, changed'. It is interesting to note that their research on identity reveals that when the term first came into use in civic discussion, it was seen to connote sameness rather than difference. For example, in 1920s South Africa policymakers rejected its use, arguing that the term didn't 'acknowledge any real difference between Europeans and natives'.

I am by no means suggesting that identity-related conflicts persist only within the remit of language. Yet because 'important and historical processes occur *within* language', as Williams said, it is important to also use language to the greatest extent possible to improve and assuage important and historical processes.

Identity erotics repurposes identity as a label that not only accounts for external circumstances such as race, gender and religion, which as we have seen are ultimately arbitrary, but it also helps us see that regardless of background, everyone carries an interior world. In his essay *What Is Metamodernism and Why Does It Matter?* in *Sideview* magazine, Greg Dember, writing about why he uses the term *interiority*, says that metamodernity 'is motivated by a need to safeguard the individual's interior experience against postmodern ironic relativism, modernist reductionism, and also from the ontological inertia of pre-modern tradition'. This playful and poetic approach is also why you could say that identity erotics is a metamodern approach. It is an attempt marked by 'a pragmatic romanticism unhindered by ideological anchorage' as artist Luke Turner (2011) writes in *The Metamodern Manifesto*.

Identity erotics can help to foster a relational sensibility of connection and care for strangers simply based on the shared, intimate complexity of being human. As mentioned, this will not in itself create world peace – and nor does it intend to – but it will make the ride in-between worlds a far less bumpy one.

References

Badiou, A. (2012). *In Praise of Love*. Serpent's Tail.

Bollier, D. (2016) Transnational Republics of Commoning: Reinventing Governance Through Emergent Networking: www.bollier.org/blog/transnational-republics-commoning

Dember, G. (2020) 'What Is Metamodernism and Why Does It Matter?' *The Side View*, https://thesideview.co/journal/what-is-metamodernism-and-why-does-it-matter/

Freinacht, H. (2017). *The Listening Society: A Guide to Metamodern Politics, Part One*. Metamoderna ApS.

Friends of the Earth (2018). *Why Women Will Save the Planet*. Zed Books.

hooks, b. (2016). *All About Love: New Visions*. HarperCollins.

Turner, L. (2011). *The Metamodernist Manifesto*. www.metamodernism.org/

Vermeulen, T. and van den Akker, R. (2010). Notes on metamodernism. *Journal of Aesthetics and Culture*, 2(1), DOI: 10.3402/jac.v2i0.5677.

Weber, A. (2017) *Matter and Desire: An Erotic Ecology*, Chelsea Green Publishing.

Whyte, D. (2003) *Footsteps: A Writing Life*. Many Rivers Press.

Williams, R. (1968/2014) *Keywords: A Vocabulary of Culture and Society*, OUP.

Notes

1 I don't capitalise the terms 'black' and 'white' in this essay to keep consistent with my writing elsewhere. While I don't address the capitalisation question directly, the chapter titled 'Blackness' in my book *Sensuous Knowledge: A Black Feminist Interpretation for Everyone* provides context for this choice.

13 On Committed Uncertainty
A dialogue concerning mystery, metaphysics and metamodernism

Jonathan Jong and Mark Vernon

Jonathan Jong

It has been about a decade since you wrote *How to be an Agnostic*, in which you propose an agnosticism that is deeply interested in and engaged with religious questions, including questions about God. I was particularly interested in your description of this position as 'committed uncertainty' because it expressed something I have noticed among my peers, both the religious and non-religious. There is, on the one hand, much lamenting about the decay of social bonds and trust in institutions and authorities, which might be diagnosed as a crisis of commitment. On the other hand, there is – in the name of humility, perhaps, or fear of hubris, at least – the problem of being bonded too tightly to any community and trusting too much in any institution and authority. Your pairing of these two intuitions speaks directly to this problem, which quite obviously manifests itself well beyond religious concerns. Let's begin our conversation here, then. It seems to me that this phrase 'committed uncertainty' can be read in two ways, either as a commitment to uncertainty or as an uncertain commitment to some religious tradition. These are, of course, not mutually exclusive readings. Which did you intend at the time? And has your orientation shifted in the decade since?

Mark Vernon

Thanks for picking that up. At the time, around 2010, I was wrestling with what felt like a gaping hole in my theological education. This was doubly striking as I studied theology while training to be ordained a priest in the Church of England. What that training and study almost wholly lacked, as I recall, is what would have been a central element in any medieval theological education, namely the fundamental unknowability of God. I discovered why this is a blessing, not a curse, while subsequently writing about Plato. My PhD was on the centrality of friendship in Platonic philosophy and, roughly, the sense I gained was that Plato thought philosophy is best done between friends because friends can happily and honestly navigate the terrain between what they know and what they don't know. This is the edge of growth for we humans, because the quality of our awareness means that we can explore our uncertainties. This can be frightening. But it is also a route to discovering more about life, not least that our life springs from a much wider life, which is its source and sustainer.

Now, that source can be experienced in many ways, from those ways that are amenable to the natural sciences, to those that would be the origin of what the natural sciences study, which theists call God. I became interested in how to develop my awareness of this 'ever-present origin', to use Jean Gebser's wonderful expression. Socrates' commitment to uncertainty became key: he felt he was wise because he knew for sure that he knew nothing for sure. This was a type of wisdom not just because it made him cautious and thorough in his investigations, but more profoundly, because it put him in touch with the wisdom that is beyond his own. Plato called that wisdom the good, beautiful and true. It also made love the centre of his philosophical way of life because love is able to reach beyond what is known, much as lovers or friends share in each other's lives not because they know everything about each other, but because their unknown dimensions are open to each other, too. This is what gives a relationship the experience of depth.

In other words, Plato's commitment to friendship and uncertainty came together not just for practical reasons – because the world is full of uncertainties and having friends in such an environment is useful – but also for ontological reasons, because in close friendship we gain an experience of what it is to be more alive in a world of impenetrable depths from which life itself springs.

So I am committed to uncertainty. In the decade since I wrote that book, the big change would be that my practice has moved on, from philosophy to psychotherapy. I felt that psychotherapy is a better inheritor of Ancient Greek philosophy than modern philosophy.

But I maintain an uncertain commitment to any religious tradition, partly because the religious tradition I know the best, Christianity, seems to have lost lots of the wisdom about uncertainty as the pathway to God; and partly because any one religious tradition is, inevitably, going to contain doctrines, images, myths and creeds that are limited as well as rich. So it's very helpful to be open to other traditions that may offer alternative pathways to the divine, too.

I've given away a bit of my biography in responding to your question, which might raise some of your biographical perspective, as you are an Anglican priest. I wonder how you experience these things?

Jonathan Jong

I got lucky; in many ways, that prepared me for my time at theological college, which was really rather theologically and philosophically uninteresting. You say that your training lacked an emphasis on God's unknowability: I don't recall being taught anything about the doctrine of God at all, besides patristic controversies about the Trinity. I had to pick that up elsewhere.

It seems to me that one can arrive at an apophatic theological disposition from two directions: beginning with human limitations or with the nature of God. I would identify the first path with what you describe as Socratic, and towards which my upbringing in Malaysia and subsequent training as a cognitive psychologist led me. There's something about growing up in a religiously pluralistic country that fosters humility about one's religious views, I think. Malaysia is constitutionally Muslim, but only 60 per cent of the population is Muslim, and growing up we tended to celebrate each other's religious festivals: Eid al-Fitr was a public holiday, but so was Good Friday and Vesak Day. In such a context, it's difficult to be unaware of how culturally and biographically contingent one's religious beliefs are: this in turn makes it difficult to be dogmatic about them.

I became a Christian among quite conservative evangelical Methodists, but even though I believed Christianity was true – with the zeal of a teenage convert, no less – I would not have gone so far as to say that Islam or Buddhism or Hinduism were *false*. It seemed obvious to me that whatever truth Christianity contained, it was incomplete. Studying psychology at university broadened my sense that human knowing is fragile, susceptible to all kinds of biases, driven by motivations other than those towards truth: religious knowledge was surely not exempt from this general rule. And actually, studying philosophy of science – my lecturer, Alan Musgrave, was one of Karl Popper's and Imre Lakatos's students – helped too: Popper's falsificationism is apophatic in spirit, of course, and Lakatos is even more cautious than Popper is about the relationship between science and truth, even though both thought that science aims at truth.

More recently, I have been coming towards apophaticism from the other direction. By the time I was in graduate school, my interest in 'science-and-religion' had led me to Herbert McCabe, for whom apophaticism is not just necessitated by human cognitive limitations but also – somewhat paradoxically – by what we do want to say about God and creation. Simply put: the creator of all things cannot be a thing, and is therefore not knowable in the way that things are knowable. This view is, I soon discovered, the 'classical' view, clearly assumed throughout most of Christian theological history, and not just among medieval mystics: McCabe got it from Aquinas, to be sure, but he got it from Pseudo-Dionysius and Augustine and so on. When I arrived in Oxford after graduate school, I was pleased to discover that Anglo-Catholicism in Oxford was – and still is – very much influenced by McCabe and that current of English Roman Catholic theology that put Aquinas, Wittgenstein and Marx together. In those days, just as I was starting at theological college, I read a lot of McCabe, Nicholas Lash and Denys Turner, whose *How to be an Atheist* book clearly affected you too. Luckily for me, as I was picking this stuff up alongside the bland stuff I was getting in my formal training, it didn't feel like I was filling a gap left behind by religious authorities, or anything like that.

I'm curious about the role this second direction plays for you, which is – if you like – apophatic on kataphatic grounds, or – to return to your phrase – uncertainty based on commitment: God's unknowability is entailed by theological claims about God's nature. Your Platonism is particularly interesting here, as this route to apophaticism has obvious Neoplatonist roots, not just in the fifth-century mystic Pseudo-Dionysius's reading of Proclus, but also in Christian Platonism of Church Fathers like Augustine and Gregory of Nyssa. Or perhaps your apophaticism only or primarily comes from that first direction?

Mark Vernon

I devoured writings by Turner and McCabe. They come like fresh revelations ringing with truth when you've only otherwise studied the ups and downs of church controversies about the Trinity, as you say. Turner is witty when he explains how hard it is to be an atheist because everything that the atheist denies, he would deny too as a theist – even to the point of God's existence. Which, as McCabe points out, is because existence itself is dependent upon God and so even existence can't be any kind of final or definitive comment about God. It's a bit like the old paradox prompted by Epimenides the Cretan remarking that all Cretans are liars (with apologies to Cretans). Wrestling with whether or not Epimenides the liar was speaking the truth generates the sense that there is a grammar of true and falsity that must be prior to the discussion itself. The grammar is akin to the intangible tangibility of God.

I also like your sense that Christianity can be true without other religions being false. I actually think that this is the sign of a religion being true. It can admit other paths and expressions because it recognises that it is a path and expression. Or to put it another way, Christianity is true because it is trying to express more than Christianity – a more that may well be found better expressed in other traditions. Only a tradition that can welcome more than itself can be true, when it comes to the truth of God, who (?) exceeds all that has ever been said because God is the reason anything can be said. Etc, etc.

Platonism went through various phases, of course, even within Plato's dialogues, including clearly dogmatic periods. Though there always seems to have been a pull-back to the more cautious and apophatic, and the sense that this is the way to what's good, beautiful and true. It's the advantage of having Socrates as your founding spirit.

So I think that's right about the apophatic coming from human limitations and the nature of God. Though I'd add a third source, which is that to be human is to be embarked upon a tremendous journey of return to the divine. I mean this in the sense captured by the Christian Platonism you mention, as opposed to the Gnostics because, as you'll know, in Christian Platonism, as in Neoplatonism, everything is ultimately good. The issue is the manner in which 'what is' reflects what is *good*. This means that there are finally no dualisms of good and evil, spirit and matter, as the Gnostics supposed. Rather, the task of return is, in a way, the struggle to perceive all things right and to see that everything lives and moves and has its being in God. The extent to which you can see that, is the extent to which you have returned.

This thought brings me back to why I feel psychotherapy is the natural inheritor of ancient philosophy, as opposed to modern philosophy. It was clear to the ancients that in order to understand something, you have to share in the being of what you seek to understand. This is why Plotinus makes his remark about no eye ever seeing the sun without being sun-like, much as no soul can see what's beautiful without becoming beautiful. The beautiful must have an adequate home in your mind for your mind to perceive it. The ugly mind will never get it, much as the unmusical person, given there is such a person, will always struggle with understanding music.

This means that you must attend to yourself in order to perceive what's good, beautiful and true. And it seems to me that psychotherapy is one of the relatively rare, living traditions in the West that attends to the self, not so that the person can flourish well enough in the world as it currently is, though that may happen; but so the person can flourish as a person. In short, psychotherapy is, at heart, a process of return as well – the return to being human. In part, this means feeling into what has happened in your life. But feeling into leads to feeling around, so the experience itself generates the sense of there being more in life: it is simultaneously an about-turn from conscious or unconscious preoccupation with the past, to a sense that there is a future that can now be different.

For the theist, that future is shaped by the divine. How could it be otherwise, when God has shaped everything to start with? However, that leads me to a sense of what is so wrong with our times today, at least in the West. Perhaps this is something you would like to pick up. But in a nutshell, my basic analysis of our troubles and failures as a society, from fostering mass extinctions to climate instability, stems from spiritual materialism: the attempt to collapse the whole of life onto the material plane alone. This is a disaster because the whole of life cannot be collapsed onto the material plane alone, and if you try it, you end up consuming the material plane until there is nothing left. To put it another way, heaven is not a place on earth, though the whole earth shines with it, seen aright. But you need to see it aright.

Jonathan Jong

I can see how psychotherapy is like philosophy as we find it in Plato's dialogues: in both cases, there is conversation, and the philosopher/therapist is not just dictating propositions at the interlocutor/client or trying to bombard her with syllogisms, but encouraging her to find resources already present in herself to come towards new understanding. This is not – I think you will agree – simply an effort to discover what one idiosyncratically believes. There has been a lot of talk in the self-help literature that draws on psychotherapeutic resources, about discovering or being in touch with one's true self, which comes across as quite individualistic, if not narcissistic. But the language you use – 'return to being human' – implies a less atomistic view, which I think is truer not just to Socrates but also to Freud and Jung, for whom the contents of the unconscious are shared by all human beings after all.

I wonder, then, if Wittgenstein – who, like you, had a sort of anti-philosophical turn towards therapy – can add something here. For Wittgenstein, it is not just the individual's confusion that needs treatment, but the confusion of language itself, which is necessarily a shared enterprise: there is no private language, as he argued. There is an obvious connection here too with what we have been saying about religion: God is very difficult to talk about, even though talking is a necessary path towards silent contemplation. The series of affirmations and negations at the heart of apophatic theology is, in this sense, linguistic therapy too. Maybe it's not only modern philosophy that should take a therapeutic turn, but modern theology too, especially as it is taught from pulpits and the lecterns of seminaries.

If spiritual materialism is the problem, I can't help but think that material spirituality is a solution. I mean by this what I think you mean by 'the whole earth shines with [heaven]': 'The world is charged with the grandeur of God', as Hopkins has it. We have, so far, been talking about the side of Christianity and related traditions that emphasises divine transcendence: God is difficult to talk about precisely because God is wholly other. But there is also a side of Christianity – and here, it is somewhat less similar to its other Abrahamic cousins – that emphasises divine *immanence*. We see this most clearly in the doctrine of the Incarnation, in which God enters the world in the same way that a baby does. This is then taken up a notch in certain views of the eucharist, in which the faithful are invited to take and eat and drink the body and blood of Christ: these common substances, bread and wine, become the vehicles of our communion with the infinite and immaterial God. Like all sacraments, the eucharist is a sign for us, which is not to say that the bread symbolises flesh and the wine blood, but that the entire thing reveals the intimacy between God and creation, even its humblest elements.

I think this means that heaven *is* a place on earth, sort of: or there's a line attributed to Paul Éluard, the Surrealist and Communist poet that goes something like: 'There is another world, and it is this one.' But this means that we don't have to *make* – inevitably by force – this world into some other world of our fantasies. It already is heaven, though not as natural science and technology perceive it in its crassest Baconian mode, to whom (through Hobbes) we owe that awful aphorism about knowledge being power.

Mark Vernon

I love that Éluard attribution. In his novel, *The Solid Mandala*, Patrick White quotes it as, 'There is another world, but it is this one', immediately following the thought with a quote from Meister Eckhart: 'It is not outside, it is inside; wholly within.'

That's my take on it: the inside of the world has been lost in modern times. I think the loss is bound up with the proliferation of prefixes to 'modern', as in postmodern, metamodern, hypermodern and so on. My sense is that they get added when philosophers know that the modern worldview isn't enough, which is to say, they feel there is more to the world than the modern worldview allows. It's the world of quality, interiority and spirit not captured in positivistic or Baconian assumptions about, say, cause and effect, or the progress of knowledge via empirical investigation, or the sovereignty of the natural sciences. So they add a prefix to express a need for something more than, or beyond, the mechanical and modern.

However, the prefixes simultaneously trap the philosophers using them by keeping them beholden to the modern worldview. They must define their 'x'-modernity in relation to modernity. It's why postmodernity or metamodernity or hypermodernity has an epicycle feel, like a series of footnotes to modernity.

The way out is to make the inward turn, to foster the capacity to perceive further dimensions to the world, upon which the world rests. To put it theistically, this is an awareness that the world is sustained by God, as opposed to being caused by God, as if in the latter case God were to the cosmos as a garage mechanic is to a car. It is the real meaning of 'In the beginning was the Word', as you know, which doesn't mean there is a beginning to everything, which there may or may not be; but that there is an ever-present, dynamic source of everything.

Leibniz put it well in his analogy of the geometry books. He imagines a country in which there have always been geometry books, copied one from another. In that country, you can always explain the cause of any particular book's existence because it has been copied from another book. However, you cannot explain why there are geometry books at all, without falling into an infinite regress – epicycles of explanation, if you like – unless you reach for another explanation for the existence of geometry books. This is another dimension of reality in addition to mere copying, though it includes the practice of copying, and it is the dimension that is the source of books, geometry and copying. You could call that dimension the intelligence wholly within and exceeding the books, geometry and copying, that loves and so sustains them.

In more Platonic terms, it is the presence of a chain of being that originates in Being itself, and I take it that this is what Hopkins is expressing in the world being charged with the grandeur of God, as well as illuminating the deep meaning of sacraments like the eucharist. They allow us to gain a feel for the infinite depth of Being, which, while transcending the tangible world around us, is simultaneously imminent, embedded in all beings and things around us. William Blake's line was seeing heaven in a grain of sand.

So yes, the transcendent is imminent and other. The material world is the tangible tip of a pyramid of being that, as it reaches down, expands into levels of being called by various names, including soul, spirit, mind, intelligence, pure consciousness, God. These are the other worlds that are here.

I'm nervous about calling that 'material spirituality'. I feel the pull towards enlarging our cosmic awareness beyond the material, if often *through* the material. But that cosmic awareness can be enlarged in other ways. Plato would say we also need to feel the expansion through our moral and aesthetic awareness, as well as our noetic or intelligent awareness. This means contemplating notions like the good, beautiful and true for their own sake, as well as in the ways in which they manifest.

Similarly, I think it's important to keep a separation between heaven and earth – perhaps the kind of separation that Coleridge highlighted, in which there is sameness with difference. It's why Heraclitus wrote of flux and change, and averred that 'it is wise to agree that all things are one'. It's why, as Dante rises into the heavens of Paradise, he's amazed to see myriad individual souls, all of whom are consciously, freely, desirously, delightfully, wholly themselves, and also fully in harmony with God. It's the unity found in diversity, and so on.

Incidentally, the inability to perceive this kind of participating separation is why, I think, many Christians struggle with the doctrine of the Trinity, with its 'three in one and one in three'. Meister Eckhart put it neatly in one of his sermons: 'Whoever can conceive of distinction without quantity, knows that three Persons are a single God.' He adds that, for any individual capable of that perception, 'If there were a hundred Persons in the Godhead, they would see only one God. Unbelievers and some uneducated Christians are astounded at this, even some priests know as little about it as a stone does, and take three in one in the sense of three cows or three stones.'

Incidentally, it's for the same reason Eckhart can affirm, 'My eye and God's eye is one eye, and one sight, and one knowledge, and one love,' and simultaneously be completely clear that he is not God.

That takes me back to what you raise about Plato, understanding and words. The term he uses, of course, is recollection: when words and understanding come together to enlarge an awareness of reality, the experience is best described as a recollection, as if realising something that, in retrospect, was half known all along. It's not individualistic or narcissistic because that realisation is of the chain of being, though it takes an individual with a full consciousness of their embeddedness in the cosmos to realise it.

It can sound mysterious but can be unpacked by considering, say, whether your words are speaking you, as much as you are speaking your words; or in the contemplative practice of observing thoughts in the moment of arising: they can be seen to have a life of their own, even as that life is also your own, owned consciousness.

My guess is that much of what I've said you will agree with. But do you think that these kinds of reflections can help with the problem of metamoderism, as I've defined it? Do you agree with the prefix problem? I feel that unless we find ways of reopening such a wider perception of and participation in reality, the epicycles will continue to ensnare. Though that also raises the question of how, of course, too, which is clearly non-trivial.

Jonathan Jong

Yes, I made that connection too between the Éluard quote and the scramble to find the 'beyond' of modernism. This reminds me that there are quite obvious Christian resources – I can't speak for other traditions – that can help with this wrestling with seemingly opposing intuitions associated with the 'modern' and with whatever people say came before or comes after it. Christians have, as we have discussed, been doing this kind of thing for a very long time, not least in the oscillation between kataphatic and apophatic modes. Over and over again, Christians have had to 'stay with the tension', to hold together commitments that may well prove, in the end, to be contradictory or paradoxical, but which in the meantime are generative when held in tension: generative of ideas, to be sure, but – at the Church's best – also generative of moves to make the world better, that is, to transform this world into the other one. The examples are legion, in the age-old and never-ending debates over the transcendence and immanence of God, the physicality and spirituality of human beings, the humanity and divinity of Christ, the real and symbolic presence of Christ in the Eucharist, the anticipation and realisation of the kingdom of God, and the related between your emphasis on separating heaven and earth and my emphasis on identifying them.

It is common to lampoon such questions as silly and irrelevant, but this judgement is mistaken, because these are, all of them, explorations of love. We have hinted at this already, in our consideration of how sacramental theology helps us to see the goodness of materiality. These examples can also be multiplied: in classic apophatic fashion, we can see the value of these tensions best when we fail to uphold them. When people have dislocated heaven from earth, we have run roughshod over creation; when we have reduced heaven to earth, we have done the same in our attempt to manufacture paradise. When people have over-spiritualised humanity, we have been blind to physical suffering; when we have over-physicalised humanity, we have fetishised individual hedonic pleasure to the detriment of a broader happiness that our Ancient Greek guides called eudaimonia.

After Christianity, we – in the West – have wanted to hold on to the goods generated by centuries of these theological labours, but it's not at all obvious to me that we have succeeded. Having exorcised metaphysics from our moral discourse, we have replaced talk of creation's goodness with utilitarian calculi and of the inherent dignity of human being with nothing except the phrase 'human rights', moored by nothing more than the agreement not to ask further questions. It is no wonder that there is so much hand-wringing in the West over what story to tell ourselves about ourselves, or even whether any stories can be told. As in political economy, in philosophy too, austerity is often the attractive error.

You ask about the 'problem of *meta*modernism', but if this incarnation of the eternal recurrence of prefixes entails a retrieval of *meta*physics – in a second naivete, as Paul Ricoeur might say – then this time, we might have a way out of our rut after all. Much depends on whether our cynicism will triumph over our courage to believe in things unseen, or at least to essay towards such mysteries.

Mark Vernon

Thanks again, and your description of the oscillation and tension makes me think of a third dynamic, to which our philosophical forebears were alert, and which has been rediscovered by some in modern times.

It's the so-called tropological moment in hermeneutics. The word comes from the Greek, *tropos*, meaning turning point. Hence the Tropics of Cancer and Capricorn are the lines on the earth's surface between which the sun's zenith turns and cycles each year. What our enlightened forebears looked for is the moment at which reading a text, engaging in a debate, contemplating a symbol or taking part in a ritual changed you because it turned your perception around.

I think this is why many of Plato's dialogues end in aporia, or a seeming hiatus in the argument. It's not that reason has failed the interlocutors and so they must stop. It's that reason has reached its limits of articulation and, with that giving up, there is a silence into which a further perception may come into view. It's a pregnant moment of fresh possibilities, which Plato artfully crafted in his dialogues because such rich disturbance mirrored meeting the historical Socrates.

It's why becoming a scientist is not really about learning the facts but about learning the art. I did a physics degree as an undergraduate and fumbled my way to the finals, at which point I realised that while I had studied physics, I hadn't become a physicist. I hadn't made that extra tropological step of being able to speak physics, you might say, which is necessary to help the science develop further.

Initiation rites recognise the same dynamic. A crisis must be reached, after which the initiate gains the capacity to see more. Bewilderment is often the word used in spiritual traditions. Much about life has been learned, much of life has been suffered. And then it all comes crashing to a seeming halt. There is a dark night of the soul, or breakdown, or raging at the apparent darkness. It is a moment of almost giving up, which is really a moment of letting go, that becomes the capacity to take in a whole lot more. That more is now able to reveal itself because it is located in a part of reality that is beyond anything the initiate of themselves possesses, though they can now connect to it. It's why initiates are sometimes called the 'perfected'. It is not that they are perfect, but they have looked beyond the horizons of their flawed perceptions, to know the presence of that which is perfect. It's a kind of death and is immensely freeing. For this reason, Cicero thought that the mystery rites of the ancient world, which took individuals through this kind of initiation, were the greatest of Greece's many legacies to the Roman world. After the tropological experience, the individual is capable of living happily and dying with hope because they are in touch with a compass that can orientate them in life, regardless of what happens.

Within Christianity, early figures like Paul and Origen were onto it. Origen explained that a religious revelation cannot be understood at the literal level, but must be grasped by the soul and spirit, domains of perception that can embrace paradox and contradiction because they know of a type of intelligence that can see beyond reason's rejection of paradox and contradiction. Paul declared, 'Behold, I show you a mystery!' when presenting the meaning of the resurrection to the Corinthians. It is not some kind of resuscitation or magic trick, but an awakening to life and vitality beyond the material body, which had sustained the material body.

Unfortunately, in my view, the value of the tropological and mystical was marginalised by the allergy that developed towards gnosticism in the early church, and then was pretty much expelled from Western Christianity at the Reformation, when Calvin and Luther branded them popish superstitions.

It has however, in part, been rediscovered by psychotherapy. For example, Jung talked of the transcendent function. He described it as the bringing together of conscious and unconscious parts of the self not simply to integrate the two aspects, but to 'arrive at a new attitude' towards life, because previously unknown aspects of life have shown up. He thought therapy can bring about the change, when therapy is understood to aim at more than alleviating symptoms. He experienced shocking synchronicities and living symbols doing it, too. They act as bridges not only between what seems irreconcilable, but also with what is beyond current perception. The transcendent function is another inner experience, felt in the rounding out of the personality, the expansion of soul, contact with unexpected, perhaps divine, dimensions of reality, now known as real.

My sense, then, is that the postmodern, metamodern, hypermodern and so on may be a necessary phase that builds the tension until it becomes too unwieldy and rationally unbearable, and so collapses, from which radically different awarenesses of reality will arise, like a phoenix from the ashes. This will happen not because the discourse has resolved anything, or the right formula has finally been articulated, but because the individuals themselves have undergone a tropological, transcendent awakening. They will know, afresh, the ever-present origin. They can align in ways that are resonant in our times with the good, beautiful and true.

Dispatches from a Time Between Worlds

14 The Metamodern Spirit
Approaching transformative integration in psyches and societies

Layman Pascal

> *When everything is separated correctly, the separate parts flow together naturally.* Lord John Pentland, President of Gurdjieff Foundation, Talk at Cave Junction Oregon, August 1983

Our metamodern moment has come

THE TWILIGHT of the gods is upon us. This uncanny dusk is not exactly a moment in history but rather a different quality of time for individuals and human civilisation. A qualitative epoch in which we stand together in a hopeful but deeply uncertain relationship to the momentum of all the histories we collectively inherit and all the radical futures that haunt us. Although the flowers continue to bloom, everything feels surreal and desperate. Our niches, identities and social control structures are being disrupted or are failing from their own successes. An all-too-obvious gap has opened between Systems and Nature. How long can we expect to keep going forward with minds, economies, technologies and philosophies that are insufficiently faithful to the true organic, historical and multi-dimensional complexity of the world?

One way or another, a reckoning is coming.

We cannot afford to become paralysed, reckless, regressive or hysterical. To survive this strange epoch we must pass through its very heart with the maximum amount of personal and collective coherence that is possible to us as beings. So what do we need to accomplish that passage?

Somehow, our instincts must be revived and revitalised and also challenged, cultivated and brought up to date, in order to handle the world of contemporary complexity. Our understanding and mental models must expand flexibly to incorporate many perspectives and discover the viable streams that are still flowing in premodern, modern and postmodern modes of being. New principles must be discerned and brought together as sturdy logs in the raft we are building together. A robust good conscience must be re-achieved. We need to be confident about when to be coolly objective and when to be passionately active; when to be maximally inclusive and when to take a stand against real dangers. More than anything else we need to regenerate and clarify, both personally and collectively, our powers of coordination. There are certain capacities that we can only access in our best modes. There are feelings of crucial meaningfulness that only feed back upon us when there is a higher degree of coherence among our parts, our functions, our tribes, our worldviews. Whatever this looks like, whoever can contribute to it and whatever kind of culture supports and is produced by it will be metamodern under any name …

Who and what are we?

The metamodern mind is a creative intelligence fed by interperspectival practices. Such a richness blossoms in proportion to our personal experience of exploring and validating many far-ranging types of perspective and value. We become fertilised by our passage through a great many – often contradictory – nuances of psychology, sociology and history. Slowly, perhaps painfully slowly, we accumulate a coherent vision of the world and, hopefully, discover that we are not alone in perceiving the broad contours of a new sensibility. We begin to gamble on the emergence of a qualitatively distinct, highly inclusive and intellectually seductive new schema, logic, operating system or paradigm.

Traces of this 'metamodernism' start to unfold among ourselves as if they were the fascinating and self-reinforcing fragments of a profound holographic image of a new world. Articulating the principles of that world, however, is no easy task. The degree of complexity and novelty involved often eludes simple representation. The need to draw from multiple disciplines is daunting. Nonetheless, we must try and keep trying.

Perhaps, we wonder, our best bet is to focus our new gaze outward? Externally, we may try to describe *a science and politics of meaning that simultaneously embraces the gifts of premodern, modern and postmodern styles of civilisation.* Or perhaps we will gaze more deeply into ourselves and seek *a mode of private living and consciousness that integrates a fuller range of the experiences and intelligences of which we are composed as human beings.* Inside or outside? No one knows better than we integrationists and inbetweensmen just how inevitable, enchanting and necessary will be the convergence of these apparently opposed domains of inquiry.

So we are allies of convergence. We are thresholders. The very cracks, loopholes, relativisms and paradoxes which postmodern studies have added to modern thought are, for us, a kind of building material for a great reconstruction. A positive effort that might keep pace with the unique cultural, psychological and technological circumstances of today and tomorrow. We experimental metamodernites have been known to take every perspective but not to take them all equally – or at face value.

Our position is not merely to affirm all possible contexts in a vast discordant panoply of relativism but instead we strive to enfold 'major types of perspective' within a supportive coherence that moves towards effective, naturalistic and abundant solutions to significant universal human problems. We are working to produce higher, deeper or meta-level patterns that enshrine and incorporate the most valuable discoveries of all the different types of perspective.

Where does the essential worth of each worldview and cognitive style come from? When is each kind of intelligence at its best? How can we borrow from each system's best insights and combine them sanely? This is fluid, exploratory, non-dogmatic, of course! Yet we are still tasked to be evaluators and to understand the sourcing of everyone's highest values in our gamble towards a world that combines the most profound contributions of all.

This is the metamodern project that I will be exploring in the remainder of this chapter. It is an attempt to invoke a general pattern of 'success' that can occur from any stage of development, any worldview, any discipline – any being.

I believe such a pattern is available in the interstitial spaces of our ontology and epistemology. A pattern which is presupposed by interaction among, and balance between, the main functional subsystems in any area of life. Once these functions are seen, dignified and teased apart, then begins an intentional balancing that can permit a degree of successful harmonisation which, in turn, may produce an 'extra' feeling. A resonant meta-spaciousness in which new patterns can be perceived, new capacity can be activated and an additional sense of energy can be discovered. A situation characterised by an amplification of our ethical motivation and the cultivation, within and between us, of a more embracing meaningfulness. Only something of this kind, it seems to me, has any chance of addressing the deep, vast and systemic challenges faced by our current and changing humanity.

This is not an entirely new form of thinking, any more than it is limited to people who call themselves metamodernists. At root, it resembles the kind of *lateral thinking* – proposed often since the time of Edward de Bono (*The Use of Lateral Thinking*, 1967) as a key element of innovation. This capacity to move sideways and access alternative perspectives and capacities is the prelude to the work of bringing them together in a way that produces a legitimate increase in empowerment. Innovation is one way of thinking about the production of novel excess harmony resulting from balanced integration of alternative experiential models in-or-between selves. We are looking for the core patterns that might give rise to innovation, religionisation, renaissance, spiritualisation and so on.

So this chapter on the 'Unfinished Project of Metamodernity' is, what I call, *an attempt to language a transrational model of Spirit that applies equally to premodern, modern and postmodern cultural consciousness for both individuals and societies.* I will dare to invoke those old and heavily laden words 'spirituality' and 'religion' to describe the project in its individual and social dimensions, but you will soon come to understand that I mean to define these in a very special way. I wish to build towards concepts that anchor their truth in an evolutionary, multi-phasic, interperspectival, humanist and developmentalist sense that could contribute to the metamodern eudaimonia. All of this I call:

The meta-state

My basic idea about the meta-state is very simple. It is based upon an almost trivial bit of wordplay. In the English language, the political status of a population and the subjective status of an individual are both called *states*.

Meta-states might therefore be imagined as special conditions in which our external interpersonal communities and our internal intrapsychic communities may periodically partake. We all experience more and less successful moments of embodiment that we describe according to the interplay among our inner and outer parts. We say: It's all coming together now! We say: Can we get our act together? Are we on the same page about the climate? Can I get beyond fighting with myself? …. Success in this domain means something like peak coordination. And failures are conceived by us as fragmentation – in which many people, many parts of the psyche, many styles of perspectives are not able to co-flourish or maximally integrate without loss of their particular dignity and idiosyncratic viewpoints? Tricky, tricky.

Our personal and social periods of peak meaningfulness seem to involve the mutually amplifying coordination of many components. Even the word 'meaningful' itself suggests this idea (John Vervaeke, 'Awakening From the Meaning Crisis: Flow, Metaphor and the Axial Revolution' 2019 www.youtube.com/watch?v=aF9HeXg65AE). Our best moments are somehow analogous to the requirements of a meaningful sentence. There is order, balance and interconnecting resonances of various different signifiers and syntactic operators creating increased understanding, offering connection to others, enabling insight into the world and opening an altered state of consciousness that we might experience as a 'new clarity'. This functional and relatively balanced conjoining of operators is not a linear process but an omnidirectional one. We know from various experiments that our brains can read scrambled words and sentences quite easily. We grasp together a collection of elements whose implications support each other up to some unique threshold at which a novel sense of empowering 'gestalt' meaningfulness is achieved.

This is a very general phenomenon. It is not unique to the metamodern way of thinking but it becomes a conscious and central metaphor in the metamodern mind. Particularly when we ponder the form of the integrated amplification of perspectives within ourselves and among each other.

I claim that this enactment of interperspectival co-recognition is the heart of metamodern progress. Arthur Koestler – father of the Holon theory, which played such a central role in the work of the first-wave metamodern theology of Ken Wilber (Integral Theory) – wrote an entire book (*Act of Creation*, 1964) about the role of conjoined bifurcations of sense in the production of art, science and understanding. He was obsessed with the balanced interaction and cross-pollination of contexts as the creative engine at work in all disciplines.

So perhaps an ultra-general pattern underlies all our efforts. For example, the compelling notion from *Nordic Ideology: A Metamodern Guide to Politics* (Hanzi Freinacht, 2019) – about how 'game denial' and 'game acceptance' must be simultaneously engaged and brought into constructive convergence to produce the social progress of 'game change' – is just one example of how this pattern permeates the insights of major metamodern thinkers.

What I might call left-wing nihilism (game denial) and right-wing nihilism (game acceptance) are united in a common structural insight whose form depends upon the prior personal experience of having encountered a sameness among these opposites without cancelling their differences.

We all know that very basic human experience of following a new route through the wilderness, or a new city, only to re-encounter a familiar location from a new angle: the developmental micro-empowerment that accompanies the interlocking of two initially diverse contexts into a local meta-context! Exquisite. I am supposing that if you do enough of this process, in enough areas of life, you will start to stand out as a *metamodernist* of some kind. So one must have explored the pattern of anti-cultural denial (the regressive forms of anti-racism, anti-sexism, anti-capitalism) and therein 'run into' something that you realise is present also in the cynical, self-serving acceptance of those who oppose our evolution into a more nuanced and beautiful society.

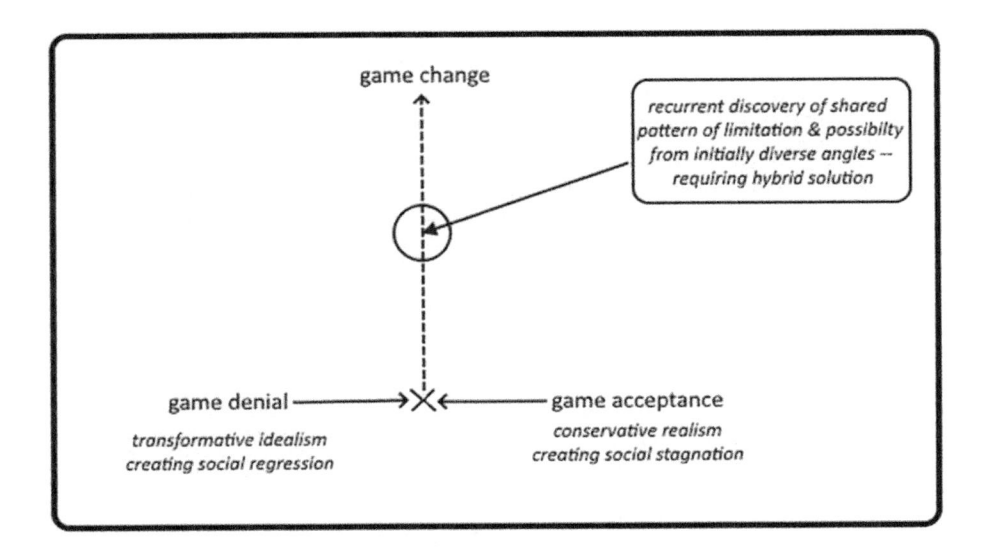

Figure 14.1 Game denial, game acceptance, game change

It is almost too obvious to mention. No one will be surprised by the aeons-old wisdom that different forces need to be combined artfully to produce a better outcome. Yet we need to get endlessly more clear about how this basic move operates as the foundation of metamodern visions and visionaries.

It is no mere social metaphor when Freinacht writes of a *listening* society, for numerous studies on the neurological effects of diverse meditation methods have discovered that 'perspective-taking practices' tend to cause growth and stimulation in the aural circuitry of the brain associated with input from the ears. Interperspectival hybrid structures depend upon a kind of listening experience which is precisely the kind of experience that media-and-technology philosophers like McLuhan suggested would become the de facto cognitive principle cultivated by the immersive and echoing information patterns of a digital society.

I propose that the production of certain kinds of interperspectival harmonisation (e.g. between social genres, between cultural codes, between psychological subpersonalities) and balanced mutual alignment can create states or peaks in which an inspirational, deeply meaningful sense of extra energy is produced in a manner analogous to the ancient dream of religious and spiritual life. This, I think, is necessary for the emergence of a meta-people and metaculture that has the flexibly inclusive but coherent vision and the generative energy (and good conscience) to exist and act responsibly and collectively in a complex, multi-epistemic world menaced by challenges and transformations whose scope is vast, whose significance is unknown and which requires us to be somehow *more than our best*.

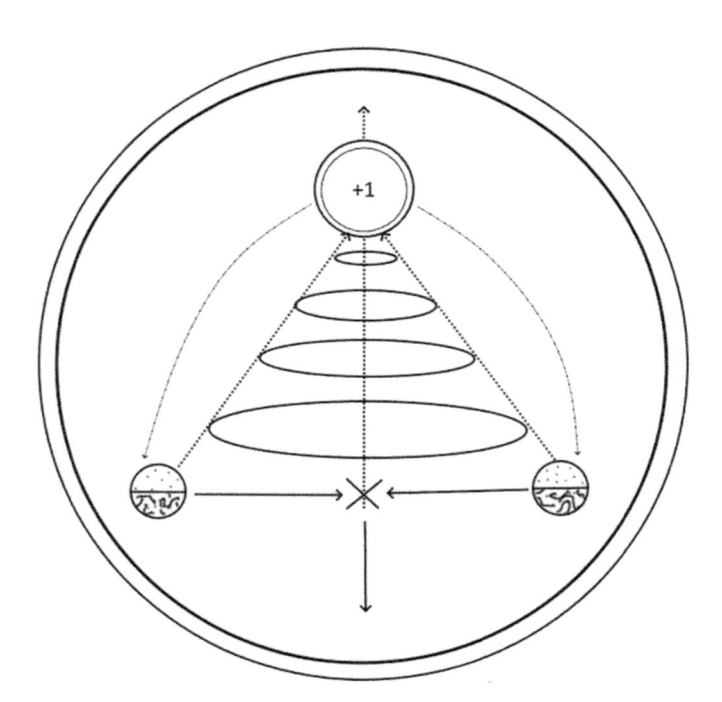

Figure 14.2 Modes, genres, subsystems

Figure 14.2 depicts modes, genres or subsystems. By teasing them part into regenerative or degenerative elements, their complementarity is freed towards an upward converge whose result will be an excess coherence that can overflow back upon those modes providing satisfaction and mobilising energy.

A little personal and cultural background

The first person I ever heard say 'meta-politics' was wily old Dr Timothy Leary. I was a boy and he was nearing the end of his life, suffering from terminal prostate cancer. Yet I found him to be more spry, lively, twinkling and, perhaps, sane than virtually any other old man I had encountered. A satyr. A true elder. I had not lived through the pluralistic carnival of the 1960s so I knew this Harvard professor and rascal-ish Irish-American psychologist much more for his work on the theory of evolutionary neurocircuits than for his brief stint as a public advocate for the human right to explore psychedelic brain change.

Turn on. Tune in. Drop out.

That was his infamous 1960s neurospiritual marketing anthem. Many folks interpreted the slogan as an invitation to 'drop out' of political and economic struggles. Frustrated and disappointed by the slow, complicated and stressful pace of institutional change, they turned instead towards a transformation of the self. Partly, they were just exhausted, partly they were beginning to understand that changing the world had to mean changing hearts and minds. One at time. Starting with themselves.

However this neo-Eastern *inward turn* was not the end of their journey. Personal growth is also slow, complicated and often stressful. And perhaps it poses a dangerous distraction from the urgent need to transform society? The pendulum swung again. And again. Today, we look back upon a long sequence of oscillations. The best of us have bounced back and forth between private and public development for many years. We can see that alternating between Society and Self is not enough. A tipping teeter-totter (see-saw) cannot be stabilised by rushing desperately back and forth from one end to the other. Instead, we must find a midpoint or else engineer a balance of weights. Thus, we need some context in which to hold both of these crucial dimensions simultaneously. They are co-essential and interdependent streams of qualitative progress. They are complementary domains in which contexts, perspectives, logics and capacities may be encouraged towards a consilience. But is there a single metamodern philosophy, science or language that can hold them both?

Yes and no.

It is unlikely that any single dogma, movement or philosophical analysis can be adequately and widely affirmed as the true vehicle of this transperspectival sensibility. However, there is also every chance that we can enrich our situation by encouraging people to flesh out and share their own meta-perspectives. We are not seeking the correct single metamodern solution, but rather a community of those who have some tacit understanding of the terrain that is being mapped by a whole set of solutions. The transformative elucidation of meta-perspectives depends on the mutually enriching interconnection of a thousand different ways of experiencing and formulating an ostensibly common vision. Our intersections, all together, are the prophet for whom we have been waiting ...

My own idea for helping this process along is not strange. It is almost too obvious to mention. We know that, in general, any kind of system will start to falter and fail if its key functional components are dramatically exaggerated or suppressed, relative to each other. You would get very sick and start to die if any of your major organs were operating twice as much or half as much as they ought to be. An appropriate balance of operations among subsystems must be mutually and creatively negotiated and maintained. Health is a gestalt effect that is sustained not only by the operation of each component but also by the reciprocal attunement, in terms of prominence and dynamism, among the components within their shared environment.

Any successful meeting of individuals, for example to address a problem, depends not only on the competence and knowledge of each person but also upon their reciprocal capacity to *share* in appropriate proportion. The components of a car engine can either 'over rev' or underfunction. Generic health, in precisely this sense of adequate complementary proportional engagement, is the precondition for strength and capacity. Our concern for self-development, and our collective capacity to face large-scale, complex and tangled meta-crises, are directly tied to whether we are strong, robust, antifragile, coordinated, healthy and so on. Our adaptive capacity is directly tied to the balance and reciprocal harmonisation of our interpersonal and intrapersonal systems. This functional harmonisation (or meta-state) is therefore analogous to a transcendental empowerment of society and of ourselves.

So what are religion and spirituality in this meta-sense?

Does spirituality describe a special realm of 'spirit powers'? Or is it merely a metaphor for intriguing existential experiences in a complexly opaque world? Or is it a particular way that we neurochemically evolve our relationship to the highest values in our personal world? Yes. It is all of that AND it is stratified into different modalities across each of the major developmental phases of individual and anthropological history, as well as being differentiated according to the understanding of disparate types of people. A meta-level understanding therefore must embrace all of this and also seek out any common principles – rather than falling back on any reductionist dismissal or dogmatic affirmation associated with some partial, conventional definition of spirituality.

And religion? Is it a belief-cult OR an ancient socio-biological evolutionary strategy OR the special hope for staving off the apocalypse and improving civilisation OR the interaction of a population with an imaginary presence OR a protective enclosure for crazy people and manipulators? Yes. So what does religiousness look like if viewed as something that must be valid in all these different frames? It will have to be quite abstract and also quite inclusive.

To a metamodern religious gaze, it seems that religion is often mixed up, in popular discourse, with mythic-membership cults. These large, easily recognised blocs of 'believers' often stand out to the modern mind as if they were the obvious and normative examples of religion – Christianity, Islam, Judaism, Buddhism .... However, these nation-like, sectarian groups, who bond over professed loyalty to a set of symbols and books, represent only one type of human religious activity. To understand more broadly we must include a larger range of phenomena. Large enough to include even many who do not self-identify as 'religious'. This is an appropriate approach because many ancient peoples would not necessarily recognise themselves as religious in the modern sense. Prehistoric, indigenous, traditional, modern, postmodern and metamodern religious activity – in both *official* and *colloquial* forms – must be included in our definition if we are to start making sense of the phenomenon.

From the perspective of developmental logic (Gebser, Piaget, Wilber, MHC, et al), this mythic-membership logic only characterises one 'stage' of religious activity. Tribal, modern, postmodern and metamodern religiosity are just as significant as the nation-like, verbal-assent based groups that are bound into official membership and mythopoetic cosmological schemes. Much other religiosity may be concealed elsewhere. Even under the idea of 'culture' itself – especially in the common or even idiosyncratic sense of individuals 'doing this (or that) *religiously*'.

In this expanded sense, a 'pagan sun-worshipper' is not only described specifically by his use of an anthropomorphic fantasy about the sun but also equally well by his performance of ritual efforts and enjoyments with regard to the sun. Perhaps it is the sacrifice of a bull in the temple of Helios or perhaps it is the regular (i.e. ritual) grilling up of a beefsteak on the BBQ when summer starts. Many of the keys to religion may be hiding in plain sight.

Of course, we might fear that this approach will lose the specificity of the definition of religion, but we should reflect upon the fact that, for example, physics has only been enriched by expanding its traditional definition of physical matter to include regimes of energy, information, multiplicity and so on. Our goal is not merely to include more examples of religiousness but to shift the specific definition into something that is more useful to the metamodern vision.

Religion in this more general form is primarily performative rather than ideological. Connective rather than cosmological. Aspirational rather than official. Coordinated by an experiential (but not necessarily consciously articulated) relationship to Powers and Principles representing the value and complex organisational patterns of Nature, Culture and Psyche.

- *Spirituality* can be defined as the cultivation and utilisation of a numinous surplus of meaningful coherence among the functional components of individual psychology.

- *Religion* may be understood as the cultivation and utilisation of a numinous surplus of meaningful coherence among the functional components of the field of culture.

And, frankly, this is the kind of religion I grew up with and the kind of spirituality I ended up teaching in my years as a meditation and yoga instructor, public lecturer and retreat leader.

Although I was raised in a very rural and patriarchal farming and fishing community, I had what I would call a 'natural' rather than 'enforced' experience of agrarian life and psychology.

Exploring apotheosis

My father was something like a rational Taoist explorer; my mother seemed to be a Christian pluralist with strong neo-pagan and theosophical tendencies. The two main impressions I received from her about religion were contained in her belief that the Gospel was a non-metaphorical set of claims about the physics of the universe ('*I think Jesus means it literally when he says he IS light* ...') and her open favouring of the Bhagavad Gita for its poetic and aesthetic elements ('*I love Krishna because he is blue* ...'). She taught me not only that many religions contain truths, but also that religious truths can be evaluated by multiple methodologies. When it came to religion, aesthetics was as important as ethical codes, and physics was as important as mythology. Religion was a phenomenon in which diverse genres of social activity and values flowed together harmoniously.

So the groundwork was laid for a sincere irony in my relationship to the notion of spiritual and religious progress ...

And I *did* feel my childhood was holy. I knew a kind of faith in the background consistency of my golden home and diaphanous local ecosystem. It was not based fundamentally on visions or , or even on my encounter with the ancient evocative ideas of our religious ancestors – although these were certainly present. It was anchored in something more general, more direct and perhaps more important. Perhaps it was the essential rightness of the world? Maybe something similar to that feeling of ancient Romans who treated their Caesar and Rome as 'gods'? Here is a mutually interweaving resonance of elements that, to some unknown degree, just *work*, hanging together and glowing in the recollected imagination, the happiness, functionality and vitalism that archaically made pagans love a 'holy rock' or treat a little mountain as 'Shiva himself'. A mechanism of apotheosis was at work.

Later, apprenticed to a Buddhist order that specialised in psychology and somatic energy healing, I tried to balance out my studies by attending a religious service from a different religion each Sunday. From the Baptists to the Scientologists, from the Sikhs to the Pentecostals, from Rama-worshippers to New Age circles invoking the global web of sentient nature. I half fell in love with Catholicism, was stimulated intellectually by the late-life conversions of Marshall McLuhan and Anne Rice, and probably also the glamour of the Renaissance. However, my aspirational feeling about Catholicism never quite jived with what I heard from people who had been 'raised Catholic'. And many of the churches seemed like they were not religious enterprises at all – but more like Museums of Religion. Here were collections of images, stories, writings and rituals all pointing back to some historical cultural moment and distant place where *religion* had actually been occurring for a while. They openly spoke of the historical sites of the actual descent of Grace.

In fact, many of these institutions and their administrators actively asserted that they were *not* doing religion – that their people could do no more than remember, hear about and trust in a time when somebody else was having real religiousness. But if they were self-admitted placeholders for religion, then where, I wondered, was the actual religion today? Upon what factors did those ancient moments of religious renaissance depend? Clearly, my use of the word religion was mutating …

Teaching yoga and meditation and giving public talks on various thorny philosophical aspects of cosmology, subtle energy and human growth put me in a situation that I slowly recognised as being analogous to a *religious figure* or a *priest* of previous epochs. After a while you are tempted to start dropping the word 'analogous' and want to say: real priests or theologians *are* organic rather than official. In every time period they were doing their version of what I am doing. A seductive temptation indeed.

I started to look for these 'organic plants of holiness' under any conditions. I started to think that Nietzsche and Kierkegaard might be exemplary Christians, in the same sense that Socrates was an exemplary Athenian despite his official excommunication and murder. There was this recurring sense of civic holiness that made me feel profoundly connected to the land, the cosmos and the community, as if *something more* was at work.

I did not ascribe metaphysical narratives to this feeling. And I did not undergo this experience equally, at all times. It seemed to be continuous in its most basic sense, but its intensity was dependent upon how well I was doing – whatever that meant. It seemed to increase in proportion to my health, my taking on challenges, my intentional efforts, successful risks of intimate sharing, nature immersion, certain acts of perception, various meditation practices, trances and dances.

And all that was everything I could think of religion meaning in its best sense. The same apotheosis of cultural activity that I beheld in Tibetan sand mandalas, the ceiling of the Sistine Chapel, the turquoise minarets of the Mohammedan cities. Luminous. Networked. Balanced diversity. Super-coordinated potencies added up to more than the sum of their parts. My love for this quality helped me find positive religious sentiment in places I had overlooked. I found it in the iconoclastic Deism of the founders of democracy. It pervaded the early geniuses of the natural sciences probably more than it ever pervaded a crowd of zealous believers.

All too clearly, it began to seem that anti-religious arguments articulated by atheists were almost entirely opposed to the cultural codes of mythic loyalists and had very little to do with what I considered the essence of religion or spirituality.

My great hope, then, is to present a plausible structural analogy between the 'inner personal' and 'outer social' dimensions of desirable human transformation and edification. If it is possible to conjoin (a concept hinted at in the etymology of both *re-ligio* and *yo-ga*) these two territories into a tandem project, then perhaps it will be possible to extend this common notion to many more zones of human concern. Little by little, we might find a very general image of meta-success.

We may explore this possibility in private and public terrains, with each consisting internally of distinct modules and developmental flows. These will be named differently in each domain. For example, the interior modules might be construed as sub-selves or subjective sub-functions, while the cultural modules could be called social genres – or perhaps modes of production? For the moment, let us only acknowledge that there may be analogous forms operating in each zone, quite appropriately, under different historical and intellectual labels. Whatever we call these *unfolding modules*, I suggest that they can be grasped individually or in clusters, independently or interdependently cultivated, more or less harmonised, meaningfully interwoven, variably combined and potentially integrated into an intermodal whole that is experientially greater than the sum of its parts.

It is this particular notion of an active gestalt of the integrated parts that will lead me towards the language of 'Spirit'. This kind of geist is produced or enacted in a manner that is roughly isomorphic between the personal and cultural spheres.

What we hope Spirit means is that we can cultivate, respond to and be enlivened by a greater wholeness or experiential resonance, whose numinous surplus is progressively expressed as 'faithful living' and as an increased personal and collective capacity to face challenges large and small.

The successful production of this greater wholeness could be treated as the implied telos of psychological and social developmental activity in the degree to which we can intelligently orient towards it as an Other, Energy, Feeling or Self. For our purposes it will make no difference whether the Numinous or Divinising experience is itself conceived as being like a 'person' or a 'chemistry' or a 'force of nature' or some permutation of psychology. We may treat these as complementary interpretive lenses for the same process. That allows us to consider the integration of a wide variety of superficially disparate religious approaches. As noted before, our most general notion of religion must straddle such superficial distinctions as that between monotheism and paganism, colloquial and official, organised and disorganised, verbally affirmed or implicit. Likewise, our notion of spirituality must be equally at home in East and West, ancient and modern and pluralistic epochs, secular and metaphysical descriptions. It must be able to be widespread or idiosyncratic, neurochemical or contemplative, priestly or shamanic, spoken or unspoken, naturalistic or digitally mediated. These are the preconditions of a metamodern understanding of religion and spirituality and they come together in a common process that places the seed-pattern of metamodern thought itself into the heart of all our definitions.

Enlightenment in a metamodern sense

Enlightenment, for example, is a word that straddles private and public domains. The famous 'Western enlightenment' suggests the great cultural illuminations of the 17th century that brought reason, experimentalism, individual dignity and intercultural humanism out of the hands of a few philosophic cabals into the general assumptions of pan-Europeanism. Conversely, the famous 'Eastern enlightenment', which became global as it flowed into Europe and America in the mid-20th century, suggested an inward practice of self-transcendence employing meditation, devotional heart-awakening, subtle energy, sacred exercise and the endless variations of the guru system to enable wisdom-cultivation and enhanced states of consciousness.

I will treat both these forms of enlightenment as successful instances of a common process. That will require defining enlightenment in a broad way that can apply to most of the current usages and also help in fine-tuning our notions of 'religion' and 'spirituality' in ways that can be maximally inclusive without being merely open-ended and vague. This will reflect work and conversations associated with the Foundation for Integral Religion and Spirituality (FIRS), as well as my own history of involvement in postmetaphysical spirituality, non-dual theology and the communities of integrative meta-theory. That is merely to say, I have thought about this already and wish to deepen and extend these ideas. The primary value will be to see if we can glimpse a common meta-developmental pattern in two distinct but interlocked domains. The secondary value will be any particular notions of religion and spirituality that might serve us personally or that might clarify the process of full spectrum cultural integration and open up benevolent pathways to the truly satisfying, truly interesting and adequately safe, planetary wisdom-civilisation that the whole species, perhaps the whole biosphere, is yearning towards. While we do not wish to make extraordinary metaphysical claims about the will of nature, we must certainly recognise that our survival and our mental health are deeply connected to thriving, bio-diverse ecological systems that are reciprocally dependent upon the collective actions of human society. We enter into deeply entangled and deeply political dimensions when we consider the implications of this view of the intrapersonal and interpersonal production of 'spirit'.

So let's try to articulate what this common meta-vision looks like and then roam through a variety of aspects of the philosophy of spirituality, personal development, religion, politics and cultural evolution to see if we frequently re-encounter this pattern and might wish to employ it in the manner of an archetype, telos or flexibly explanatory vision-logic structure that might be able to yoke together (yo-ga, re-ligio) the meta-movement in many distinct domains.

This metamodern notion of religion has to validate but exceed the subset of religious examples that modernity has too often taken as its dogmatic, superstitious adversary. Our view is closer to transcendental agnosticism – a *sincere irony* – but it is flexible enough to make use of (and support) healthy and functional practices that are encoded in many of the mysteries, myths and rituals of the traditional membership cults.

Clearly metamodern religiosity is not existentially confined by questions like: Is there really a soul? A god? Another world? These questions are interesting to explore but fundamentally secondary to an inclusive, postmetaphysical and meta-level analysis of what we are calling spirituality and religion.

Although I tend to use the language of 'production' to describe the emergence of the Numinous, there is nothing that prevents this same picture from being interpreted as 'gaining access' to a pre-existing reality. Historically, the immediately obvious impression of access to pregiven Other has dominated human interpretations, but under modern and postmodern conditions a stream of vital scepticism has arisen, informed both by the success of material science and by radical trends in philosophy. To clarify a metamodern position we must think in terms of structures that have explanatory power and which can be utilised in either way.

In this chapter I am fundamentally agnostic about the ontological status of the 'spirit' that is the outcome and organisational referent of successful developmental integration in private and public spheres. What's more, I think that this transcendental agnosticism allows us the widest and most flexible meta-analysis for our own experiences and for dealing with all kinds of people who may hold very apparently secular or very apparently 'metaphysical' ideas. We need to be able to affirm the procedures and statements, provided we can give them our own twist.

Consider your own intimations about history and our world.

What do you think are successful and unsuccessful examples of a society? We find it difficult to make such evaluations because we have incomplete information and an unknown degree of personal bias. Our hope is that we can get better if we make an honest attempt. The pluralistic cultural operating system seems to get confused by the sheer diversity of styles and often loses faith in its own values. It has trouble validating itself in the face of the multiverse. Metamodern minds and their allies must get beyond this trap.

Our advantage is that the very principles of meta-society – principles which allow for and arise from the balanced validation of diverse historical paradigms – can operate as a standard with which to evaluate historical paradigms. Within the context of meta-society's own values, tools and cognitions, its own world, how well does it evolve without losing structural consistency, diversity and adequate homogeneity? How well does it allow people to transition into other paradigms and cultivate the cross-pollination of various social categories in a broadly shared cultural satisfaction that mobilises our collective problem-solving insights and activities. This is the return to alignment (*re-ligio*) and the birth of a novel spirit (*re-naissance*) that harmonises the disparate characters in the general organic wellbeing (*eudaimonium*) of social creatures.

Let's take a short tour of examples that occur to my version of a metamodern mind.

You may be familiar with the old excitement surrounding the 'integral movement', whose millennial spokesman was the American philosopher-sage Ken Wilber. Fans of Wilber were aroused by the spectre of a greater integration of all the dynamic parts (quadrants, states, stages, shadows, lines, etc.) of multi-dimensional human beings. This arousal involved a sense of emergent higher spirit and an optimism that their vision could spread around the world to help overcome a massively fragmented, polarised, untethered and haunted world. That was a moment, in a sense, of the meta-crisis that brought people together around principles and techniques of integration – sensing that new shared fields of meaning are necessary in order to summon together the many forces that must work in a complementary fashion to address complex, deep and large-scale issues.

It seems that a regular crisis can be approached by leveraging one of our existing methods (e.g. sending the police to a crime scene, getting a babysitter for your children). However, it is plausible that a higher level or multiplicative convergence of crises requires us to exceed and enfold our many different methods. We must be as complex as the combined sources of our emerging trouble. Therefore, our best chance always relies upon the functional and spirited coordination of the maximum number of different insights, skills and capacities. Only a renaissance can fight a meta-crisis.

A renaissance – an *integrative sacralisation of culture* – involves a new birth of style, harmony, revivified instincts and hopeful innovation. This results from the integrative assimilation of many diverse sources into shared experiential coherence. If there is a chance that we can deal with the dangerous and confusing challenges that face our current society, we will expect it to resemble those historical moments in which a similar uptake-and-update occurred.

Saul of Tarsus organised numerous experimental 'religious' communities within the Roman Empire. He worked according to a principle of *integration*. Greeks, Jews and Romans surrendered their traditional identities to voluntarily cooperate in a new scheme of ethics, diet, mysticism, politics, sexuality, education, art, mythology, risk, hope, literacy and more. All these genres of social activity were brought together in a shared energising spirit that would soon transform the empire. Their new harmony was breathed together (*con-spiracy*) to produce a whole new style of human being. It also shook up the world and transformed social systems on a transhuman scale. The results were not immediate nor uniformly positive. Of course not. However, they did initiate a current of cultural transformation.

And this current of transformation was communally acknowledged and constantly referenced as a 'holy spirit'. Everyone confessed to the experience of an edifying and galvanising creative impulse shared among the members of the community. A real surplus was being produced and they entered into a relationship with this extra quality that was their touchstone and telos.

Whether we imagine this phenomenon as descending from heaven or rising from the people, we nonetheless must envision it as occurring on a meta-level relative to the group identities and social practices of the time period. Emergent Christianity was 'meta' relative to ethnicity, class, profession, education and so on. It put emperors and slaves, fools and wise men, realists and idealists in the same boat. And it did this not merely by providing a framing context or a social agenda, but rather by embodying or producing an experiential 'spirit' that seemed to govern, justify and make seductive a new pattern of action derived from the consilience of many cultural genres and extended into changes in the complex overarching condition of humanity.

This period – which many nostalgic Christians today look back upon as a special period in which the 'spirit was still active on the earth' – has many similarities to other renaissance-like moments in history. The ongoing spirit of China is deeply entangled, at its source, with the divinisation of the First Emperor following his integration of the Warring States in a new system of language, technology, peace, war, etiquette, alchemy and art. Whatever glow or sheen makes *Chin* and *China* still vibrate with a resonant meaning and possible destiny for many people is entwined with an historical moment that tried to harmonise many disparate cultural segments. The later renaissances in 16th- and 17th-century Europe likewise seem to be still pregnant with an aura of successful integration, world-changing confidence, new style and emerging insights.

Heidegger famously said, towards the end of his life, that only a new god can save us now. Well, new gods are born in renaissances. We may scold Heidegger for thinking that the German National Socialist party was actually a progressive and integrative revolution, but we can sympathise with his desperate desire for such a revolution to emerge – as his deeply considered position that only such an emergence was capable of grappling with the problematic ecological, economic, sociological and technological consequences of modernity.

The infamous Nazi focus on racial and cultural purity epitomises the failure to create renaissance conditions. We look back upon that period with a fear and contempt that is primarily centred on Germany's aggressive cultural fragmentation. Their inability to incorporate ethnic, physiological and neurological diversity was a symptom of their social distress and the essential characteristic of their production of hellish rather than heavenly world conditions. They were not able to handle the higher-level complex crises of their time period because they were not robust or flexible enough to accomplish a harmonious consilience of many diverse functions and types of people. The regressive attempt to pare down the cultural situation until it seems more homogeneously manageable is among the most frequent characteristics of epochs that we look back upon with the exact opposite of that seductive golden glow of renaissance.

Most criticism of the Catholic Church today focuses upon its history of physical abuse and its support for science-inhibiting dogmatism. Yet we can also critique it from the point of view of its oscillating relationship with successful cultural integration. *Catholicity* was originally synonymous with *universality*. In that notion is a very clear idea that all people, all nations and all classes of society ought to be brought together in a great mandalic cathedral. A cathedral in which 'God's glory' names the luminous and numinous 'additional spirit' generated by the meta-cultural engine, overflowing back down upon it as both proof of success and as a teleological orientation for the more cohesive self-wielding of the multitude towards solving civilisation's problems (as they were understood at the time).

The laudable shift from Pope Benedict to Pope Francis in the 21st century demonstrates one oscillation away from a more puritan refinement towards an attempt to assimilate the energies and concerns of the current period. The relevance of this institution has always depended upon its ability to 'get on top of' the Euro-global situation. If it retracts towards purity, then it undercuts its future relevance. The 16th-century Renaissance in Europe was, partly, a success of the Catholic Church, which still haunts us today with its oddly 'unorthodox' pontifical embrace of radical artists, new technologies and every aspect of European culture, no matter how lewd or unsavoury from the point of view of the puritans. This organisational plasticity of embrace was a successful move by this organisation much in the same manner as was Pope Leo I's moving of the official birthday of Jesus to coincide with the pagan solstice festival. The empowerment of the Church might be said to depend upon the investments that take the form of assimilating, incorporating and 'owning' the different cultural energies, mood and practices already existing in the world.

The Inquisition was a sign of Catholic decline in much the same way that the Cult of Mary and the production of beautiful paintings and exalted cathedrals was a sign of Catholic renewal. And the downstream influence of the people organised in this mode and mood depends very greatly upon how well they can draw together diverse perspectives to elicit the motivating and trans-conscious human experience of collective meaning and capacity. Without that 'power', we are significantly limited in our capacity to make change to the complex inherited social and technological systems in which we are embedded.

How can this idea be brought up to the meta-level beyond simply stating that all renaissance provides an integrative context that operates around and between many cultural genres? A first step in this direction will be to consider how this phenomena looks across different sets of cultural codes.

We have been looking at successful religionisation or *integrative renewal* in traditional, premodern societies. We might even fear the association of cultural progress with religion because we have learned to over-associate the process with the many famous examples of pre-rational, pre-humanist, pre-individualistic and uniformal religiosity. However, those are features of the orthodox premodern cultural codes – not specifically of the social process analogous to religionisation. Such a process can certainly succeed or fail through the modern or postmodern cultural codes. In fact, these worldspaces, capacities and value-systems might even be 'more religious' when they succeed.

The more contemporary cosmos is more expansive. Today's potential psyche may attain higher degrees of rational self-organisation, and the culture honours the divine spirit more completely by discovering it as the intrinsic dignity of every human being, regardless of membership affiliation. And we can look at the poles of more and less *successful meta-social activation* in a modern context.

There are many reasons why the so-called West had, after the Second World War, such a productive period of cultural progress that it simultaneously suggests both the right-wing American fantasy of 1950s greatness to which the nation should return AND the left-wing fantasy of the origin conditions for the progressive cultural leap of the 1960s. Too often these reasons are reduced merely to economic advantage created by the mass increase of industrial production coupled with the smoking ruin of Japanese and German economic competitors. It is just as relevant to consider the way in which society was organised under the unique conditions of mobilisation for the Second World War. There was an unprecedented *mixing of types* in American culture. Rural White boys who might have dwelled in parochial isolation from racial integration at home found themselves working and fighting alongside negroes. Urban and agricultural boys were likewise co-mingled in the disciplines, horrors and pleasures faced by soldiers. On the home front, there was an unprecedented call for people to leave their standard occupations and join together in the industrial and organisational war effort, elbow to elbow, with women and men from various races, educational backgrounds and economic classes, in a common current of joint pleasures, efforts and distresses.

A simple metaphor of an electrically conductive fluid composed of various mechanically mixed chemicals may present itself. Consider this mixture in a jar and imagine that its ability to conduct electricity is analogous to the 'current' of evolutionary potential or even deep, developmental civic spirit in a population. The individual chemicals are not strongly electrically conductive – so when the mixture separates into its subcomponents there is a loss of this shared emergent property. Disintegration into the component chemicals is natural and occurs spontaneously whenever the active mixing of substances is not present.

Using such a mental image as if it were an hypothesis, we would speculate that the 'glow' of national spirit – including both its unique conservative and naturally progressive aspects – is produced around situations where large functional blocs of the culture are intermingled. Not just nominally for a parade or a tour, but operationally in ways that lead to shared humanity, shared struggle and shared enjoyments. And in the absence of such intermingling circumstances, including 'free choice of consumer lifestyles and employment', the natural process of separation would occur – leading to a widely proclaimed loss of progressive consensus, shared community, confidence in the structure of the nation and cooperative sacrifice as a moral guideline for business and governance. And the natural extension of this loss of electrical conductivity would be a pandemic search for an alternative grouping in which such conductivity might be present – from a return to the conservative forms of the last great period of public spirit to a progressive fragmentation into gender, racial or religious tribalisms.

The internal division within societies around the issue of immigration is, inter alia, emblematic of the meta-social need for harmony of diversity. We want as much diversity as can be harmonised. Anti-diversity complaints ought to rise dramatically if our harmonisation procedures are inadequate. Indeed, people might even become phobic about the concept of assimilation in the degree to which we cease to be any good at that necessary organic task. Retribalisation of the public ethos is a predictable result of the failure to produce any satisfying shared spirit among many different types of people. This spirit is so important to the function and health of beings that they instinctively begin to fall back towards more primitive groupings in which they might (and believe they historically did or might be more able to do locally) achieve a balance of homogeneity and heterogeneity. Too much of one stifles the other. This is again a strictly metamodern observation because it validates and integrates different epochal perspective sets within a single health-and-development oriented function.

Again, the image here is that of a surplus harmonious creativity inculcated by effective integration of naturally distinct functional sub-dimensions. And this is not so far from the Marxist view that the gap between the 'workers' and the 'capitalists' (and between the social academics and the proletariat) is the structural contradictory inhibiting the actual production of modern civilisation correlated to our new technologies.

The actual praxis of cultivating this kind of quasi-transcendent interdisciplinarity must have common threads in all situations, but will of course have significantly different optics and particular procedures depending on the kind of 'world' that is being integrated. As a radical example, we might look to the highly aesthetic, highly functional and astonishingly symbiotic realm of the terrestrial biosphere. Here we find not only extraordinary degrees of complementary interpenetration by various 'genres' of life (e.g. the hyper-coordination between insects, bacteria, mycelial webs and trees that are required to secure a 'forest'), but also a recurrent pattern in which solutions solve many problems simultaneously. The types of chemical and physical architecture that the field of biomimicry is now trying to harvest represents a set of solutions and an approach to large-scale problem-solving (a) in which many symbiotic functions seeking different goals are yoked together in a shared, self-sustaining tangle, and (b) whereby structural and functional solutions resulting from this deep combining of functions do not simply solve one problem but create cascades of helpfulness whose full range may not be discovered for a long time.

These are the sorts of effects we see in historical examples of 'peak culture' and which we therefore seek to intelligently inculcate in our emerging meta-societies. We have problems that are diverse, complex and operate at scales that transcend tribal, traditional and modern geopolitics and have not been adequately resolved by the emergence of the pluralistic-relativistic sensibility. It is of the utmost urgency that we pay attention to the production of functional cultural moods in which many diverse types of people and activity can be brought together in a self-sustaining tangle, whose resultant patterns may be able to address problems on higher complex scales, as well as cascades of problems in all directions.

What I am proposing here is that this is not simply a matter of implementing new socio-economic and technological strategies but that it requires, both as a supplement and, in part, a precursor to the willingness-to-implement, the cultivation of a 'holy' mood. Each culture that has done well in the base – relative to whatever situations, ideas, values and worldview existed for them – needed to mobilise in a shared and uplifting manner. They needed some degree of religiosity, under many diverse names, implicit in their social experience. They needed this not only to act as an experiential point of mutual coordination but also to provide the satisfaction and allure that motivates individuals of disparate disciplines and temperaments to want to work together and solve problems. And to situate this willingness not merely in their conscious minds and stress responses but also deep in their biological, emotional and unconscious instincts such that their full complement of resources come to bear upon addressing, directly *and* indirectly, the problems that loom over the world we now inhabit.

We have a benevolent neo-futurist tendency that demands the embrace of other epochs and layers of psychocultural experience. We seek to encourage a wise world of engineered stable abundance in which people feel naturalised and creatively contemplate their civilisation with a good conscience. Otherwise we have no idea how much damage and retardation of progress is occurring because people's best ideas and efforts are uncoordinated, too reliant upon the conscious mind and occurring within the latent context of a fragmentary, separative and one-sidedly critical view of their own culture.

Unless our definition of *our* culture appeals to us viscerally as something greater, something worthwhile, something analogous to 'holy', then we are all the enemies of collective wellbeing even while we pursue disparate plans and actions to improve the world situation. No one works hard, with all of their capacities, to help out a loveless marriage.

New gods are born in renaissances.

The very same situation that fluctuates between more or less successful historical cultural pools (in the meta-social sense) also obtains within each human individual. The inner society also does better or worse when it comes to functional integration of its subjective parts into a great whole that can mobilise its capacities for new insights and provides the energy for actions that grow our heart, mind, body and relationships.

> I think of spiritual sensibility as a disposition towards reality characterised by concern for the fullness of life and experienced through simultaneous intimations of aliveness, goodness, understanding and meaning. Those glimpses of wholeness and integration have a texture that is at once emotional, ethical, epistemic and existential – the feeling of being alive, the conviction that something matters, the intuition that the world makes sense, and the experience that life is meaningful respectively. More substantively,
> … cultivating spiritual sensibility is about deepening our engagement with questions of being(death), belonging(love), becoming(self) and beyondness(soul).

That's metamodern author Jonathan Rowson, reflecting upon the core insights of his book *Spiritualise* in the updated foreword of that volume (*Spiritualise: Cultivating spirituality sensibility to address 21st century challenges*, 2017). He describes spirituality as a 'disposition' that enfolds 'fullness concerns' and appears in the form of 'intimations' of positive meaningful principles that experientially validate our lives. And it involves multiple basic forms of human intelligence (emotional, ethical, etc.). It can be cultivated by a certain approach to engaging things like being, belonging, becoming and beyondness. What does that tell us?

It tells us that we are dealing with a view of spirituality that is concerned to access a special condition. A condition in which many functions are brought together and a sense of transformational fullness is intimated. A surplus coherent condition that is suggested by our personal sense of meaningful beingness as much as it is by our interpersonal experience of love and belonging. This spiritual sensibility is an improved engagement with our power to transform ourselves properly and to resonate with a factor that promises meaning and harmony beyond the fragmented contents of the world. Rowson describes the accessing (or producing) of a coherent incorporative field of feeling that enfolds multiple facets of the psyche – empowering, organising and justifying our experience of being in the world.

Where does more depth come from? What is it that our interpretive capacity enacts during our peak experiences and hints to us in lingering intuitive intimations? What strangely familiar and numinous *something* may be equally well perceived as being, belonging, becoming and beyondness – and how is that something cultivated in our experience? How does it stand in relation to the mutuality of facets, capacities and human functions whose coordination appears enhanced in these successful moments that provide the justification of existence?

My argument is that this meta-state is not merely coincidentally related to the increased wholeness of the mandala of different human psychological functions, but that it is actually cultivated by our attempts to produce this balance among our psychic subcategories. What are psychic subcategories? They are the different intelligences such as emotion, ethics, somatic, cognitives. They are the right and left sides of our nervous system. They are the perception of self and the perception of others and environments. They are light and shadow, male and female, conscious and unconscious, disparate sub-selves or chakra-like operational regions of our subjective anatomy. All these different functional components can operate more or less well together. Those moments in which we discern more clearly the meta-state towards which the spiritual sensibility is inclined reveal a beautiful harmony of all these subparts of ourselves which seem to be held wondrously by subtly permeating overtones of instinctively valorised 'fits-together-ness'.

We could certainly adopt the naive metaphysical impression of our ancestors, who viewed these moments as breakthroughs into the primal, timeless and underlying condition of the cosmos. Such interpretations give, appropriately, great honour to these meta-states, but they do not fully incorporate the postmetaphysical and deeply constructive vision of reality that emerged in modern and postmodern philosophies. Metamodern spirituality must at least risk the notion that the appearance of harmonised psychological factors occurring in tandem with the felt-enhancement of our beingness is because these are moments in which the harmonisation of those qualities has succeeded and produces this epiphanic side effect.

The risk of such an interpretation of spirituality is well worth the gamble because it lays before us an image of the successful spiritual event that resembles not only the production of empowered culture but also the developmental shifts that occur in moments of growth and realisation in any aspect of life.

Renaissance vs metacrisis (or: who we need to be, inside and out?)

How do we cultivate coherence, both interpersonally and intrapersonally? This is a practical question upon which, more than any other, the production of metamodern culture and the success of metamodern movements of all kinds will depend. A robust sense of meaningful identity, a full complement of organic capacity, regular access to satisfying community and peak experiences, and an ongoing developmental approach to self and others – these are the key areas in which we must succeed. We could call these spiritual and religious territories but we are under no obligation to do so. What matters is engaging them, under any terminology, and trying to think out the procedures that secure and promulgate the condition upon which metamodernism depends. Only that can empower us as the many reckonings of the near future come to bear upon civilisation. This chapter has been trying to explore the general patterns that produce metamodern psychology and upon which its optimism may be based.

The short aphorism *transcend and include* is still an excellent summary of our overall meta-orientation. We are meta (sic) in the degree to which we go beyond (which is also between) the structures that we inherit into our psyche and our society. However, we have not truly gone beyond if we reject and condemn those structures upon which we stand. A comprehensive exploration, appreciation and remixing of our received realities is needed. Cultivating a deeper or higher phase of being-in-the-world means that we must go more deeply into things – into their nuances, gaps and interstitial zones – and then work them together into new and inspiring balances. We must do this with as much grace, sensitivity and energy as possible. And this is not just a matter of the self-validating aesthetics of the self. It is also a profound moral requirement.

We do not need to spend much time enumerating the uncanny and dangerous trends of the meta-crisis that sprawls across all domains of human existence today. And be sure that there are many more tendrils of radical change and destabilisation than you have heard about so far. A reckoning is coming. A battlefield is being laid out before us. A flood is coming and those who can build rafts have an extraordinary responsibility and opportunity.

Raft building means the ability to discern viable logs from within their embedded environment and to successfully lash them together to produce a situation of floating, escape and new functionality. Sound familiar? And who will discover and yoke together the great panoply today and tomorrow if not the metamodernists, in the broadest sense of that word?

As *metamoderns-in-spirit* we can affirm and bring together radical postmodern insights, premodern naturalism and the modern need for humanistic reason and scientific development. In all of this we serve the ancient alchemical law of depth development – *solve et coagula*. First, we must discover the different functional subcomponents of what previously appeared to be obvious unitary blocs or systems. Then, we work to combine these operational facets harmoniously, without cancelling their differences. This very general process, when it succeeds, characterises both our kind of vision and the kind of world we have to make efforts to cultivate. Unless we can create and secure new coherent platforms of individual and collective experience, we will fail in the face of the storm of interlocking crises that characterise the epoch into which our species is now travelling. We will fail if we cannot achieve empowering, validating and world-justifying moods and motivation both within and among ourselves. And we will fail if we cannot, personally and collectively, access the emergent capacities and insights that arise from the production of transcendent-seeming meta-states.

Action and insight extend from some kind of meta-stability. This is a fundamental aspect of emergence theory. There is a distinction between the aggregate activity of many interacting objects or entities and the far less frequent appearance of a qualitatively unique, new form of organisation that integrates many entities into a new entity with new options for engagement. Among many interacting beings there emerges a shared platform or premise. These beings begin to inhere and cohere within a meta-stability.

This new state – this meta-state – must be preserved and constantly regenerated or else the new functions will destabilise and decohere back into the aggregate assembly of the components. An adequate, harmonious interactivity of components that maintains a general set of functional capacities of the new totality is called *health*, if we think about it in biological terms. Health is required for strength and creative actions. It is the necessary launching ground for adaptive efforts at a new scale.

If my overall temperature average goes off by even a few degrees, then I must suddenly leave Christmas dinner, abandon the business meeting, stop writing my poem and retreat into a feverish puddle from which I can only hope that I will emerge again. The analogy to our collective situation is quite dramatic. How can nations, social transformative movements, international agencies, educational institutions or human development teams hope to grapple successfully with the meta-crisis if they do not have access to the full range of capacities produced by their balanced co-functioning? Without a deep existential pleasure in our shared activity, how will we hope to mobilise any real change? How will we even remember the qualities that are worth fighting for? How will we access the territories in which we can at least try to take action on the scales at which the problems are nested? The meta-crisis that faces our world consists of challenges and dangers at a very high scale.

The inner component of the meta-crisis is the loss of meaning, and the outer component is the onrushing convergence of ecological destabilisation, technological transformations of the basic parameters of organic and psychological life and uncontrolled information explosions in world, whose collective meaning has been shredded. It is not necessary to call these spiritual life and religious life, respectively, but such naming would not be out of place historically. Our physical health must be joined with a sense of subjective meaning and a shared social coordination capable of evading mass conflict, mobilising nation states towards streamlined, non-oppressive progressive action. Citizens require enough naturalistic pleasure in their shared diversity and enough similarity that they are willing to make sacrifices for each other and to spend minimal time cultivating grievances amplified through media and to feel the kind of stable confidence that leads to benevolent and interesting futuristic goals.

The problems that thwart our capacity to collectively deal with the meta-crisis to the best of our ability relate to (a) lack of collective coordination, (b) lack of adaptation to new information and tools and (c) lack of shared spirit. These are impeded by partisanship, strife between genders, races, creeds and sensibilities, disparity of economic engagement, control over profits between classes, collective cynicism and ennui, and an inability to connect with confidence, inspiration and mutual benevolent feelings on a large and stable scale. Individually, there are analogous problems. We do not uptake our knowledge into action. Our conscious and unconscious, left and right, heart, mind and body, and various factional sub-selves seldom achieve a stable individuation with a correlative feeling of super-coordination, a meaning that lets us engage our full capacities and follow through with a clarity of purpose that might be coordinated with the masses.

The objective threats to our complex adaptive cultural systems and our need for improvement live or die based on the experiential realities the developing beings undergo. Do we understand enough to confront our challenges? Do we have the confidence and energy needed? Are we in touch with our values to the point that we can act as their agents in the world? Do we have enough clarity, wisdom and being within ourselves and our social networks to even approach the challenges? We exist in powerful, technologically advanced and information-rich societies, but informational environments are not educational environments (Zachary Stein, *Education in a Time Between Worlds: Essays on the Future of Schools, Technology and Society*, 2019). The mere presence of mediated data does not imply the successful communicatory and integrative work that converts it into empowering understanding any more than gross national product tells us the qualitative experience of wealth for the citizens. Therefore, the extra meaningful quality – of wisdom and higher radiance – so long projected upon the teacher or the dharma, is not produced within us or among us. The praxis of understanding has always been under assault by cultural forces that benefit from the superficiality of public knowledge. Now, however, it is powered up technologically and economically to hack attention itself.

There are very many interesting philosophies and very many potentially useful social and political programmes. There are very many promising technologies, both new and old. In the end, no part of this promise will be realised unless we have more stable access to a higher degree of integration within ourselves and across the population divides in such a way that we are willing to face great challenges and have the coordination, appetite and extended capacities to do so.

> **Meta-state** (1) A state of consciousness that transcends, integrates and/or negotiates between other more common states, skills or intelligences; (2) A general platform of psychology that cultivates, clarifies and extends the experience of interperspectival intelligence; (3) A form of society that both deepens and exceeds our conventional inherited notions of cultural organisation; (4) In thermodynamics, a meta-stable state in which a phenomenon persists despite transformations or chaotic flux in its underlying materials; (5) Colloquial variant of metastasis – i.e. the growth of a phenomenon beyond one region into the rest of a whole structure.

Index

A

aesthetics 18, 79, 136, 139, 170, 187, 193, 235, 288, 302, 311, 314
agency(ies) 18, 35, 63, 74, 77, 86, 141, 151–152, 201–213, 265
agnosticism 221, 281–291, 305–306
Anthropocene 60, 73–75, 227
aperspectival xxxix
apotheosis 244, 302–304
Aurobindo, Sri 22, 87
autonomy 27, 35, 60, 122, 164, 210, 231, 278

B

between 29, 44, 99, 101, 106–107, 113, 119–121, 124–125, 127
  in(-)between 54, 58–59, 66, 69, 78, 246, 252, 254, 271, 294
beyond 29–30, 44, 72, 77, 90, 116, 120, 245, 252–255, 260, 263
  beyondness 250, 255
Bildung xxxvi, 20, 39, 170, 274, 277
biosphere 68, 72, 76, 137, 305, 311

C

capitalism 86–89, 95, 105, 108, 139, 157–158, 169, 176–178, 183, 186–187, 194,
  198–199, 201, 213, 220, 225–227, 276
Cartesian 77, 140
China 34, 142, 185–187, 195, 308
Christianity 16, 36, 220, 220–221, 225, 228–232, 231–232, 235, 244, 282–291, 302–
  303, 307–308
Chronos 57, 221
civilisation 16, 22–28, 47, 55, 72–73, 76–77, 90, 95, 101, 219, 225–226, 228, 235–236,
  293–294, 300, 311

Arendt 62
climate 30, 41, 63–64, 74, 184, 192. *See also global warming*
  climate emergency 18–19, 25–26, 44, 77
cliodynamics viii
cognition 107–108, 111, 114, 117–118, 126, 222, 234, 245–247
  cognitive complexity 38, 109, 114–115, 117, 120–121
  cognitive styles 116, 122
  distributed cognition 242, 264, 266
cognitive architecture 116
cognitive dissonance 201–211. *See also dissonance*
coherence 34, 66, 71, 90, 118–120, 205, 234, 294–295, 301, 312–315
commons 32, 277–279
Commons, Michael 108, 116, 124, 139, 152
communism 176
community 42, 47, 101–102, 146, 151, 185, 193–194, 235, 300, 310, 313
complexity 18, 26–27, 42, 54–58, 63–64, 67–69, 105–127, 105–128, 176, 180, 193, 197–198, 293–294
  cognitive complexity 108, 114–115, 117, 119–120, 152
  complex adaptive systems 65–66
  paradoxical complexity (paradexity) 231
  releasing complexity 106–110, 124, 126–127
consciousness 22–23, 42–43, 46, 53–58, 72–73, 78, 89–90, 111–112, 221–222, 225–226, 246–247, 275–276, 287–288, 294, 296, 316
contingency 35, 54, 283
coronavirus 183, 207. *See also Covid-19*
cosmovision 44–46
Covid-19 19–20, 24–25, 36, 44, 59, 76, 157, 236. *See also coronavirus*
crisis 16, 19, 26–33, 60, 62–63, 76, 85–86, 89, 98, 101, 127, 211, 225, 233, 241–266, 281, 307
cultural codes 37, 175–199, 298, 303, 309
culture wars 85–102, 107, 140, 272

D

Dalí, Salvador 141
Darwin, Charles 181
Darwinian 59, 64–66
de Chardin, Teilhard 121
deconstruction 54, 106, 108, 110, 112, 115, 117, 122, 124–128, 137, 187, 196
  Derrida 145
deep ecology 228
deep time 72
development(al) 85–86, 93, 97, 101, 105–129, 136–154, 181, 183, 185–186, 196, 212, 225–226, 242, 247, 266–267, 278, 295, 297, 299–301, 304–306, 310, 313–315

developmentalist/m 149, 296
moral development 186
dialectic 106, 138, 241–267
dialogos 41, 242–267
dissonance 20, 24–26, 42–43, 201–212. *See also cognitive dissonance*
dividual 152

E

Earth 72–73, 77–78, 184, 277
ecology(ical) 24–28, 32, 35–38, 61, 180, 249. *See also deep ecology*
  information ecology 43, 98
economic model 175–177, 183, 190, 198
economy(ic) 18, 28, 32, 36, 42–43, 60, 78, 101, 139, 151, 154, 158, 176–199, 275, 309
  macroeconomics 25
  political economy 24, 289
  socio-economic 27, 32, 311
education 18, 32, 38–39, 85–101, 85–102, 115, 170, 178, 189, 194, 258, 271, 307, 316
ego development 107–108, 122, 125–126. *See also development*
Éluard, Paul 286, 289
embodied imagination 247–248
enlightenment/Enlightenment 63, 102, 121, 142, 186, 194, 219, 231, 243, 251, 305–311
episteme(ic/ology) 18, 29, 32, 40–41, 45–47, 65, 77, 119, 124, 139, 146, 176, 187, 243, 245, 251–253, 256–264
  epistemic bubble 40
eros 236, 244, 252, 256–264
  erotic 276–277, 279
Eros 121
eschatology 61, 233
ethics(al) 18, 27–28, 63, 64, 108, 110, 112, 114, 116, 119, 120, 125–129, 139, 143, 146–147, 164, 210, 219, 226, 251, 275, 277, 295, 307, 313
evolution 17–18, 22, 56, 58–59, 72, 77, 79, 92–94, 106–108, 114, 121–122, 136, 143–149, 181, 300

F

faith 15, 149, 233, 235, 302
feminine 277
feminism 147, 228, 232–234, 275
Foucault, Michel xxxiv, 144, 147, 223–224
Freinacht, Hanzi 135–154

G

Gaia xli, 72–76, 235
Game B 27, 42
Gebser, Jean 46, 53–58, 62, 73, 75, 78, 122, 139, 282, 301
global warming 25, 38
gnosis 241–267
God 16, 46, 146, 267, 278, 281–288

H

Hall, Jordan 41
Hegel, G.W.F. 149, 210, 212
Heidegger, Martin 246, 249, 253, 255, 265, 308
hierarchy 119
　developmental hierarchy 107
　dominatory hierarchy 119
historiography 37–38, 137
history (historical) 17, 53, 61, 86, 136–139, 143, 149, 162, 175–199, 210, 220–225, 228, 272, 279, 283, 293, 300, 306–314
humanity 25, 57, 86–87, 105, 146, 237, 248, 273, 276, 289, 295, 308, 310
hypermodern 220, 235, 287
hyperobject 74, 77

I

identity 23, 34
　identity erotics 271–279
　identity politics 37, 272–279
imaginal 44, 111, 250, 260
imaginary 39, 43–44, 275, 300
　collective imaginary 37, 185
　social imaginary 71–79
indigenous 38, 45, 56, 175–176, 189–190, 278, 301
　indigenous economy 183–185, 190
　indigenous knowledge 195, 228
individual 35–36, 40, 58, 64–65, 67, 76, 89, 108, 116, 122, 140, 151–152, 170, 175–179, 176–181, 184–185, 189, 197, 219, 222, 242–244, 254, 257, 259, 264–265, 279, 286, 288–291, 296, 300–301, 311–312
　individual agency 201–213
individualism 27, 105
integral 23, 46, 57, 78–79, 275
　Integral Theory xxxi, 139, 150, 297, 306
　integral thinking 73

post-integral xxxii
integration 45, 116–122, 176, 233, 293–315
intellectual property (IP) 157–170
intelligence 61, 107, 242, 244, 264–266, 287, 290, 294–295, 312–313
  artificial intelligence 99
  collective intelligence 24, 140, 152, 219, 264
interconnected 28, 72, 76, 87, 138, 158, 179, 191, 198, 273
interiority 37–38, 275, 279, 287
intimacy 87, 253, 276–277, 286
irony(ic) 37, 135–154, 149, 187, 231, 244–245, 273, 279
  sincere irony 138–139, 140, 143, 148, 302, 305
  Socratic irony 230, 258

J

juxtaposition 234–235, 277

K

kainos 57–58
kairos 57
  Kairos 221

L

Landry, Forrest 27
language 17, 21–22, 31, 40, 41–42, 55, 56–58, 61, 64–66, 89, 95, 145–146, 151, 167, 184, 187, 222–224, 245, 247, 260, 274–276, 279, 286, 296, 304, 306
liberation theology 231–234
logos 47, 243–267
loops 181–187, 190–198

M

market economy 176–177, 183
McLuhan, Marshall 75, 79, 298, 302
meaning 19, 27–28, 57, 85, 117, 135, 146, 149, 154, 160, 162, 189–190, 192–199, 211, 220, 223–224, 227, 253, 257–259, 264, 266, 272, 277–279, 294, 301, 303, 307–308, 312, 315
  meaning crisis 108, 242, 265
  meaningfulness 16, 142, 150, 175, 254, 294–296
meaning-making 30, 68, 107, 114, 119, 121, 125–127, 139, 146, 151, 154, 242, 267, 274–275
meta 54, 73–75

going meta 29–30, 71, 73
  meta-state 296–300, 313–316
meta-crisis (metacrisis) 15–48, 54–55, 73
meta-history viii, xli
metamodern 29, 37–38, 54–55, 71
  metamodernity 30, 54, 106, 136–138, 153, 176, 274–275, 279, 287
  metamodern spirit 220, 293–323
  political metamodernism 38
metanoia 20, 29, 219–228
metaphysics 29, 46–47, 54–55, 67, 112, 118, 225, 235, 272, 289, 305–306, 313
meta-theory 118, 136, 140, 148–155, 220, 305
metaxy 29, 78, 254–255, 258
Model of Hierarchical Complexity (MHC) 108, 116, 124, 301
modern 37, 45, 54–68, 73, 92, 100, 106, 114, 186–188, 194–195, 243, 286–287, 294–296, 309, 311
monotheism 185, 304
morality 109–110, 120, 143, 153, 169, 184, 187–188, 222–223, 288, 310, 314
  moral development 37, 186, 274–275

N

nature 27, 175, 179–180, 184, 188, 192, 197, 278
Nietzsche, Friedrich 145–146, 230, 246, 258, 303
nihilism 97, 124, 221, 223, 297

O

ontology 118, 136, 139–140, 145, 220, 242–243, 250–252, 255–256, 258, 260, 263–266, 279, 282, 295, 306
oscillation 29, 37, 140, 289–290, 299, 308

P

paganism 221, 304
panarchy 59–60, 67
pandemics 16, 25, 62, 98–102, 159, 188, 310. *See also Covid-19; See also coronavirus*
paradigm 37, 54, 119, 138–139, 141–142, 151–152, 169, 198, 219, 228–229, 231, 251, 294, 306
participatory knowing 242, 246–248, 250–256, 259–260, 263–267
pedagogy 219, 242, 256–257
peer-to-peer (P2P) 76, 92, 100
periodisation 137–138, 141–142
perspectival 114, 127, 139, 148, 246–247, 249–250, 254–256, 260, 262–263, 272
  interperspectival 294, 296–299, 316

Perspectiva (Perspectiva Press) 38, 42–43, 47
  Praxis 40, 47
perspectives 115, 120–121, 138–140, 143, 145, 145–154, 181, 185, 195, 197–198, 207, 212, 223, 227, 233–234, 242, 245–263, 294–296, 309–310
  meta-perspective 118, 299–300
planetary 33, 36, 46, 54–55, 71–79, 87, 101, 105, 235, 305
Plato (Platonic/ism) 68, 220, 224, 236, 241–266, 282, 284–285, 287–288, 290
  Neoplatonism 244, 263–264, 266, 284–285
  platonic 220, 263
politics 25, 33, 147, 169, 186, 189, 202–212, 229, 234–235
  meta-politics 299
polytheism 185–186
posthuman 71, 76–78, 137
postmetaphysics 305–306, 313
postmodern(ism/ity) 29–30, 37–38, 54–55, 86–87, 95, 106, 113, 115, 118–119, 126–127, 136–152, 176, 187–189, 196–197, 220, 228, 231–233, 235, 241–242, 295
praxis 41–42, 44, 220, 223, 230, 234, 242, 244, 254, 311, 316
premodern 45, 141, 176, 193–194, 242, 294, 296, 309, 314
  premodern economy 184–187
Prigogine, Ilya 27
progress 26, 31, 37–38, 55–56, 67–68, 78, 137–148, 193, 212, 297, 309–311
psyche 109, 111–112, 118, 120, 255, 262, 293–316
psychedelics 219, 224–225
psychology 35, 45, 88, 92, 110–111, 139, 142–143, 202–213, 298, 301–304, 313–314
  depth psychology 44, 151–153, 228
Puer xxxi

Q

quadrants xxiv, xxxi–xxxii
  four-quadrant map xl

R

relationship 18, 24, 29–30, 36–37, 41–47, 56–66, 72, 116–119, 227, 232–234, 250–254, 276–278, 300–302
  educational 95
releasing complexity 108
religion(ious) 46, 110, 145, 185–187, 220, 229–231, 236–237, 278, 281–290, 300–315. *See also paganism; monotheism; polytheism*
renaissance 295, 307
  Renaissance 186–187

S

Sanders, Bernie 235
Schmachtenberger, Daniel 26, 41–43
science 55, 64, 78, 100, 117, 122, 143–146
Senex xxxi
sensemaking 30–31, 73–78, 112, 127, 271
simplexity 106, 120–124
simplicity 108–112
socialism 36, 144, 177, 225, 235
  socialist 144, 195, 234
social justice 87, 96, 186, 219, 229, 231
society(ies) 27, 32, 76, 135–154, 175–199, 210, 273, 279, 293–316
sociology 135–154, 227–229
Socrates 243–247, 256–267, 282
spirit 56–58, 251–254, 257–261, 265–267, 287, 293–316
spirituality 15–17, 21, 32, 44–46, 107–125, 140, 191, 219–236, 289
  spiritual materialism 285–286
superimposition xxix
surreal 293
  surrealism 229, 286
symbiotic 311
system 26–28, 36, 59–68, 76–78, 92, 106–109, 113–120, 242–243, 293–316
  belief 204
  ecological 181, 228, 277
  economic 175–199
  information 89, 97, 158–168
  nervous system 251–252, 258, 260, 262, 313
  school 98–100

T

Taoism 185
Taylor, Charles 44, 72, 75
teleology 121, 143, 233
  telos 120–124, 243, 259, 304–307
temporics 56–58
theology 228, 231, 286. *See also liberation theology*
time 23, 53–69, 264–266. *See also deep time; Chronos*
  asymmetry 193
  real-time 92, 101, 158, 196
transcendence 29, 106–107, 118–128, 220, 276, 286–291, 314
  self-transcendence 242–243, 305
  sensibility transcendence 251–266

transcendental agnosticism 305–306
transcendental design 20, 27, 42
trauma 125, 152–153, 222

V

Vivekananda 15–16, 44

W

Wallerstein, Immanuel 27
West, the 34, 62–63, 68, 142, 179, 185–198, 225, 241, 285, 289, 305, 309
Wilber, Ken xxxi, 17–18, 107, 118–119, 121, 297, 306
wisdom 42, 56, 107–112, 230, 242–244, 252–253, 256–267, 282
Wittgenstein, Ludwig 247, 284, 286
worldviews 114, 145–146, 220, 248, 287, 295